Ken Akamatsu

TRANSLATED BY
Toshifumi Yoshida

ADAPTED BY
T. Ledoux

LETTERING AND RETOUCH BY
Steve Palmer

BALLANTINE BOOKS · NEW YORK

A Word from the Author

As of this book, *Negima!* Volume 9, we're heading right into the largest event ever to be held at Mahora Academy, the Mahora Festival story arc!... Or so I complacently thought, before realizing that the entirety of Volume 9 would end up covering only the preparations for the Festival. (^^;) Will Negi and his students make it through all three days in one piece?... All I can say is, I'll draw it for you best I can!

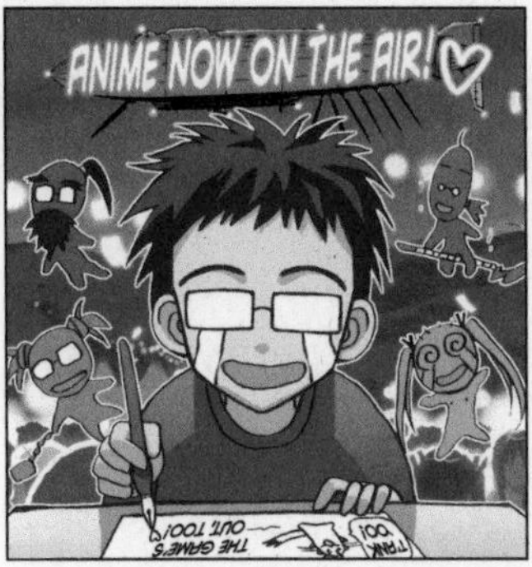
ANIME NOW ON THE AIR!

Oh, and also, before I forget—the animated *Magister Negi Magi* is now on the air (in Japan)! Watching the 31 voice actors play the 31 students is really something, let me tell you. Seriously, it's more like a classroom in an all-girl boarding school than a recording studio. Oh, would that I were Negi...! (Heh.)

Ken Akamatsu
www.ailove.net

Note: The video game and anime are currently available in Japan. At the time of publication, we do not know when they will be released in North America.

Negima! Volume 9 is a work of fiction. Names, characters, places, and incidents are the products of the author's imagination or are used fictitiously. Any resemblance to actual events, locales, or persons, living or dead, is entirely coincidental.

A Del Rey Trade Paperback Original

Published in the United States by Del Rey Books, an imprint of The Random House Publishing Group, a division of Random House, Inc., New York.

Del Rey is a registered trademark and the Del Rey colophon is a trademark of Random House, Inc.

First published in serial form by Shonen Magazine Comics and subsequently published in book form in Japan in 2004 by Kodansha Ltd., Tokyo. Publication rights arranged through Kodansha Ltd. All rights reserved.

Library of Congress Control Number: 2004090830

ISBN 0-345-48273-5

Printed in the United States of America

www.delreymanga.com

5 6 7 8 9

Translator —Toshifumi Yoshida
Adaptor—T. Ledoux
Lettering and retouch—Steve Palmer
Cover Design—David Stevenson

Honorifics

Throughout the Del Rey Manga books, you will find Japanese honorifics left intact in the translations. For those not familiar with how the Japanese use honorifics and, more important, how they differ from American honorifics, we present this brief overview.

Politeness has always been a critical facet of Japanese culture. Ever since the feudal era, when Japan was a highly stratified society, use of honorifics—which can be defined as polite speech that indicates relationship or status—has played an essential role in the Japanese language. When addressing someone in Japanese, an honorific usually takes the form of a suffix attached to one's name (example: "Asuna-san"), or as a title at the end of one's name or in place of the name itself (example: "Negi-sensei," or simply "Sensei!").

Honorifics can be expressions of respect or endearment. In the context of manga and anime, honorifics give insight into the nature of the relationship between characters. Many translations into English leave out these important honorifics, and therefore distort the "feel" of the original Japanese. Because Japanese honorifics contain nuances that English honorifics lack, it is our policy at Del Rey not to translate them. Here, instead, is a guide to some of the honorifics you may encounter in Del Rey Manga.

-*san:* This is the most common honorific, and is equivalent to Mr., Miss, Ms., or Mrs. It is the all-purpose honorific and can be used in any situation where politeness is required.

-*sama:* This is one level higher than "-san." It is used to confer great respect.

-*dono:* This comes from the word "tono," which means "lord." It is an even higher level than "-sama," and confers utmost respect.

-kun: This suffix is used at the end of boys' names to express familiarity or endearment. It is also sometimes used by men among friends, or when addressing someone younger or of lower station.

-chan: This is used to express endearment, mostly toward girls. It is also used for little boys, pets, and even among lovers. It gives a sense of childish cuteness.

Bozu: This is an informal way to refer to a boy, similar to the English term "kid" or "squirt."

Senpai/sempai: This title suggests that the addressee is one's senior in a group or organization. It is most often used in a school setting, where underclassmen refer to their upperclassmen as "senpai." It can also be used in the workplace, such as when a newer employee addresses an employee who has seniority in the company.

Kohai: This is the opposite of "sempai," and is used toward underclassmen in school or newcomers in the workplace. It connotes that the addressee is of lower station.

Sensei: Literally meaning "one who has come before," this title is used for teachers, doctors, or masters of any profession or art.

Anesan: *Anesan* (or *nesan*) is a generic term for a girl, usually older, that means sister.

Ojôsama: *Ojôsama* is a way of referring to the daughter or sister of someone with high political or social status.

-[blank]: Usually forgotten in these lists, but perhaps the most significant difference between Japanese and English. The lack of honorific means that the speaker has permission to address the person in a very intimate way. Usually, only family, spouses, or very close friends have this kind of permission. Known as *yobisute*, it can be gratifying when someone who has earned the intimacy starts to call one by one's name without an honorific. But when that intimacy hasn't been earned, it can also be very insulting.

魔法先生ネギま!

MAGISTER NEGI MAGI

9

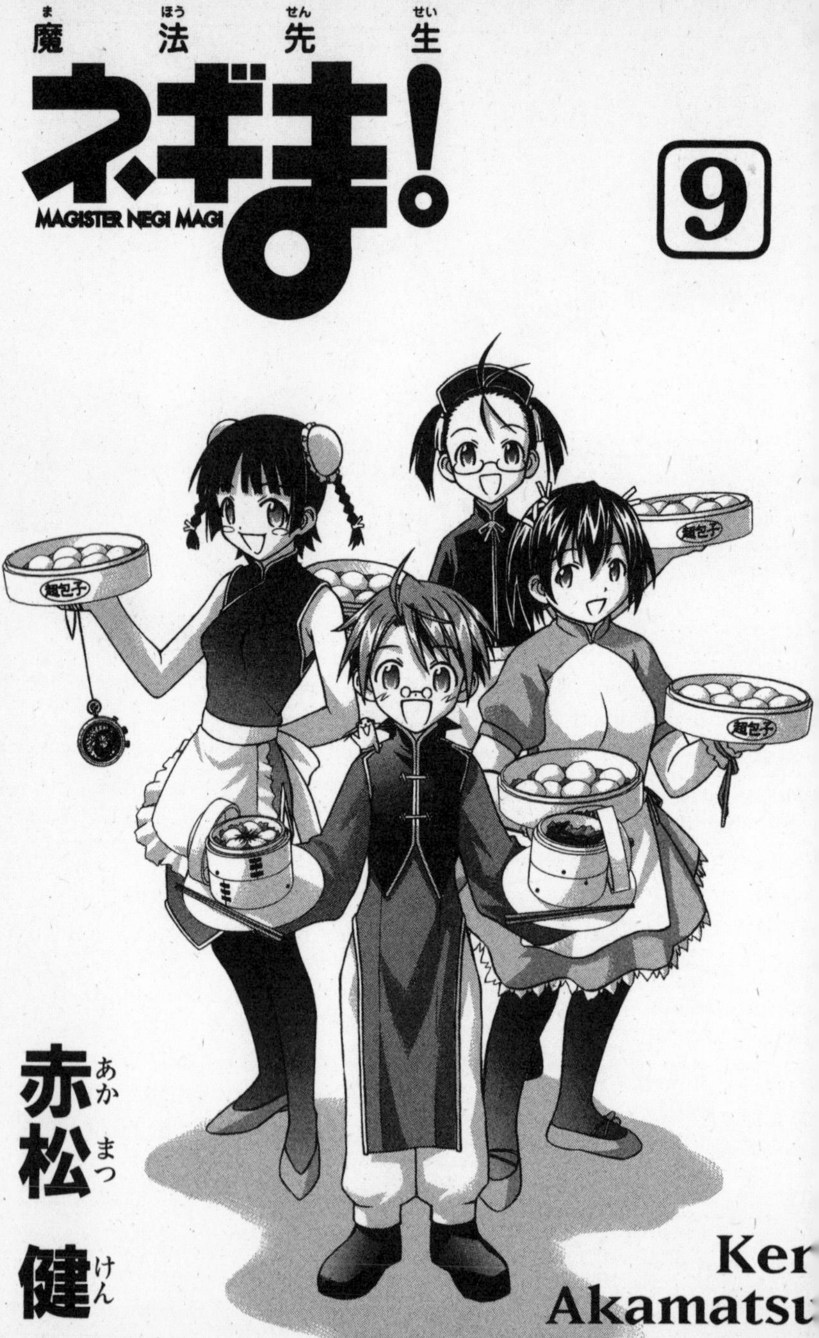
超包子

赤松健

Ken Akamatsu

CONTENTS

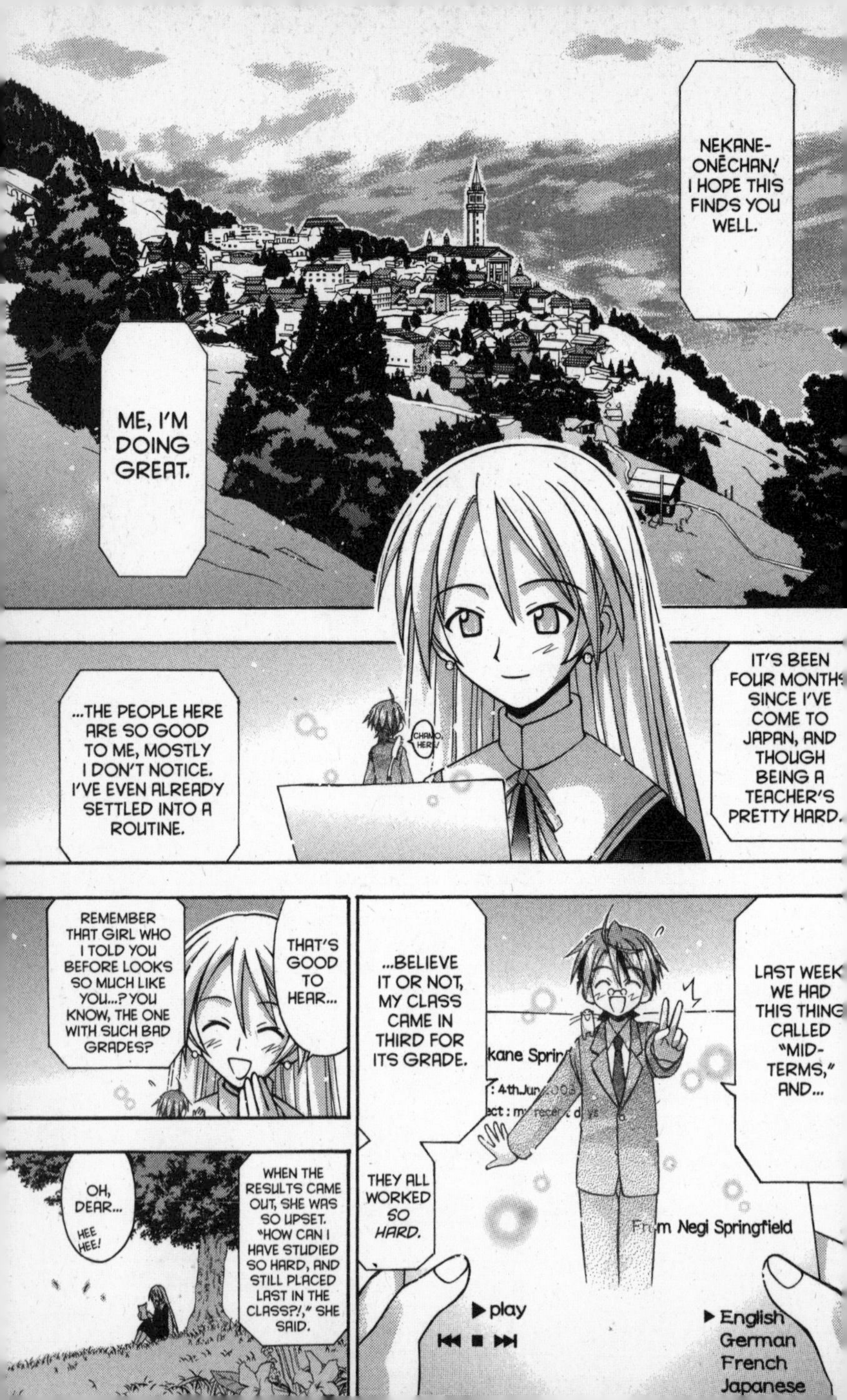
NEKANE-ONĒCHAN! I HOPE THIS FINDS YOU WELL.
ME, I'M DOING GREAT.
IT'S BEEN FOUR MONTHS SINCE I'VE COME TO JAPAN, AND THOUGH BEING A TEACHER'S PRETTY HARD.
CHAMO, HERE!
...THE PEOPLE HERE ARE SO GOOD TO ME, MOSTLY I DON'T NOTICE. I'VE EVEN ALREADY SETTLED INTO A ROUTINE.
LAST WEEK WE HAD THIS THING CALLED "MID-TERMS," AND...
...BELIEVE IT OR NOT, MY CLASS CAME IN THIRD FOR ITS GRADE.
From Negi Springfield
THEY ALL WORKED SO HARD.
▶play
▶English
German
French
Japanese
THAT'S GOOD TO HEAR...
REMEMBER THAT GIRL WHO I TOLD YOU BEFORE LOOKS SO MUCH LIKE YOU...? YOU KNOW, THE ONE WITH SUCH BAD GRADES?
WHEN THE RESULTS CAME OUT, SHE WAS SO UPSET. "HOW CAN I HAVE STUDIED SO HARD, AND STILL PLACED LAST IN THE CLASS?!," SHE SAID.
OH, DEAR...
HEE HEE!

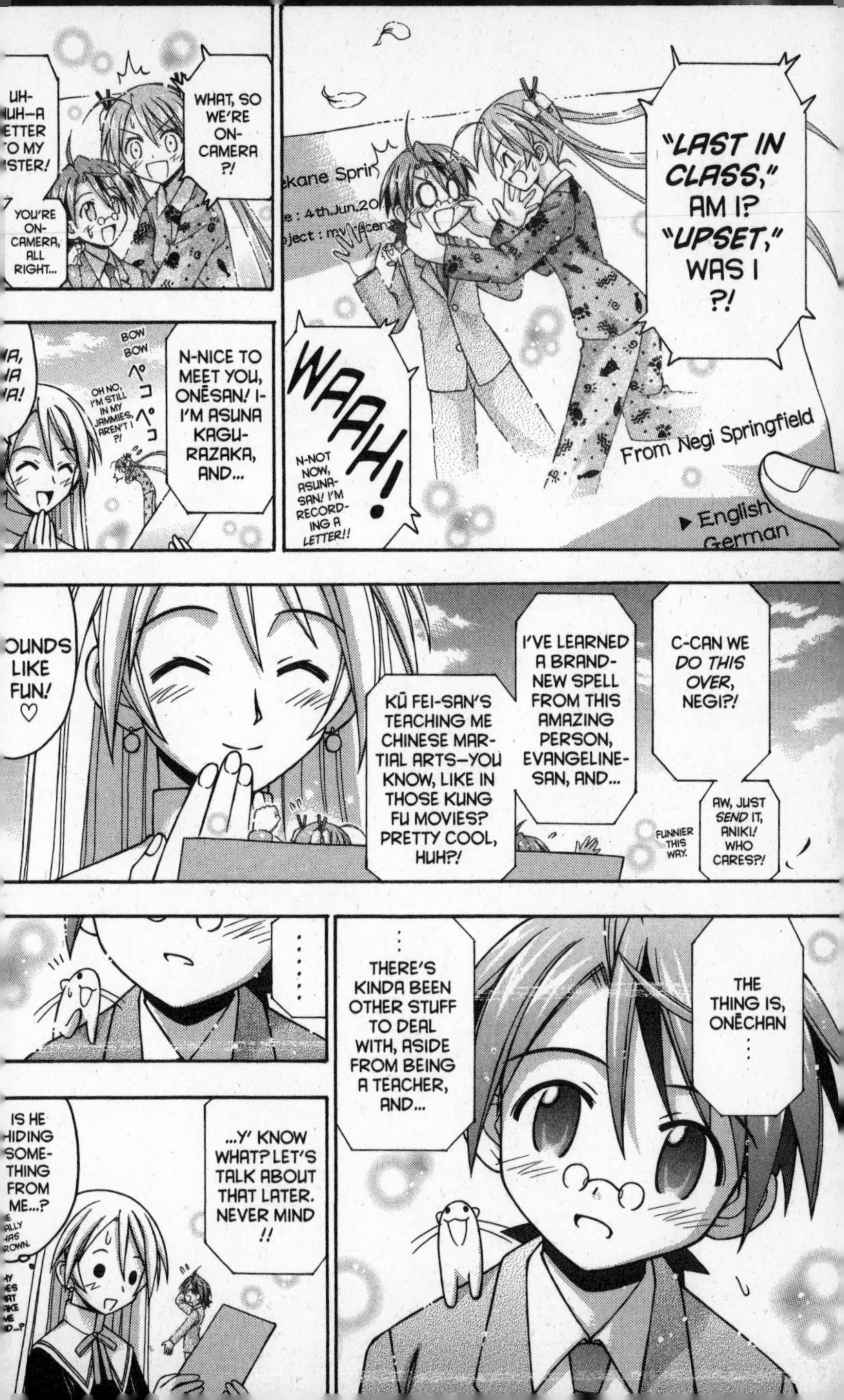
"LAST IN CLASS," AM I? "UPSET," WAS I ?!
From Negi Springfield
▶ English
German
WAAH!
N-NOT NOW, ASUNA-SAN! I'M RECORDING A LETTER!!
WHAT, SO WE'RE ON-CAMERA ?!
UH-UH—A ETTER O MY STER!
YOU'RE ON-CAMERA, ALL RIGHT...
N-NICE TO MEET YOU, ONĒSAN! I-I'M ASUNA KAGURAZAKA, AND...
BOW BOW
OH NO, I'M STILL IN MY JAMMIES, AREN'T I ?!
C-CAN WE DO THIS OVER, NEGI?!
AW, JUST SEND IT, ANIKI! WHO CARES?!
FUNNIER THIS WAY.
I'VE LEARNED A BRAND-NEW SPELL FROM THIS AMAZING PERSON, EVANGELINE-SAN, AND...
KŪ FEI-SAN'S TEACHING ME CHINESE MARTIAL ARTS—YOU KNOW, LIKE IN THOSE KUNG FU MOVIES? PRETTY COOL, HUH?!
OUNDS LIKE FUN! ♡
THE THING IS, ONĒCHAN...
...THERE'S KINDA BEEN OTHER STUFF TO DEAL WITH, ASIDE FROM BEING A TEACHER, AND...
......
...Y' KNOW WHAT? LET'S TALK ABOUT THAT LATER. NEVER MIND!!
IS HE HIDING SOMETHING FROM ME...?

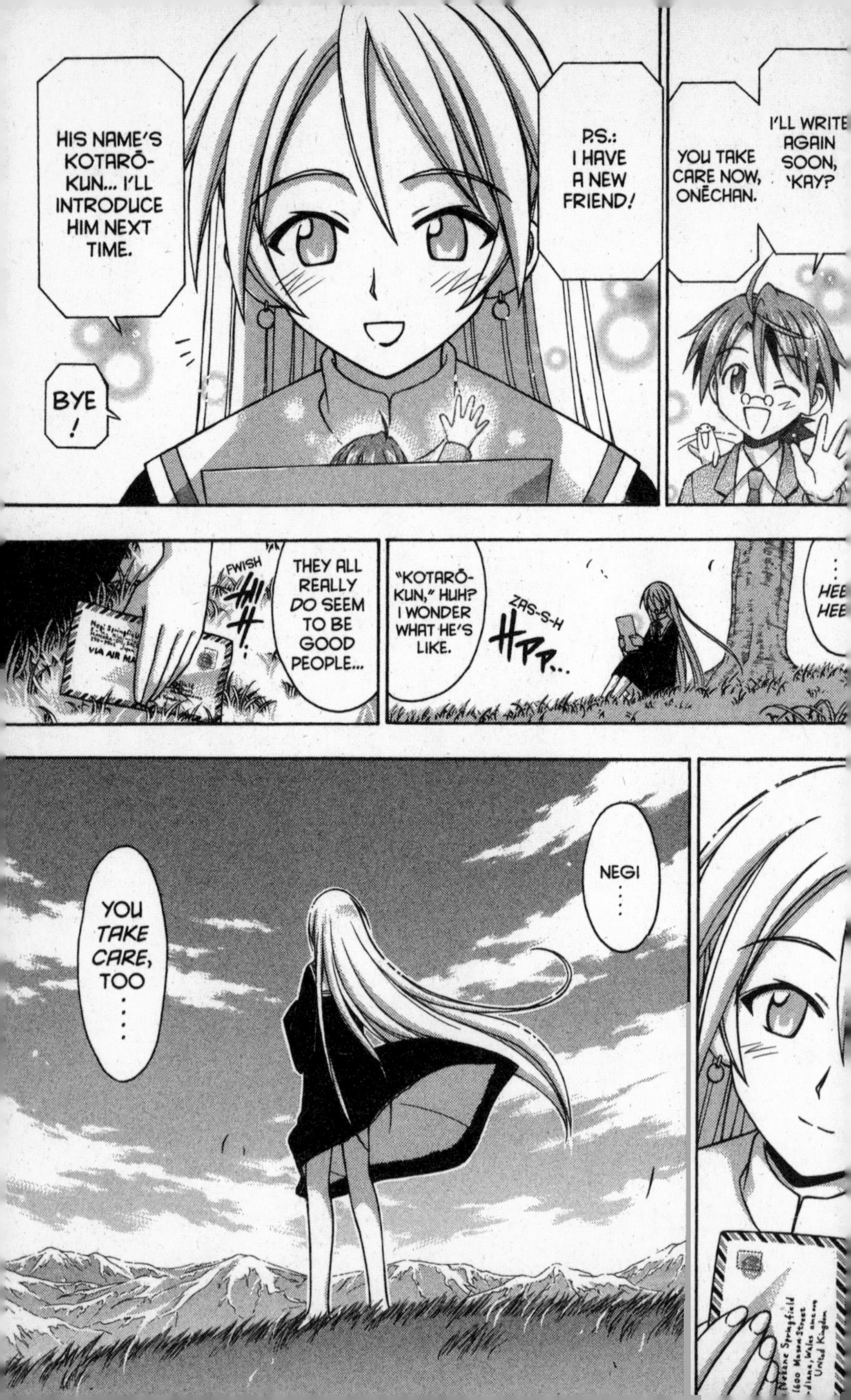
I'LL WRITE AGAIN SOON, 'KAY?
YOU TAKE CARE NOW, ONĒCHAN.
P.S.: I HAVE A NEW FRIEND!
HIS NAME'S KOTARŌ-KUN... I'LL INTRODUCE HIM NEXT TIME.
BYE!
...HEE HEE
ZAS-S-H
"KOTARŌ-KUN," HUH? I WONDER WHAT HE'S LIKE.
THEY ALL REALLY DO SEEM TO BE GOOD PEOPLE...
FWISH
NEGI.....
YOU TAKE CARE, TOO.....

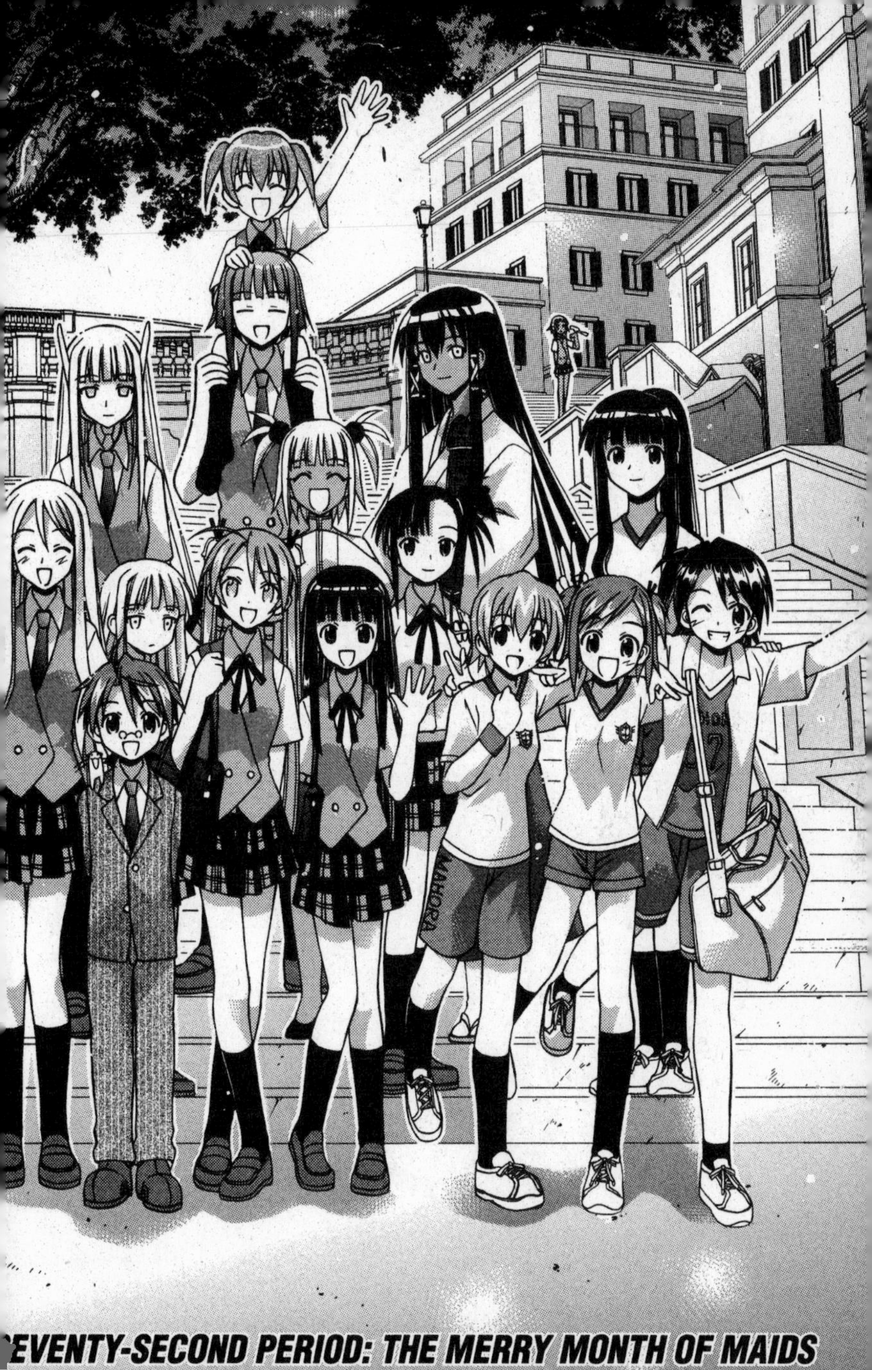
MAHORA

SEVENTY-SECOND PERIOD: THE MERRY MONTH OF MAIDS

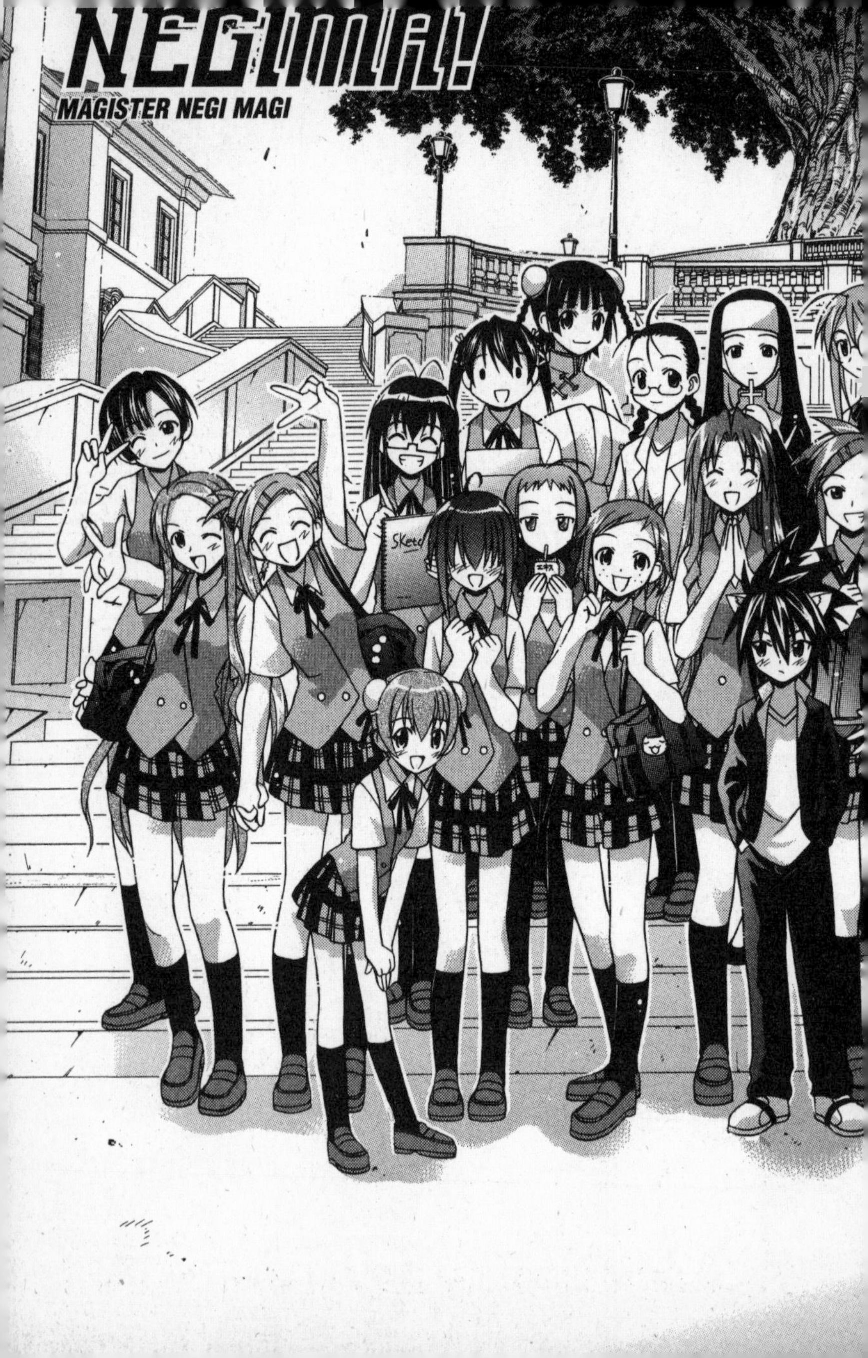
NEGIMA!
MAGISTER NEGI MAGI

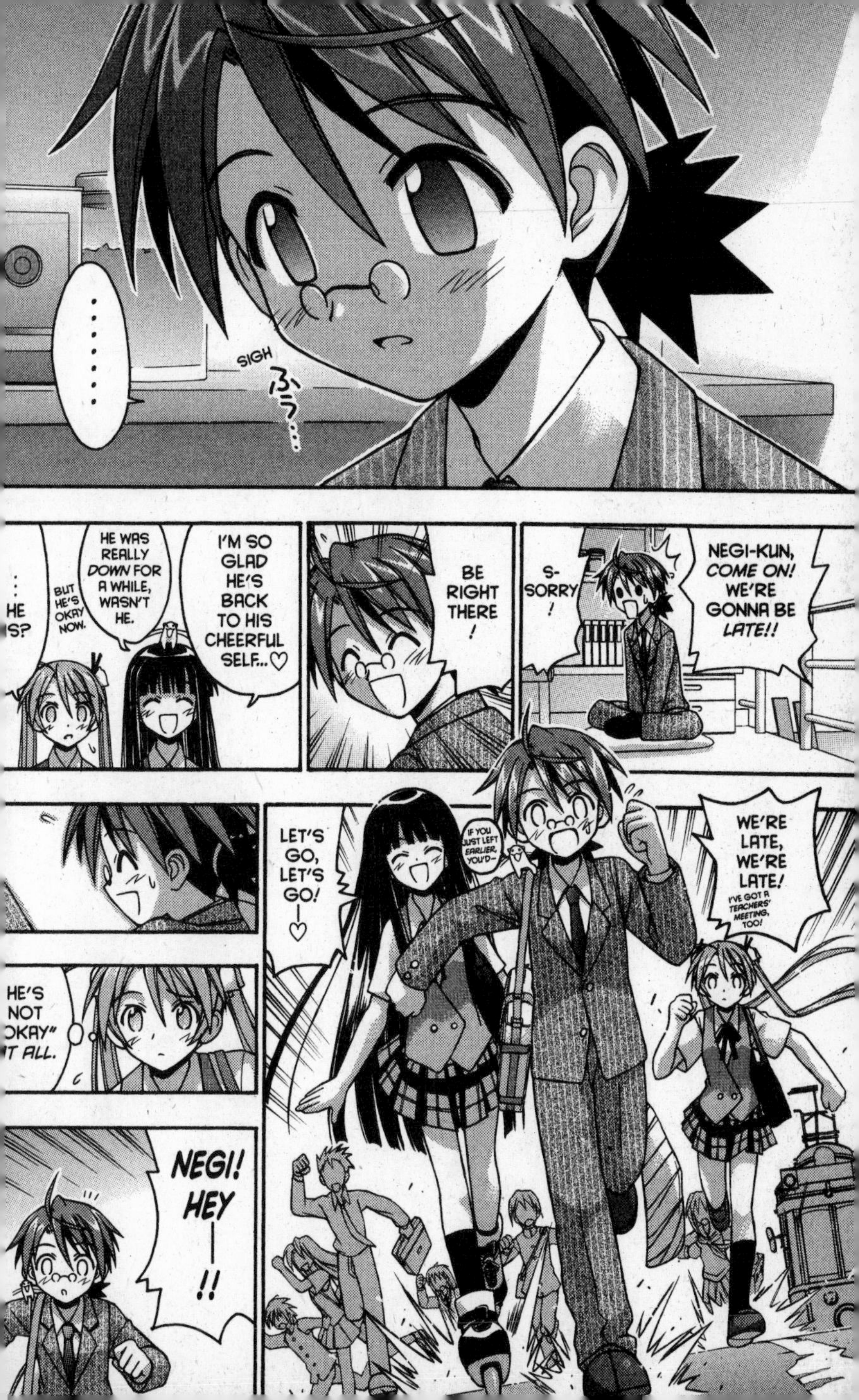
......
SIGH
ふう...
NEGI-KUN, COME ON! WE'RE GONNA BE LATE!!
S-SORRY!
BE RIGHT THERE!
I'M SO GLAD HE'S BACK TO HIS CHEERFUL SELF...♡
HE WAS REALLY DOWN FOR A WHILE, WASN'T HE.
BUT HE'S OKAY NOW.
... HE
WE'RE LATE, WE'RE LATE!
I'VE GOT A TEACHERS' MEETING, TOO!
IF YOU JUST LEFT EARLIER, YOU'D—
LET'S GO, LET'S GO! ♡
HE'S NOT OKAY" T ALL.
NEGI! HEY—!!

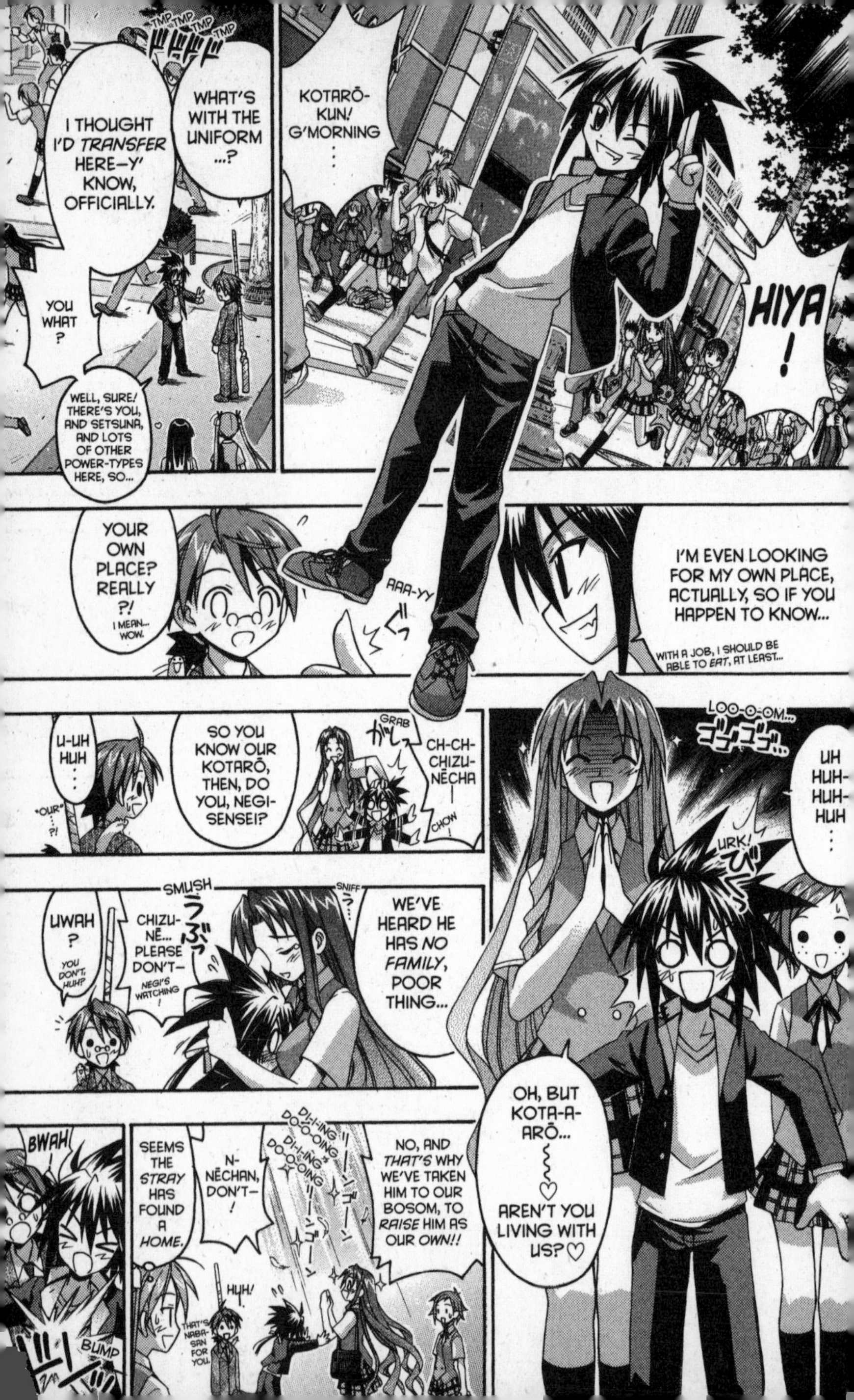
HIYA!
KOTARŌ-KUN! G'MORNING...
WHAT'S WITH THE UNIFORM...?
TMP TMP TMP TMP
I THOUGHT I'D TRANSFER HERE—Y' KNOW, OFFICIALLY.
YOU WHAT?
WELL, SURE! THERE'S YOU, AND SETSUNA, AND LOTS OF OTHER POWER-TYPES HERE, SO...
I'M EVEN LOOKING FOR MY OWN PLACE, ACTUALLY, SO IF YOU HAPPEN TO KNOW...
WITH A JOB, I SHOULD BE ABLE TO EAT, AT LEAST...
AAA-YY
YOUR OWN PLACE? REALLY?!
I MEAN... WOW.
LOO-O-OM...
UH HUH-HUH-HUH...
URK!
OH, BUT KOTA-A-ARŌ... AREN'T YOU LIVING WITH US?♡
SO YOU KNOW OUR KOTARŌ, THEN, DO YOU, NEGI-SENSEI?
GRAB
CH-CH-CHIZU-NĒCHA—!
CHOW!
U-UH HUH...
OUR...?!
WE'VE HEARD HE HAS NO FAMILY, POOR THING...
SNIFF
SMUSH
CHIZU-NĒ... PLEASE DON'T—
NEGI'S WATCHING!
UWAH?
YOU DON'T, HUH?
NO, AND THAT'S WHY WE'VE TAKEN HIM TO OUR BOSOM, TO RAISE HIM AS OUR OWN!!
DI-I-ING DO-O-OING!!
DI-I-ING DO-O-OING!!
N-NĒCHAN, DON'T—!
HUH!
THAT'S NABA-SAN FOR YOU.
SEEMS THE STRAY HAS FOUND A HOME.
BWAH!
BUMP

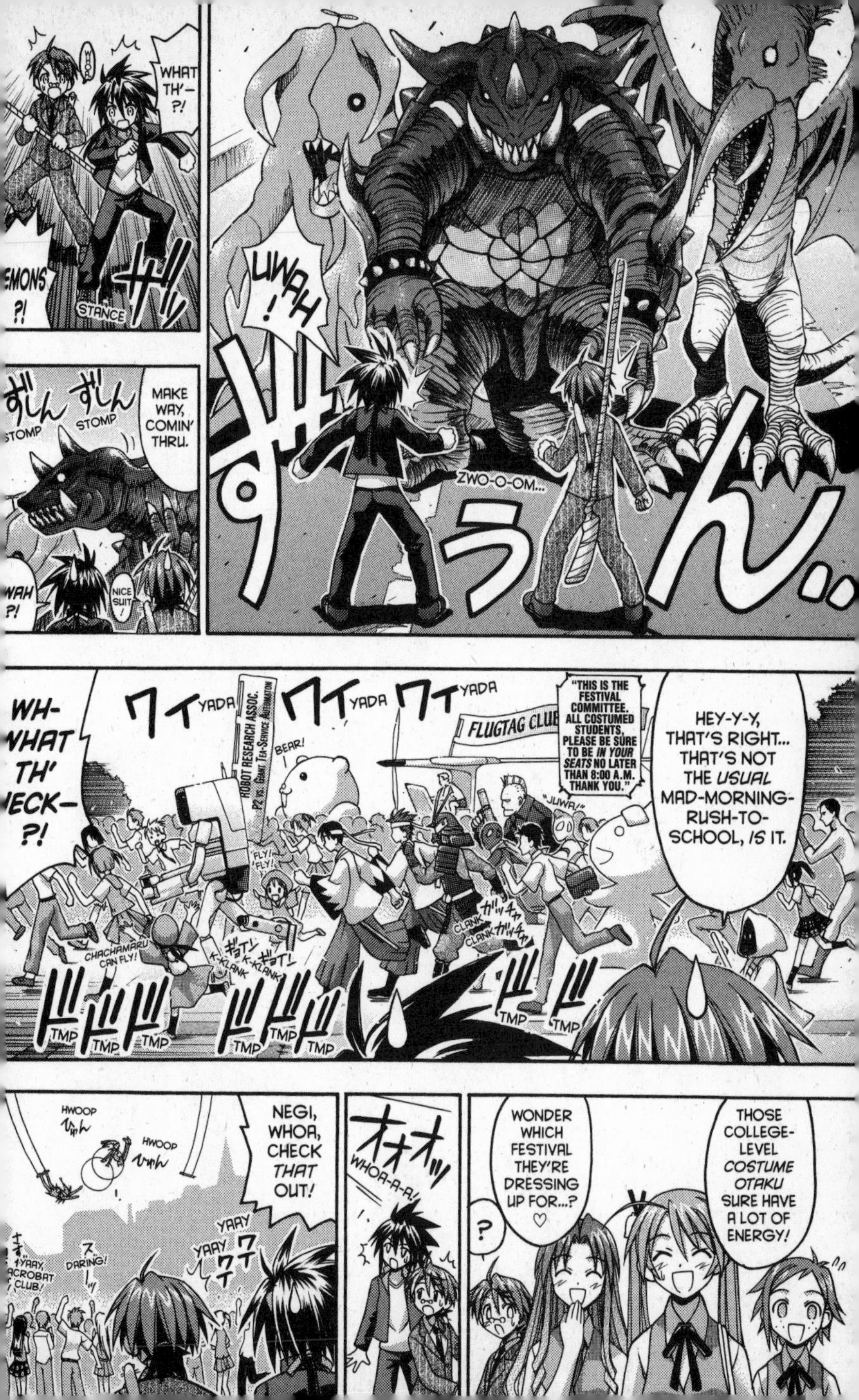
UWAH!
ZWO-O-OM...
ずうん..
WHOA
WHAT TH'—?!
EMONS ?!
ザッ
STANCE
MAKE WAY, COMIN' THRU.
ずしん STOMP
ずしん STOMP
NICE SUIT!
WAH ?!
HEY-Y-Y, THAT'S RIGHT... THAT'S NOT THE *USUAL* MAD-MORNING-RUSH-TO-SCHOOL, *IS* IT.
"THIS IS THE FESTIVAL COMMITTEE. ALL COSTUMED STUDENTS, PLEASE BE SURE TO BE *IN YOUR SEATS* NO LATER THAN 8:00 A.M. THANK YOU."
"JUWA!"
FLUGTAG CLUB
BEAR!
ROBOT RESEARCH ASSOC.
P2 vs. GIANT TEA-SERVICE AUTOMATON
ワイ YADA
ワイ YADA
ワイ YADA
FLY! FLY!
CHACHAMARU CAN FLY!
CLANK CLANK
K-KLANK K-KLANK
TMP TMP TMP TMP TMP TMP TMP TMP
WH-WHAT TH' HECK—?!
THOSE COLLEGE-LEVEL *COSTUME OTAKU* SURE HAVE A LOT OF ENERGY!
WONDER WHICH FESTIVAL THEY'RE DRESSING UP FOR...? ♡
?
オオオッ
WHOA-A-A!
NEGI, WHOA, CHECK *THAT* OUT!
HWOOP
HWOOP
YAAY
YAAY
DARING!
YAAY, ACROBAT CLUB!

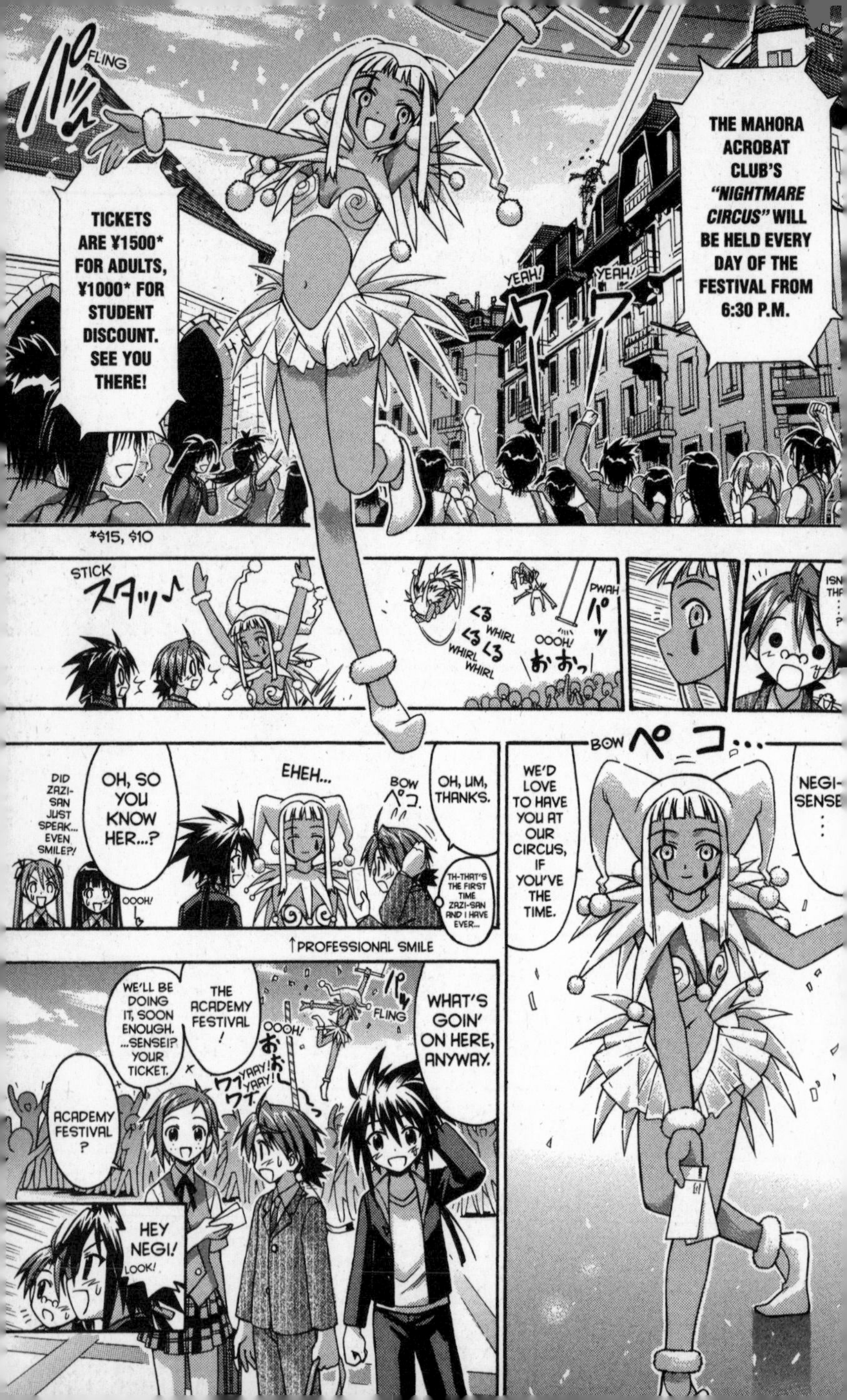
THE MAHORA ACROBAT CLUB'S "NIGHTMARE CIRCUS" WILL BE HELD EVERY DAY OF THE FESTIVAL FROM 6:30 P.M.
YEAH! YEAH!
FLING
TICKETS ARE ¥1500* FOR ADULTS, ¥1000* FOR STUDENT DISCOUNT. SEE YOU THERE!
*$15, $10
ISN THA...?
PWAH
OOOH!
WHIRL WHIRL WHIRL WHIRL
STICK
BOW
NEGI-SENSE...
WE'D LOVE TO HAVE YOU AT OUR CIRCUS, IF YOU'VE THE TIME.
OH, UM, THANKS.
BOW
EHEH...
TH-THAT'S THE FIRST TIME ZAZI-SAN AND I HAVE EVER...
OH, SO YOU KNOW HER...?
DID ZAZI-SAN JUST SPEAK... EVEN SMILE?!
OOOH!
↑PROFESSIONAL SMILE
WHAT'S GOIN' ON HERE, ANYWAY.
FLING
OOOH!
YAAY! YAAY!
THE ACADEMY FESTIVAL!
WE'LL BE DOING IT, SOON ENOUGH. ...SENSEI? YOUR TICKET.
ACADEMY FESTIVAL?
HEY NEGI!
LOOK!

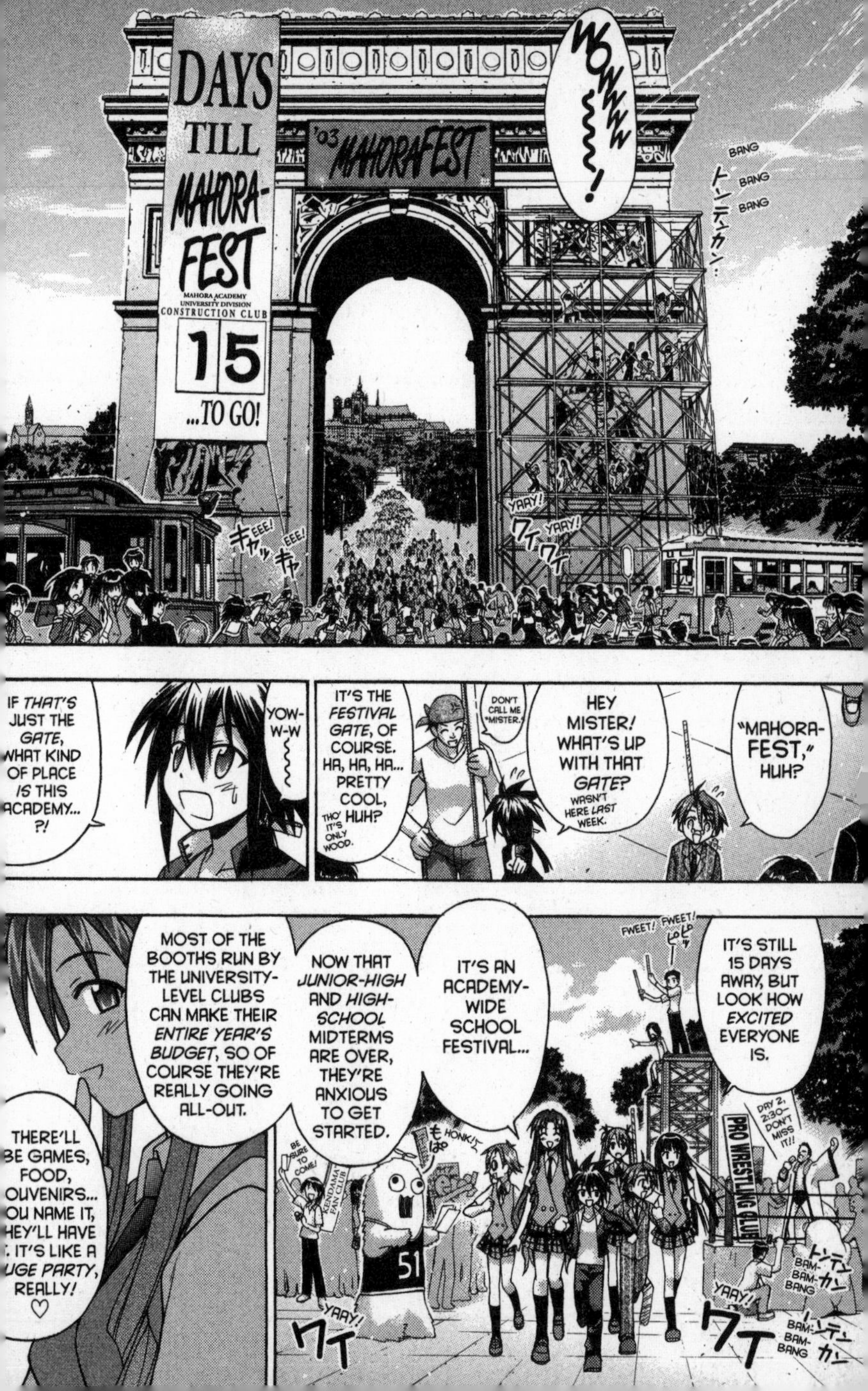
DAYS TILL MAHORA-FEST
MAHORA ACADEMY UNIVERSITY DIVISION CONSTRUCTION CLUB
15
...TO GO!
'03 MAHORAFEST
WOWWWW~~~!
BANG BANG BANG
YAAY! YAAY!
EEE! EEE!
"MAHORA-FEST," HUH?
HEY MISTER! WHAT'S UP WITH THAT GATE?
WASN'T HERE LAST WEEK.
DON'T CALL ME "MISTER."
IT'S THE FESTIVAL GATE, OF COURSE. HA, HA, HA... PRETTY COOL, HUH?
THO' IT'S ONLY WOOD.
YOW-W-W~~
IF THAT'S JUST THE GATE, WHAT KIND OF PLACE IS THIS ACADEMY...?!
FWEET! FWEET!
IT'S STILL 15 DAYS AWAY, BUT LOOK HOW EXCITED EVERYONE IS.
IT'S AN ACADEMY-WIDE SCHOOL FESTIVAL...
NOW THAT JUNIOR-HIGH AND HIGH-SCHOOL MIDTERMS ARE OVER, THEY'RE ANXIOUS TO GET STARTED.
MOST OF THE BOOTHS RUN BY THE UNIVERSITY-LEVEL CLUBS CAN MAKE THEIR ENTIRE YEAR'S BUDGET, SO OF COURSE THEY'RE REALLY GOING ALL-OUT.
DAY 2, 2:30— DON'T MISS IT!!
PRO WRESTLING CLUB
BAM-BAM-BANG
YAAY!
BAM-BAM-BANG
HONK!
BE SURE TO COME!
KENDAMA FAN CLUB
51
YAAY!
THERE'LL BE GAMES, FOOD, SOUVENIRS... YOU NAME IT, THEY'LL HAVE IT. IT'S LIKE A HUGE PARTY, REALLY! ♡

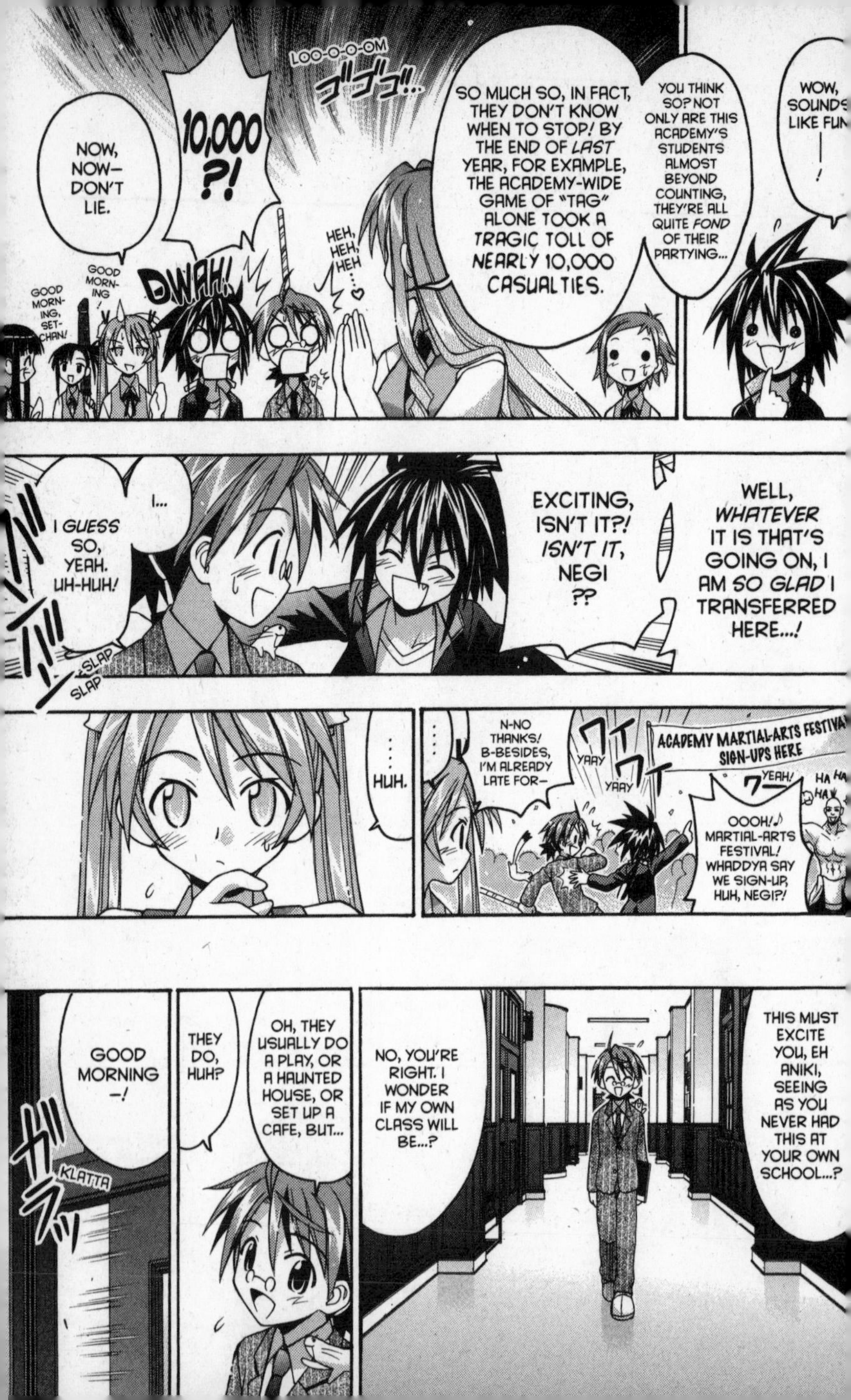
WOW, SOUNDS LIKE FUN—!
YOU THINK SO? NOT ONLY ARE THIS ACADEMY'S STUDENTS ALMOST BEYOND COUNTING, THEY'RE ALL QUITE *FOND* OF THEIR PARTYING...
SO MUCH SO, IN FACT, THEY DON'T KNOW WHEN TO STOP! BY THE END OF *LAST* YEAR, FOR EXAMPLE, THE ACADEMY-WIDE GAME OF "TAG" ALONE TOOK A *TRAGIC* TOLL OF *NEARLY* 10,000 CASUALTIES.
LOO-O-O-OM
HEH, HEH, HEH...♡
10,000?!
DWAH!
NOW, NOW— DON'T LIE.
GOOD MORNING!
GOOD MORNING, SET-CHAN!
WELL, *WHATEVER* IT IS THAT'S GOING ON, I AM *SO GLAD* I TRANSFERRED HERE...!
EXCITING, ISN'T IT?! *ISN'T IT*, NEGI??
I...
I *GUESS* SO, YEAH. UH-HUH!
SLAP SLAP
ACADEMY MARTIAL-ARTS FESTIVAL SIGN-UPS HERE
HA HA HA
YEAH!
OOOH!♪ MARTIAL-ARTS FESTIVAL! WHADDYA SAY WE SIGN-UP, HUH, NEGI!?
YAAY
YAAY
N-NO THANKS! B-BESIDES, I'M ALREADY LATE FOR—
....
... HUH.
THIS MUST EXCITE YOU, EH ANIKI, SEEING AS YOU NEVER HAD THIS AT YOUR OWN SCHOOL...?
NO, YOU'RE RIGHT. I WONDER IF MY OWN CLASS WILL BE...?
OH, THEY USUALLY DO A PLAY, OR A HAUNTED HOUSE, OR SET UP A CAFE, BUT...
THEY DO, HUH?
GOOD MORNING —!
KLATTA

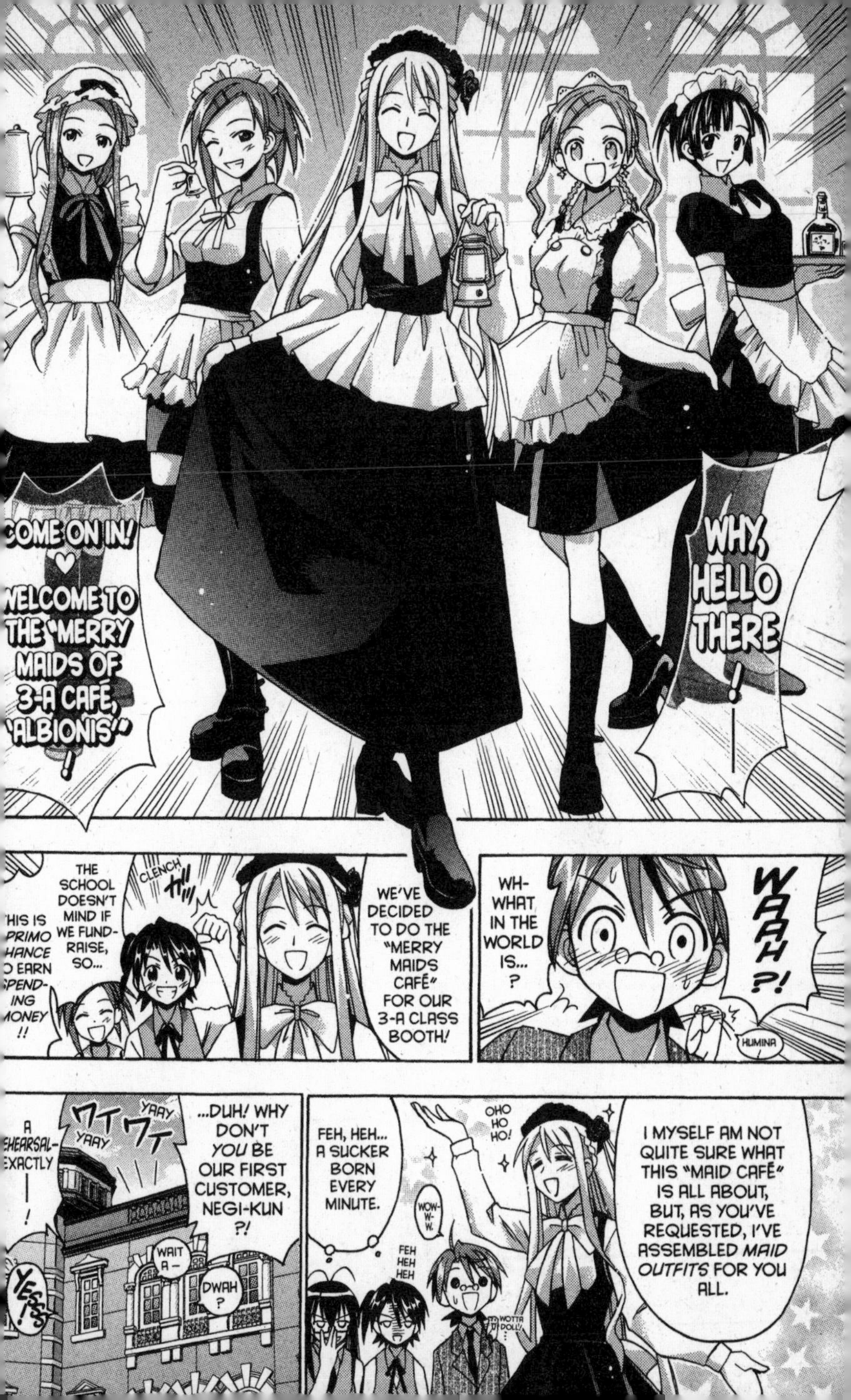
WHY, HELLO THERE!
COME ON IN! ♥ WELCOME TO THE "MERRY MAIDS OF 3-A CAFÉ, 'ALBIONIS'"!
WAAH?!
WH- WHAT IN THE WORLD IS...?
HUMINA
WE'VE DECIDED TO DO THE "MERRY MAIDS CAFÉ" FOR OUR 3-A CLASS BOOTH!
CLENCH
THE SCHOOL DOESN'T MIND IF WE FUND-RAISE, SO...
THIS IS PRIMO HANCE O EARN SPEND-ING MONEY!!
I MYSELF AM NOT QUITE SURE WHAT THIS "MAID CAFÉ" IS ALL ABOUT, BUT, AS YOU'VE REQUESTED, I'VE ASSEMBLED *MAID OUTFITS* FOR YOU ALL.
OHO HO HO!
FEH, HEH... A SUCKER BORN EVERY MINUTE.
WOW-W-W.
FEH HEH HEH
WOTTA DOLL!...
...DUH! WHY DON'T *YOU* BE OUR FIRST CUSTOMER, NEGI-KUN?!
YAAY
YAAY
WAIT A—
DWAH?
A EHEARSAL-EXACTLY—!
YESSS!

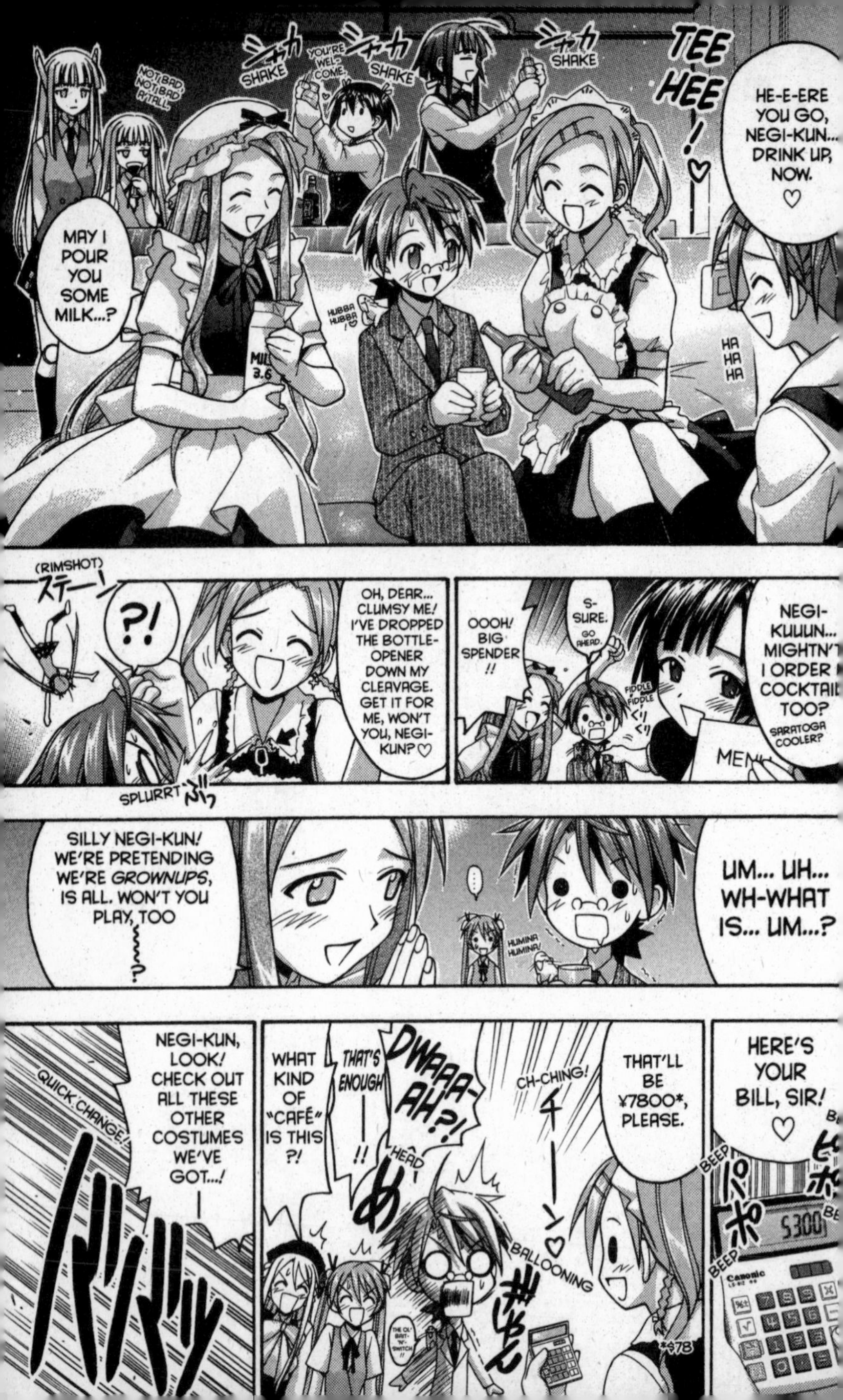
HE-E-ERE YOU GO, NEGI-KUN... DRINK UP, NOW. ♡
TEE HEE! ♡
SHAKE
SHAKE
YOU'RE WEL-COME.
SHAKE
NOT BAD, NOT BAD AT ALL.
HA HA HA
HUBBA HUBBA!
MAY I POUR YOU SOME MILK...?
NEGI-KUUUN... MIGHTN'T I ORDER COCKTAIL TOO?
SARATOGA COOLER?
MEN
S-SURE.
GO AHEAD.
OOOH! BIG SPENDER!!
FIDDLE FIDDLE
OH, DEAR... CLUMSY ME! I'VE DROPPED THE BOTTLE-OPENER DOWN MY CLEAVAGE. GET IT FOR ME, WON'T YOU, NEGI-KUN? ♡
?!
(RIMSHOT)
SPLURRT
UM... UH... WH-WHAT IS... UM...?
HUMINA HUMINA!
...
SILLY NEGI-KUN! WE'RE PRETENDING WE'RE GROWNUPS, IS ALL. WON'T YOU PLAY, TOO?
HERE'S YOUR BILL, SIR! ♡
BEEP
BEEP
5300
THAT'LL BE ¥7800*, PLEASE.
CH-CHING!
BALLOONING
*$78
DWAAAA-AH?!
THAT'S ENOUGH!!
WHAT KIND OF "CAFÉ" IS THIS?!
HEAD
THE OL' BAIT-'N'-SWITCH!!
NEGI-KUN, LOOK! CHECK OUT ALL THESE OTHER COSTUMES WE'VE GOT...!
QUICK CHANGE!

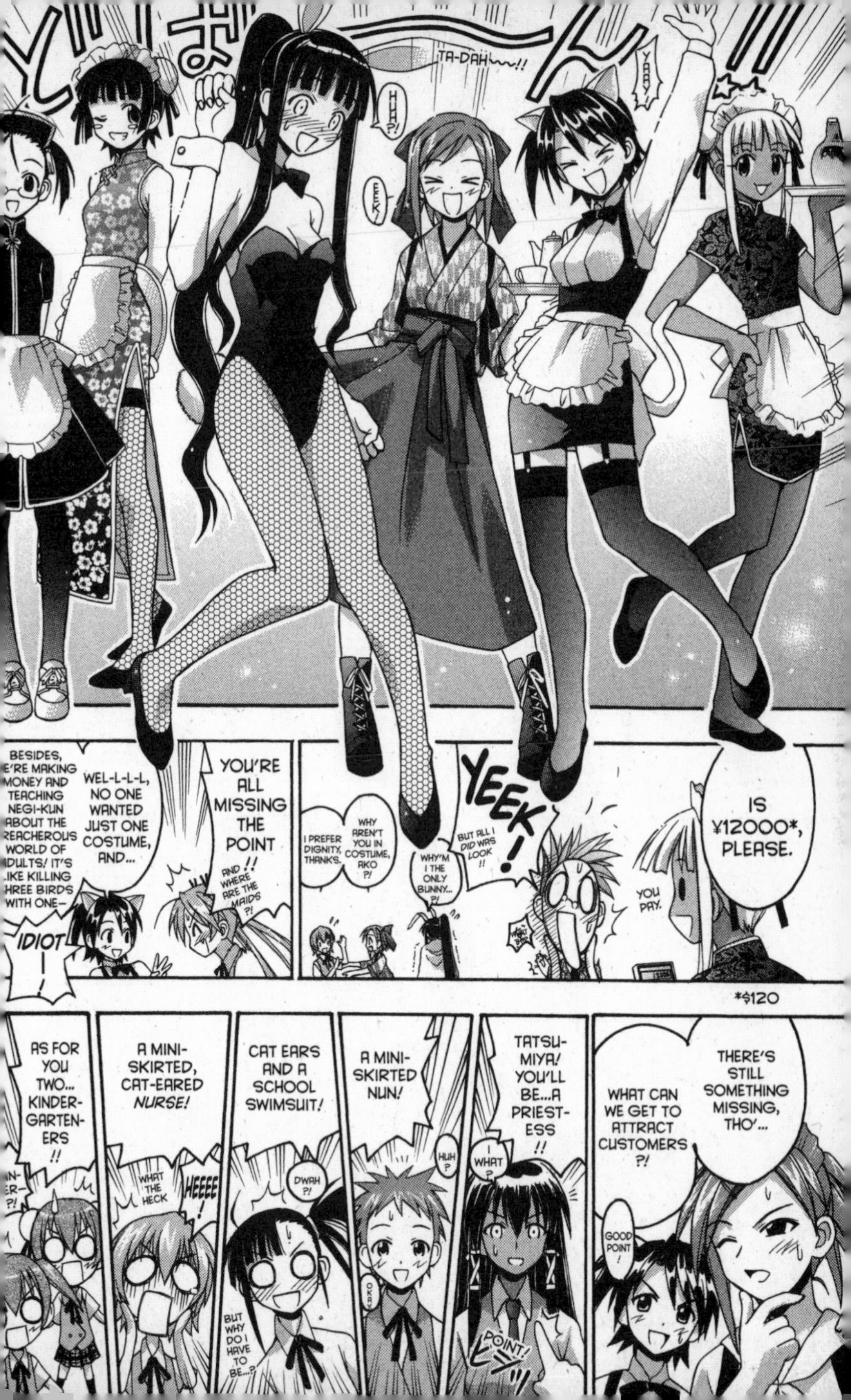
TA-DAH~~!!
YAAY!
HUH?!
EEK!
IS ¥12000*, PLEASE.
YOU PAY.
YEEK!
BUT ALL I DID WAS LOOK!!
WHY AREN'T YOU IN COSTUME, AKO?!
I PREFER DIGNITY, THANKS.
WHY'M I THE ONLY BUNNY...?!
YOU'RE ALL MISSING THE POINT!!
AND WHERE ARE THE MAIDS?!
WEL-L-L-L, NO ONE WANTED JUST ONE COSTUME, AND...
BESIDES, E'RE MAKING MONEY AND TEACHING NEGI-KUN ABOUT THE TREACHEROUS WORLD OF DULTS! IT'S IKE KILLING HREE BIRDS WITH ONE—
IDIOT!
*$120
THERE'S STILL SOMETHING MISSING, THO'...
WHAT CAN WE GET TO ATTRACT CUSTOMERS?!
GOOD POINT!
TATSUMIYA! YOU'LL BE...A PRIESTESS!!
I WHAT?
A MINI-SKIRTED NUN!
HUH?
OKAY
CAT EARS AND A SCHOOL SWIMSUIT!
DWAH?!
BUT WHY DO I HAVE TO BE...?
POINT!
A MINI-SKIRTED, CAT-EARED NURSE!
WHAT THE HECK
HEEEE!
AS FOR YOU TWO... KINDERGARTENERS!!

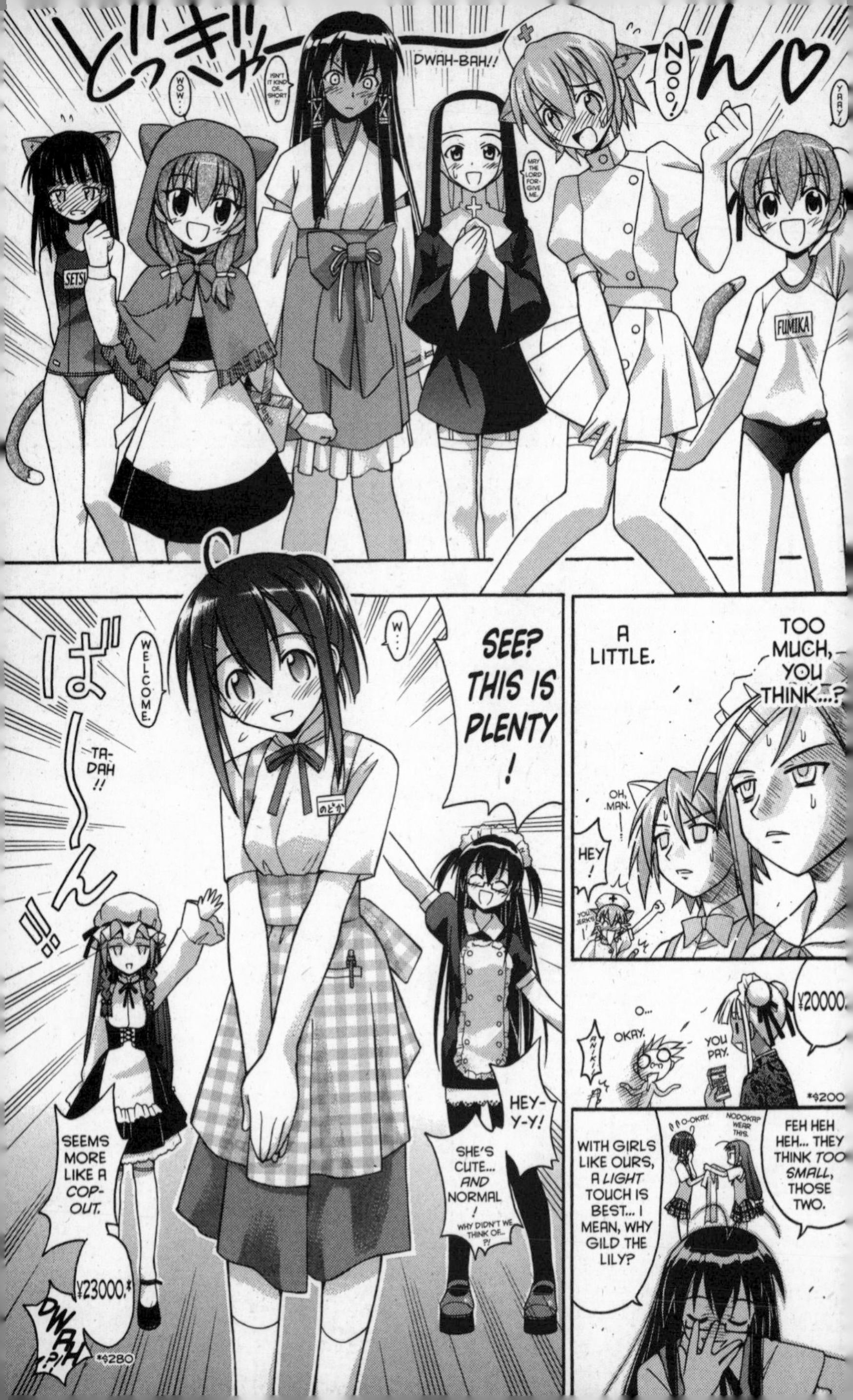

どっぎゃーーーん♡
YAAY!
FUMIKA
NOOO!
DWAH-BAH!!
MAY THE LORD FORGIVE ME.
AIN'T IT KIND OF... SHORT?!
WOW...
SETSU
TOO MUCH, YOU THINK...?
A LITTLE.
OH, MAN.
HEY!
YOU JERKS!
¥20000.
YOU PAY.
O... OKAY.
ANIKI!
*$200
FEH HEH HEH... THEY THINK TOO SMALL, THOSE TWO.
NODOKA? WEAR THIS.
O-OKAY.
WITH GIRLS LIKE OURS, A LIGHT TOUCH IS BEST... I MEAN, WHY GILD THE LILY?
SEE? THIS IS PLENTY!
W...
WELCOME.
ばーーん!!
TA-DAH!!
のどか
HEY-Y-Y!
SHE'S CUTE... AND NORMAL!
WHY DIDN'T WE THINK OF...?!
SEEMS MORE LIKE A COP-OUT.
¥23000.*
DWAH?!
*$280

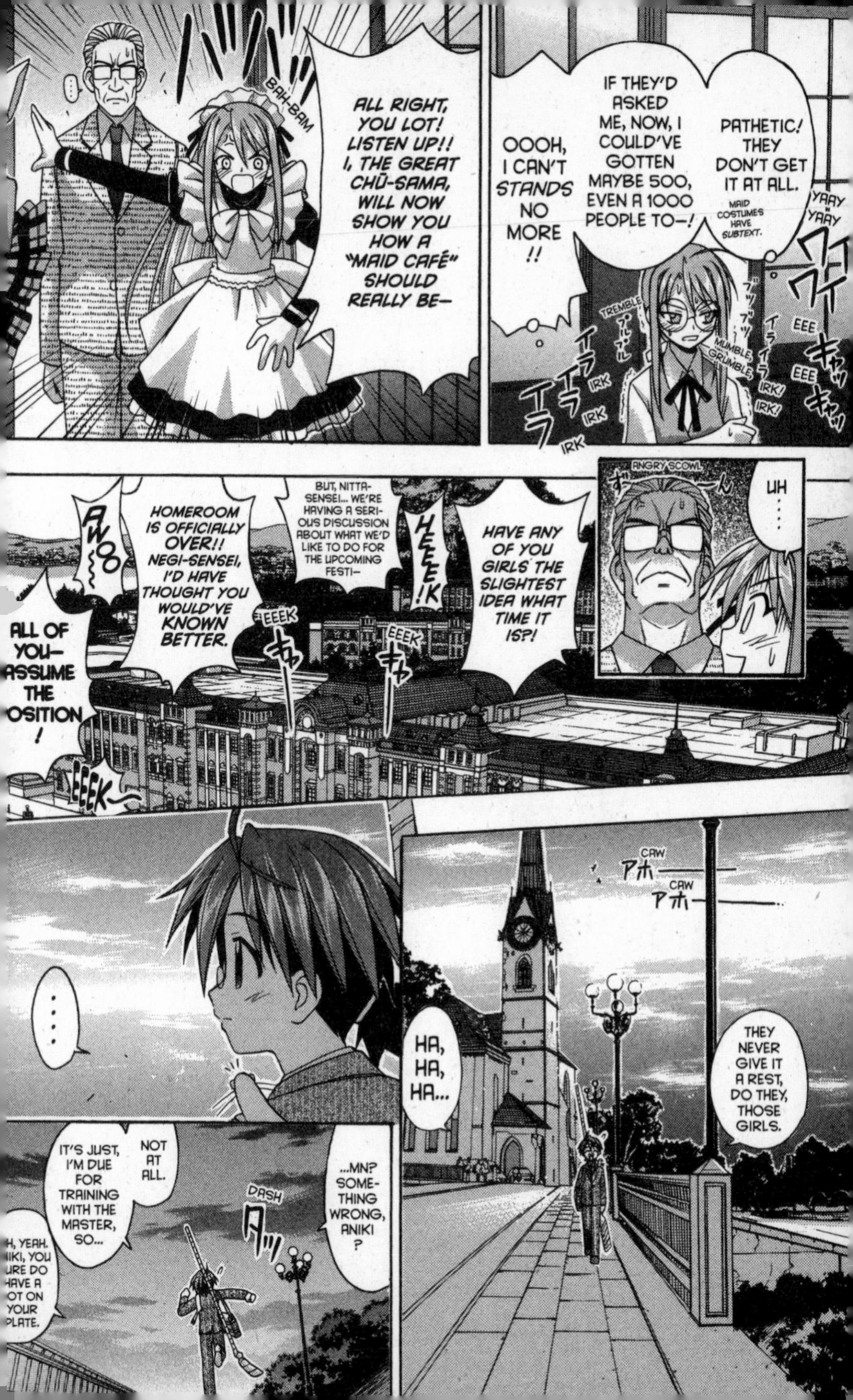
PATHETIC! THEY DON'T GET IT AT ALL.
MAID COSTUMES HAVE SUBTEXT.
YAAY YAAY
EEE EEE
IF THEY'D ASKED ME, NOW, I COULD'VE GOTTEN MAYBE 500, EVEN A 1000 PEOPLE TO—!
MUMBLE, GRUMBLE,
IRK! IRK!
TREMBLE
IRK IRK IRK
OOOH, I CAN'T STANDS NO MORE !!
ALL RIGHT, YOU LOT! LISTEN UP!! I, THE GREAT CHŪ-SAMA, WILL NOW SHOW YOU HOW A "MAID CAFÉ" SHOULD REALLY BE—
BAH-BAM
...
UH ....
ANGRY SCOWL
HAVE ANY OF YOU GIRLS THE SLIGHTEST IDEA WHAT TIME IT IS?!
HEEEEK!
EEEK
BUT, NITTA-SENSEI... WE'RE HAVING A SERIOUS DISCUSSION ABOUT WHAT WE'D LIKE TO DO FOR THE UPCOMING FESTI—
EEEK
HOMEROOM IS OFFICIALLY OVER!! NEGI-SENSEI, I'D HAVE THOUGHT YOU WOULD'VE KNOWN BETTER.
AWOO~~
ALL OF YOU— ASSUME THE OSITION !
EEEK~
CAW
CAW
THEY NEVER GIVE IT A REST, DO THEY, THOSE GIRLS.
HA, HA, HA...
....
...MN? SOMETHING WRONG, ANIKI?
DASH
NOT AT ALL.
IT'S JUST, I'M DUE FOR TRAINING WITH THE MASTER, SO...
H, YEAH. NIKI, YOU URE DO HAVE A OT ON YOUR PLATE.

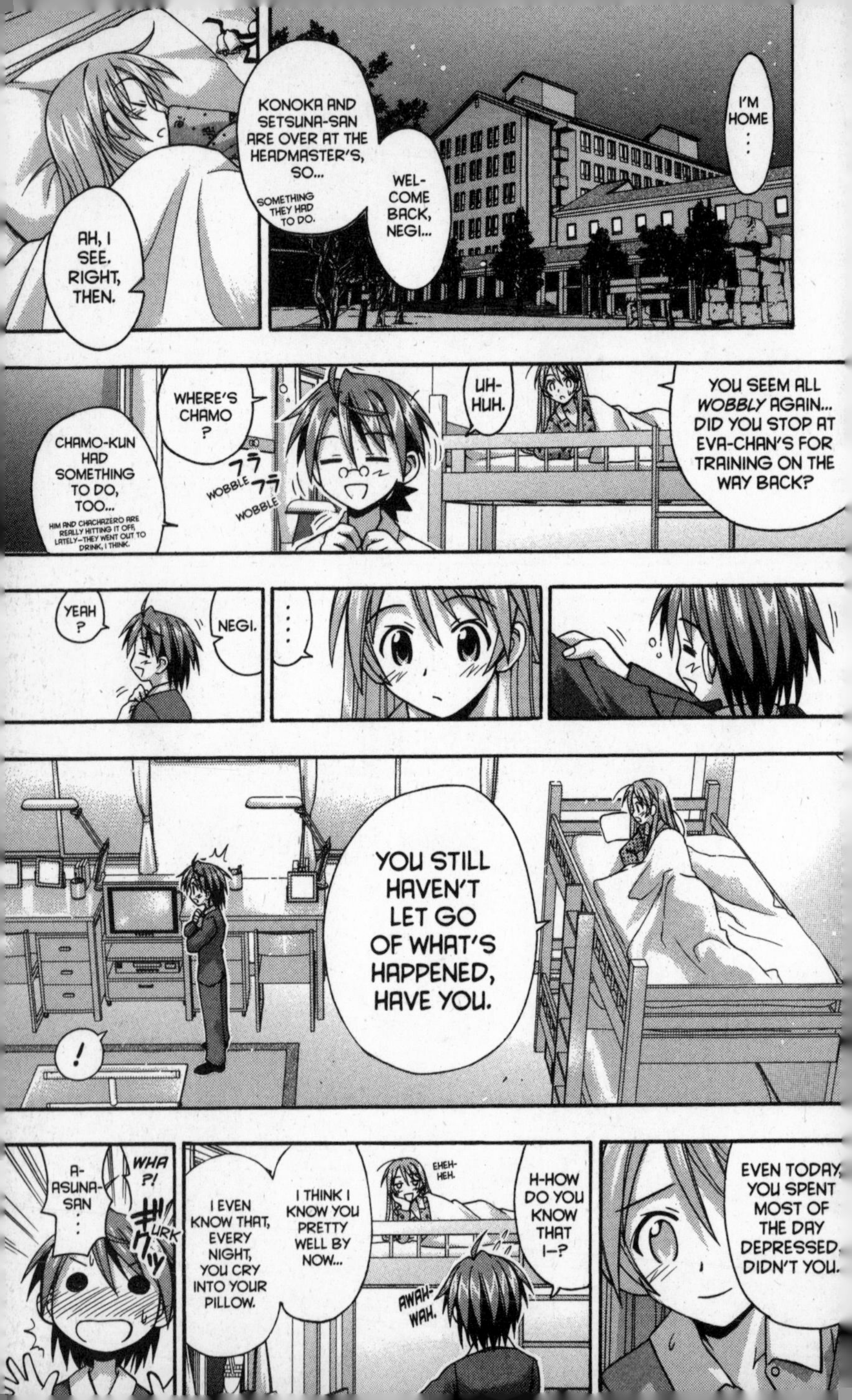

I'M HOME . . .
WEL-COME BACK, NEGI...
KONOKA AND SETSUNA-SAN ARE OVER AT THE HEADMASTER'S, SO...
SOMETHING THEY HAD TO DO.
AH, I SEE. RIGHT, THEN.
YOU SEEM ALL *WOBBLY* AGAIN... DID YOU STOP AT EVA-CHAN'S FOR TRAINING ON THE WAY BACK?
UH-HUH.
WHERE'S CHAMO?
フラ WOBBLE
フラ WOBBLE
CHAMO-KUN HAD SOMETHING TO DO, TOO...
HIM AND CHACHAZERO ARE REALLY HITTING IT OFF, LATELY—THEY WENT OUT TO DRINK, I THINK.
. . . .
NEGI.
YEAH?
YOU STILL HAVEN'T LET GO OF WHAT'S HAPPENED, HAVE YOU.
!
EVEN TODAY, YOU SPENT MOST OF THE DAY DEPRESSED, DIDN'T YOU.
H-HOW DO YOU KNOW THAT I–?
EHEH-HEH.
I THINK I KNOW YOU PRETTY WELL BY NOW...
I EVEN KNOW THAT, EVERY NIGHT, YOU CRY INTO YOUR PILLOW.
AWAH-WAH.
WHA?!
ギクッ URK
A-ASUNA-SAN . . .

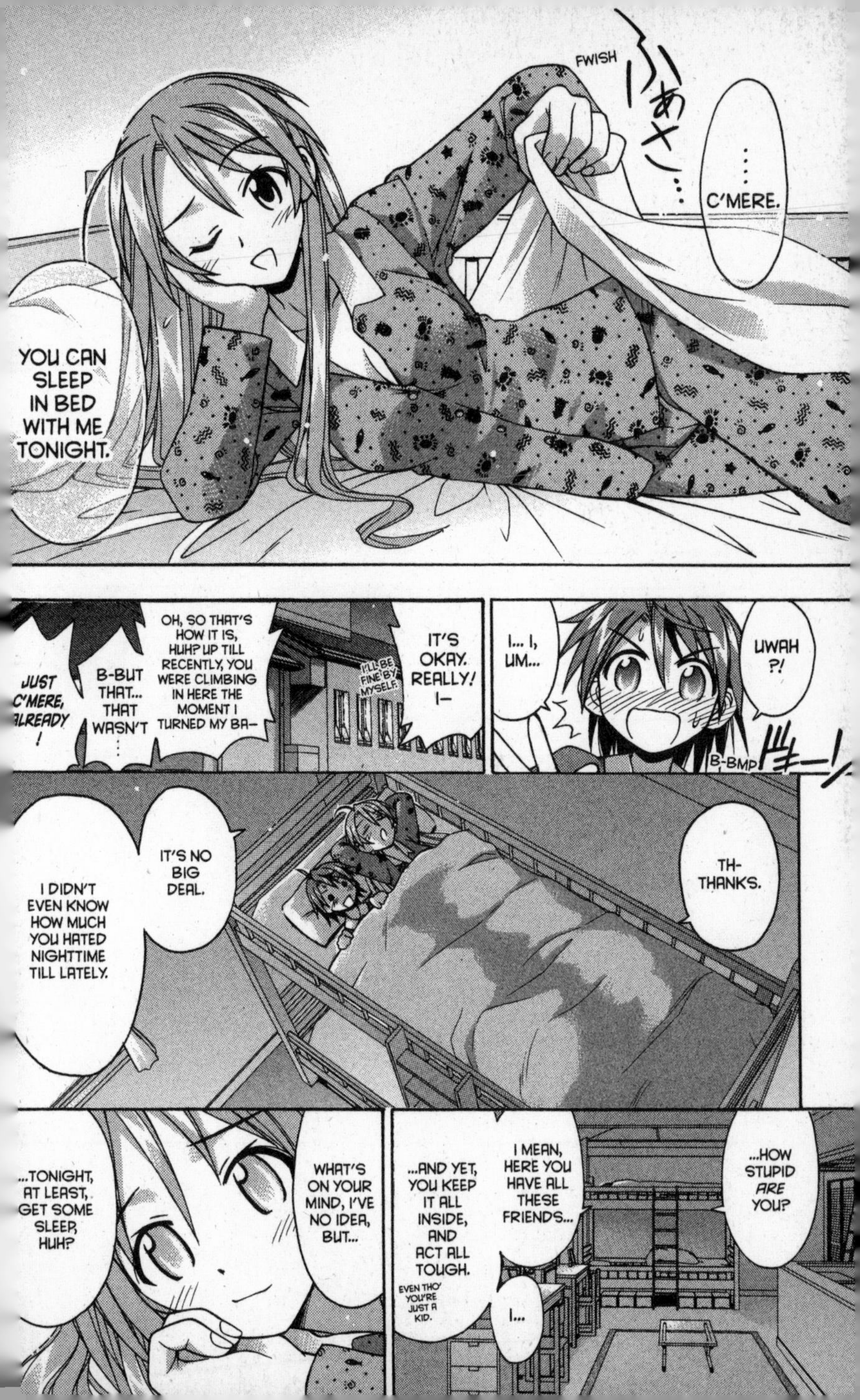
FWISH
ふぁさ…
…… C'MERE.
YOU CAN SLEEP IN BED WITH ME TONIGHT.
UWAH ?!
I... I, UM...
B-BMP
IT'S OKAY. REALLY! I—
I'LL BE FINE BY MYSELF.
OH, SO THAT'S HOW IT IS, HUH? UP TILL RECENTLY, YOU WERE CLIMBING IN HERE THE MOMENT I TURNED MY BA—
B-BUT THAT... THAT WASN'T ...
JUST C'MERE, ALREADY!
TH- THANKS.
IT'S NO BIG DEAL.
I DIDN'T EVEN KNOW HOW MUCH YOU HATED NIGHTTIME TILL LATELY.
...HOW STUPID *ARE* YOU?
I MEAN, HERE YOU HAVE ALL THESE FRIENDS...
I...
...AND YET, YOU KEEP IT ALL INSIDE, AND ACT ALL TOUGH.
EVEN THO' YOU'RE JUST A KID.
WHAT'S ON YOUR MIND, I'VE NO IDEA, BUT...
...TONIGHT, AT LEAST, GET SOME SLEEP, HUH?

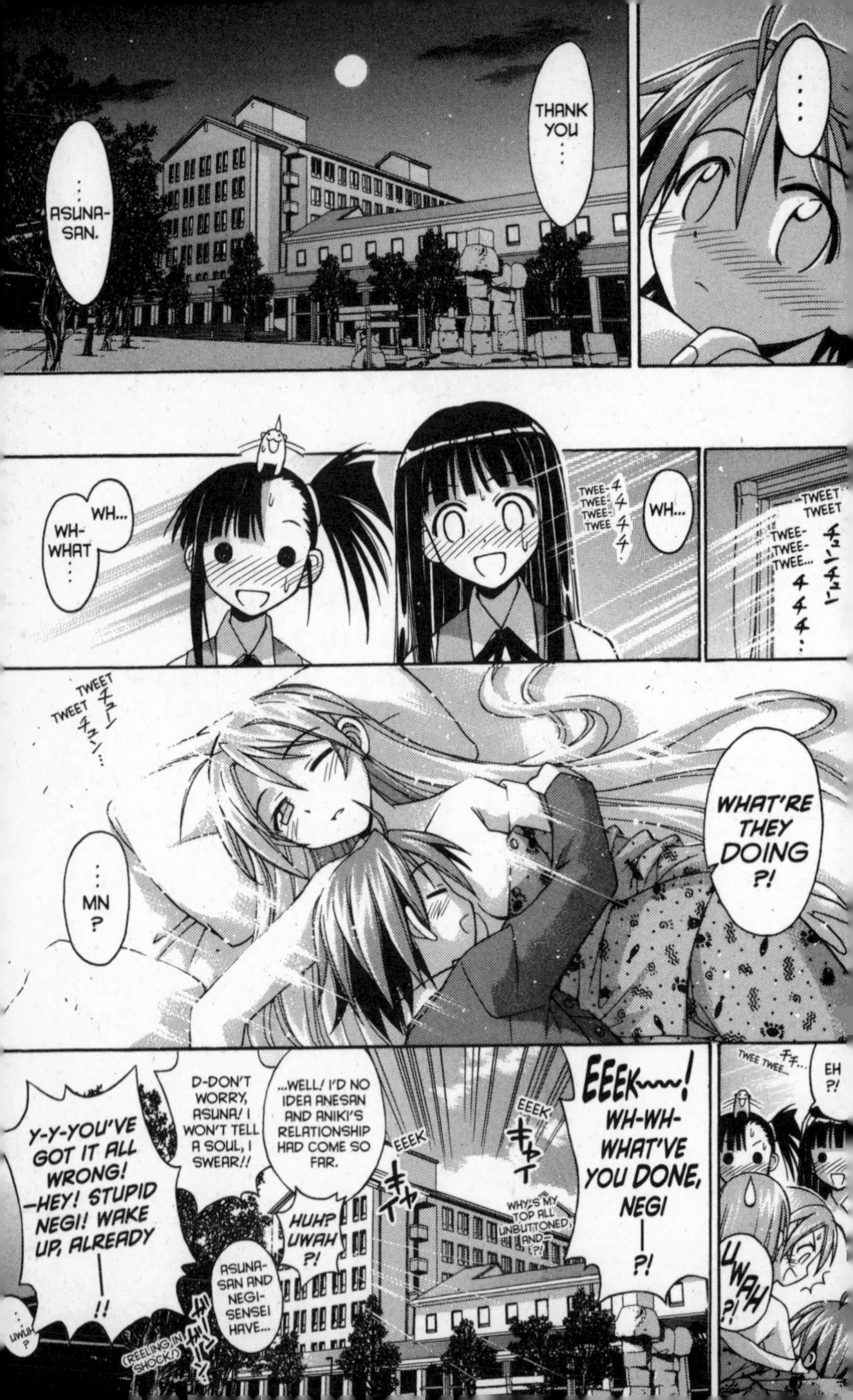
....
THANK YOU ...
... ASUNA-SAN.
TWEET TWEET
TWEE- TWEE- TWEE...
チュンチュン
チチチ...
TWEE- TWEE- TWEE- TWEE
チチチチ
WH...
WH... WH-WHAT ...
WHAT'RE THEY DOING ?!
TWEET TWEET
チュン チュン...
... MN ?
TWEE TWEE...
チチ...
EH ?!
UWAH ?!
EEEK~~~!
WH-WH-WHAT'VE YOU DONE, NEGI —?!
EEEK
キャ
WHY'S MY TOP ALL UNBUTTONED, AND—?!
EEEK
キャ
...WELL! I'D NO IDEA ANESAN AND ANIKI'S RELATIONSHIP HAD COME SO FAR.
HUH? UWAH ?!
D-DON'T WORRY, ASUNA! I WON'T TELL A SOUL, I SWEAR!!
ASUNA-SAN AND NEGI-SENSEI HAVE...
(REELING IN SHOCK)
Y-Y-YOU'VE GOT IT ALL WRONG! —HEY! STUPID NEGI! WAKE UP, ALREADY —!!
... UWUH ?

STUDENT NUMBER 30
YOTSUBA, SATSUKI
BORN: 12 MAY 1988
BLOODTYPE: A
LIKES: COOKING; HAVING OTHERS
       ENJOY MY COOKING; TAKING IT
       EASY
DISLIKES: NOTHING IN PARTICULAR...
       COMPETITION, MAYBE?
AFFILIATIONS: CHAIRMAN, "HOT LUNCH"
       COMMITTEE; MEMBER, COOKING
       RESEARCH CIRCLE

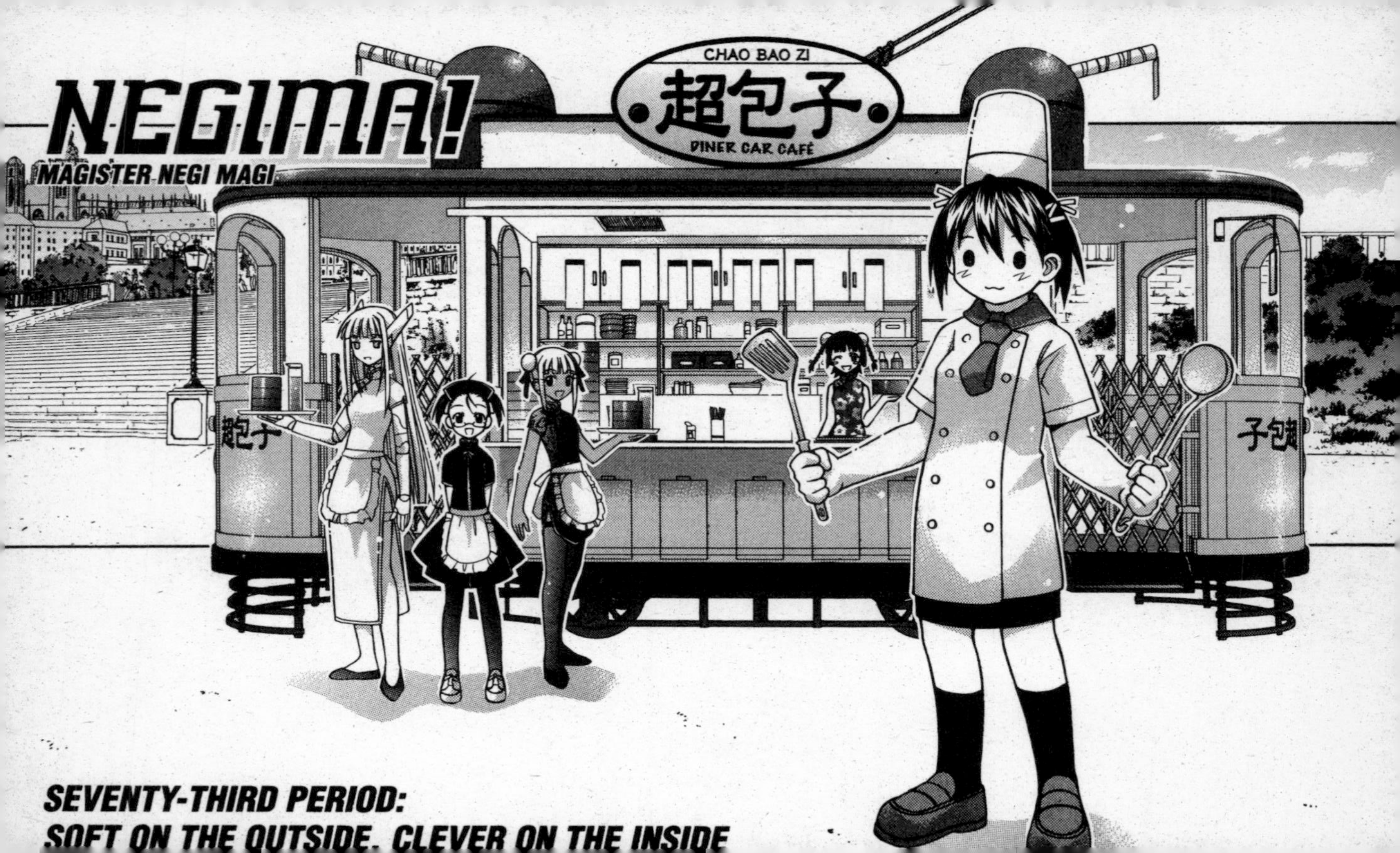
NEGIMA!
MAGISTER NEGI MAGI
CHAO BAO ZI
超包子
DINER CAR CAFÉ
超包子
子包超
SEVENTY-THIRD PERIOD:
SOFT ON THE OUTSIDE, CLEVER ON THE INSIDE

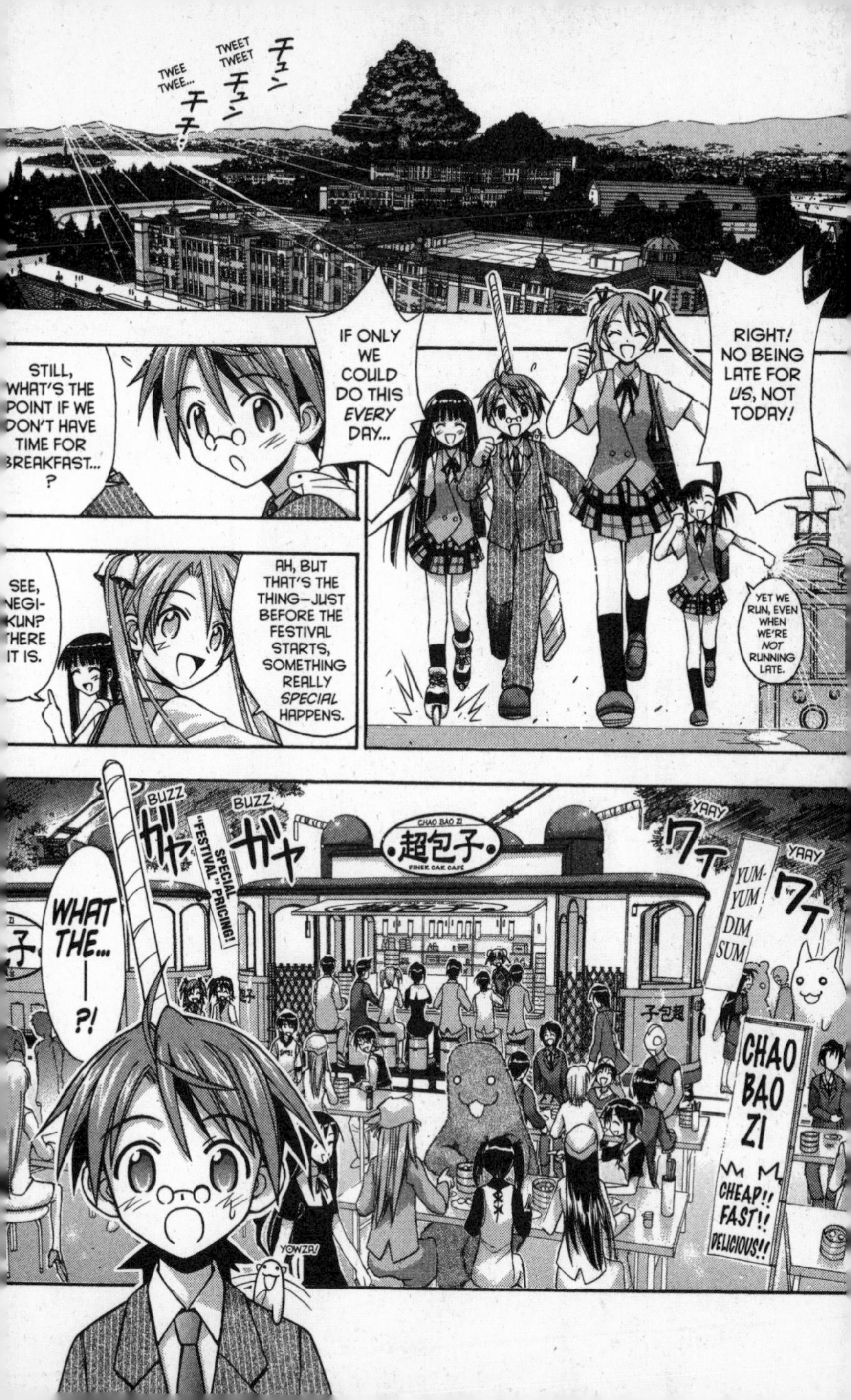
TWEET TWEET
チュン チュン
TWEE TWEE...
チチ
RIGHT! NO BEING LATE FOR *US*, NOT TODAY!
IF ONLY WE COULD DO THIS *EVERY* DAY...
YET WE RUN, EVEN WHEN WE'RE *NOT* RUNNING LATE.
STILL, WHAT'S THE POINT IF WE DON'T HAVE TIME FOR BREAKFAST...?
AH, BUT THAT'S THE THING—JUST BEFORE THE FESTIVAL STARTS, SOMETHING REALLY *SPECIAL* HAPPENS.
SEE, NEGI-KUN? THERE IT IS.
YAAY
ワァ
YAAY
ワァ
YUM-YUM DIM SUM
CHAO BAO ZI
超包子
DINER CAR CAFE
BUZZ
ガヤ
BUZZ
ガヤ
SPECIAL "FESTIVAL" PRICING!
WHAT THE...—?!
CHAO BAO ZI
CHEAP!! FAST!! DELICIOUS!!
YOWZA!

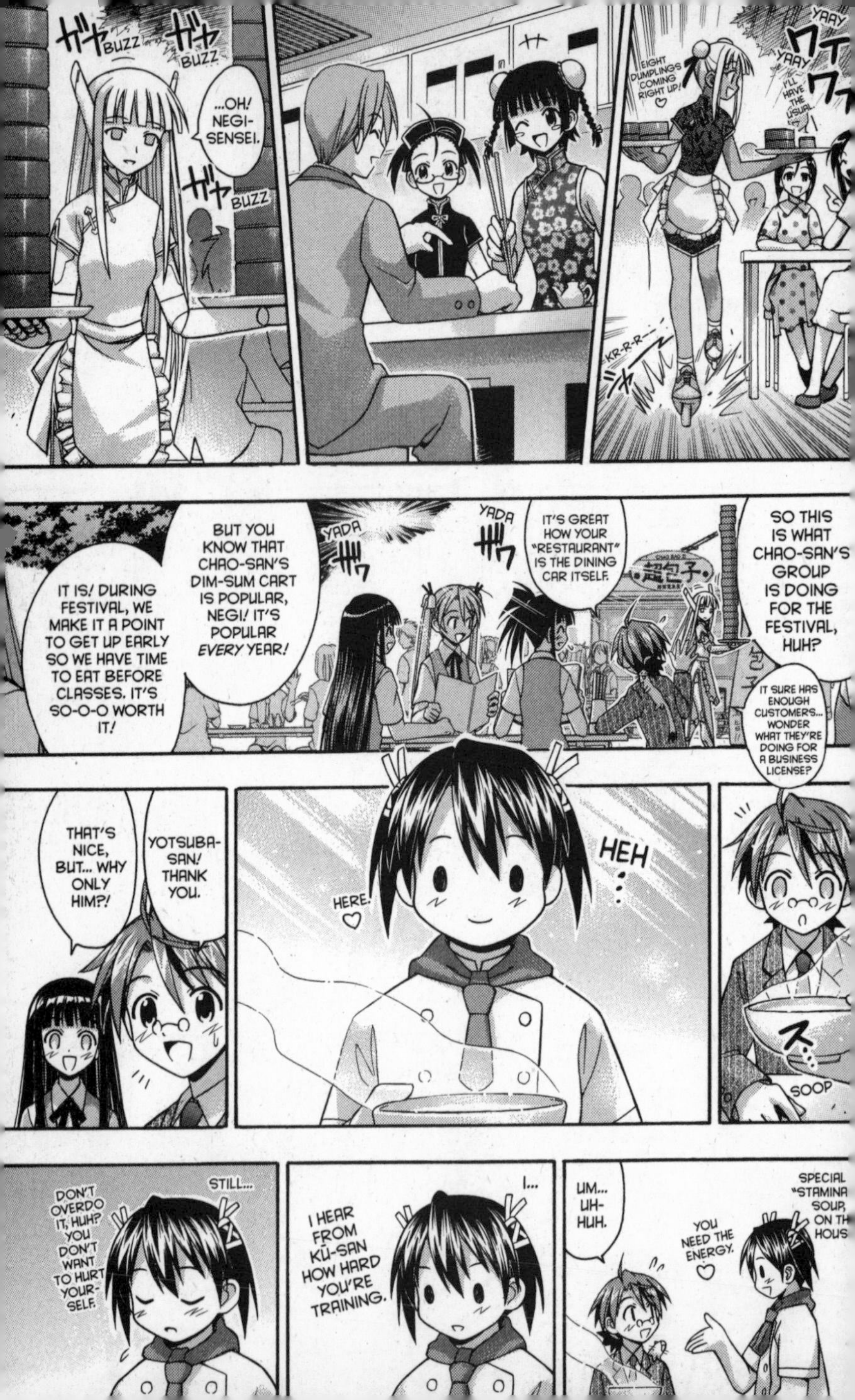
YAAY ワイ
YAAY ワイ
EIGHT DUMPLINGS COMING RIGHT UP! ♡
I'LL HAVE THE USUAL.
KR-R-R- ジャ
ガヤ BUZZ
ガヤ BUZZ
...OH! NEGI-SENSEI.
ガヤ BUZZ
SO THIS IS WHAT CHAO-SAN'S GROUP IS DOING FOR THE FESTIVAL, HUH?
IT SURE HAS ENOUGH CUSTOMERS... WONDER WHAT THEY'RE DOING FOR A BUSINESS LICENSE?
超包子
IT'S GREAT HOW YOUR "RESTAURANT" IS THE DINING CAR ITSELF.
YADA ザワ
YADA ザワ
BUT YOU KNOW THAT CHAO-SAN'S DIM-SUM CART IS POPULAR, NEGI! IT'S POPULAR *EVERY* YEAR!
IT IS! DURING FESTIVAL, WE MAKE IT A POINT TO GET UP EARLY SO WE HAVE TIME TO EAT BEFORE CLASSES. IT'S SO-O-O WORTH IT!
ス… SOOP
HEH…
HERE. ♡
YOTSUBA-SAN! THANK YOU.
THAT'S NICE, BUT... WHY ONLY HIM?!
SPECIAL "STAMINA" SOUP, ON TH HOUS
YOU NEED THE ENERGY. ♡
UM... UH-HUH.
I...
I HEAR FROM KŪ-SAN HOW HARD YOU'RE TRAINING.
STILL...
DON'T OVERDO IT, HUH? YOU DON'T WANT TO HURT YOURSELF.

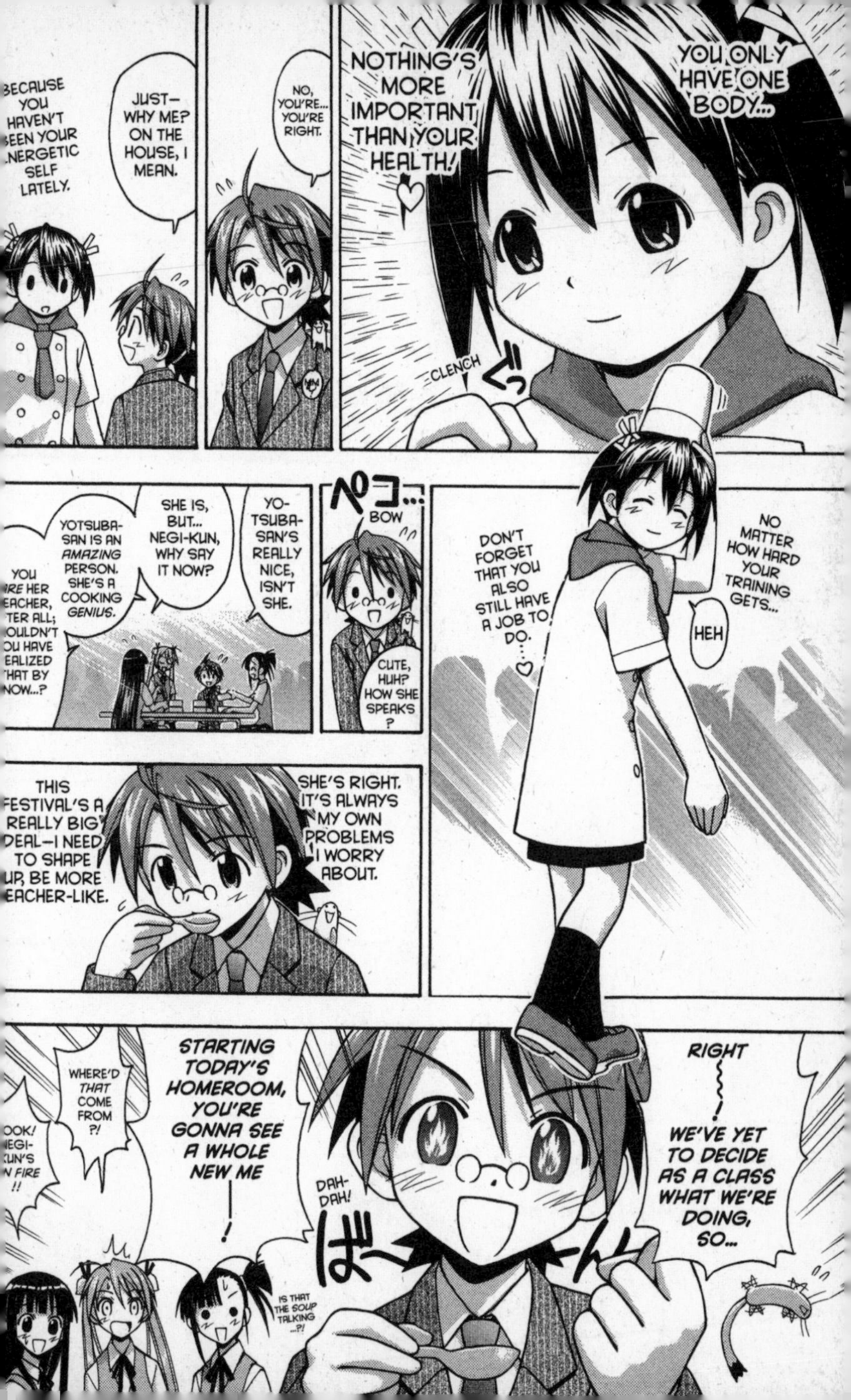
YOU ONLY HAVE ONE BODY...
NOTHING'S MORE IMPORTANT THAN YOUR HEALTH!
CLENCH
NO, YOU'RE... YOU'RE RIGHT.
JUST— WHY ME? ON THE HOUSE, I MEAN.
BECAUSE YOU HAVEN'T BEEN YOUR NERGETIC SELF LATELY.
NO MATTER HOW HARD YOUR TRAINING GETS...
HEH
DON'T FORGET THAT YOU ALSO STILL HAVE A JOB TO DO.
BOW
YO-TSUBA-SAN'S REALLY NICE, ISN'T SHE.
CUTE, HUH? HOW SHE SPEAKS?
SHE IS, BUT... NEGI-KUN, WHY SAY IT NOW?
YOTSUBA-SAN IS AN AMAZING PERSON. SHE'S A COOKING GENIUS.
YOU RE HER EACHER, TER ALL; OULDN'T OU HAVE EALIZED THAT BY NOW...?
SHE'S RIGHT. IT'S ALWAYS MY OWN PROBLEMS I WORRY ABOUT.
THIS FESTIVAL'S A REALLY BIG DEAL—I NEED TO SHAPE UP, BE MORE EACHER-LIKE.
RIGHT~~~! WE'VE YET TO DECIDE AS A CLASS WHAT WE'RE DOING, SO...
STARTING TODAY'S HOMEROOM, YOU'RE GONNA SEE A WHOLE NEW ME!
DAH-DAH!
IS THAT THE SOUP TALKING...?!
WHERE'D THAT COME FROM?!
OOK! NEGI-KUN'S N FIRE!!

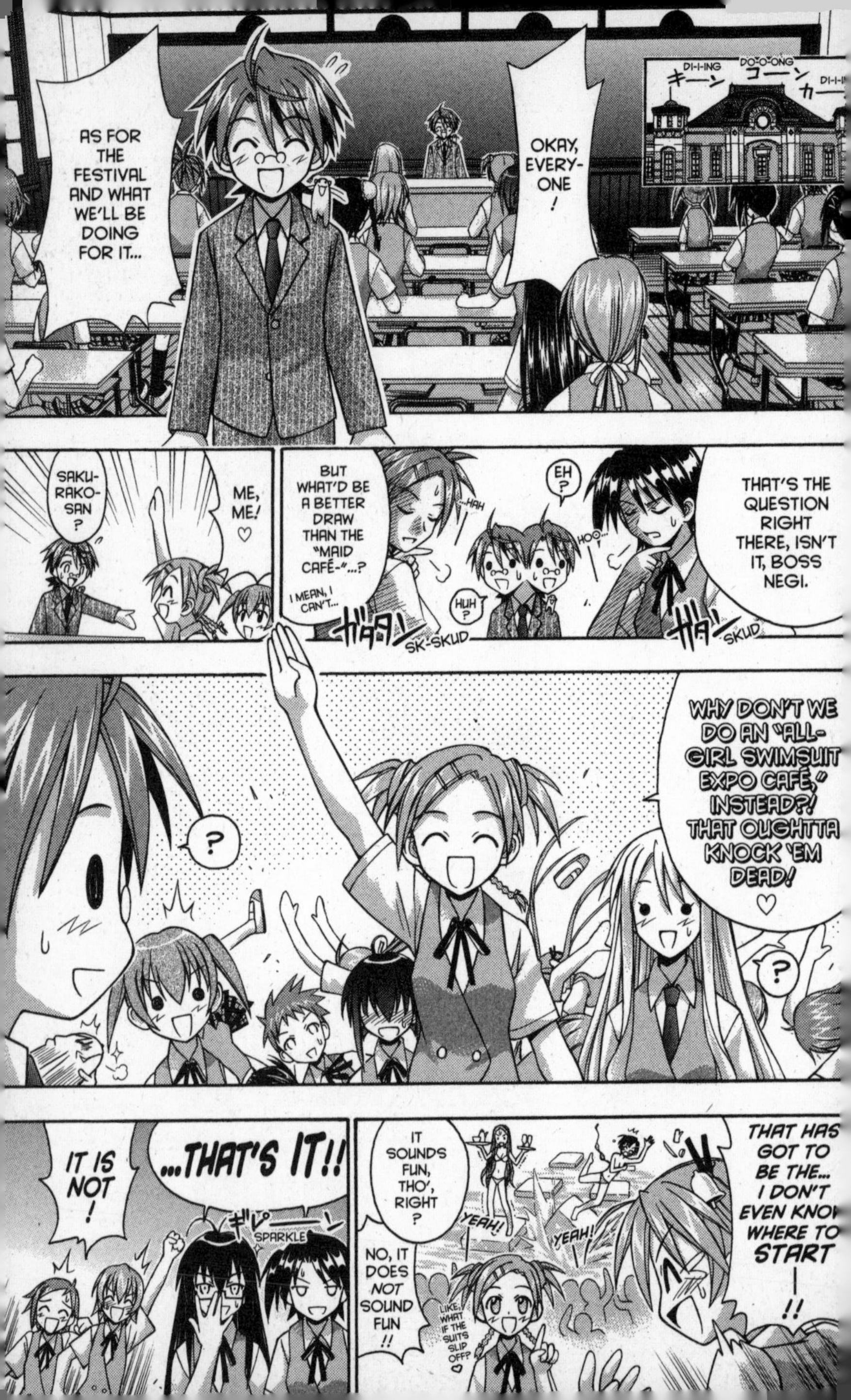
DI-I-ING
キーン
DO-O-ONG
コーン
DI-I-I
カー
OKAY, EVERY-ONE!
AS FOR THE FESTIVAL AND WHAT WE'LL BE DOING FOR IT...
THAT'S THE QUESTION RIGHT THERE, ISN'T IT, BOSS NEGI.
HOO...
SKUD
EH?
HUH?
...HAH
BUT WHAT'D BE A BETTER DRAW THAN THE "MAID CAFÉ-"...?
I MEAN, I CAN'T...
SK-SKUD
ME, ME! ♡
SAKU-RAKO-SAN?
WHY DON'T WE DO AN "ALL-GIRL SWIMSUIT EXPO CAFÉ," INSTEAD?! THAT OUGHTTA KNOCK 'EM DEAD! ♡
?
?
THAT HAS GOT TO BE THE... I DON'T EVEN KNOW WHERE TO START—!!
IT SOUNDS FUN, THO', RIGHT?
YEAH!
YEAH!
NO, IT DOES NOT SOUND FUN!!
LIKE, WHAT IF THE SUITS SLIP OFF? ♡
...THAT'S IT!!
IT IS NOT!
SPARKLE

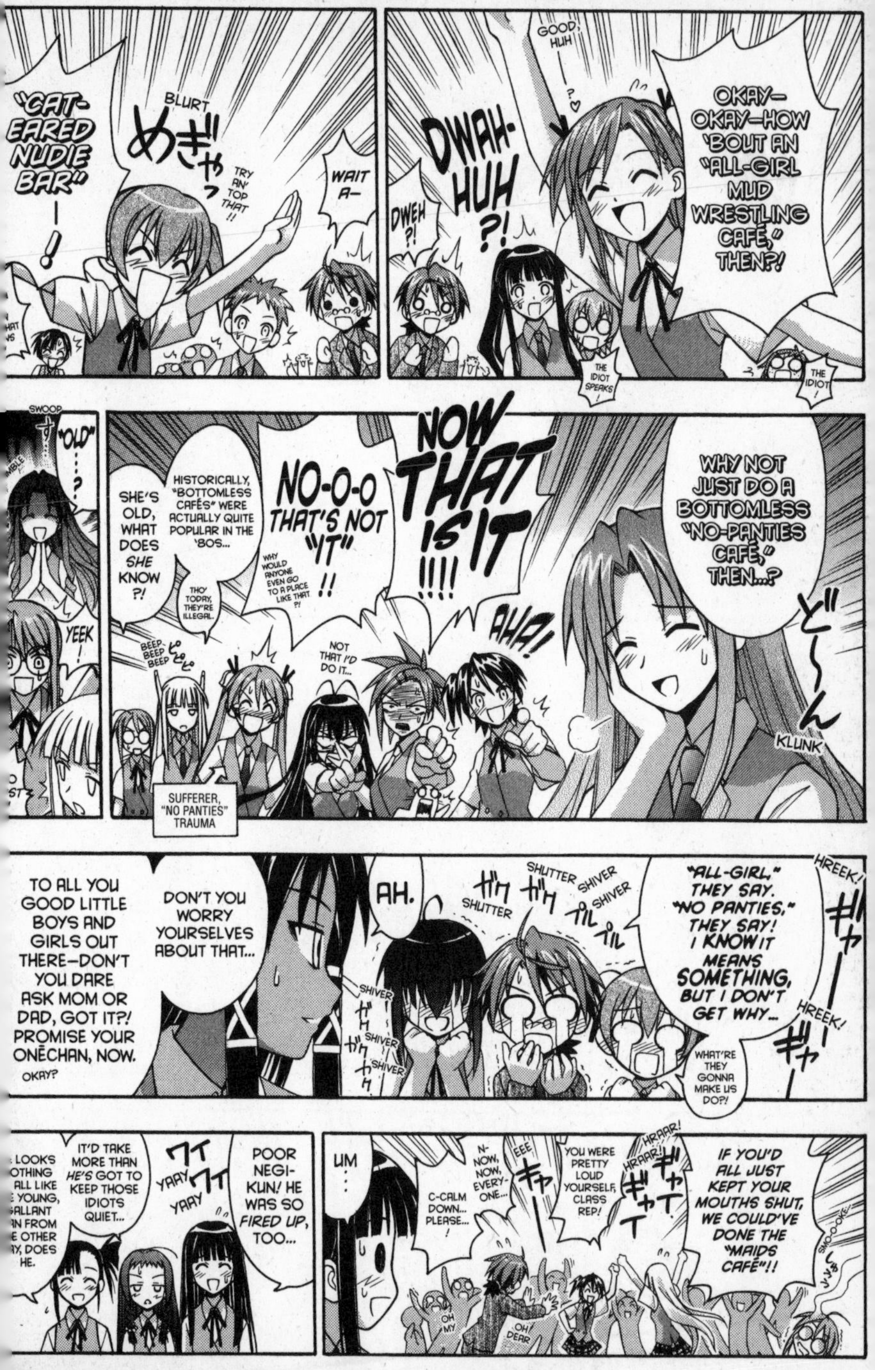
GOOD, HUH—?♡
OKAY—OKAY—HOW 'BOUT AN "ALL-GIRL MUD WRESTLING CAFÉ," THEN?!
DWAH-HUH?!
DWEH?!
THE IDIOT!
THE IDIOT SPEAKS!
WAIT A—
TRY AN' TOP THAT!!
BLURT めぎゃっ
"CAT-EARED NUDIE BAR"—!
WHY NOT JUST DO A BOTTOMLESS "NO-PANTIES CAFÉ," THEN...?
ど～ん KLUNK
NOW THAT IS IT!!!!
AHA!
NO-O-O THAT'S NOT "IT"!!
WHY WOULD ANYONE EVEN GO TO A PLACE LIKE THAT?!
NOT THAT I'D DO IT...
HISTORICALLY, "BOTTOMLESS CAFÉS" WERE ACTUALLY QUITE POPULAR IN THE '80S...
THO' TODAY, THEY'RE ILLEGAL.
SHE'S OLD, WHAT DOES SHE KNOW?!
BEEP-BEEP BEEP ぴぴぴ
SUFFERER, "NO PANTIES" TRAUMA
YEEK!
SWOOP す
"OLD"...?
HREEK! ギャー
"ALL-GIRL," THEY SAY. "NO PANTIES," THEY SAY! I KNOW IT MEANS SOMETHING, BUT I DON'T GET WHY...
HREEK! ギャ
WHAT'RE THEY GONNA MAKE US DO?!
SHUTTER SHIVER ガクガク プルプル SHIVER SHUTTER
AH.
SHIVER ガクガク SHIVER SHIVER
DON'T YOU WORRY YOURSELVES ABOUT THAT...
TO ALL YOU GOOD LITTLE BOYS AND GIRLS OUT THERE—DON'T YOU DARE ASK MOM OR DAD, GOT IT?! PROMISE YOUR ONĒCHAN, NOW.
OKAY?
SMO-O-OKE しゅ～
IF YOU'D ALL JUST KEPT YOUR MOUTHS SHUT, WE COULD'VE DONE THE "MAIDS CAFÉ"!!
HRAAR! HRAAR! ギャ ギャ ギャー
YOU WERE PRETTY LOUD YOURSELF, CLASS REP!
EEE キャー
N-NOW, NOW, EVERY-ONE...
C-CALM DOWN... PLEASE...!
OH! DEAR
OH MY
UM...
POOR NEGI-KUN! HE WAS SO FIRED UP, TOO...
YAAY ワイ YAAY ワイ
IT'D TAKE MORE THAN HE'S GOT TO KEEP THOSE IDIOTS QUIET...

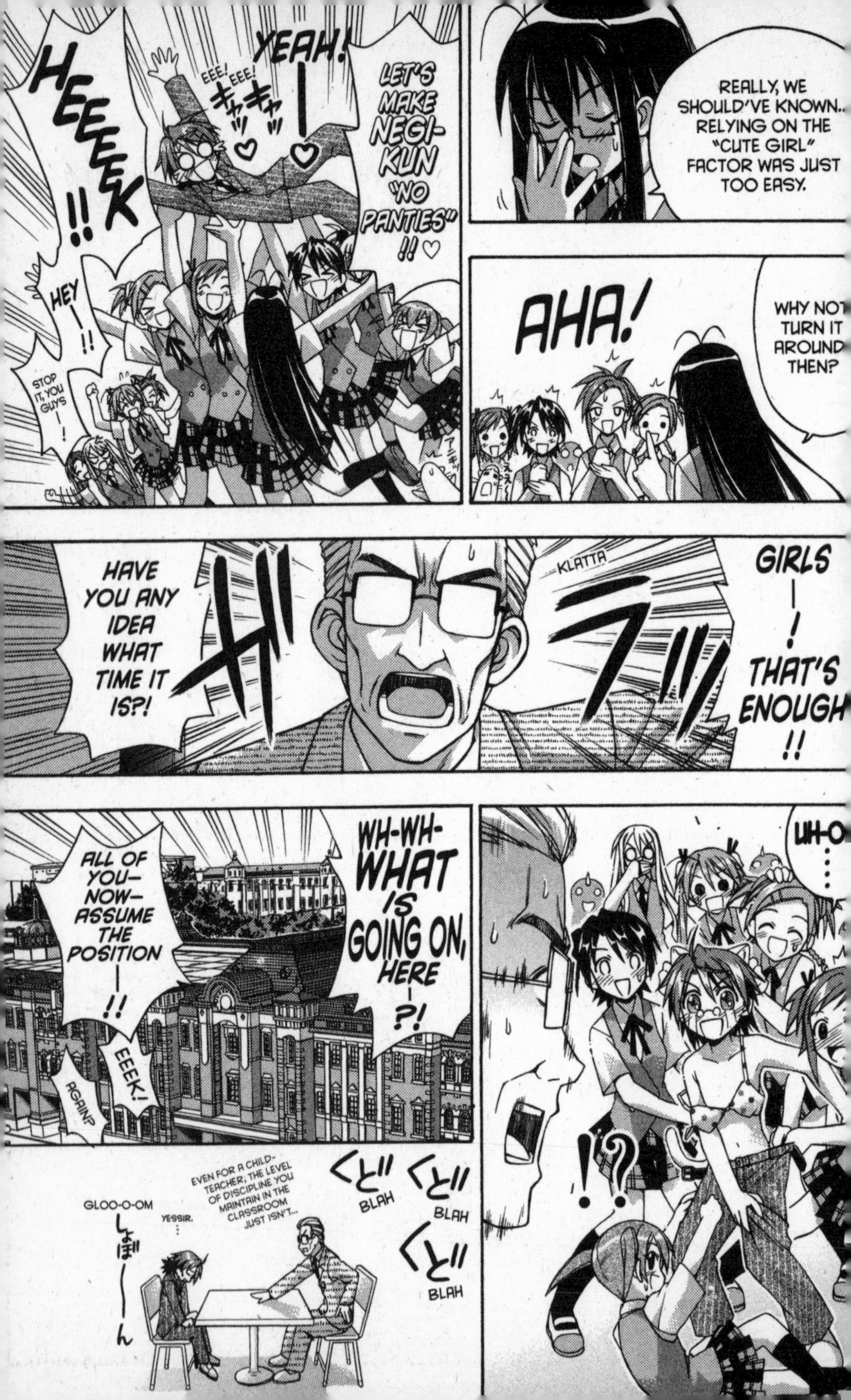
REALLY, WE SHOULD'VE KNOWN.. RELYING ON THE "CUTE GIRL" FACTOR WAS JUST TOO EASY.
AHA!
WHY NOT TURN IT AROUND THEN?
LET'S MAKE NEGI-KUN "NO PANTIES" !! ♡
YEAH! ♡
EEE! キャッ ♡
EEE! キャッ
HEEEEEK !!
HEY !!
STOP IT, YOU GUYS !
GIRLS ! THAT'S ENOUGH !!
KLATTA
ガラッ
HAVE YOU ANY IDEA WHAT TIME IT IS?!
UH-O...
!?
WH-WH-WHAT IS GOING ON, HERE?!
ALL OF YOU—NOW—ASSUME THE POSITION !!
EEEK!
AGAIN?
くどくど BLAH
くどくど BLAH
くどくど BLAH
EVEN FOR A CHILD-TEACHER, THE LEVEL OF DISCIPLINE YOU MAINTAIN IN THE CLASSROOM JUST ISN'T...
YESSIR. ...
GLOO-O-OM しょぼーん

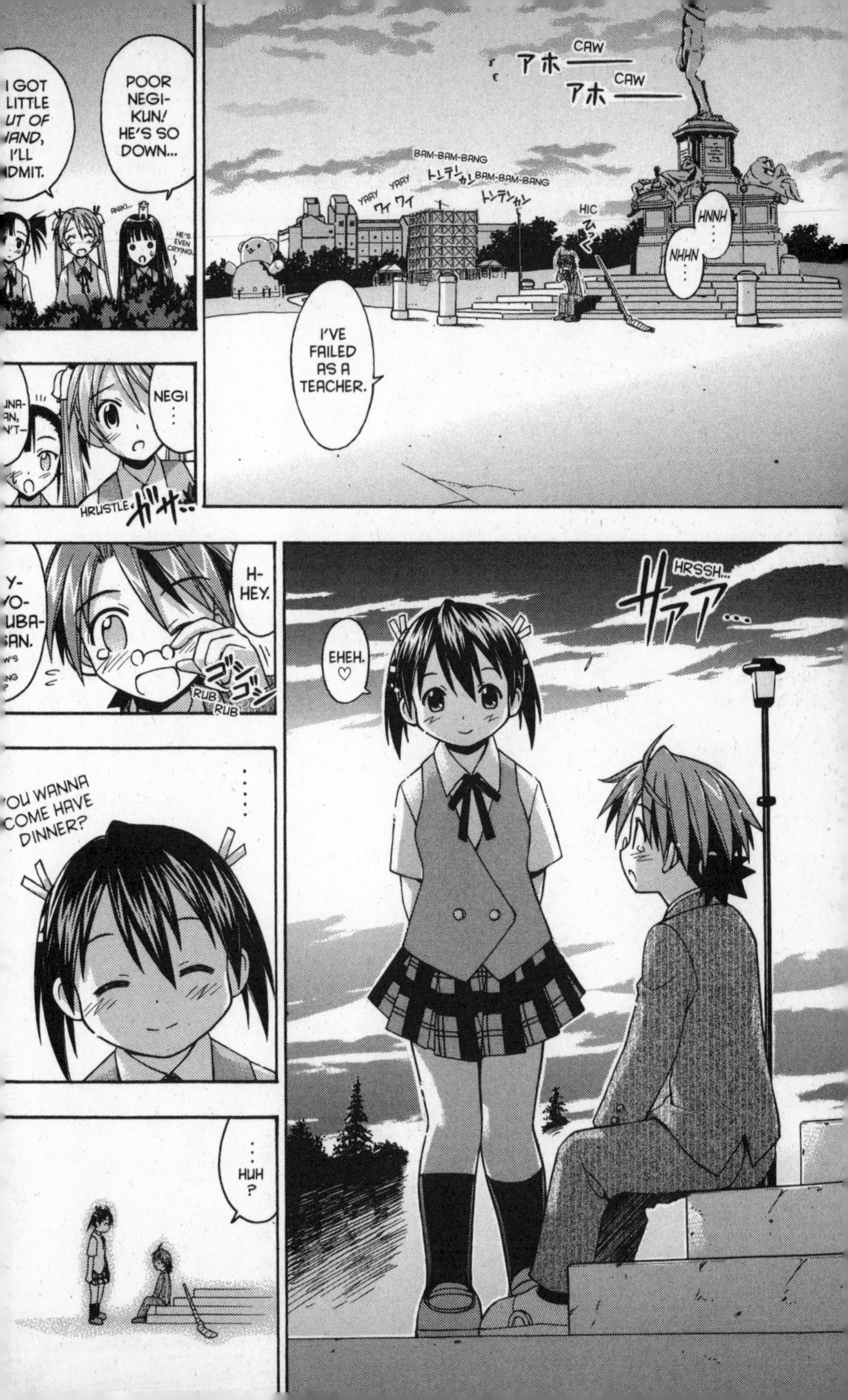

アホー CAW
アホー CAW
BAM-BAM-BANG
YAAY YAAY ワイワイ
トンテンカン BAM-BAM-BANG
トンテンカン
HIC
HNNH...
NHHN...
I'VE FAILED AS A TEACHER.
POOR NEGI-KUN! HE'S SO DOWN...
I GOT LITTLE UT OF AND, I'LL DMIT.
ANIKI...
HE'S EVEN CRYING.
NEGI...
UNA-AN, N'T—
HRUSTLE ガサ
HRSSH... サァア...
EHEH. ♡
H-HEY.
Y-YO-UBA-SAN.
RUB RUB ゴシゴシ
......
YOU WANNA COME HAVE DINNER?
...HUH?

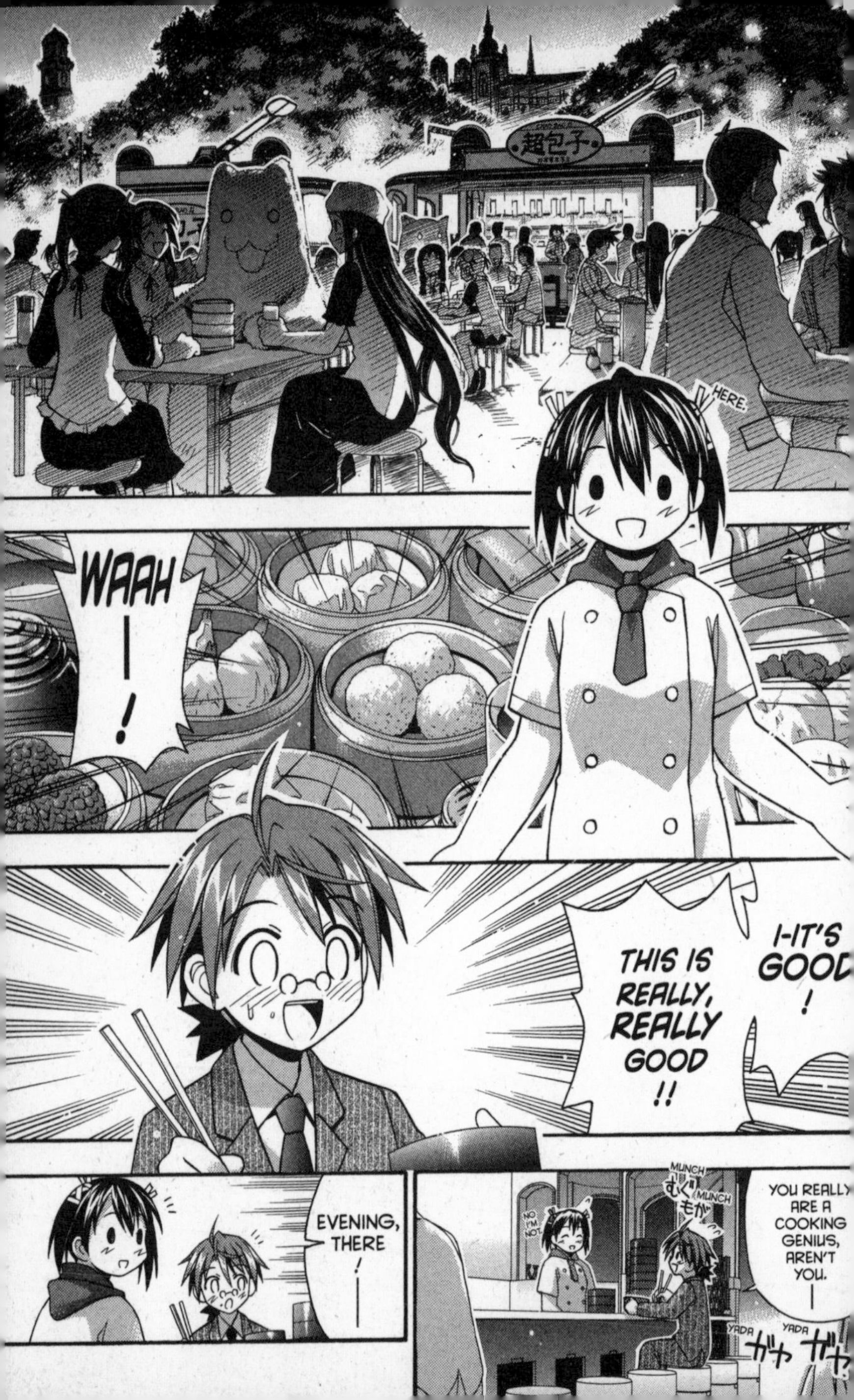

超包子
HERE.
WAAH—!
I-IT'S GOOD!
THIS IS REALLY, REALLY GOOD!!
YOU REALLY ARE A COOKING GENIUS, AREN'T YOU.—
MUNCH むぐ
MUNCH もが
NO I'M NOT.
YADA ガヤ
YADA ガヤ
EVENING, THERE!—

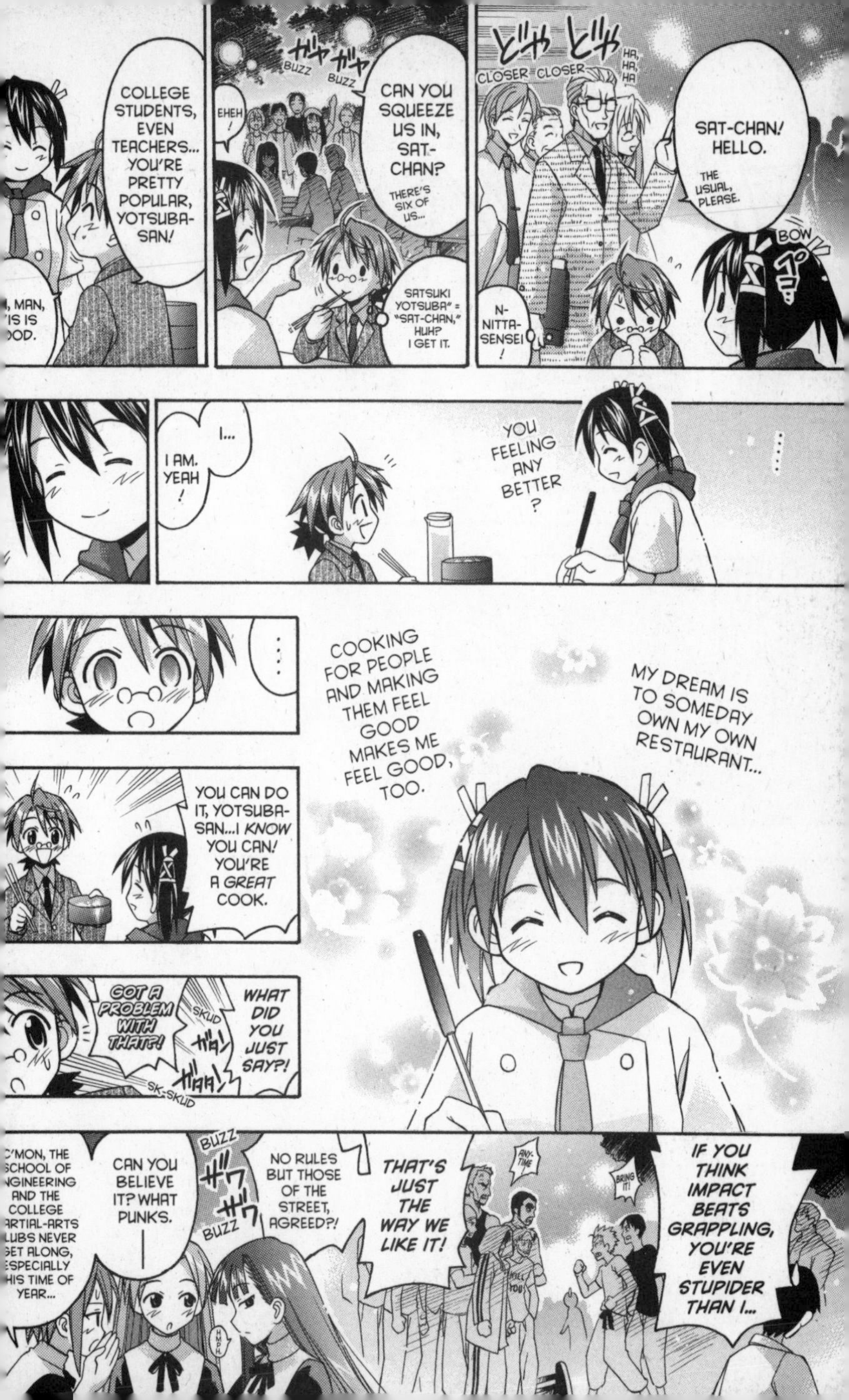
SAT-CHAN! HELLO.
THE USUAL, PLEASE.
BOW
HA, HA, HA
CLOSER CLOSER
N-NITTA-SENSEI!
CAN YOU SQUEEZE US IN, SAT-CHAN?
THERE'S SIX OF US...
BUZZ BUZZ
EHEH!
SATSUKI YOTSUBA" = "SAT-CHAN," HUH? I GET IT.
COLLEGE STUDENTS, EVEN TEACHERS... YOU'RE PRETTY POPULAR, YOTSUBA-SAN!
, MAN, 'IS IS OOD.
....
YOU FEELING ANY BETTER?
I... I AM. YEAH!
MY DREAM IS TO SOMEDAY OWN MY OWN RESTAURANT...
COOKING FOR PEOPLE AND MAKING THEM FEEL GOOD MAKES ME FEEL GOOD, TOO.
...
YOU CAN DO IT, YOTSUBA-SAN...I KNOW YOU CAN! YOU'RE A GREAT COOK.
WHAT DID YOU JUST SAY?!
GOT A PROBLEM WITH THAT?!
SKUD
SK-SKUD
IF YOU THINK IMPACT BEATS GRAPPLING, YOU'RE EVEN STUPIDER THAN I...
BRING IT!
ANY-TIME
THAT'S JUST THE WAY WE LIKE IT!
NO RULES BUT THOSE OF THE STREET, AGREED?!
BUZZ BUZZ
CAN YOU BELIEVE IT? WHAT PUNKS.
HMPH.
C'MON, THE SCHOOL OF NGINEERING AND THE COLLEGE ARTIAL-ARTS LUBS NEVER ET ALONG, SPECIALLY HIS TIME OF YEAR...

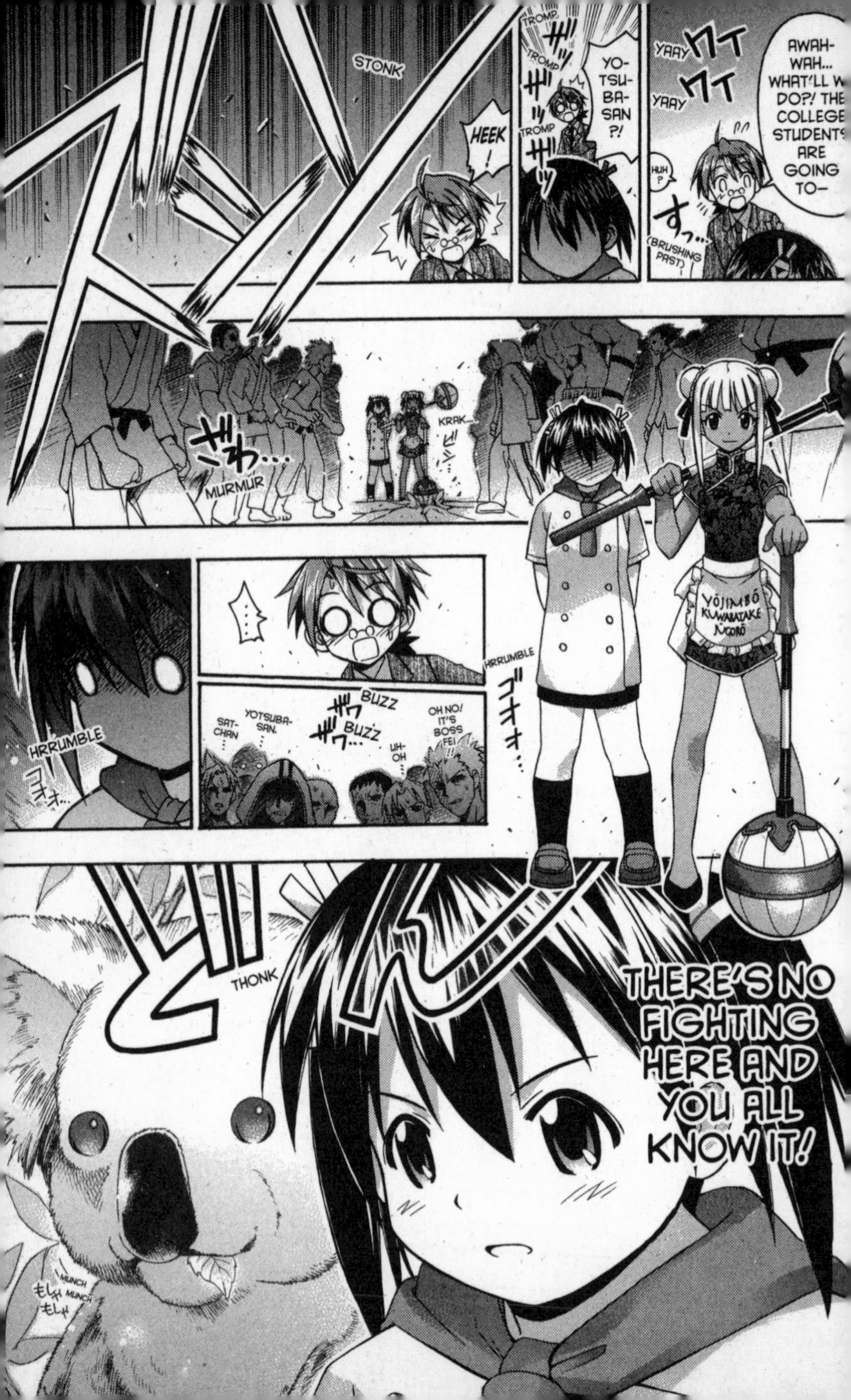
AWAH-WAH... WHAT'LL WE DO?! THE COLLEGE STUDENTS ARE GOING TO—
YAAY
YAAY
HUH?
(BRUSHING PAST)
TROMP
TROMP
TROMP
YO-TSU-BA-SAN?!
STONK
HEEK!
KRAK...
MURMUR
HRRUMBLE
YŌJIMBŌ KUWABATAKE JŪGORŌ
...!
OH NO! IT'S BOSS FEI!!
UH-OH...
BUZZ
BUZZ
YOTSUBA-SAN.
SAT-CHAN...
HRRUMBLE
THERE'S NO FIGHTING HERE AND YOU ALL KNOW IT!
THONK
MUNCH
MUNCH

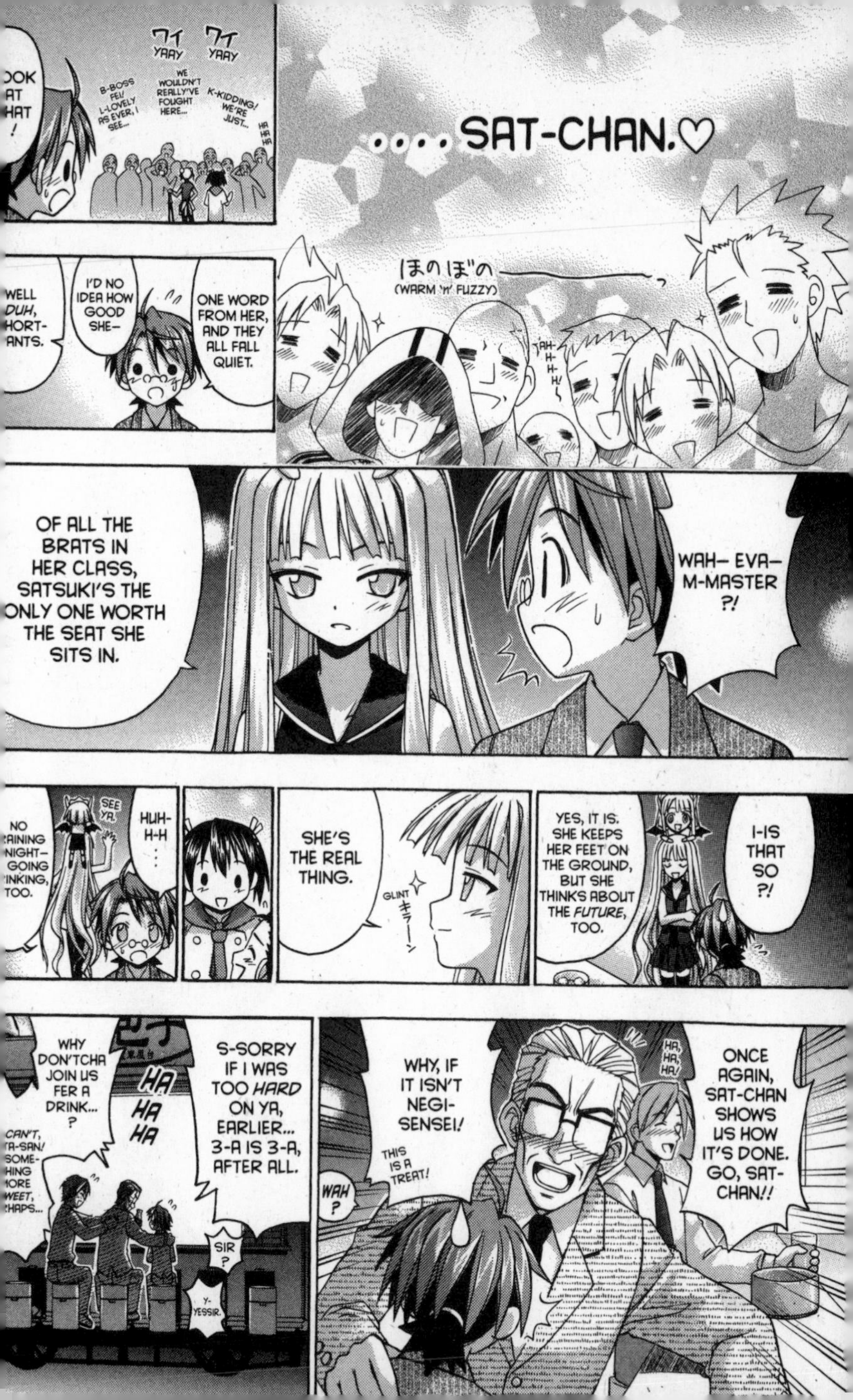
....SAT-CHAN.♡
ほのぼの
(WARM 'N' FUZZY)
AH-H-H-H!
ワイ YAAY ワイ YAAY
K-KIDDING! WE'RE JUST...
HA HA HA
WE WOULDN'T REALLY'VE FOUGHT HERE...
B-BOSS FEI! L-LOVELY AS EVER, I SEE...
OOK AT HAT!
ONE WORD FROM HER, AND THEY ALL FALL QUIET.
I'D NO IDEA HOW GOOD SHE—
WELL DUH, HORT-ANTS.
WAH— EVA— M-MASTER ?!
OF ALL THE BRATS IN HER CLASS, SATSUKI'S THE ONLY ONE WORTH THE SEAT SHE SITS IN.
I-IS THAT SO ?!
YES, IT IS. SHE KEEPS HER FEET ON THE GROUND, BUT SHE THINKS ABOUT THE FUTURE, TOO.
SHE'S THE REAL THING.
GLINT キラーン
HUH-H-H...
SEE YA.
NO RAINING NIGHT-GOING INKING, TOO.
ONCE AGAIN, SAT-CHAN SHOWS US HOW IT'S DONE. GO, SAT-CHAN!!
HA, HA, HA!
WHY, IF IT ISN'T NEGI-SENSEI!
THIS IS A TREAT!
WAH?
S-SORRY IF I WAS TOO HARD ON YA, EARLIER... 3-A IS 3-A, AFTER ALL.
HA HA HA
WHY DON'TCHA JOIN US FER A DRINK...?
CAN'T, A-SAN! SOME-HING MORE WEET, CHAPS...
SIR?
Y-YESSIR.

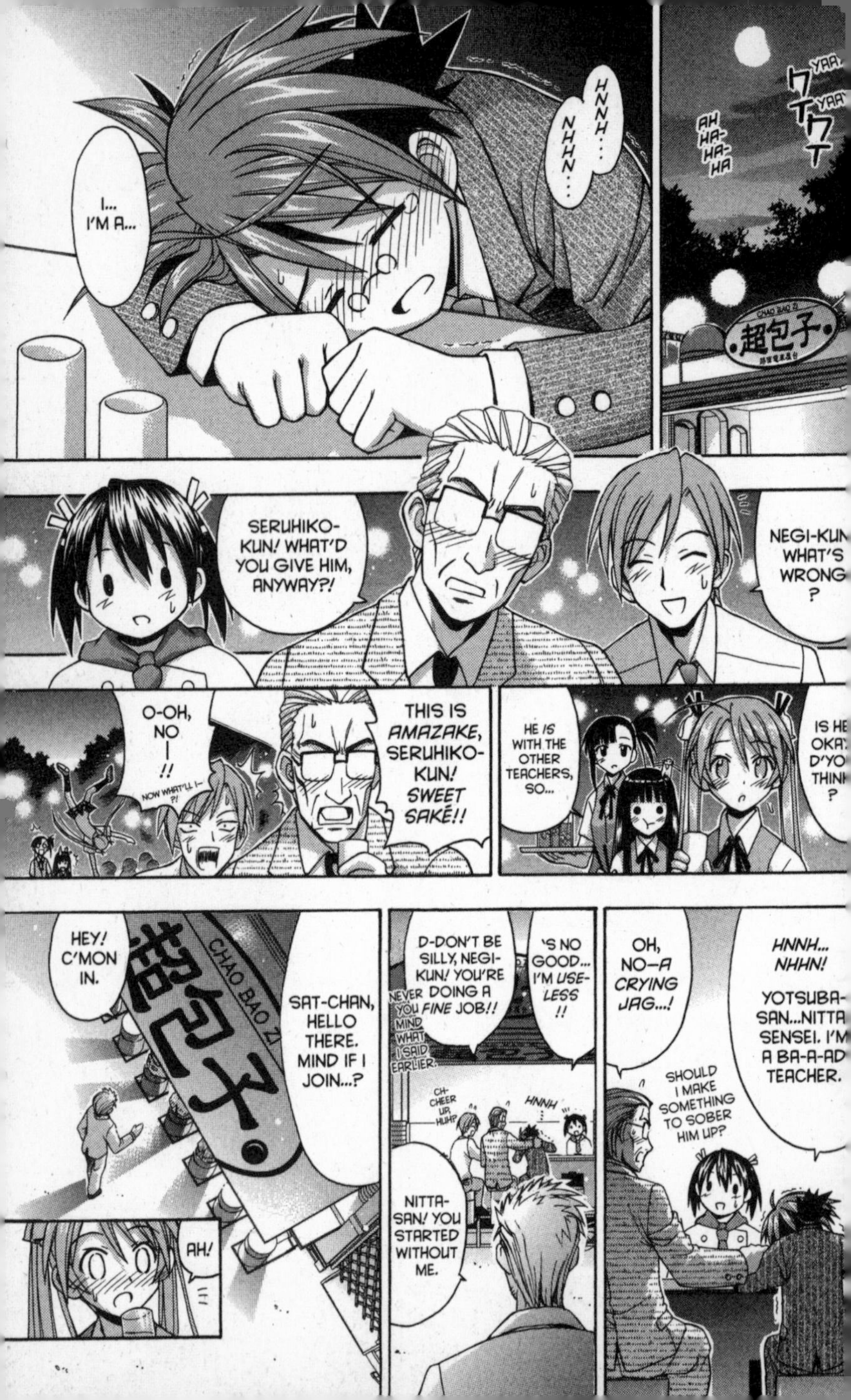
YAA YAA
AH HA-HA-HA
CHAO BAO ZI
超包子
HNNH... NHHN...
I... I'M A...
NEGI-KUN WHAT'S WRONG?
SERUHIKO-KUN! WHAT'D YOU GIVE HIM, ANYWAY?!
IS HE OKAY D'YOU THINK?
HE *IS* WITH THE OTHER TEACHERS, SO...
THIS IS *AMAZAKE*, SERUHIKO-KUN! *SWEET SAKÉ!!*
O-OH, NO-!!
NOW WHAT'LL I-?!
HNNH... NHHN!
YOTSUBA-SAN...NITTA SENSEI. I'M A BA-A-AD TEACHER.
OH, NO—A CRYING JAG...!
SHOULD I MAKE SOMETHING TO SOBER HIM UP?
'S NO GOOD... I'M *USE-LESS!!*
D-DON'T BE SILLY, NEGI-KUN! YOU'RE DOING A *FINE* JOB!!
NEVER YOU MIND WHAT I SAID EARLIER.
HNNH
CH-CHEER UP, HUH?
NITTA-SAN! YOU STARTED WITHOUT ME.
SAT-CHAN, HELLO THERE. MIND IF I JOIN...?
HEY! C'MON IN.
CHAO BAO ZI
超包子
AH!

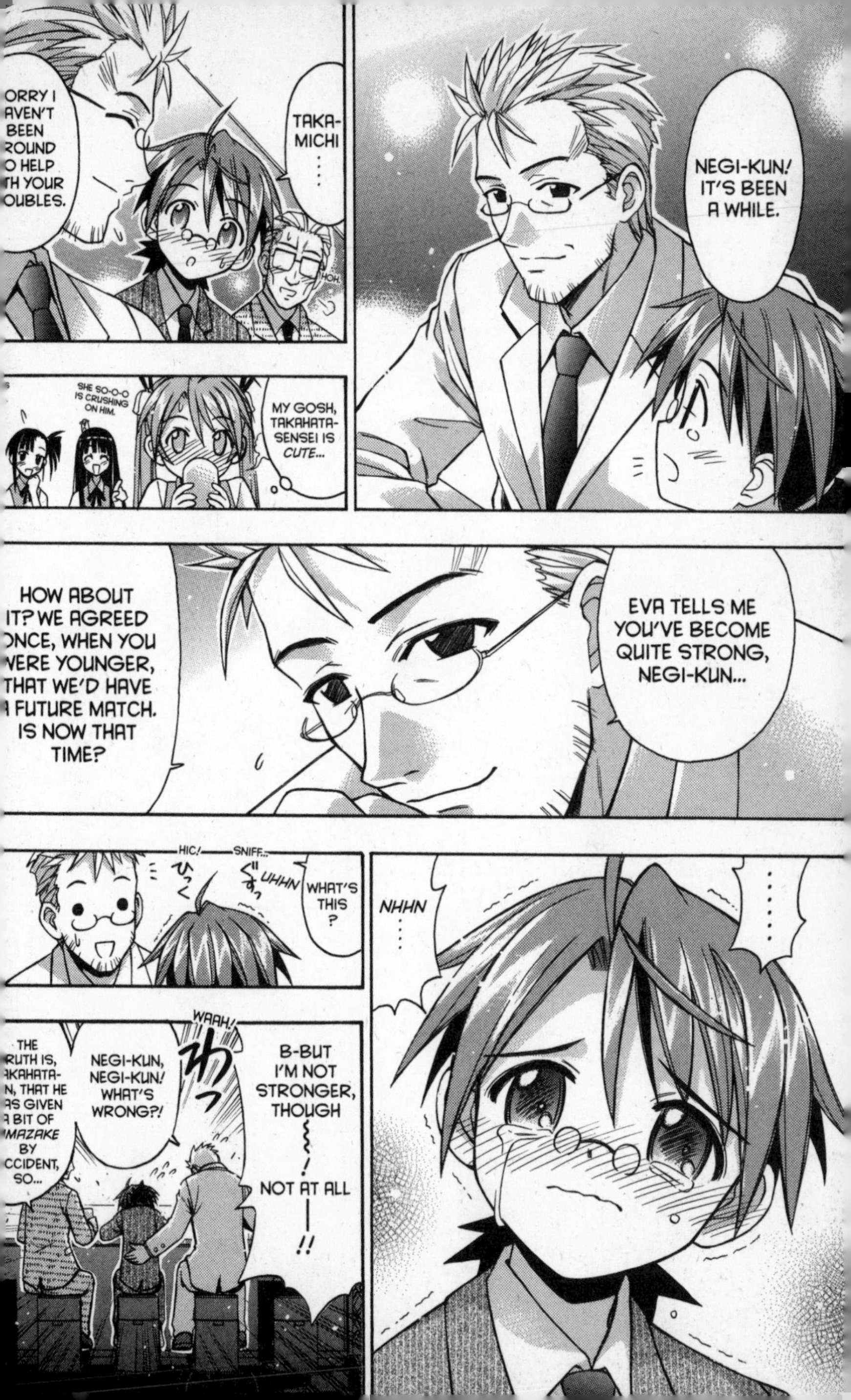
NEGI-KUN! IT'S BEEN A WHILE.
TAKA-MICHI ....
ORRY I AVEN'T BEEN ROUND O HELP TH YOUR OUBLES.
HOH.
MY GOSH, TAKAHATA-SENSEI IS CUTE...
SHE SO-O-O IS CRUSHING ON HIM.
EVA TELLS ME YOU'VE BECOME QUITE STRONG, NEGI-KUN...
HOW ABOUT IT? WE AGREED NCE, WHEN YOU ERE YOUNGER, THAT WE'D HAVE FUTURE MATCH. IS NOW THAT TIME?
......
NHHN ....
WHAT'S THIS ?
UHHN
SNIFF...
HIC!
B-BUT I'M NOT STRONGER, THOUGH ~~! NOT AT ALL —!!
WAAH!
NEGI-KUN, NEGI-KUN! WHAT'S WRONG?!
THE RUTH IS, AKAHATA-N, THAT HE AS GIVEN A BIT OF MAZAKE BY CCIDENT, SO...

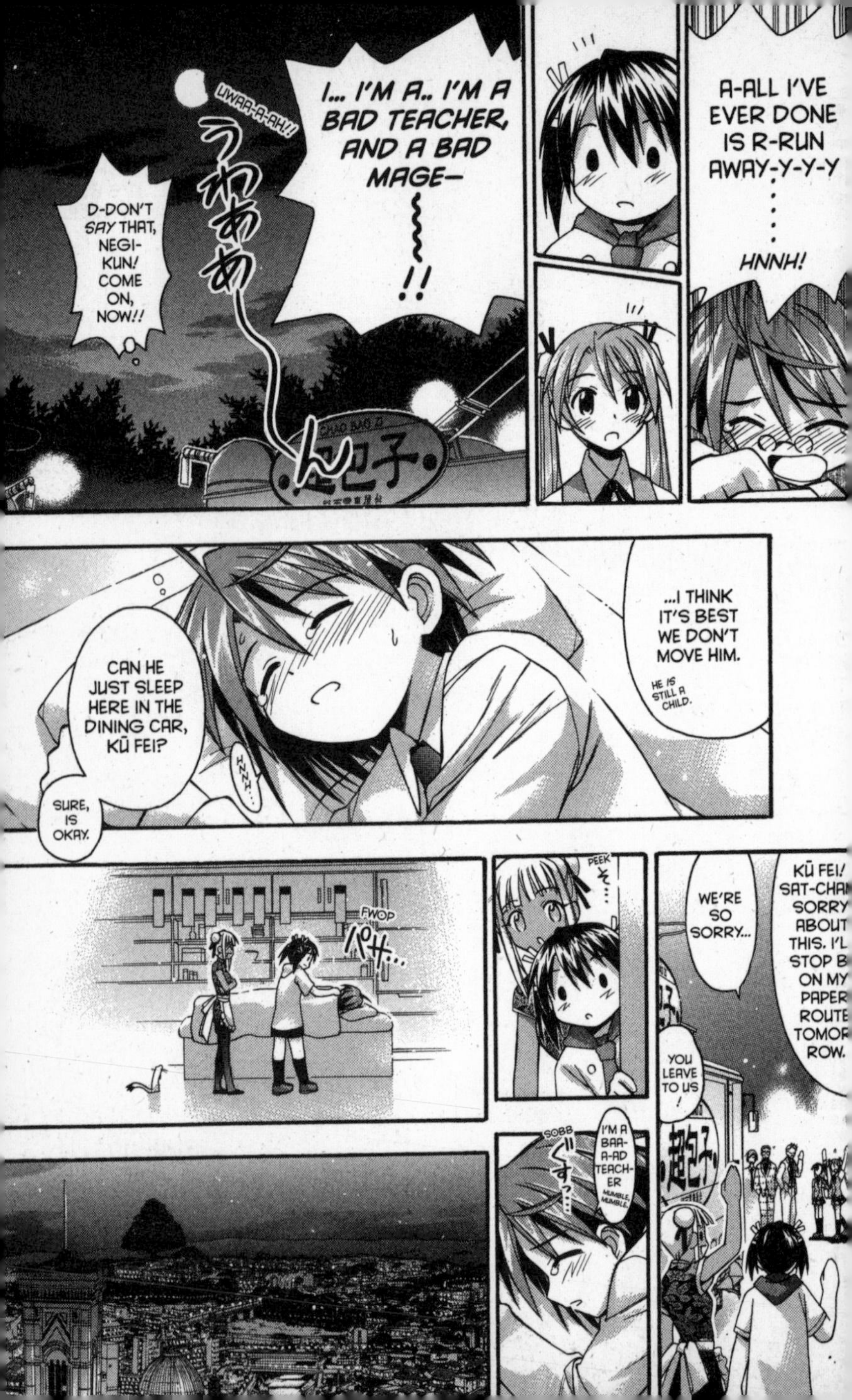
A-ALL I'VE EVER DONE IS R-RUN AWAY-Y-Y-Y . . . .
HNNH!
I... I'M A.. I'M A BAD TEACHER, AND A BAD MAGE-~~~!!
UWAA-A-AH!!
うわああ～ん
D-DON'T SAY THAT, NEGI-KUN! COME ON, NOW!!
CHAO BAO ZI
超包子
...I THINK IT'S BEST WE DON'T MOVE HIM.
HE IS STILL A CHILD.
CAN HE JUST SLEEP HERE IN THE DINING CAR, KŪ FEI?
HNNH...
SURE, IS OKAY.
KŪ FEI! SAT-CHAN SORRY ABOUT THIS. I'L STOP B ON MY PAPER ROUTE TOMOR ROW.
WE'RE SO SORRY...
YOU LEAVE TO US!
PEEK
そ…
FWOP
パサ…
超包子
I'M A BAA-A-AD TEACH-ER
MUMBLE, MUMBLE.
SOBB
ぐすっ…

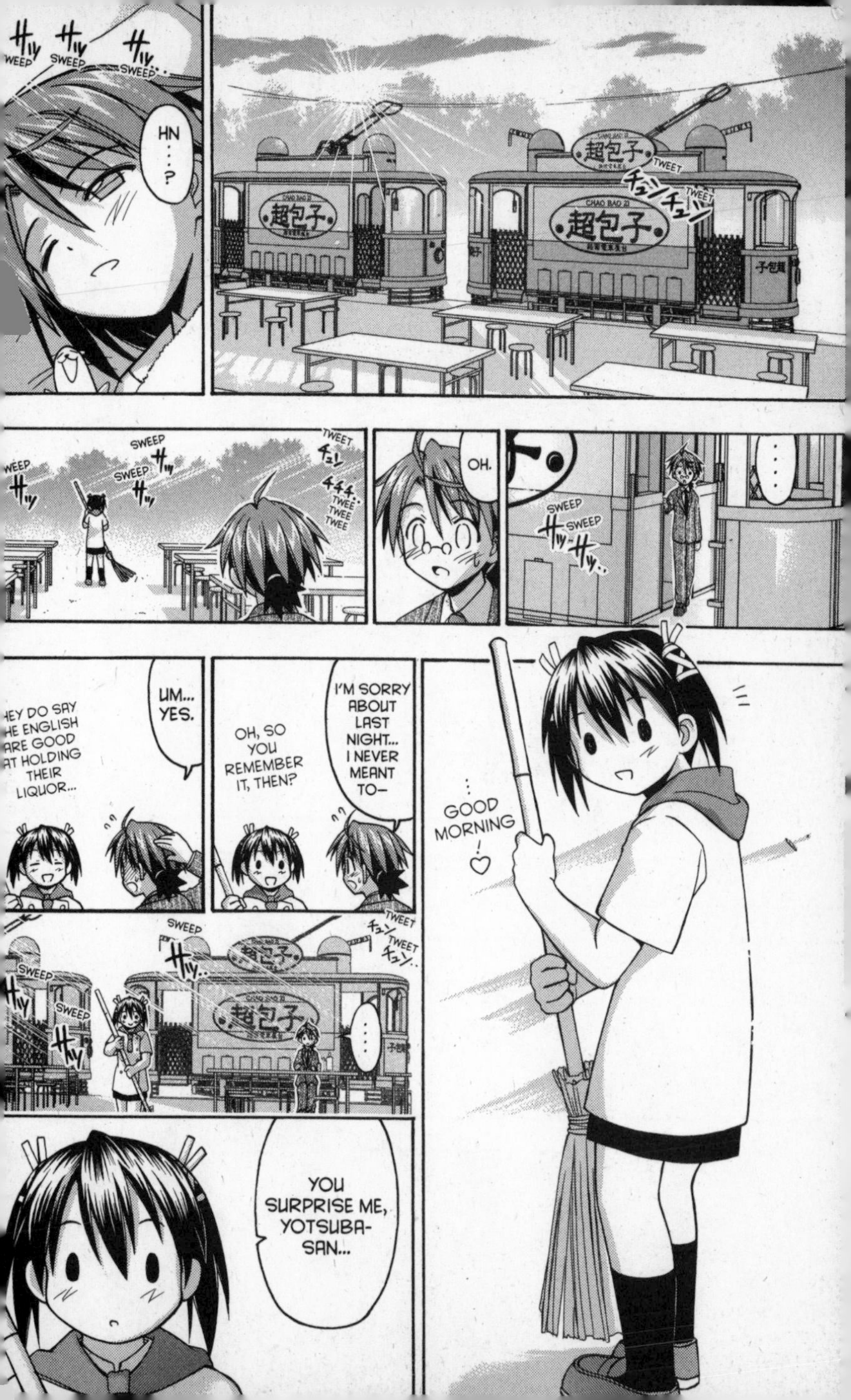

TWEET
TWEET
チュンチュン
SWEEP
SWEEP
SWEEP
HN...?
SWEEP
SWEEP
...
OH.
TWEET
TWEE TWEE TWEE
SWEEP
SWEEP
WEEP
...GOOD MORNING!
I'M SORRY ABOUT LAST NIGHT... I NEVER MEANT TO—
OH, SO YOU REMEMBER IT, THEN?
UM... YES.
HEY DO SAY HE ENGLISH ARE GOOD AT HOLDING THEIR LIQUOR...
TWEET
TWEET
SWEEP
SWEEP
SWEEP
...
YOU SURPRISE ME, YOTSUBA-SAN...

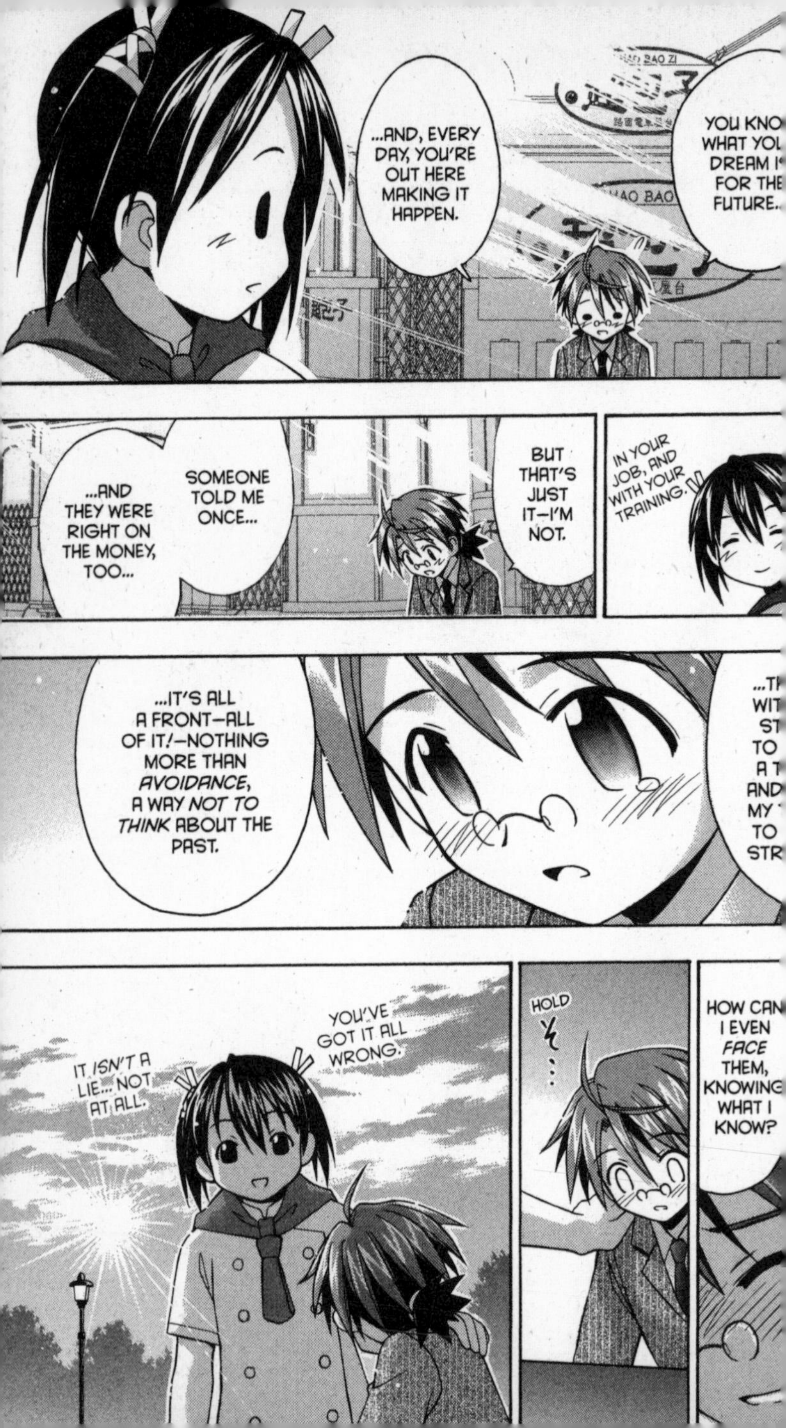
YOU KNO WHAT YOL DREAM I' FOR THE FUTURE..
...AND, EVERY DAY, YOU'RE OUT HERE MAKING IT HAPPEN.
IN YOUR JOB, AND WITH YOUR TRAINING.
BUT THAT'S JUST IT—I'M NOT.
SOMEONE TOLD ME ONCE...
...AND THEY WERE RIGHT ON THE MONEY, TOO...
...IT'S ALL A FRONT—ALL OF IT!—NOTHING MORE THAN *AVOIDANCE*, A WAY *NOT TO THINK* ABOUT THE PAST.
HOW CAN I EVEN *FACE* THEM, KNOWING WHAT I KNOW?
HOLD
YOU'VE GOT IT ALL WRONG.
IT *ISN'T* A LIE... NOT AT ALL.

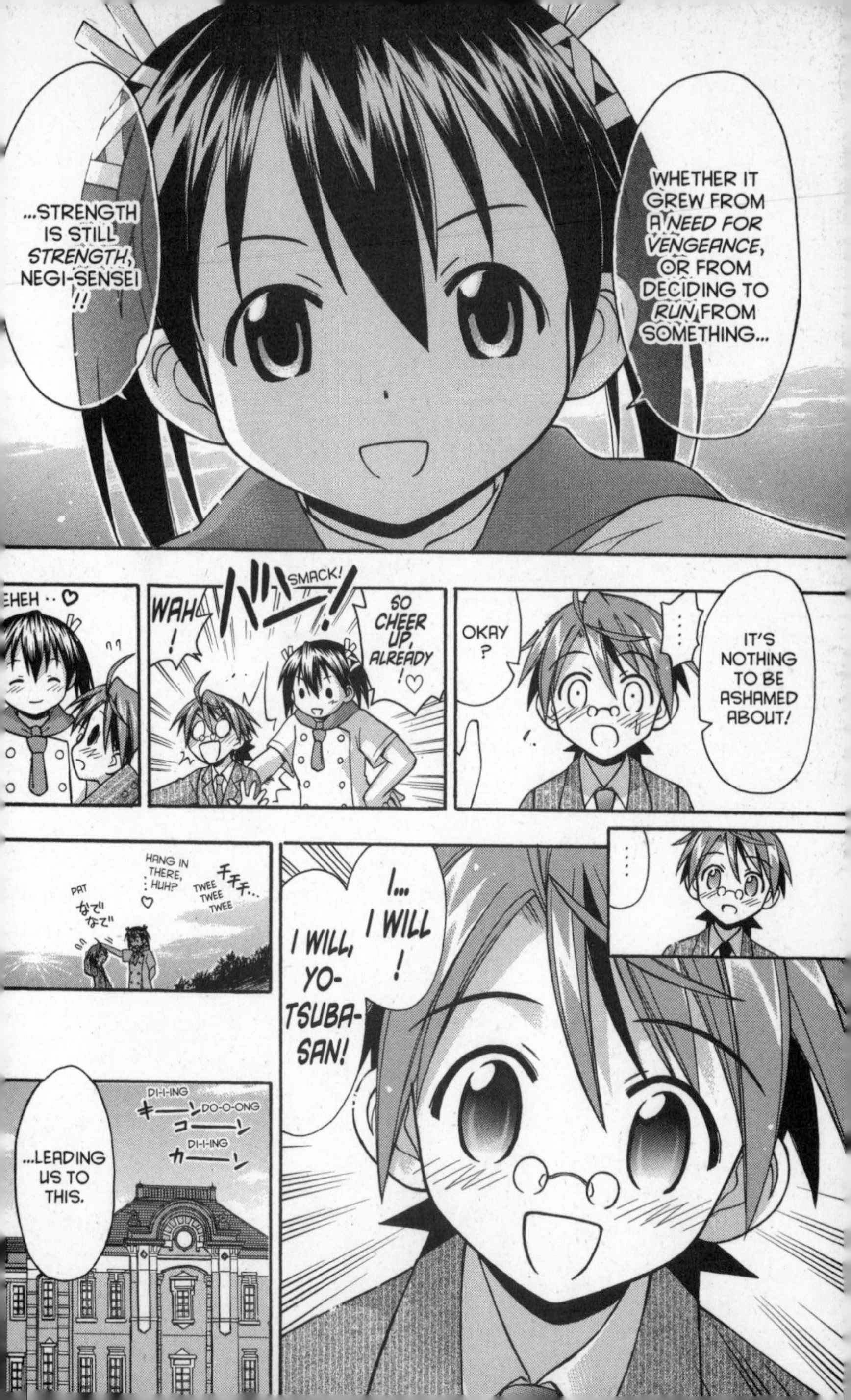
WHETHER IT GREW FROM A NEED FOR VENGEANCE, OR FROM DECIDING TO RUN FROM SOMETHING...
...STRENGTH IS STILL STRENGTH, NEGI-SENSEI!!
IT'S NOTHING TO BE ASHAMED ABOUT!
...
OKAY?
SO CHEER UP, ALREADY!♡
SMACK!
WAH!
EHEH..♡
...
I... I WILL!
I WILL, YO-TSUBA-SAN!
HANG IN THERE, HUH?♡
TWEE TWEE TWEE
チチチ...
PAT
なでなで
...LEADING US TO THIS.
DI-I-ING
キーン
DO-O-ONG
コーン
DI-I-ING
カーン

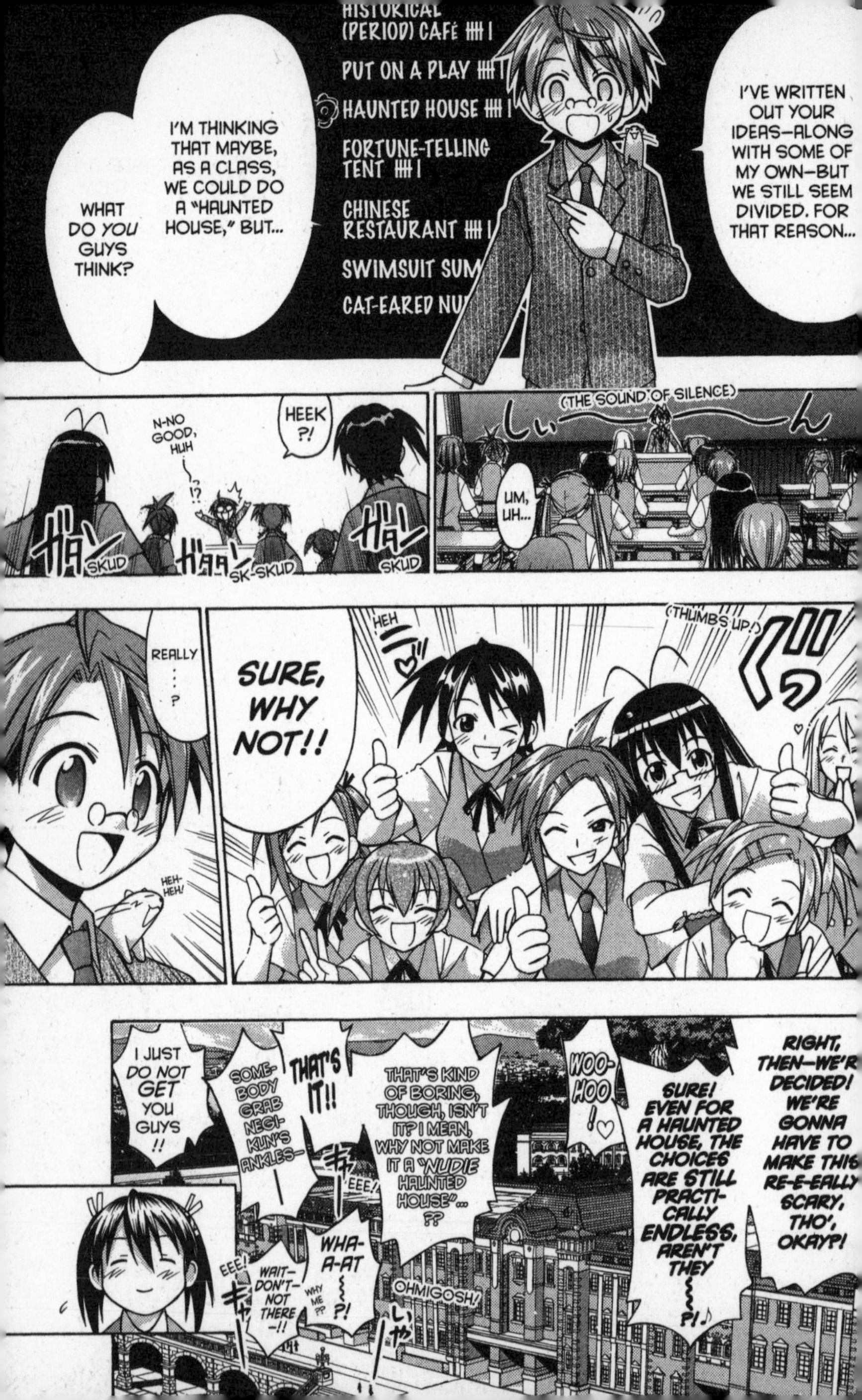
I'VE WRITTEN OUT YOUR IDEAS—ALONG WITH SOME OF MY OWN—BUT WE STILL SEEM DIVIDED. FOR THAT REASON...
HISTORICAL (PERIOD) CAFÉ
PUT ON A PLAY
HAUNTED HOUSE
FORTUNE-TELLING TENT
CHINESE RESTAURANT
SWIMSUIT SUM
CAT-EARED NU
I'M THINKING THAT MAYBE, AS A CLASS, WE COULD DO A "HAUNTED HOUSE," BUT...
WHAT DO YOU GUYS THINK?
(THE SOUND OF SILENCE)
UM, UH...
HEEK ?!
N-NO GOOD, HUH
!?
SKUD
SK-SKUD
SKUD
(THUMBS UP!)
HEH
SURE, WHY NOT!!
REALLY ...?
HEH-HEH!
RIGHT, THEN—WE'R DECIDED! WE'RE GONNA HAVE TO MAKE THIS RE-E-EALLY SCARY, THO', OKAY?!
SURE! EVEN FOR A HAUNTED HOUSE, THE CHOICES ARE STILL PRACTI-CALLY ENDLESS, AREN'T THEY ~~?!♪
WOO-HOO!♡
THAT'S KIND OF BORING, THOUGH, ISN'T IT? I MEAN, WHY NOT MAKE IT A "NUDIE HAUNTED HOUSE"...??
EEE!
THAT'S IT!!
SOME-BODY GRAB NEGI-KUN'S ANKLES—
I JUST DO NOT GET YOU GUYS!!
OHMIGOSH!
WHA-A-AT ~~?!
WHY ME ??
WAIT—DON'T—NOT THERE—!!
EEE!

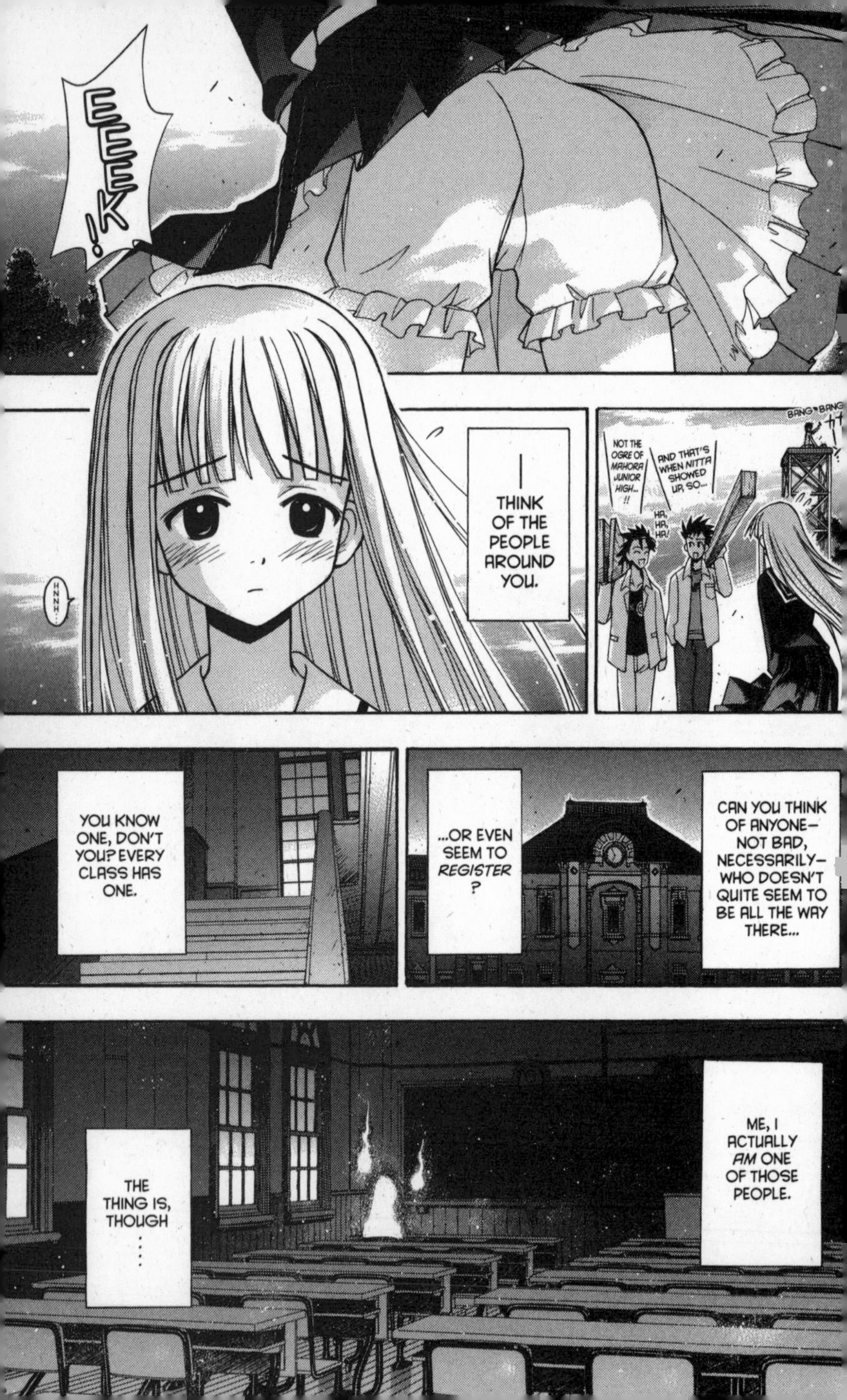
EEEEK!
BANG BANG
AND THAT'S WHEN NITTA SHOWED UP, SO...
NOT THE OGRE OF MAHORA JUNIOR HIGH...!!
HA, HA, HA!
I THINK OF THE PEOPLE AROUND YOU.
HNNH...
CAN YOU THINK OF ANYONE— NOT BAD, NECESSARILY— WHO DOESN'T QUITE SEEM TO BE ALL THE WAY THERE...
...OR EVEN SEEM TO *REGISTER*?
YOU KNOW ONE, DON'T YOU? EVERY CLASS HAS ONE.
ME, I ACTUALLY *AM* ONE OF THOSE PEOPLE.
THE THING IS, THOUGH....

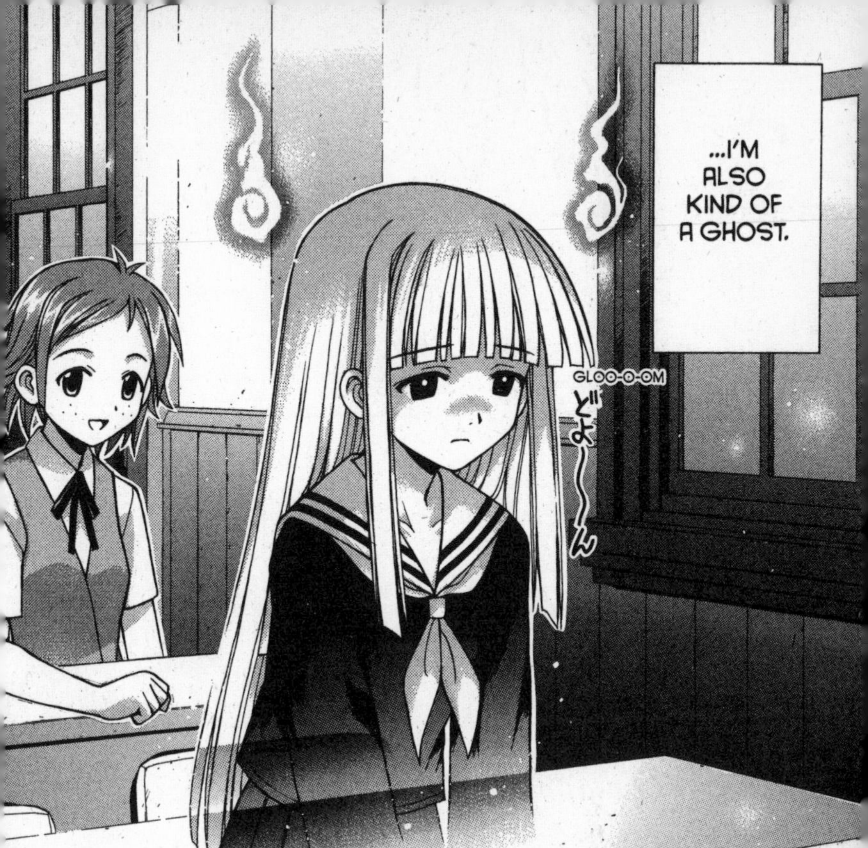
...I'M ALSO KIND OF A GHOST.
GLOO-O-OM
どよ〜〜ん

NEGIMA!

MAGISTER NEGI MAGI

SEVENTY-FOURTH PERIOD: HERE, THERE, AND NOWHERE

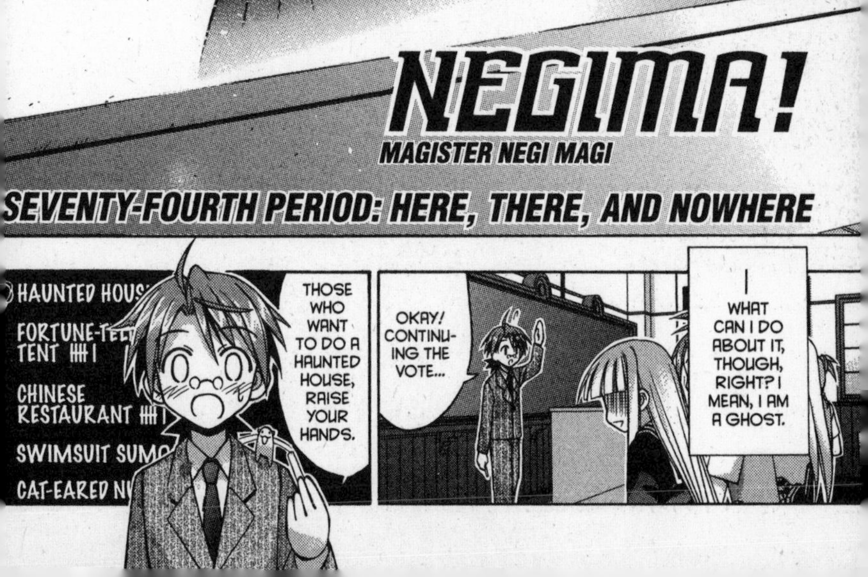
I
WHAT CAN I DO ABOUT IT, THOUGH, RIGHT? I MEAN, I AM A GHOST.
OKAY! CONTINUING THE VOTE...
THOSE WHO WANT TO DO A HAUNTED HOUSE, RAISE YOUR HANDS.
HAUNTED HOUS
FORTUNE-TELL TENT 卌I
CHINESE RESTAURANT 卌I
SWIMSUIT SUMO
CAT-EARED N

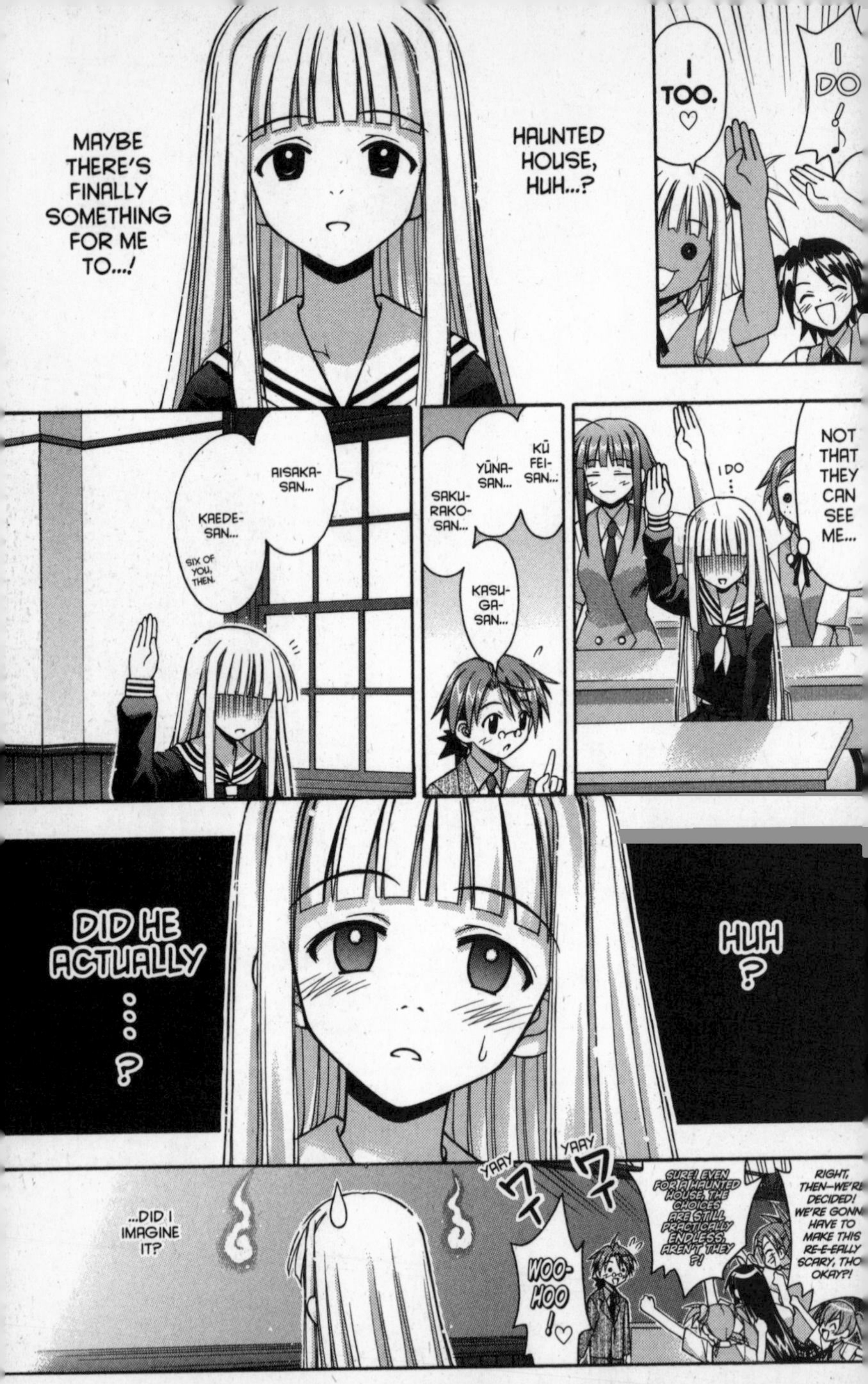

I DO!
I TOO. ♡
HAUNTED HOUSE, HUH...?
MAYBE THERE'S FINALLY SOMETHING FOR ME TO...!
NOT THAT THEY CAN SEE ME...
I DO...
KŪ FEI-SAN...
YŪNA-SAN...
SAKURAKO-SAN...
KASUGA-SAN...
AISAKA-SAN...
KAEDE-SAN...
SIX OF YOU, THEN.
HUH?
DID HE ACTUALLY...?
RIGHT, THEN—WE'RE DECIDED! WE'RE GONNA HAVE TO MAKE THIS RE-E-EALLY SCARY, THO OKAY?!
SURE! EVEN FOR A HAUNTED HOUSE, THE CHOICES ARE STILL PRACTICALLY ENDLESS, AREN'T THEY?!
YAAY
YAAY
WOO-HOO! ♡
...DID I IMAGINE IT?

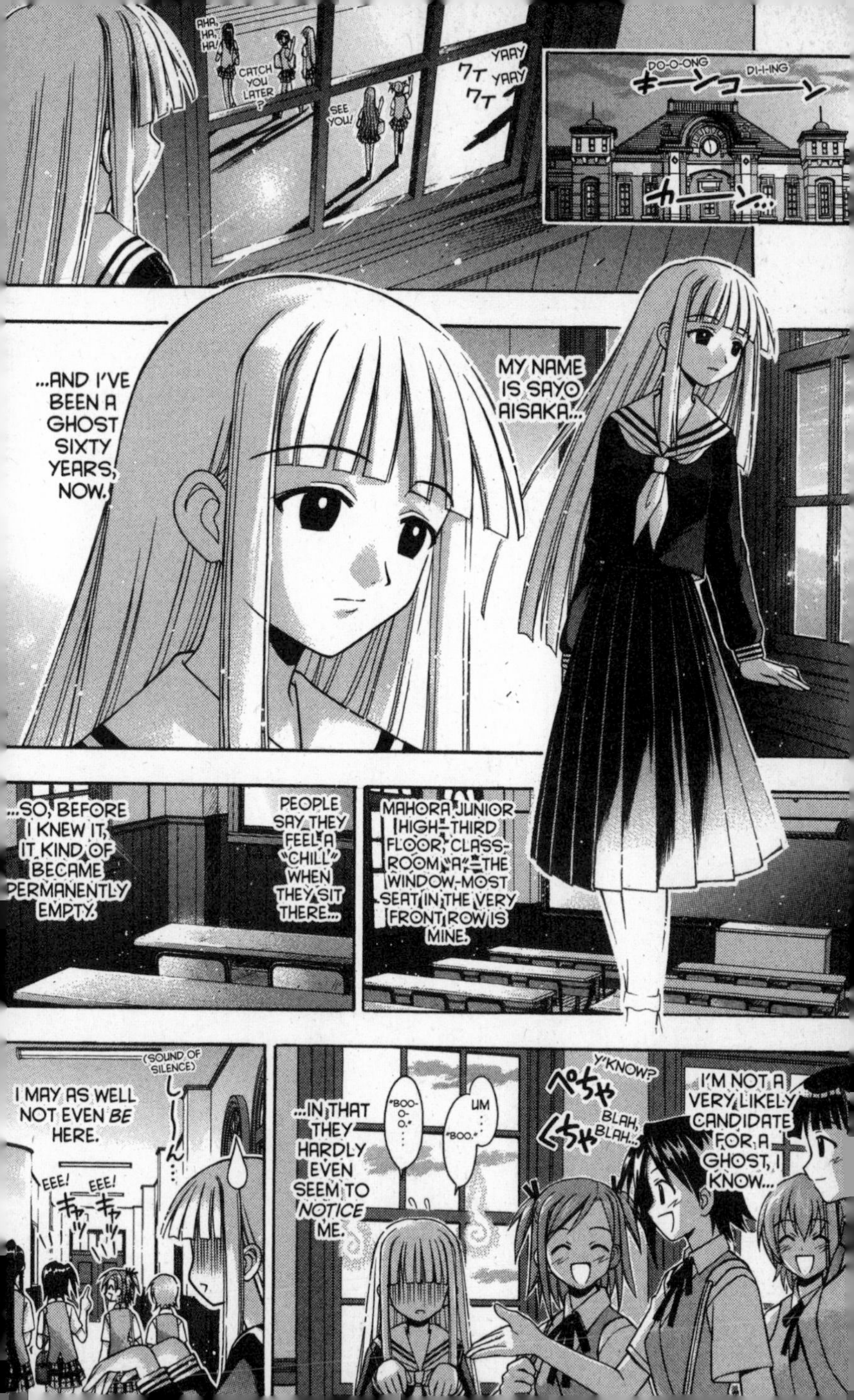
DO-O-ONG
DI-I-ING
キーンコーン
カーン…
YAAY YAAY
ワイワイ
SEE YOU!
AHA, HA, HA!
CATCH YOU LATER?
MY NAME IS SAYO AISAKA...
...AND I'VE BEEN A GHOST SIXTY YEARS, NOW.
MAHORA JUNIOR HIGH—THIRD FLOOR, CLASSROOM "A"—THE WINDOW-MOST SEAT IN THE VERY FRONT ROW IS MINE.
PEOPLE SAY THEY FEEL A "CHILL" WHEN THEY SIT THERE...
...SO, BEFORE I KNEW IT, IT KIND OF BECAME PERMANENTLY EMPTY.
I'M NOT A VERY LIKELY CANDIDATE FOR A GHOST, I KNOW...
Y'KNOW?
ぺちゃ
くちゃ
BLAH, BLAH...
UM
"BOO."
"BOO-O-O."
...IN THAT THEY HARDLY EVEN SEEM TO *NOTICE* ME.
(SOUND OF SILENCE)
しーん
I MAY AS WELL NOT EVEN *BE* HERE.
EEE! EEE!
キャーキャー

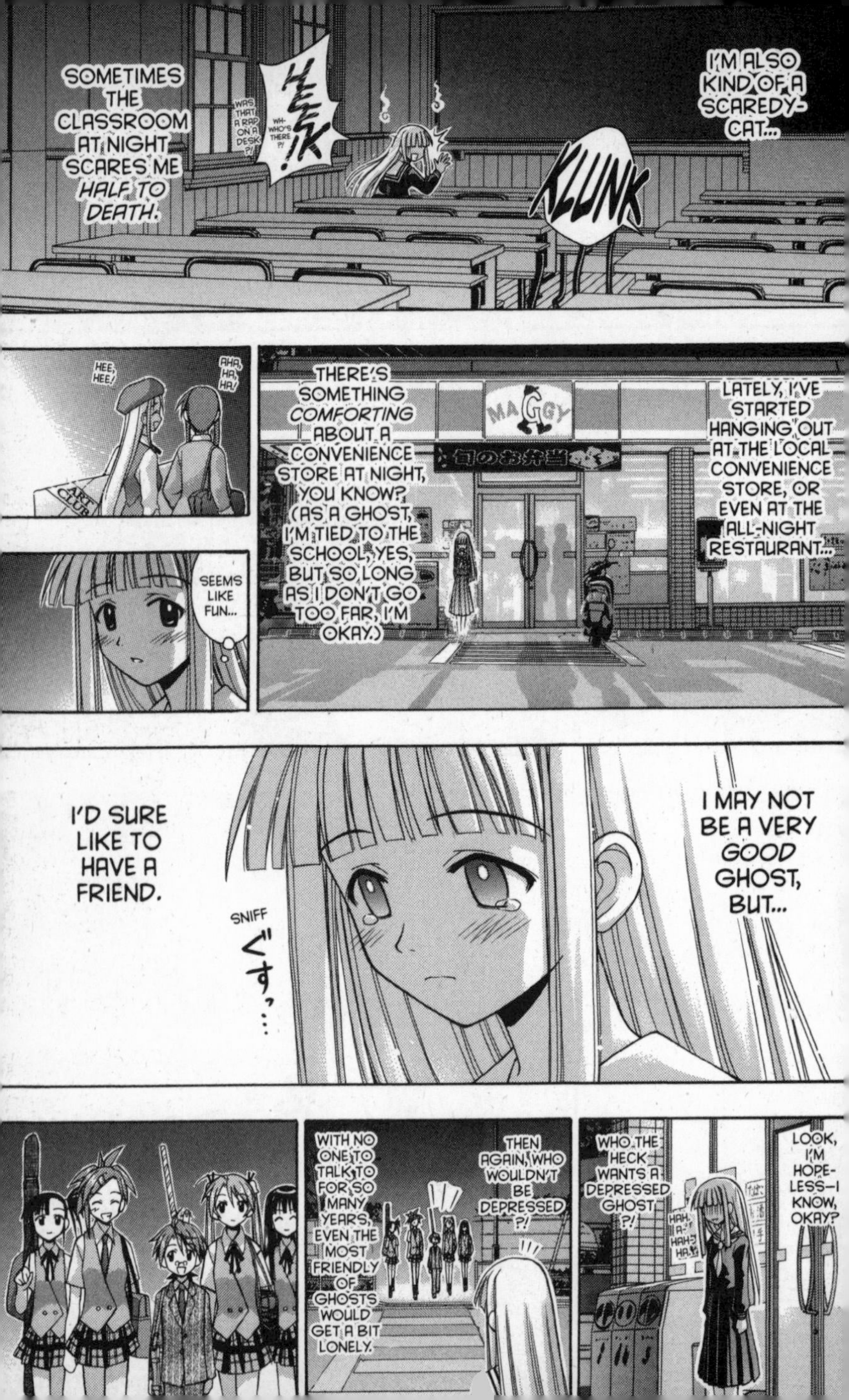
I'M ALSO KIND OF A SCAREDY-CAT...
KLUNK
HEEK!
WH-WHO'S THERE?!
WAS THAT A RAP ON A DESK?!
SOMETIMES THE CLASSROOM AT NIGHT SCARES ME *HALF TO DEATH.*
LATELY, I'VE STARTED HANGING OUT AT THE LOCAL CONVENIENCE STORE, OR EVEN AT THE ALL-NIGHT RESTAURANT...
MAGGY
旬のお弁当
THERE'S SOMETHING *COMFORTING* ABOUT A CONVENIENCE STORE AT NIGHT, YOU KNOW? (AS A GHOST, I'M TIED TO THE SCHOOL, YES, BUT SO LONG AS I DON'T GO TOO FAR, I'M OKAY.)
AHA, HA, HA!
HEE, HEE!
ART CLUB
SEEMS LIKE FUN...
I MAY NOT BE A VERY *GOOD* GHOST, BUT...
SNIFF
ぐすっ…
I'D SURE LIKE TO HAVE A FRIEND.
LOOK, I'M HOPELESS—I KNOW, OKAY?
HAH, A-HAH HA
WHO THE HECK WANTS A DEPRESSED GHOST?!
THEN AGAIN, WHO WOULDN'T BE DEPRESSED?!
WITH NO ONE TO TALK TO FOR SO MANY YEARS, EVEN THE MOST FRIENDLY OF GHOSTS WOULD GET A BIT LONELY.

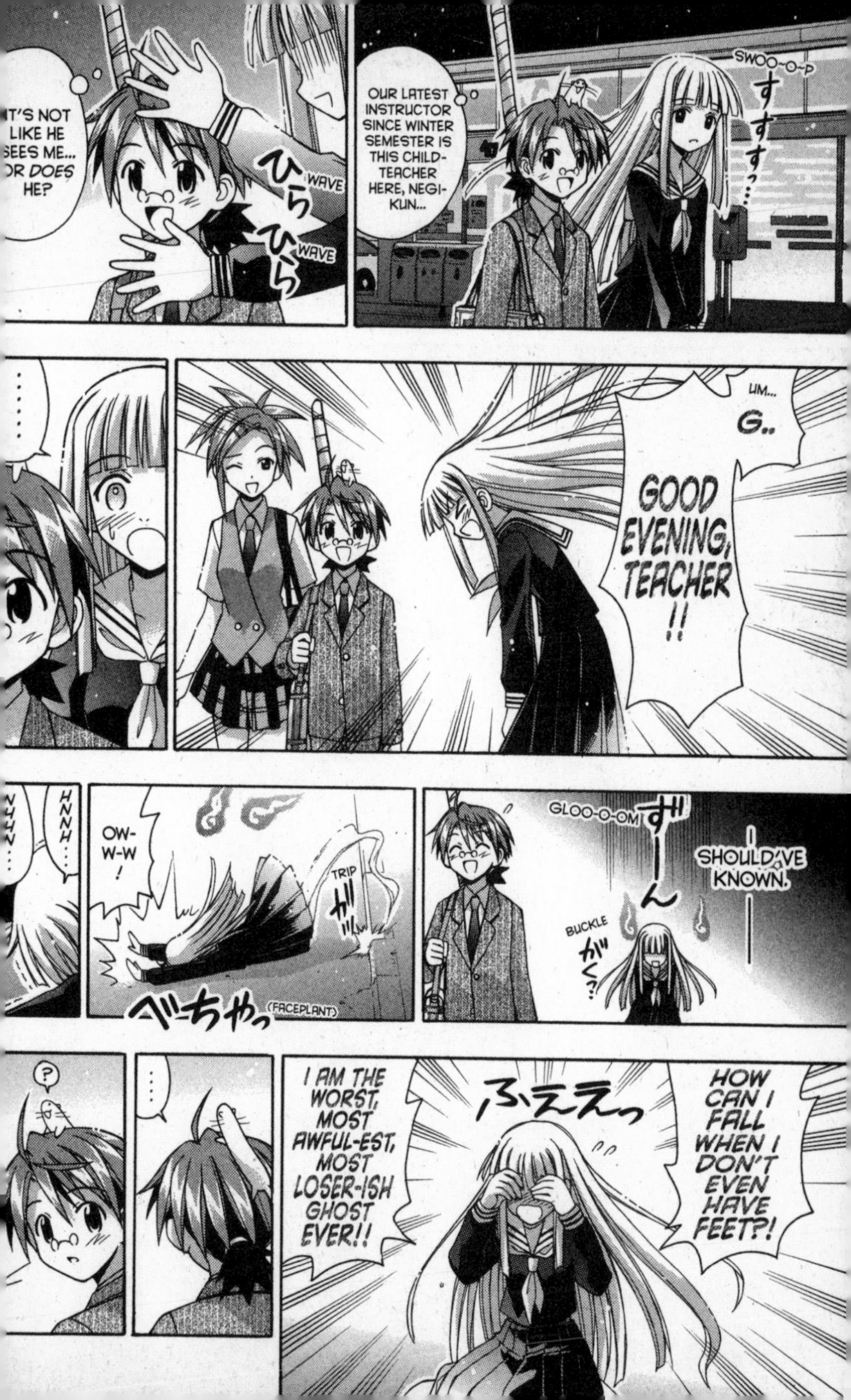
SWOO~O~P
すすすっ…
OUR LATEST INSTRUCTOR SINCE WINTER SEMESTER IS THIS CHILD-TEACHER HERE, NEGI-KUN...
ひら WAVE
ひら WAVE
T'S NOT LIKE HE SEES ME... R DOES HE?
UM...
G..
GOOD EVENING, TEACHER!!
......
GLOO-O-OM ずーん
SHOULD'VE KNOWN.
BUCKLE がくっ
TRIP ガッ
OW-W-W!
べちゃっ (FACEPLANT)
HNNH...
NHHN...
HOW CAN I FALL WHEN I DON'T EVEN HAVE FEET?!
ふえぇっ
I AM THE WORST, MOST AWFUL-EST, MOST LOSER-ISH GHOST EVER!!
....
?

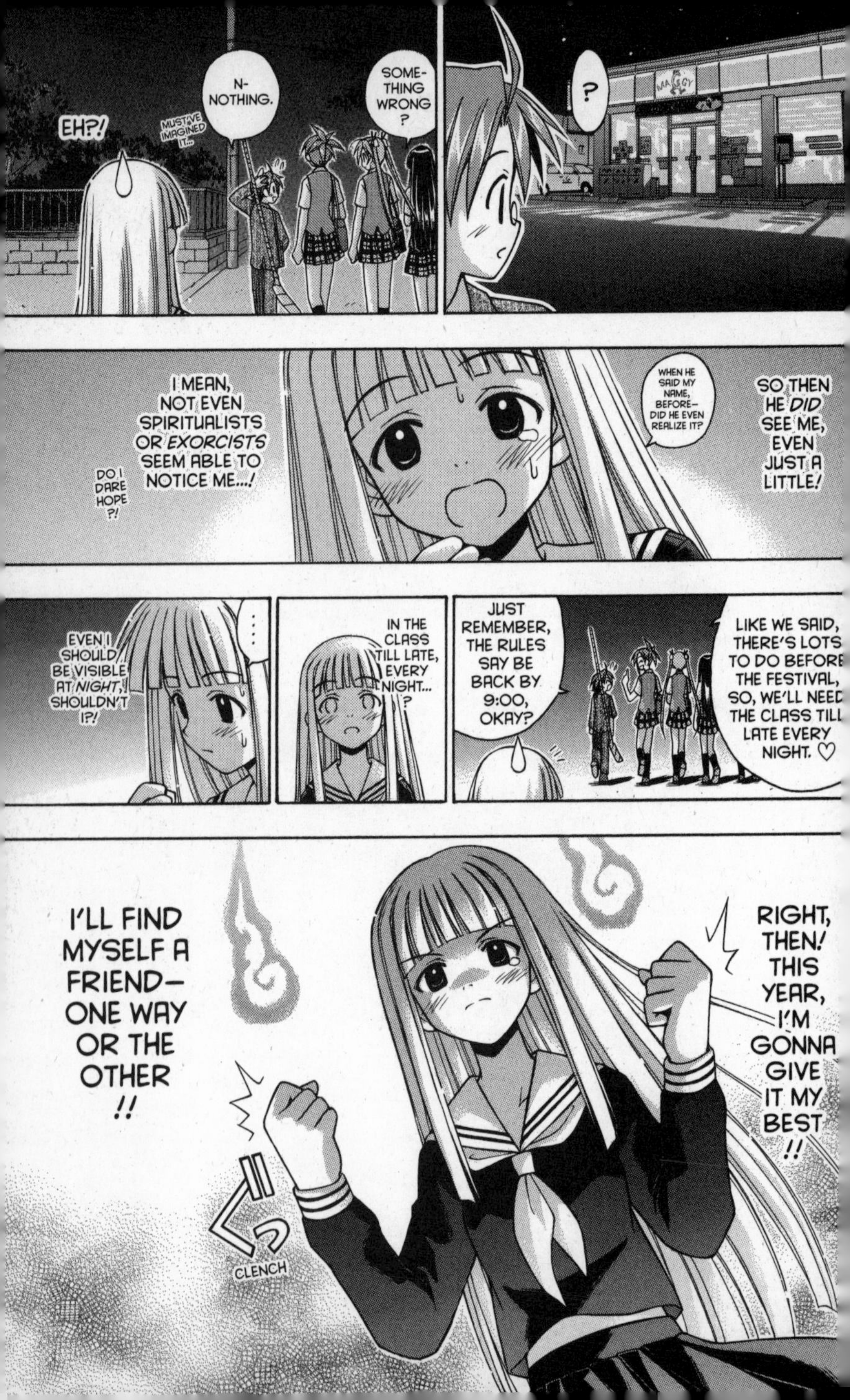
?
SOME-THING WRONG?
N-NOTHING.
MUST'VE IMAGINED IT...
EH?!
SO THEN HE *DID* SEE ME, EVEN JUST A LITTLE!
WHEN HE SAID MY NAME, BEFORE— DID HE EVEN REALIZE IT?
I MEAN, NOT EVEN SPIRITUALISTS OR *EXORCISTS* SEEM ABLE TO NOTICE ME...!
DO I DARE HOPE?!
LIKE WE SAID, THERE'S LOTS TO DO BEFORE THE FESTIVAL, SO, WE'LL NEED THE CLASS TILL LATE EVERY NIGHT. ♡
JUST REMEMBER, THE RULES SAY BE BACK BY 9:00, OKAY?
IN THE CLASS TILL LATE, EVERY NIGHT...?
...
EVEN I SHOULD BE VISIBLE AT *NIGHT*, SHOULDN'T I?!
RIGHT, THEN! THIS YEAR, I'M GONNA GIVE IT MY BEST!!
I'LL FIND MYSELF A FRIEND— ONE WAY OR THE OTHER!!
CLENCH

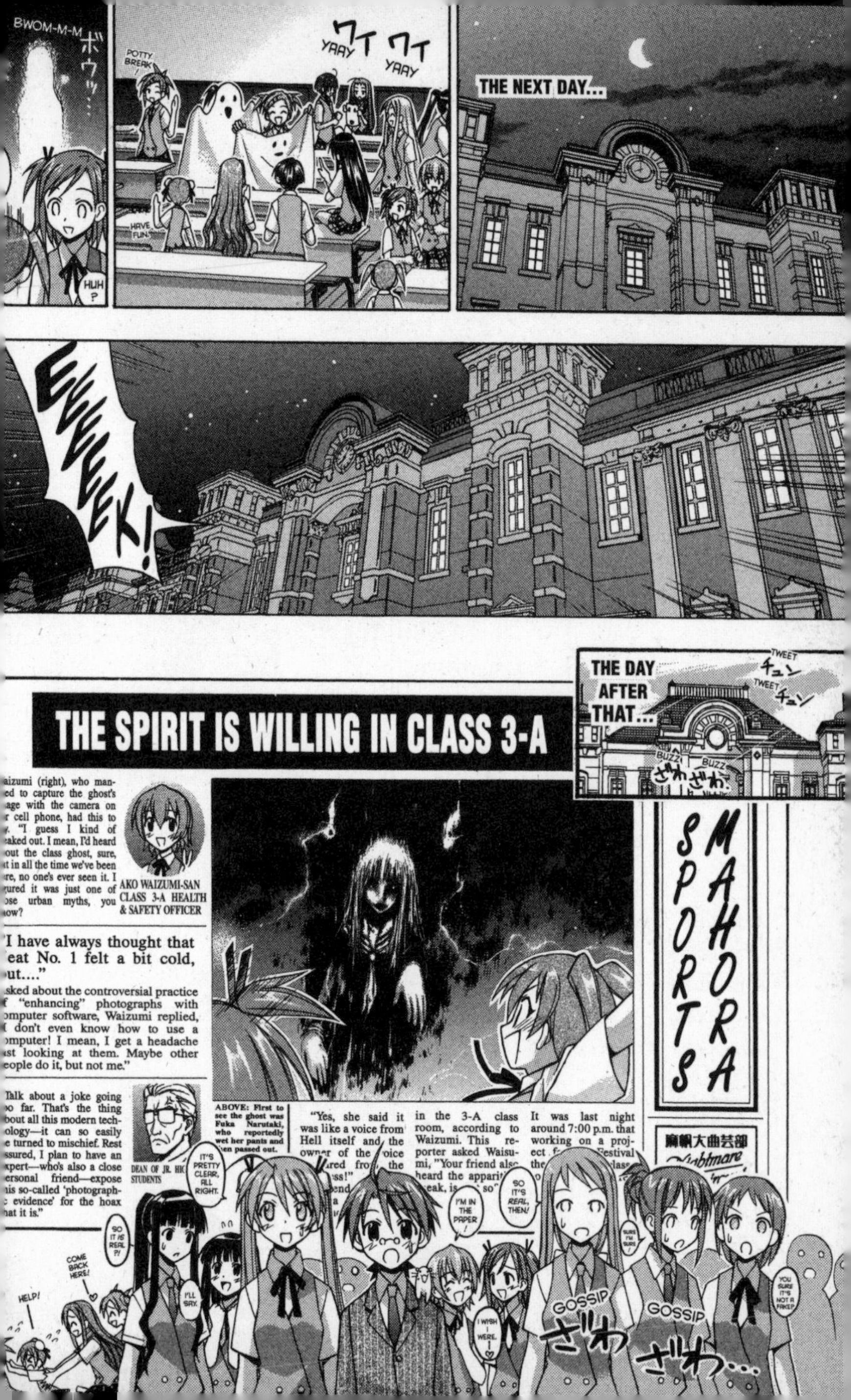

THE NEXT DAY...
ワイ YAAY ワイ YAAY
POTTY BREAK
HAVE FUN.
BWOM-M-M ボウッ…
HUH?
EEEEEK!
THE DAY AFTER THAT...
TWEET チュン
TWEET チュン
BUZZ BUZZ ざわざわ
MAHORA SPORTS
THE SPIRIT IS WILLING IN CLASS 3-A
aizumi (right), who maned to capture the ghost's age with the camera on r cell phone, had this to . "I guess I kind of eaked out. I mean, I'd heard out the class ghost, sure, t in all the time we've been re, no one's ever seen it. I ured it was just one of se urban myths, you ow?
AKO WAIZUMI-SAN CLASS 3-A HEALTH & SAFETY OFFICER
'I have always thought that eat No. 1 felt a bit cold, ut...."
sked about the controversial practice f "enhancing" photographs with omputer software, Waizumi replied, I don't even know how to use a omputer! I mean, I get a headache st looking at them. Maybe other eople do it, but not me."
Talk about a joke going o far. That's the thing bout all this modern techology—it can so easily e turned to mischief. Rest ssured, I plan to have an xpert—who's also a close ersonal friend—expose is so-called 'photographc evidence' for the hoax at it is."
DEAN OF JR. HIG STUDENTS
ABOVE: First to see the ghost was Fuka Narutaki, who reportedly wet her pants and hen passed out.
"Yes, she said it was like a voice from Hell itself and the owner of the oice ared fro the ss!" end a
in the 3-A class room, according to Waizumi. This reporter asked Waisumi, "Your friend also heard the apparit eak, is so"
It was last night around 7:00 p.m. that working on a project f Festival the class o
麻帆大曲芸部
YOU SURE IT'S NOT A FAKE?
GOSSIP ざわ
GOSSIP ざわ…
SURE I'M SURE!
SO IT'S REAL, THEN!
I'M IN THE PAPER!
I WISH I WERE.
IT'S PRETTY CLEAR, ALL RIGHT.
I'LL SAY.
SO IT IS REAL?!
COME BACK HERE!
HELP!

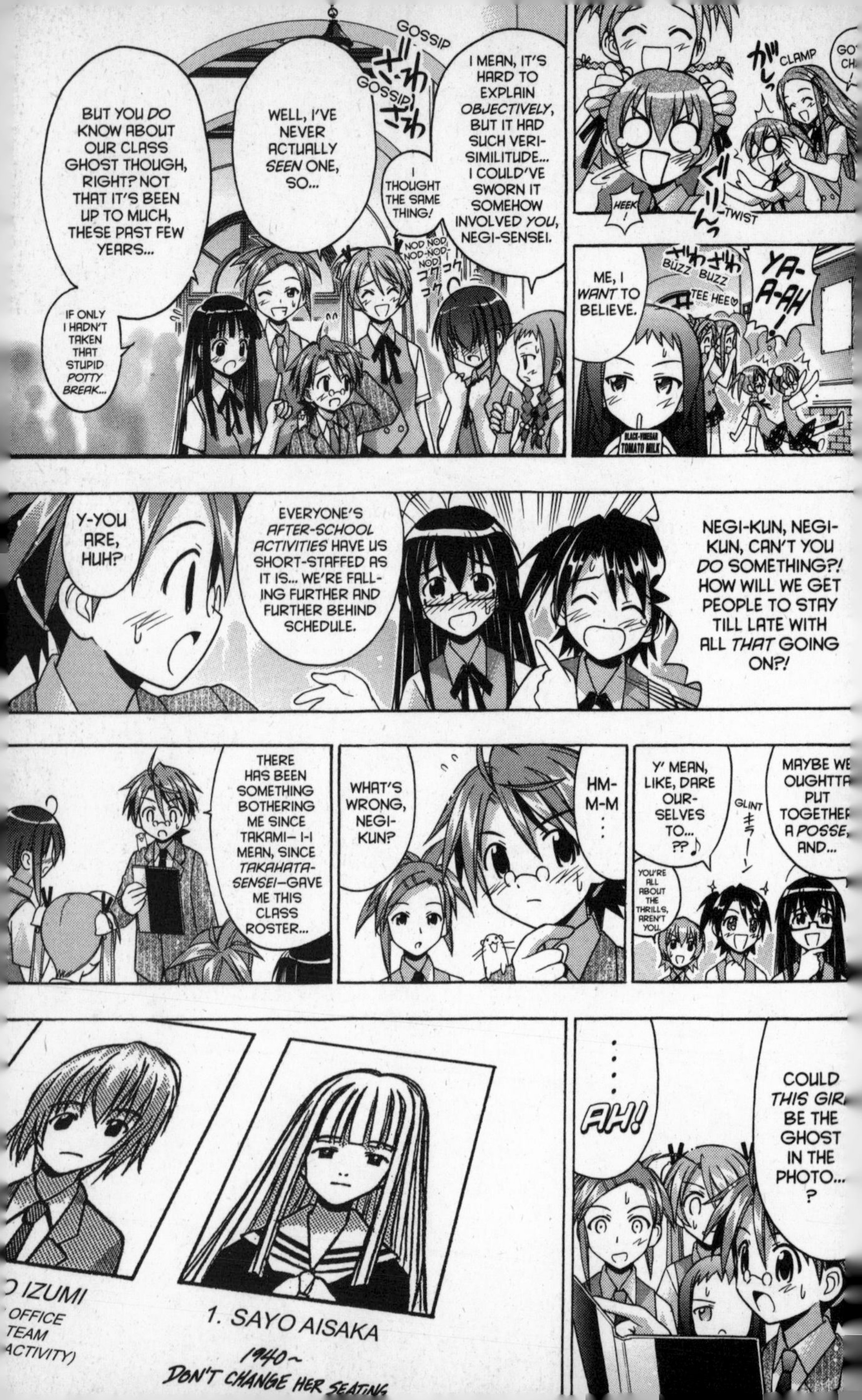
GO' CH
がしっ
CLAMP
HEEK!
ぐりんっ
TWIST
ざわざわ
BUZZ BUZZ
TEE HEE♡
YA-A-AH!
ME, I *WANT* TO BELIEVE.
BLACK-VINEGAR TOMATO MILK
GOSSIP
ざわ
GOSSIP
ざわ
I MEAN, IT'S HARD TO EXPLAIN *OBJECTIVELY*, BUT IT HAD SUCH VERISIMILITUDE... I COULD'VE SWORN IT SOMEHOW INVOLVED *YOU*, NEGI-SENSEI.
I THOUGHT THE SAME THING!
NOD NOD NOD-NOD-NOD!
コクコクコク
WELL, I'VE NEVER ACTUALLY *SEEN* ONE, SO...
BUT YOU *DO* KNOW ABOUT OUR CLASS GHOST THOUGH, RIGHT? NOT THAT IT'S BEEN UP TO MUCH, THESE PAST FEW YEARS...
IF ONLY I HADN'T TAKEN THAT STUPID *POTTY* BREAK...
NEGI-KUN, NEGI-KUN, CAN'T YOU *DO* SOMETHING?! HOW WILL WE GET PEOPLE TO STAY TILL LATE WITH ALL *THAT* GOING ON?!
EVERYONE'S *AFTER-SCHOOL ACTIVITIES* HAVE US SHORT-STAFFED AS IT IS... WE'RE FALLING FURTHER AND FURTHER BEHIND SCHEDULE.
Y-YOU ARE, HUH?
MAYBE WE OUGHTTA PUT TOGETHER A *POSSE*, AND...
Y' MEAN, LIKE, DARE OURSELVES TO...??♪
GLINT
YOU'RE ALL ABOUT THE THRILLS, AREN'T YOU.
HM-M-M...
WHAT'S WRONG, NEGI-KUN?
THERE HAS BEEN SOMETHING BOTHERING ME SINCE TAKAMI— I-I MEAN, SINCE *TAKAHATA-SENSEI*—GAVE ME THIS CLASS ROSTER...
......
AH!
COULD *THIS GIRL* BE THE GHOST IN THE PHOTO...?
O IZUMI
OFFICE
TEAM
ACTIVITY)
1. SAYO AISAKA
1940~
DON'T CHANGE HER SEATING

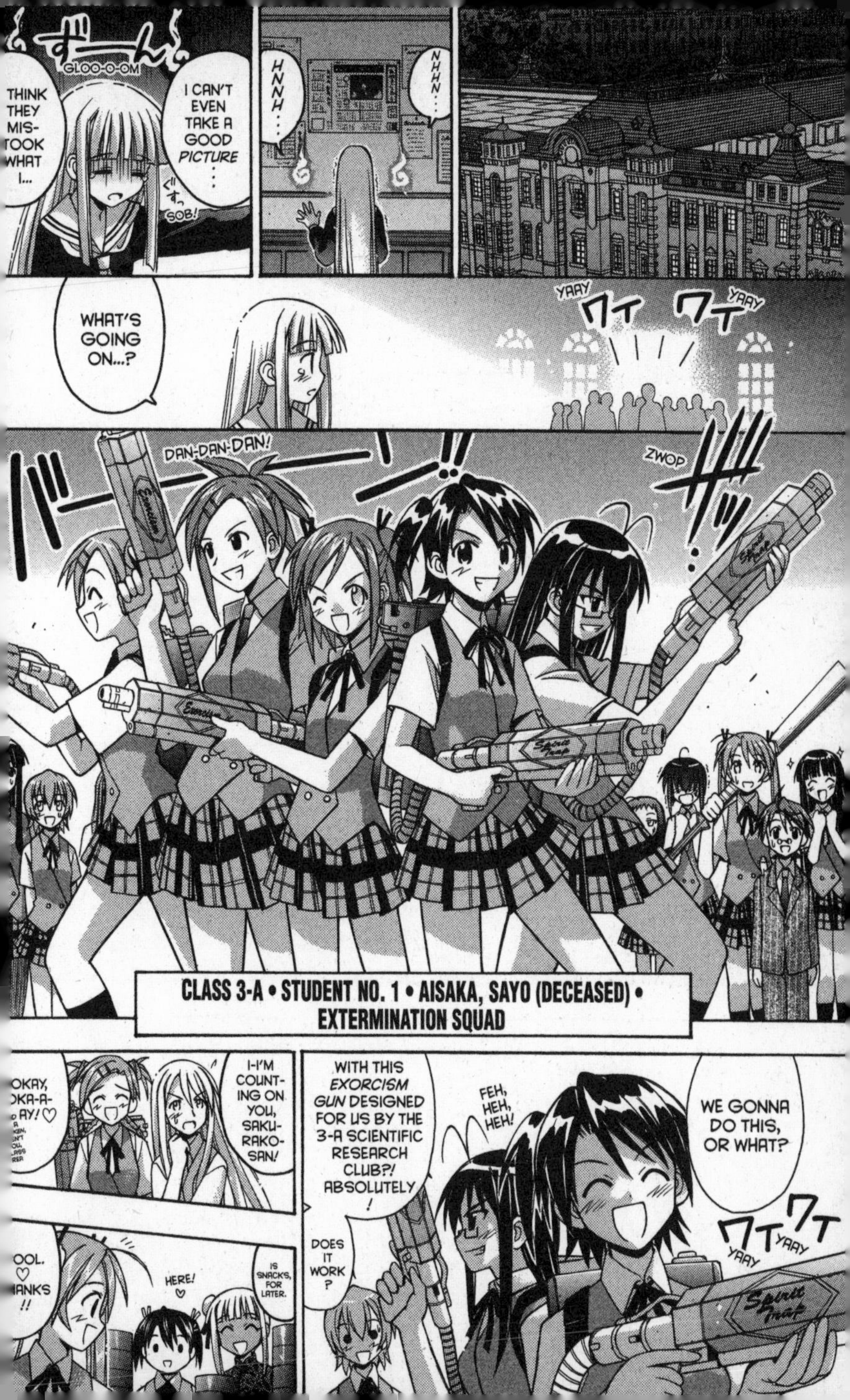
NHHN...
HNNH...
GLOO-O-OM
I CAN'T EVEN TAKE A GOOD PICTURE...
THINK THEY MIS-TOOK WHAT I...
SOB!
YAAY
YAAY
WHAT'S GOING ON...?
ZWOP
DAN-DAN-DAN!
CLASS 3-A • STUDENT NO. 1 • AISAKA, SAYO (DECEASED) • EXTERMINATION SQUAD
WE GONNA DO THIS, OR WHAT?
FEH, HEH, HEH!
WITH THIS EXORCISM GUN DESIGNED FOR US BY THE 3-A SCIENTIFIC RESEARCH CLUB?! ABSOLUTELY!
DOES IT WORK?
YAAY
YAAY
I-I'M COUNTING ON YOU, SAKURAKO-SAN!
OKAY, OKA-A-AY! ♡
IS SNACKS, FOR LATER.
HERE! ♡
OOL. ♡ HANKS!!

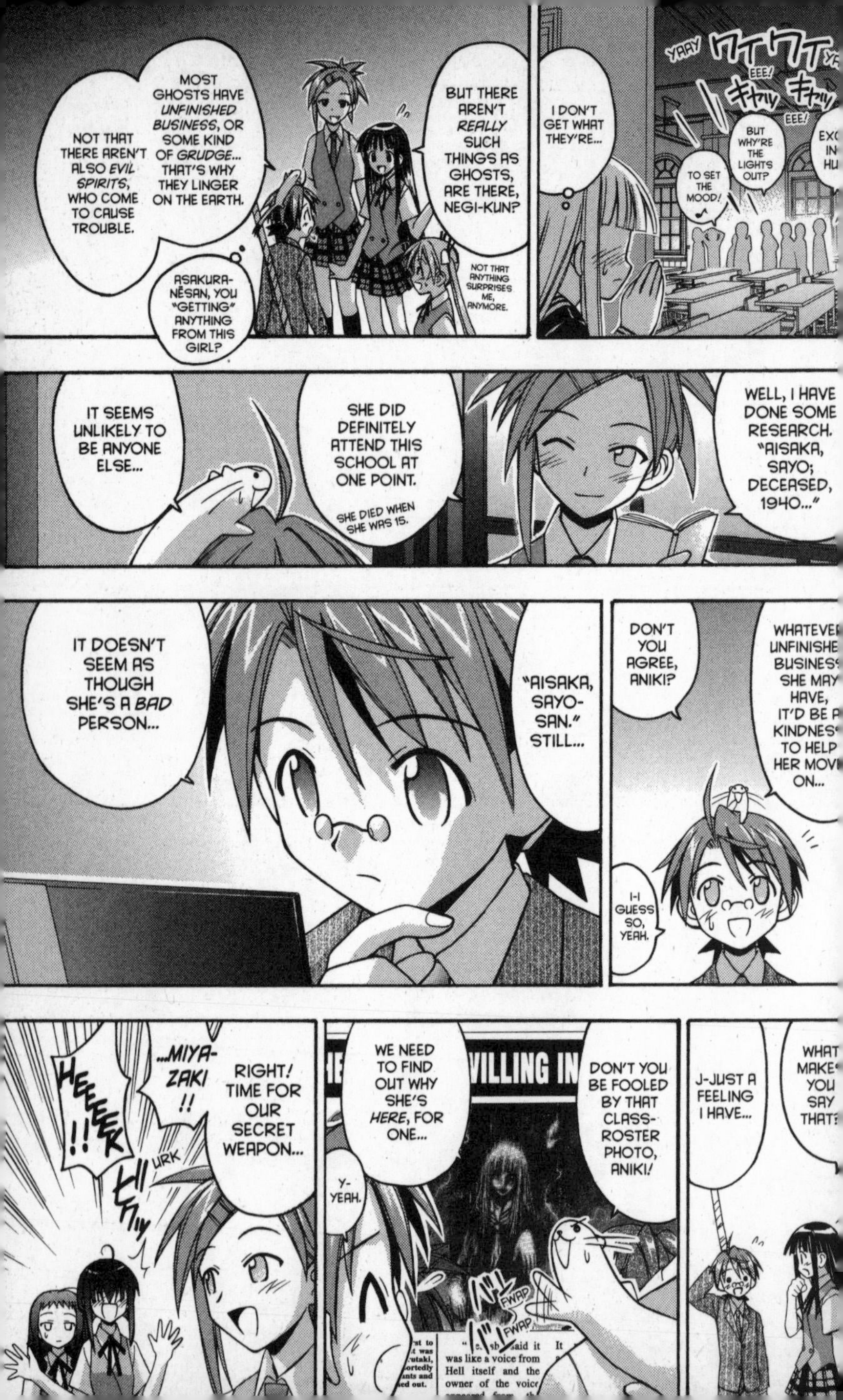
YAAY
EEE!
EEE!
BUT WHY'RE THE LIGHTS OUT?
TO SET THE MOOD!
I DON'T GET WHAT THEY'RE...
BUT THERE AREN'T *REALLY* SUCH THINGS AS GHOSTS, ARE THERE, NEGI-KUN?
MOST GHOSTS HAVE *UNFINISHED BUSINESS*, OR SOME KIND OF *GRUDGE*... THAT'S WHY THEY LINGER ON THE EARTH.
NOT THAT THERE AREN'T ALSO *EVIL SPIRITS*, WHO COME TO CAUSE TROUBLE.
NOT THAT ANYTHING SURPRISES ME, ANYMORE.
ASAKURA-NÊSAN, YOU "GETTING" ANYTHING FROM THIS GIRL?
WELL, I HAVE DONE SOME RESEARCH. "AISAKA, SAYO; DECEASED, 1940..."
SHE DID DEFINITELY ATTEND THIS SCHOOL AT ONE POINT.
SHE DIED WHEN SHE WAS 15.
IT SEEMS UNLIKELY TO BE ANYONE ELSE...
WHATEVE UNFINISHE BUSINES SHE MAY HAVE, IT'D BE A KINDNES TO HELP HER MOV ON...
DON'T YOU AGREE, ANIKI?
I-I GUESS SO, YEAH.
"AISAKA, SAYO-SAN." STILL...
IT DOESN'T SEEM AS THOUGH SHE'S A *BAD* PERSON...
WHAT MAKE YOU SAY THAT
J-JUST A FEELING I HAVE...
DON'T YOU BE FOOLED BY THAT CLASS-ROSTER PHOTO, ANIKI!
VILLING IN
was like a voice from Hell itself and the owner of the voice
FWAP
FWAP
WE NEED TO FIND OUT WHY SHE'S *HERE*, FOR ONE...
Y-YEAH.
RIGHT! TIME FOR OUR SECRET WEAPON...
...MIYA-ZAKI !!
HEEEEK!!
URK

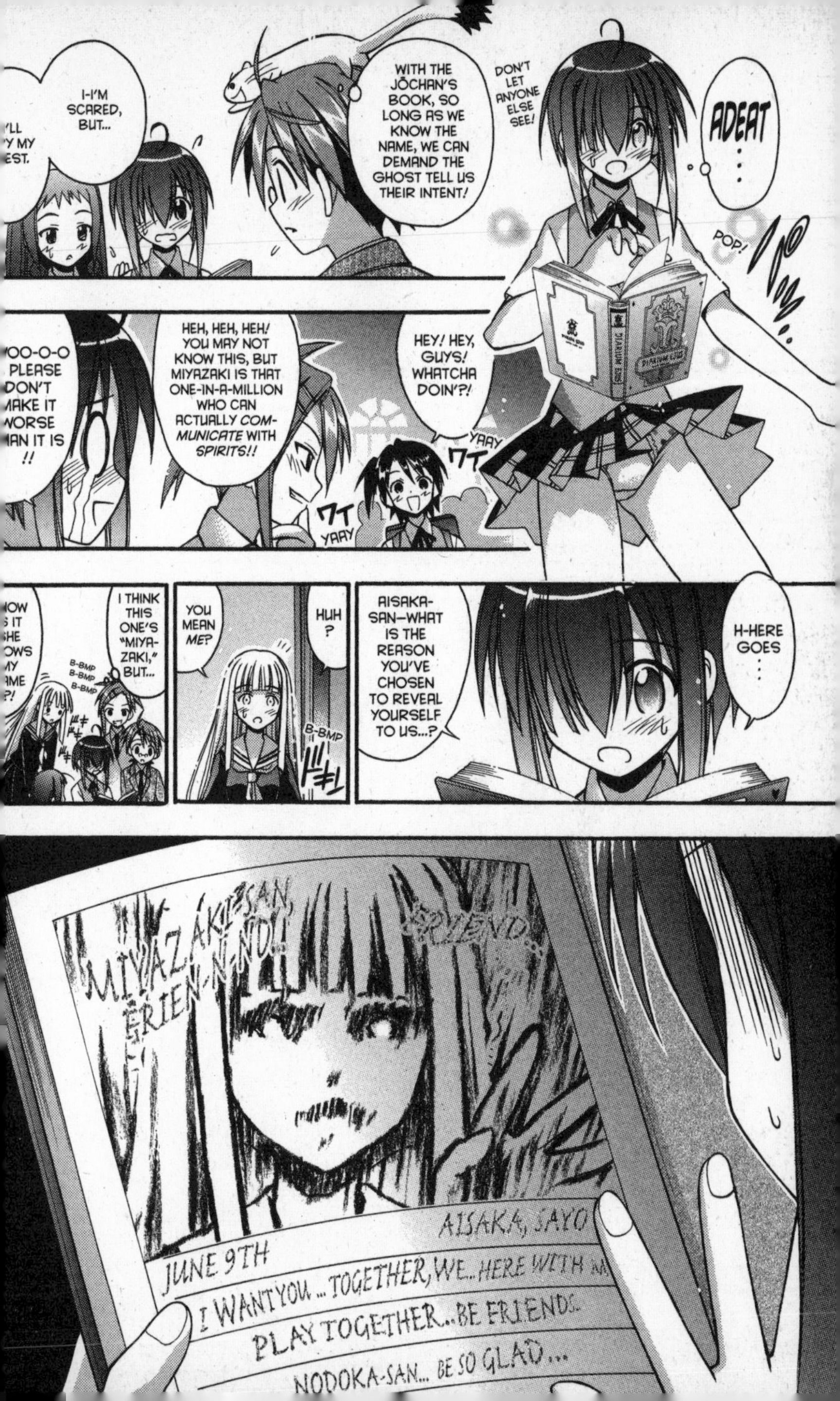
ADEAT . . .
DON'T LET ANYONE ELSE SEE!
POP!
WITH THE JŌCHAN'S BOOK, SO LONG AS WE KNOW THE NAME, WE CAN DEMAND THE GHOST TELL US THEIR INTENT!
I-I'M SCARED, BUT...
HEY! HEY, GUYS! WHATCHA DOIN'?!
YAAY
YAAY
HEH, HEH, HEH! YOU MAY NOT KNOW THIS, BUT MIYAZAKI IS THAT ONE-IN-A-MILLION WHO CAN ACTUALLY COM-MUNICATE WITH SPIRITS!!
H-HERE GOES . . .
AISAKA-SAN—WHAT IS THE REASON YOU'VE CHOSEN TO REVEAL YOURSELF TO US...?
HUH?
B-BMP
YOU MEAN ME?
I THINK THIS ONE'S "MIYAZAKI," BUT...
B-BMP B-BMP B-BMP
MIYAZAKI-SAN, FRIEN-N-ND!!
FRIEND...
AISAKA, SAYO
JUNE 9TH
I WANT YOU ... TOGETHER, WE... HERE WITH
PLAY TOGETHER... BE FRIENDS
NODOKA-SAN... BE SO GLAD...

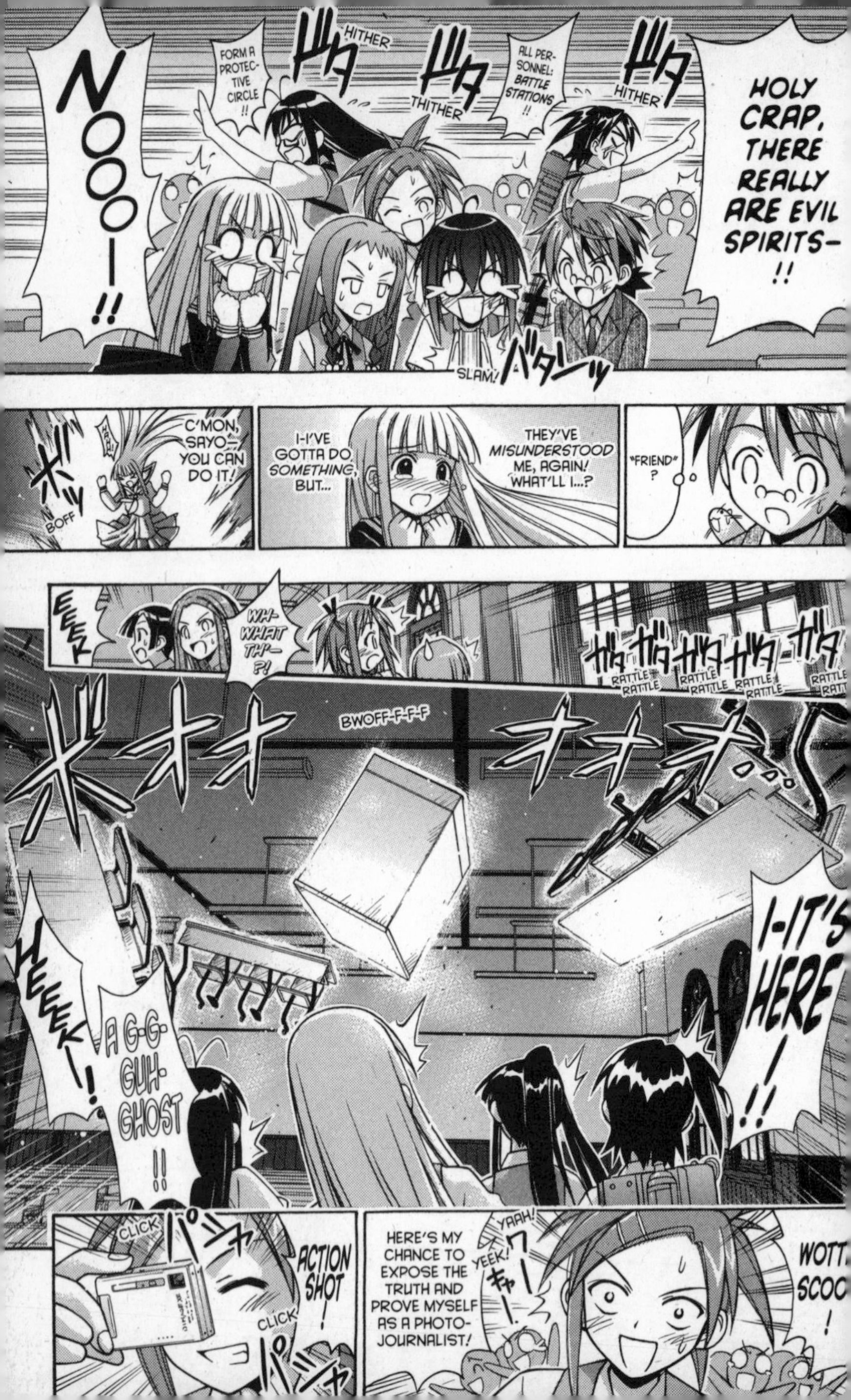
HOLY CRAP, THERE REALLY ARE EVIL SPIRITS—!!
HITHER
ALL PERSONNEL: BATTLE STATIONS!!
THITHER
HITHER
FORM A PROTECTIVE CIRCLE!!
NOOOO—!!
SLAM!
"FRIEND"?
THEY'VE MISUNDERSTOOD ME, AGAIN! WHAT'LL I...?
I-I'VE GOTTA DO SOMETHING, BUT...
C'MON, SAYO—YOU CAN DO IT!
BOFF
RATTLE RATTLE
RATTLE RATTLE
RATTLE RATTLE
RATTLE RATTLE
WH-WHAT TH'—?!
EEEK
BWOFF-F-F-F
I-IT'S HERE—!!
A G-G-GUH-GHOST!!
HEEEEK—!!
YAAH!
YEEK!
HERE'S MY CHANCE TO EXPOSE THE TRUTH AND PROVE MYSELF AS A PHOTO-JOURNALIST!
ACTION SHOT!
CLICK
CLICK

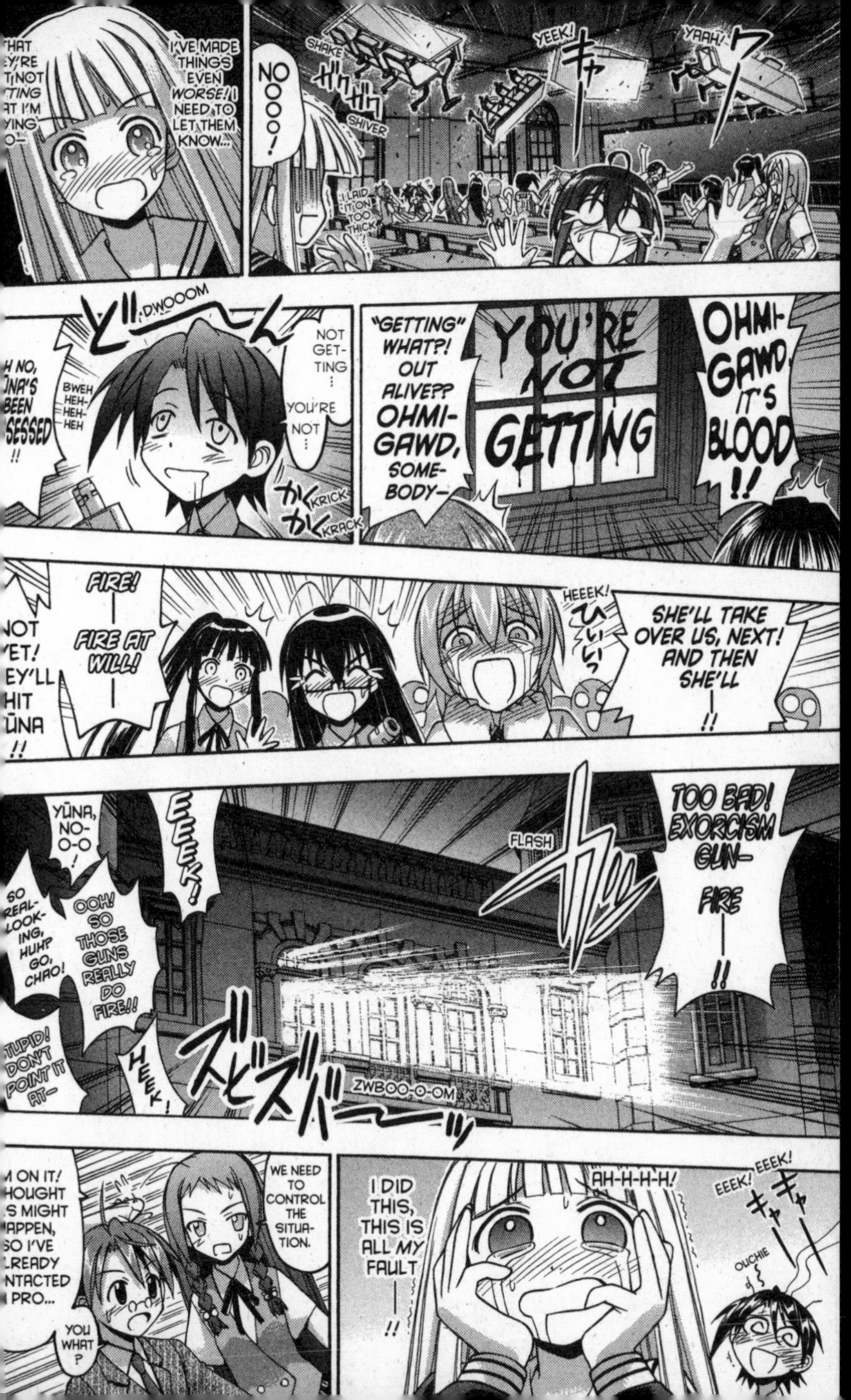

YAAH!
YEEK!
SHAKE
SHIVER
NOOOOO!
I LAID IT ON TOO THICK!
I'VE MADE THINGS EVEN WORSE! I NEED TO LET THEM KNOW...
THAT EY'RE T NOT TTING AT I'M YING O—
OHMI-GAWD, IT'S BLOOD!!
YOU'RE NOT GETTING
"GETTING" WHAT?! OUT ALIVE?? OHMI-GAWD, SOMEBODY—
NOT GETTING... YOU'RE NOT...
DWOOOM
BWEH HEH-HEH-HEH
KRICK KRACK
H NO, YŪNA'S BEEN SESSED!!
HEEEK!
SHE'LL TAKE OVER US, NEXT! AND THEN SHE'LL—!!
FIRE! —FIRE AT WILL!—
NOT YET! EY'LL HIT YŪNA!!
TOO BAD! EXORCISM GUN—FIRE—!!
FLASH
EEEEK!
YŪNA, NO-O-O!
OOH! SO THOSE GUNS REALLY DO FIRE!!
SO REAL-LOOKING, HUH? GO, CHAO!
ZWBOO-O-OM
HEEEK!
TUPID! DON'T POINT IT AT—
EEEK! EEEK!
AH-H-H-H!
OUCHIE
I DID THIS, THIS IS ALL MY FAULT—!!
WE NEED TO CONTROL THE SITUATION.
M ON IT! HOUGHT S MIGHT APPEN, SO I'VE LREADY NTACTED PRO...
YOU WHAT?

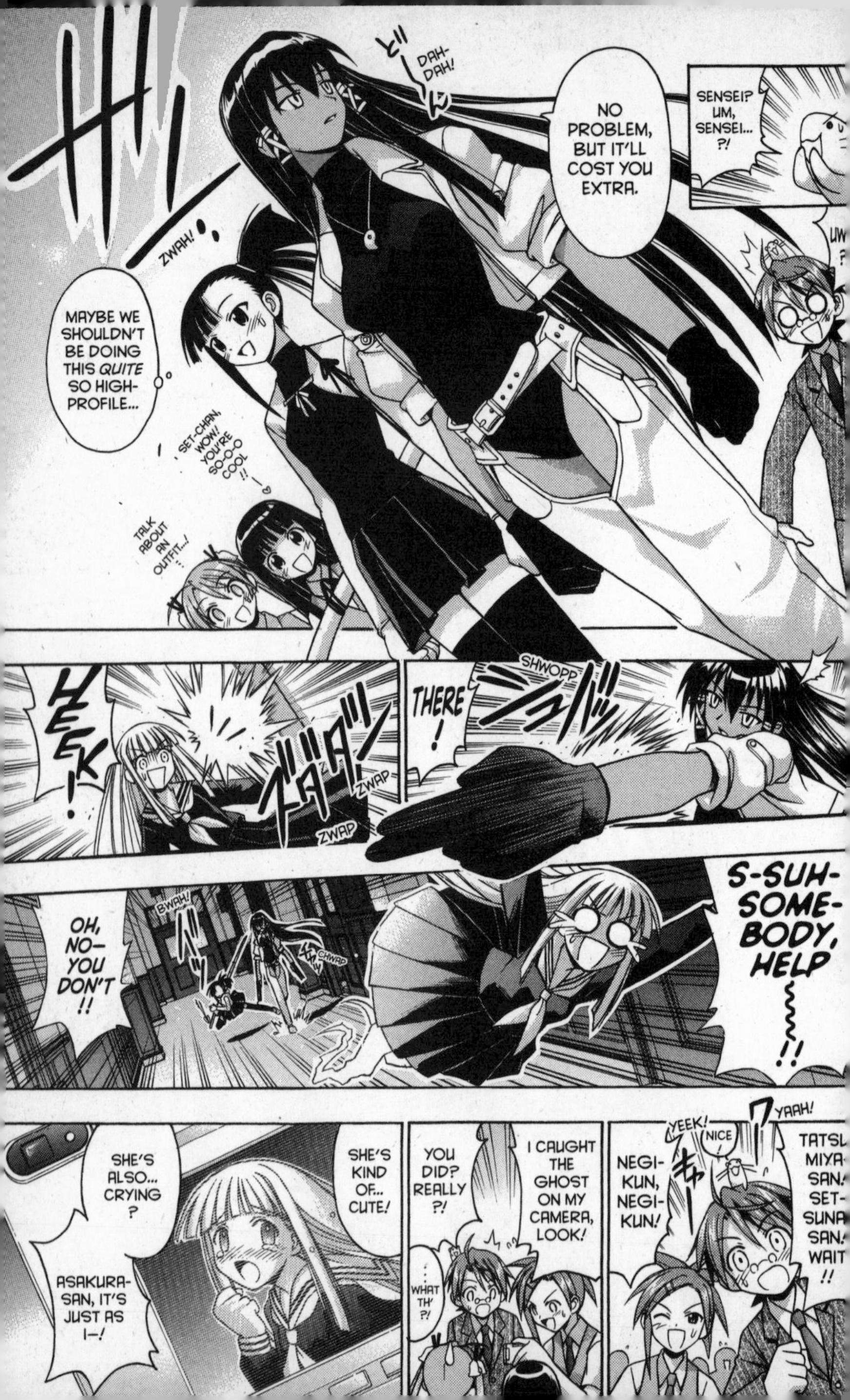
SENSEI? UM, SENSEI...?!
UW...?
DAH-DAH!
NO PROBLEM, BUT IT'LL COST YOU EXTRA.
ZWAH!
MAYBE WE SHOULDN'T BE DOING THIS QUITE SO HIGH-PROFILE...
SET-CHAN, WOW! YOU'RE SO-O-O COOL!!
TALK ABOUT AN OUTFIT...!
SHWOPP
THERE!
HEEEK!
ZWAP
ZWAP
S-SUH-SOMEBODY, HELP~~~!!
CHWAP
BWAH!
OH, NO—YOU DON'T!!
YAAAH!
YEEK!
NICE!
TATSU... MIYA-SAN! SET-SUNA-SAN! WAIT!!
NEGI-KUN, NEGI-KUN!
I CAUGHT THE GHOST ON MY CAMERA, LOOK!
YOU DID? REALLY?!
...WHAT TH'?!
SHE'S KIND OF... CUTE!
SHE'S ALSO... CRYING?
ASAKURA-SAN, IT'S JUST AS I—!

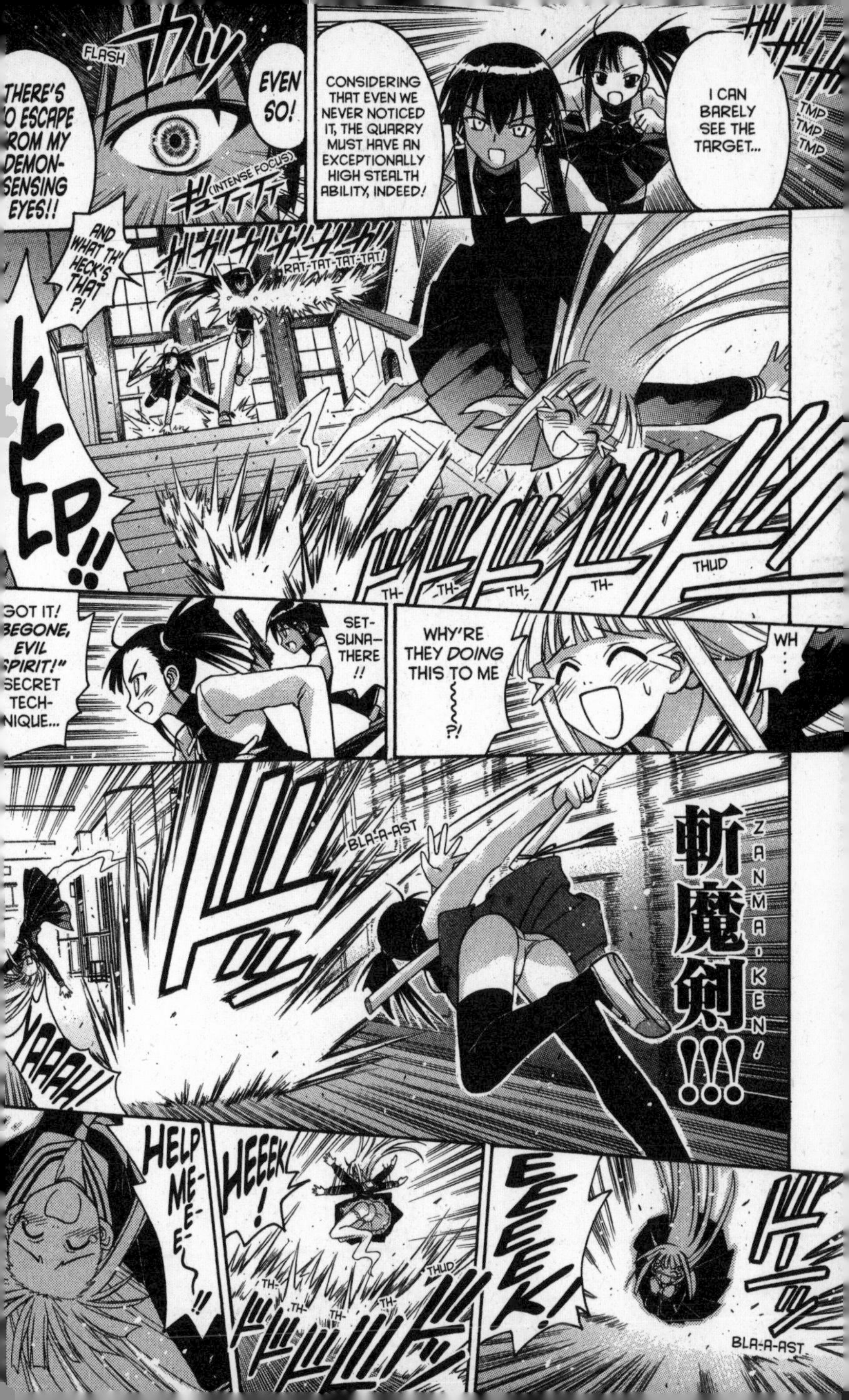

I CAN BARELY SEE THE TARGET...
TMP TMP TMP
CONSIDERING THAT EVEN WE NEVER NOTICED IT, THE QUARRY MUST HAVE AN EXCEPTIONALLY HIGH STEALTH ABILITY, INDEED!
EVEN SO!
FLASH
THERE'S O ESCAPE ROM MY DEMON-SENSING EYES!!
(INTENSE FOCUS)
AND WHAT TH' HECK'S THAT ?!
RAT-TAT-TAT-TAT!
EEP!!
TH- TH- TH- TH-
THUD
WH...
WHY'RE THEY *DOING* THIS TO ME ~?!
SET-SUNA-THERE !!
GOT IT! BEGONE, EVIL SPIRIT!" SECRET TECH-NIQUE...
斬魔剣!!!
ZANMA-KEN!
BLA-A-AST
AAAH!
BLA-A-AST
EEEEEK!
HEEEK!
THUD
TH- TH- TH-
HELP ME-E-E-E~!!

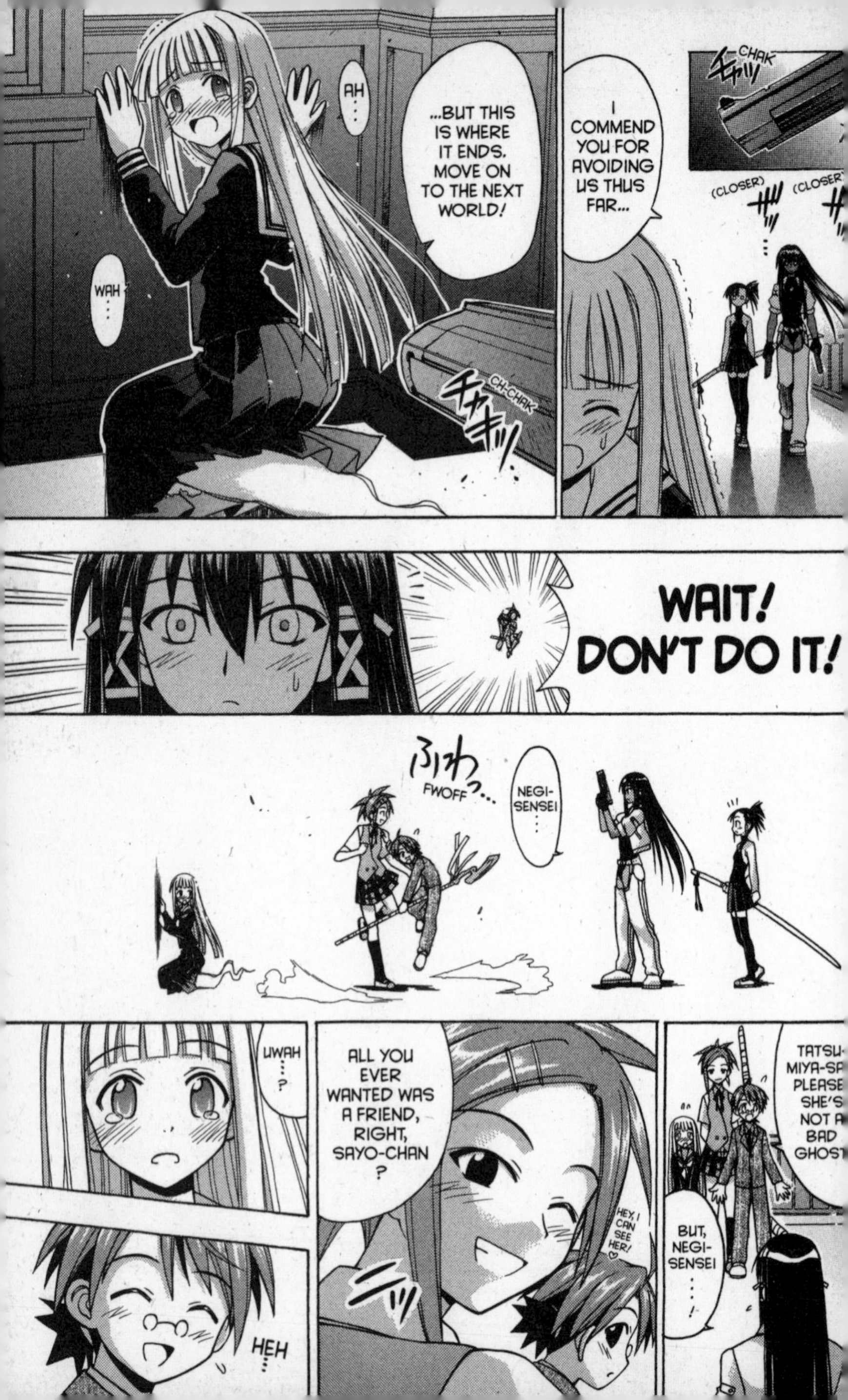
CHAK
(CLOSER)
(CLOSER
I COMMEND YOU FOR AVOIDING US THUS FAR...
...BUT THIS IS WHERE IT ENDS. MOVE ON TO THE NEXT WORLD!
AH...
WAH...
CH-CHAK
WAIT! DON'T DO IT!
FWOFF...
NEGI-SENSEI...
TATSU-MIYA-SA PLEASE SHE'S NOT A BAD GHOST
BUT, NEGI-SENSEI...!
ALL YOU EVER WANTED WAS A FRIEND, RIGHT, SAYO-CHAN?
HEY, I CAN SEE HER! ♡
UWAH...?
HEH...

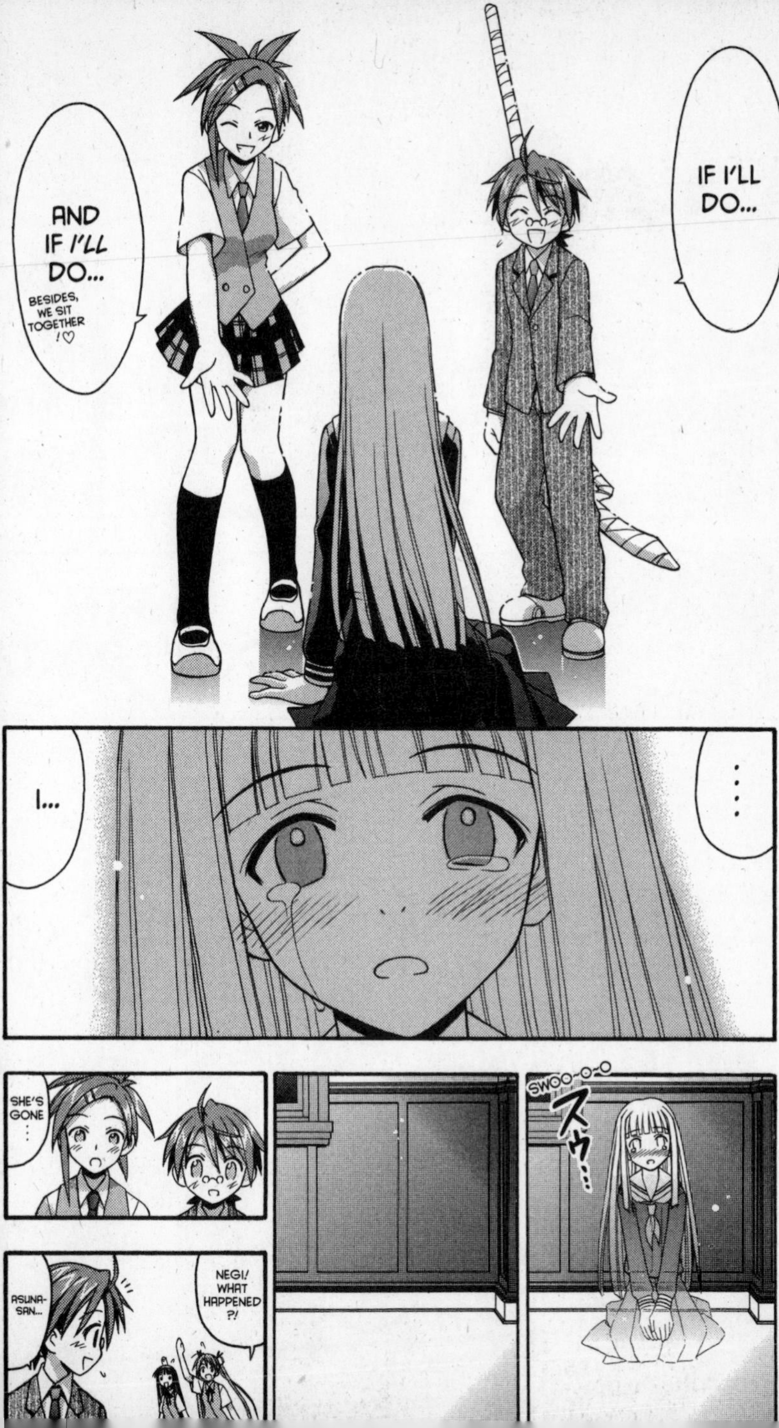
IF I'LL DO...
AND IF I'LL DO...
BESIDES, WE SIT TOGETHER !♡
....
I...
SWOO-O-O
スゥ...
SHE'S GONE ...
NEGI! WHAT HAPPENED ?!
ASUNA-SAN...

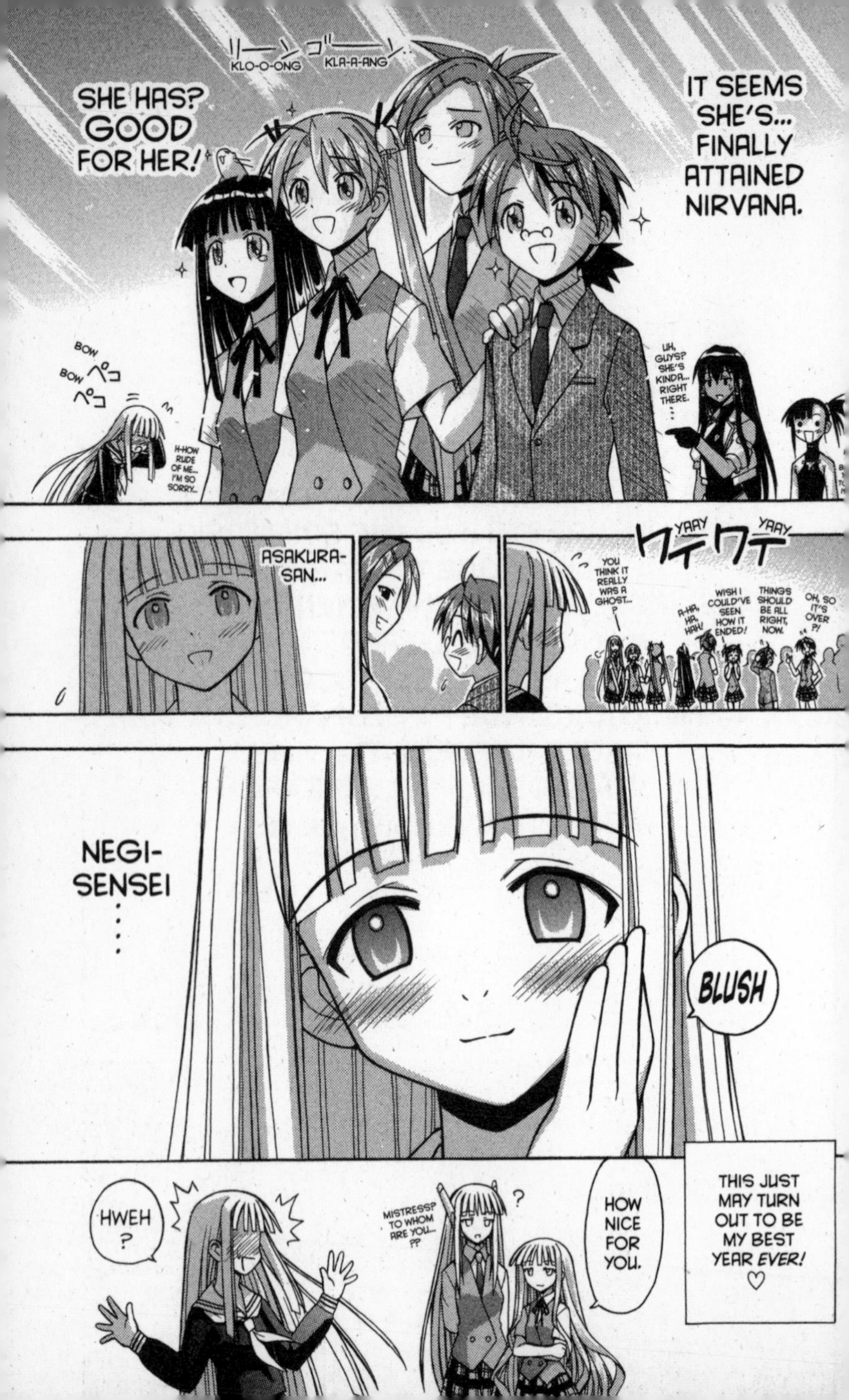
IT SEEMS SHE'S... FINALLY ATTAINED NIRVANA.
KLO-O-ONG KLA-A-ANG
SHE HAS? GOOD FOR HER!
UH, GUYS? SHE'S KINDA... RIGHT THERE. ...
BOW BOW
H-HOW RUDE OF ME... I'M SO SORRY...
YAAY YAAY
OH, SO IT'S OVER?!
THINGS SHOULD BE ALL RIGHT, NOW.
WISH I COULD'VE SEEN HOW IT ENDED!
A-HA, HA, HAH!
YOU THINK IT REALLY WAS A GHOST...?
ASAKURA-SAN...
BLUSH
NEGI-SENSEI ....
THIS JUST MAY TURN OUT TO BE MY BEST YEAR *EVER!* ♡
HOW NICE FOR YOU.
MISTRESS? TO WHOM ARE YOU...??
HWEH?

STUDENT NUMBER 24
HAKASE, SATOMI
BORN: 14 JULY 1988
BLOODTYPE: B
LIKES: ROBOTS; CURRENT RESEARCH
INTERESTS (i.e., THE SCIENTIFIC
APPLICATIONS OF MAGIC)
DISLIKES: ANYTHING UN-SCIENTIFIC
(MAGIC USED TO FURTHER MY
RESEARCH DOESN'T COUNT)
AFFILIATIONS: ROBOT RESEARCH
CIRCLE (UNIVERSITY-LEVEL);
JET-PROPULSION RESEARCH
CIRCLE (UNIVERSITY-LEVEL)

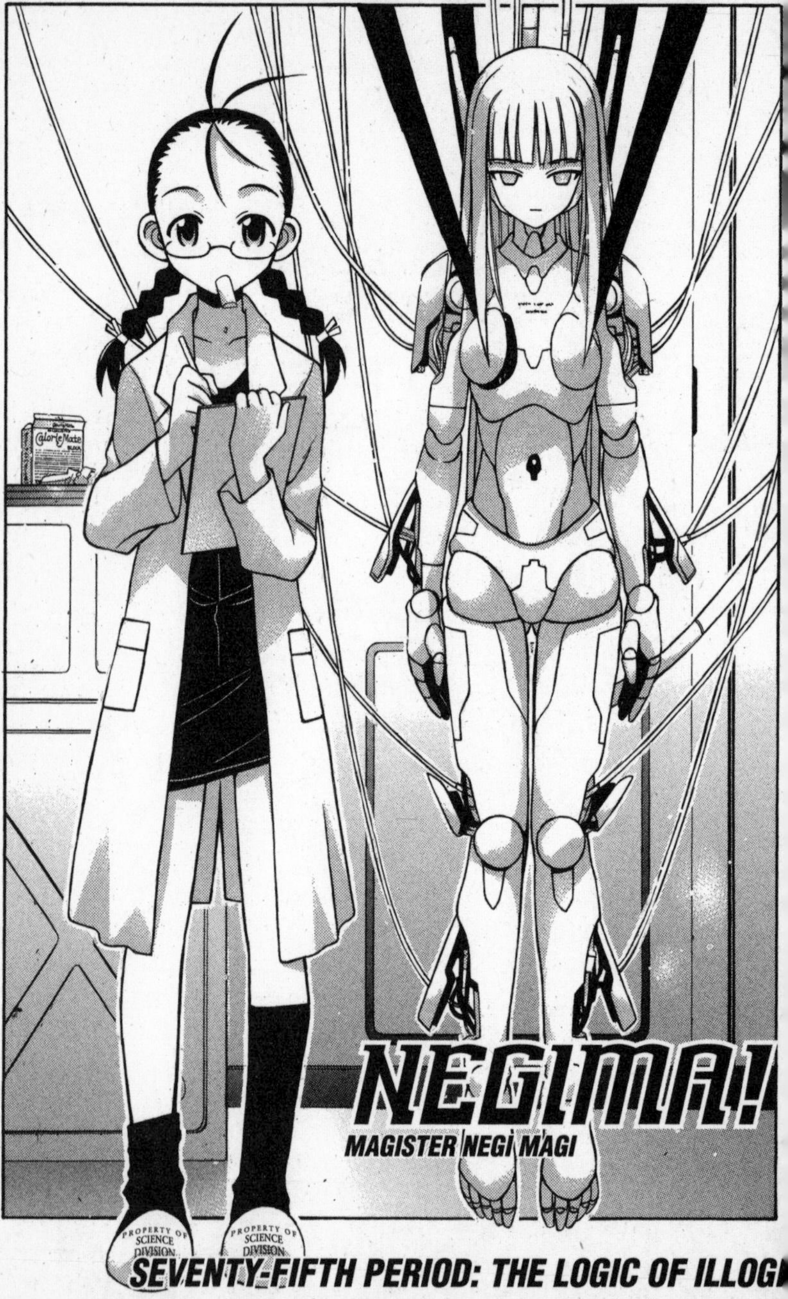
CalorieMate
NEGIMA!
MAGISTER NEGI MAGI
PROPERTY OF SCIENCE DIVISION
PROPERTY OF SCIENCE DIVISION

SEVENTY-FIFTH PERIOD: THE LOGIC OF ILLOG

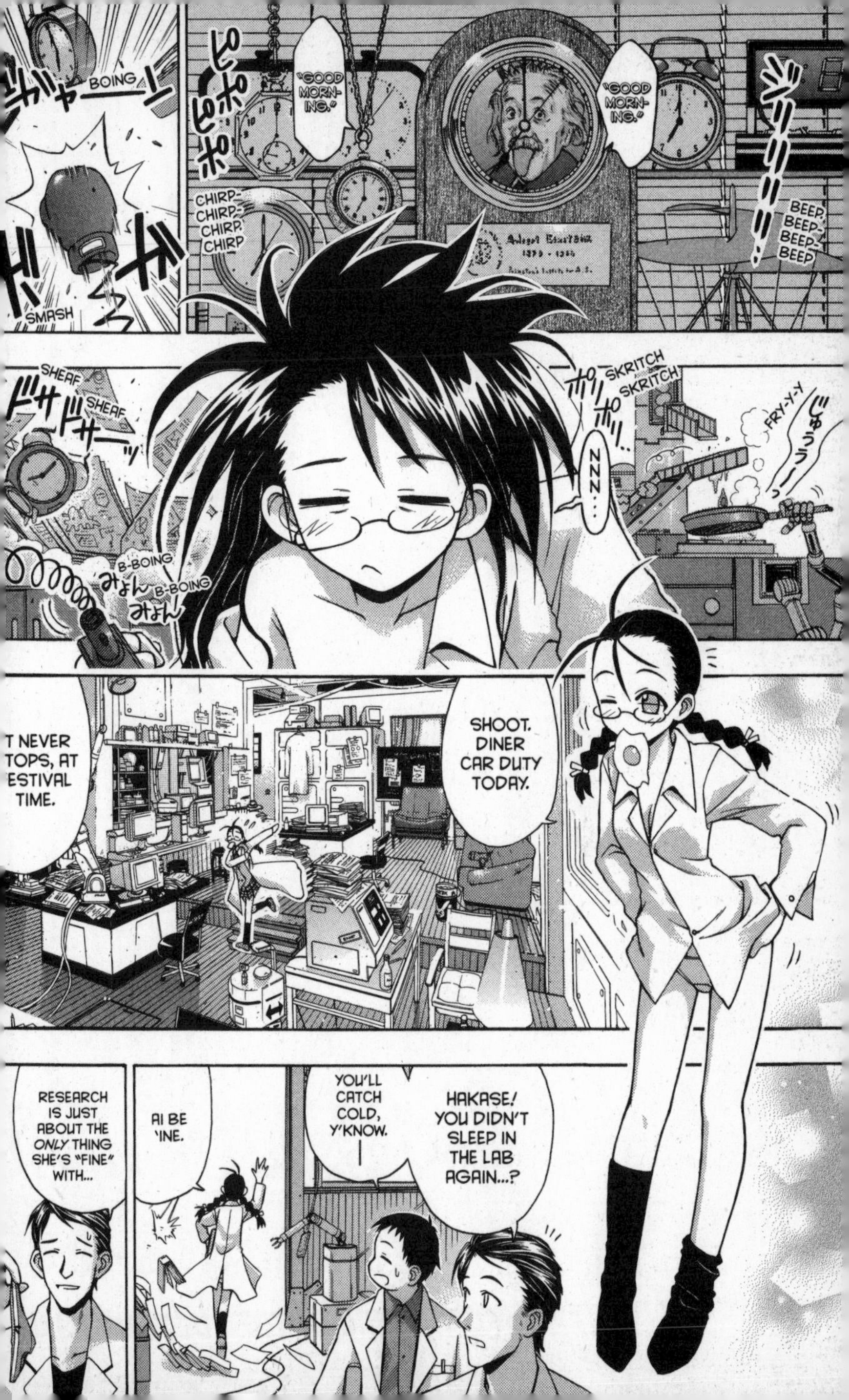
BEEP, BEEP-BEEP-BEEP
"GOOD MORN-ING."
"GOOD MORN-ING."
ピポピポ
CHIRP-CHIRP-CHIRP. CHIRP
BOING
SMASH
SKRITCH SKRITCH
NNN...
FRY-Y-Y
SHEAF SHEAF
ドサドサーッ
B-BOING みょん B-BOING みょん
SHOOT. DINER CAR DUTY TODAY.
T NEVER TOPS, AT ESTIVAL TIME.
HAKASE! YOU DIDN'T SLEEP IN THE LAB AGAIN...?
YOU'LL CATCH COLD, Y'KNOW.
AI BE 'INE.
RESEARCH IS JUST ABOUT THE *ONLY* THING SHE'S "FINE" WITH...

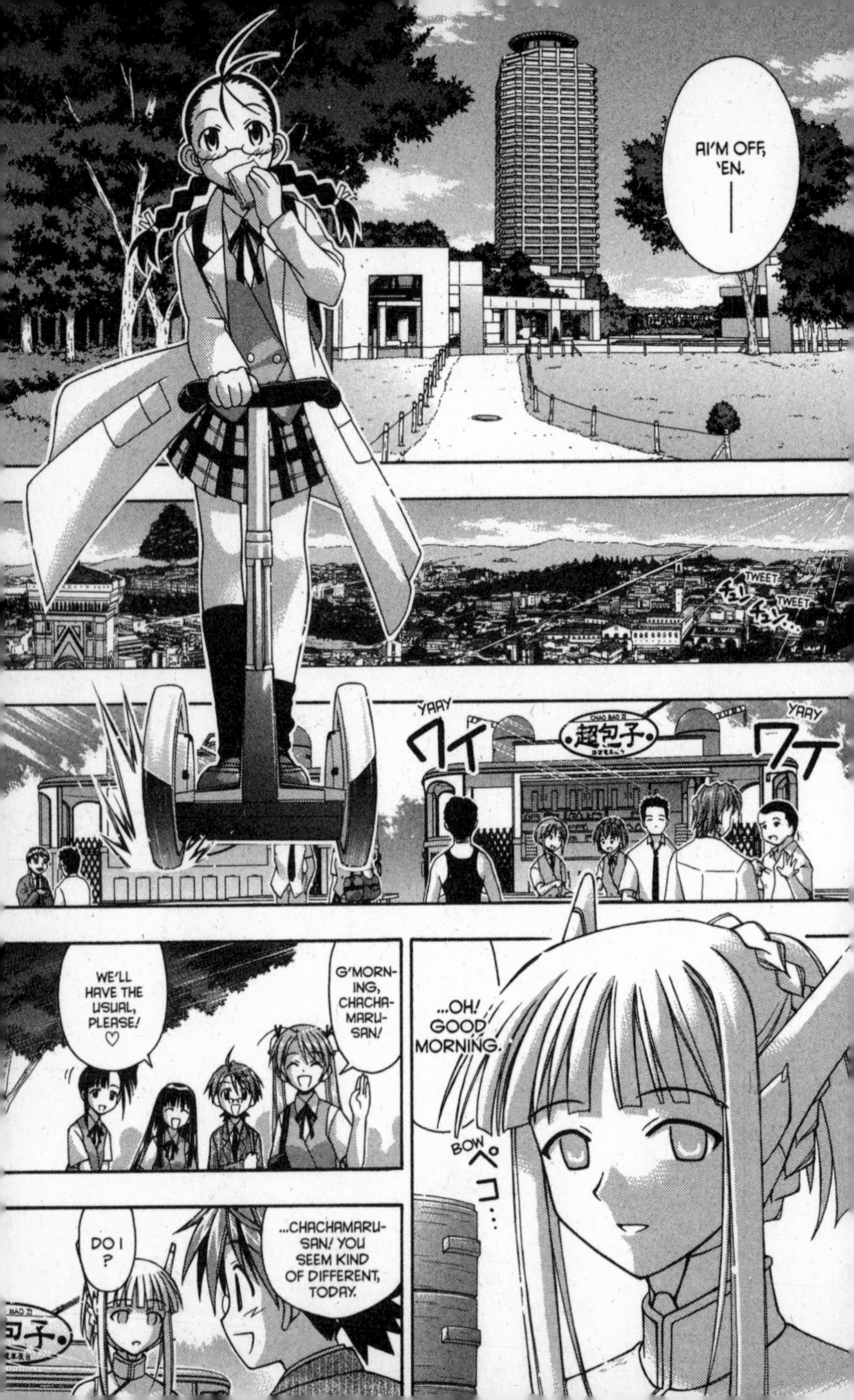
AI'M OFF, 'EN.
TWEET
TWEET
YAAY
CHAO BAO ZI
超包子
YAAY
...OH! GOOD MORNING.
BOW
G'MORNING, CHACHAMARU-SAN!
WE'LL HAVE THE USUAL, PLEASE! ♡
...CHACHAMARU-SAN! YOU SEEM KIND OF DIFFERENT, TODAY.
DO I ?

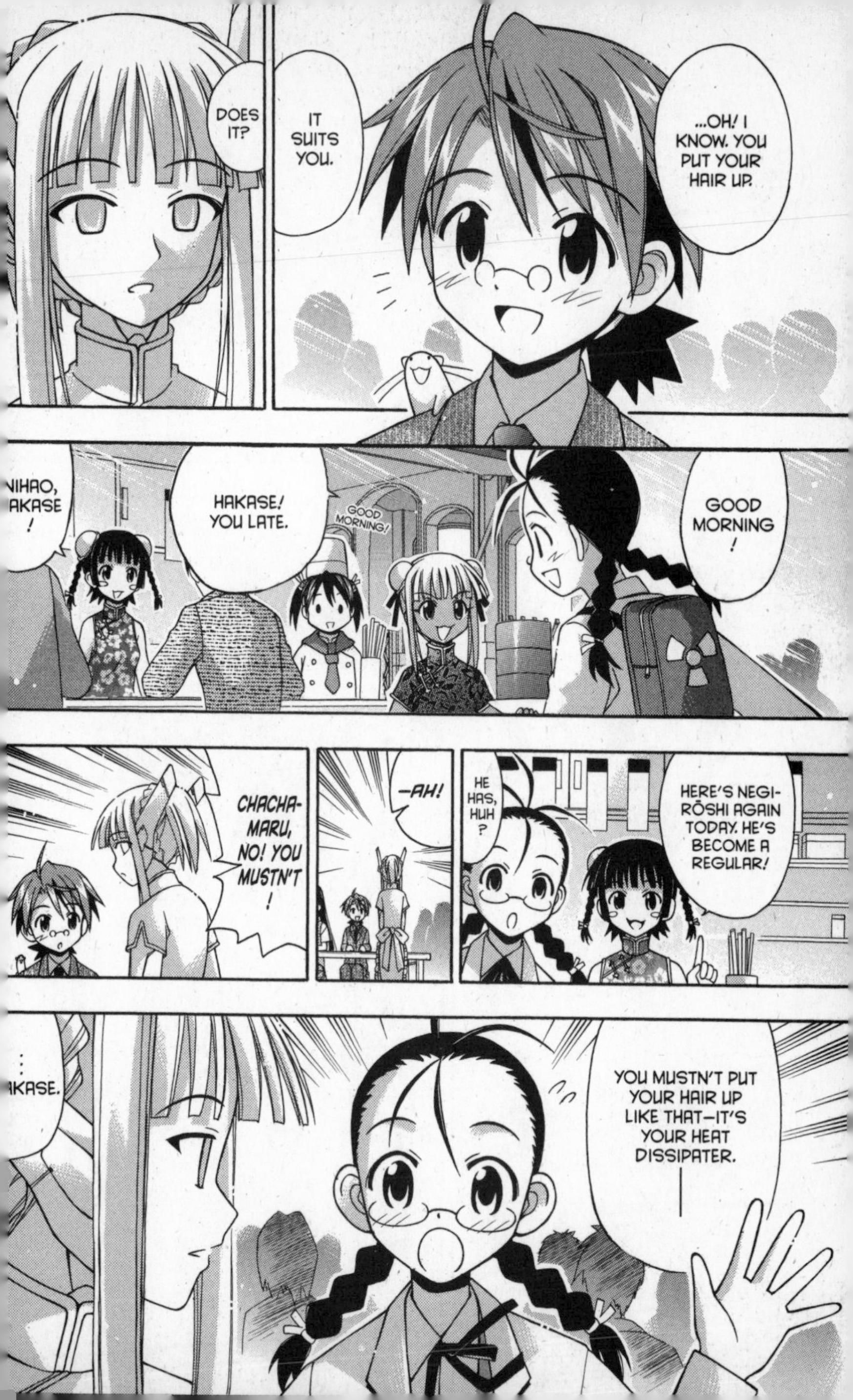
...OH! I KNOW. YOU PUT YOUR HAIR UP.
IT SUITS YOU.
DOES IT?
GOOD MORNING!
GOOD MORNING!
HAKASE! YOU LATE.
NIHAO, AKASE!
HERE'S NEGI-RŌSHI AGAIN TODAY. HE'S BECOME A REGULAR!
HE HAS, HUH?
—AH!
CHACHA-MARU, NO! YOU MUSTN'T!
YOU MUSTN'T PUT YOUR HAIR UP LIKE THAT—IT'S YOUR HEAT DISSIPATER.
...AKASE.

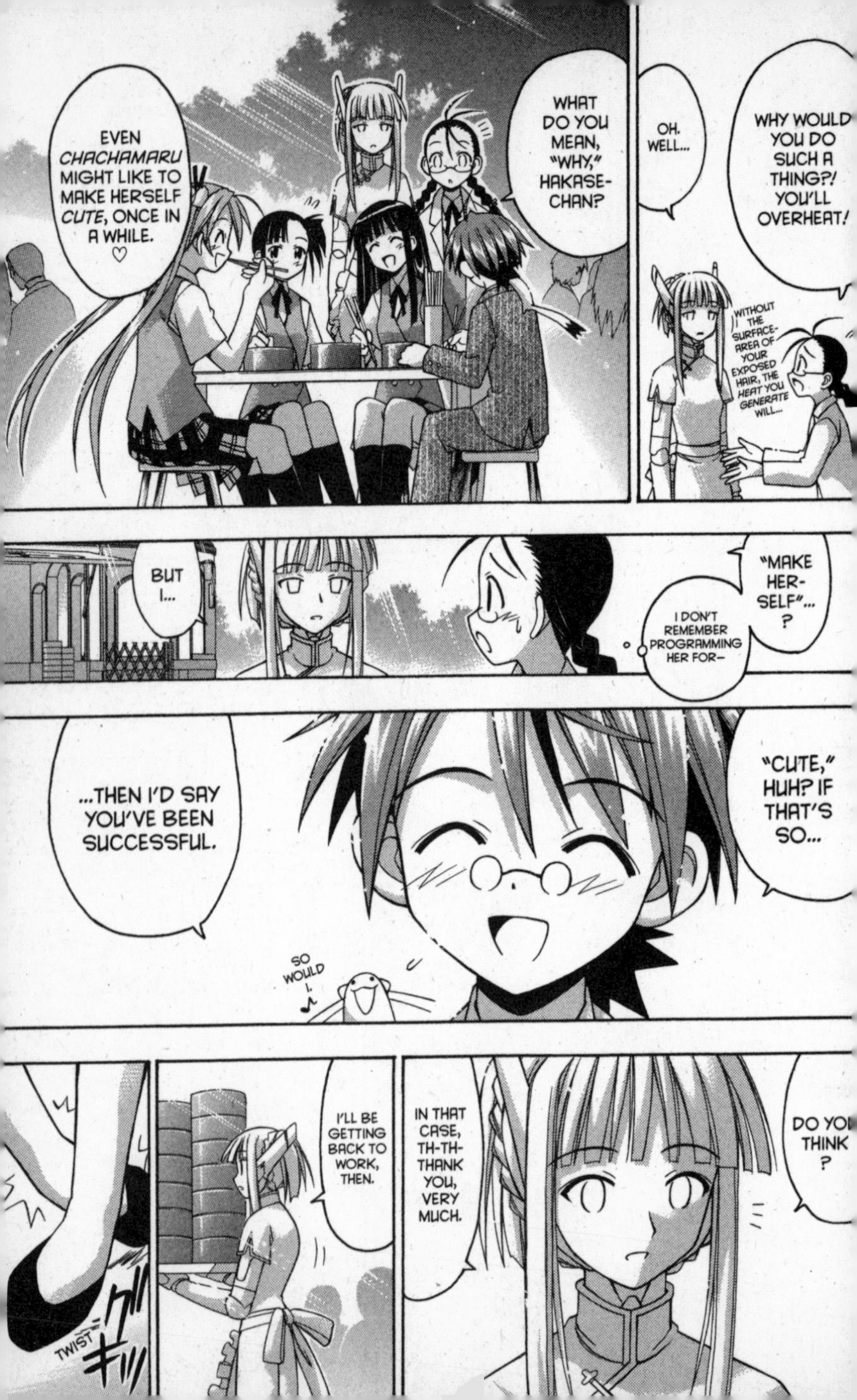
WHY WOULD YOU DO SUCH A THING?! YOU'LL OVERHEAT!
WITHOUT THE SURFACE-AREA OF YOUR EXPOSED HAIR, THE HEAT YOU GENERATE WILL...
OH. WELL...
WHAT DO YOU MEAN, "WHY," HAKASE-CHAN?
EVEN CHACHAMARU MIGHT LIKE TO MAKE HERSELF CUTE, ONCE IN A WHILE. ♡
"MAKE HER-SELF"...?
I DON'T REMEMBER PROGRAMMING HER FOR—
BUT I...
"CUTE," HUH? IF THAT'S SO...
...THEN I'D SAY YOU'VE BEEN SUCCESSFUL.
SO WOULD I. ♪
DO YOU THINK?
IN THAT CASE, TH-TH-THANK YOU, VERY MUCH.
I'LL BE GETTING BACK TO WORK, THEN.
TWIST

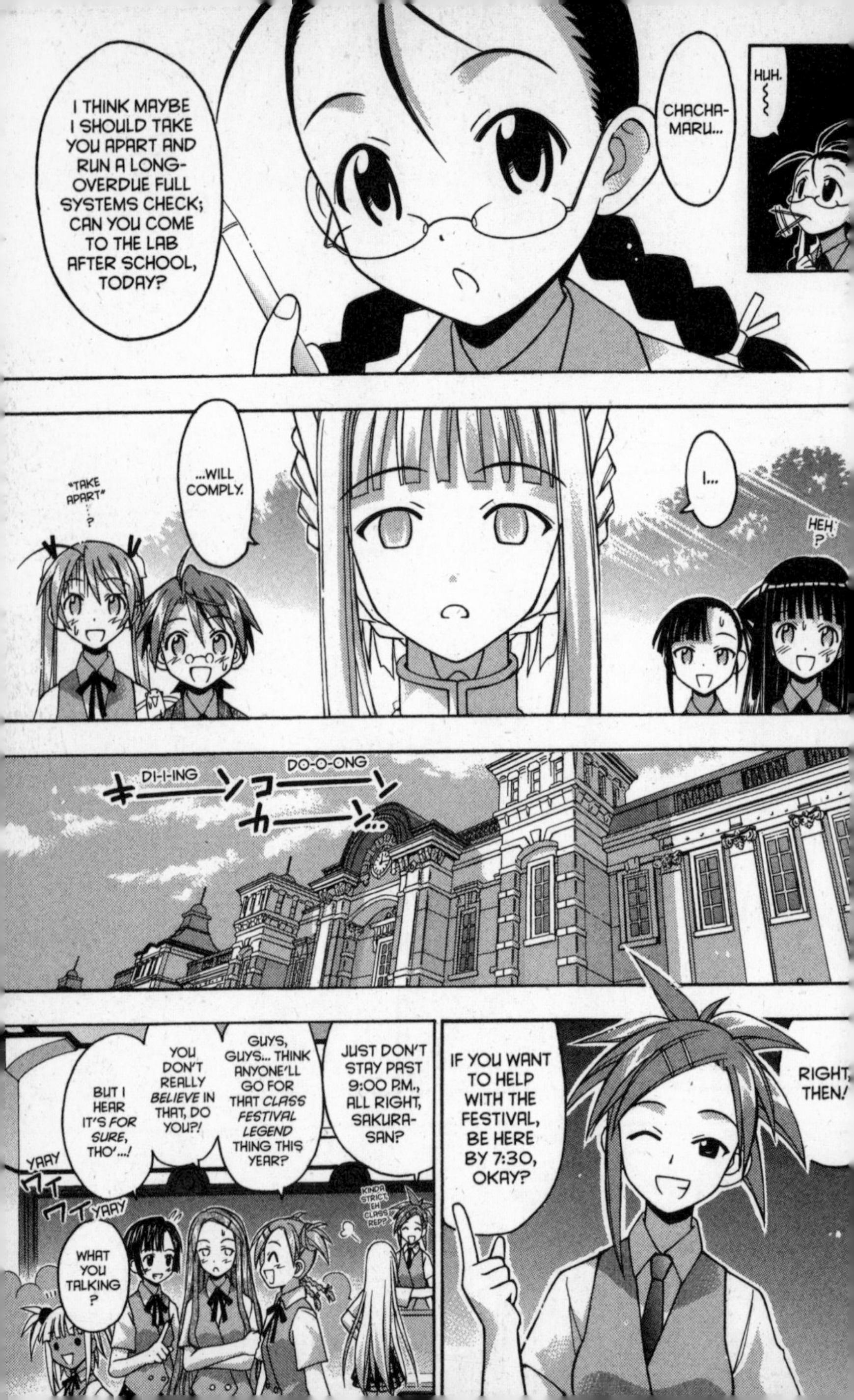
HUH.
CHACHA-MARU...
I THINK MAYBE I SHOULD TAKE YOU APART AND RUN A LONG-OVERDUE FULL SYSTEMS CHECK; CAN YOU COME TO THE LAB AFTER SCHOOL, TODAY?
I...
HEH?
...WILL COMPLY.
TAKE APART...?
DI-I-ING
DO-O-ONG
RIGHT, THEN!
IF YOU WANT TO HELP WITH THE FESTIVAL, BE HERE BY 7:30, OKAY?
JUST DON'T STAY PAST 9:00 P.M., ALL RIGHT, SAKURA-SAN?
GUYS, GUYS... THINK ANYONE'LL GO FOR THAT *CLASS FESTIVAL LEGEND* THING THIS YEAR?
YOU DON'T REALLY *BELIEVE* IN THAT, DO YOU?!
BUT I HEAR IT'S *FOR SURE*, THO'...!
KINDA STRICT, EH CLASS REP?
YAAY
YAAY
WHAT YOU TALKING ?

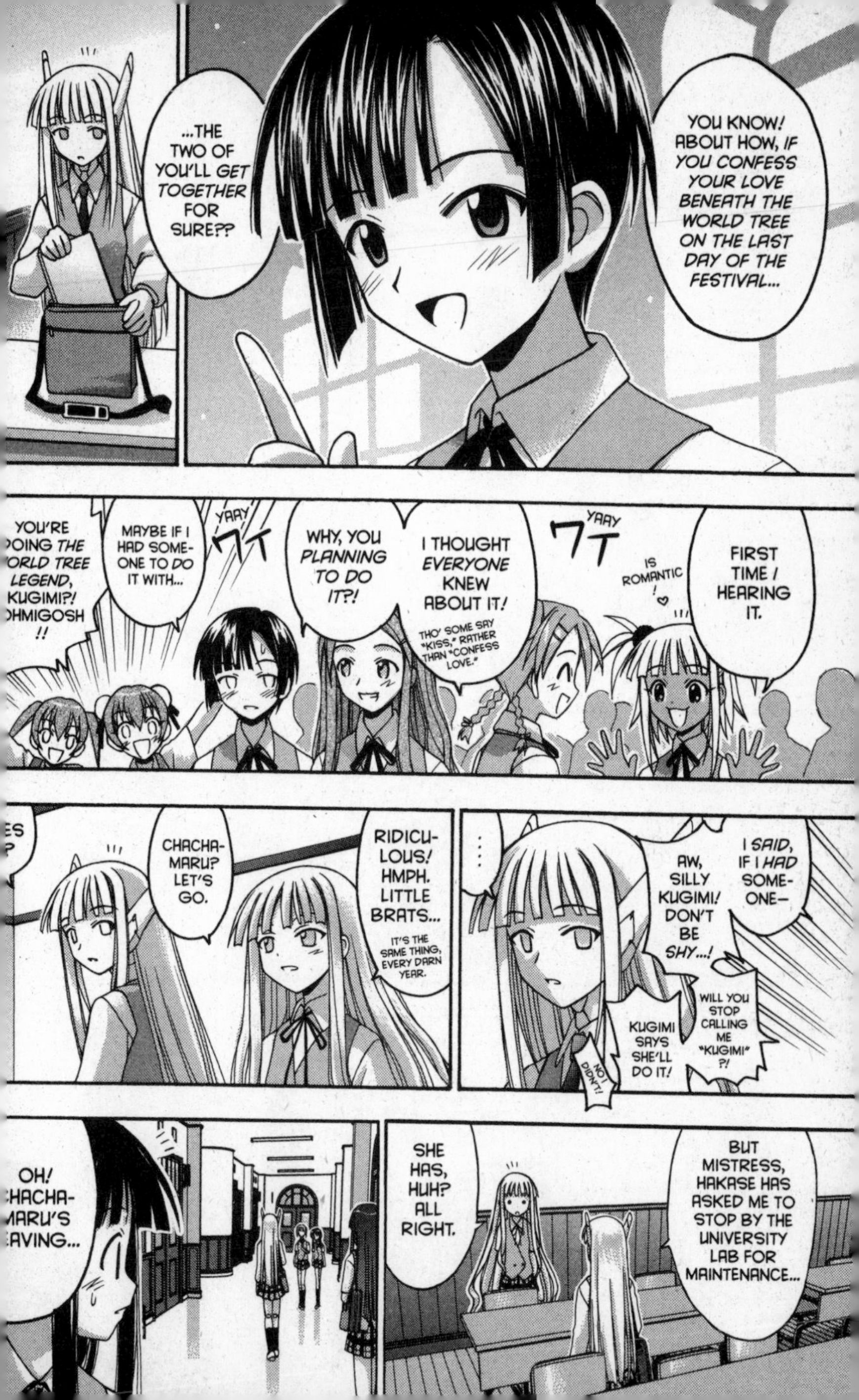
YOU KNOW! ABOUT HOW, IF YOU CONFESS YOUR LOVE BENEATH THE WORLD TREE ON THE LAST DAY OF THE FESTIVAL...
...THE TWO OF YOU'LL GET TOGETHER FOR SURE??
FIRST TIME I HEARING IT.
IS ROMANTIC! ♡
YAAY
I THOUGHT EVERYONE KNEW ABOUT IT!
THO' SOME SAY "KISS," RATHER THAN "CONFESS LOVE."
WHY, YOU PLANNING TO DO IT?!
YAAY
MAYBE IF I HAD SOME-ONE TO DO IT WITH...
YOU'RE OING THE ORLD TREE LEGEND, KUGIMI?! OHMIGOSH !!
I SAID, IF I HAD SOME-ONE—
AW, SILLY KUGIMI! DON'T BE SHY...!
WILL YOU STOP CALLING ME "KUGIMI"?!
KUGIMI SAYS SHE'LL DO IT!
NO! DIDN'T!
....
RIDICULOUS! HMPH. LITTLE BRATS...
IT'S THE SAME THING, EVERY DARN YEAR.
CHACHA-MARU? LET'S GO.
BUT MISTRESS, HAKASE HAS ASKED ME TO STOP BY THE UNIVERSITY LAB FOR MAINTENANCE...
SHE HAS, HUH? ALL RIGHT.
OH! HACHA-MARU'S EAVING...

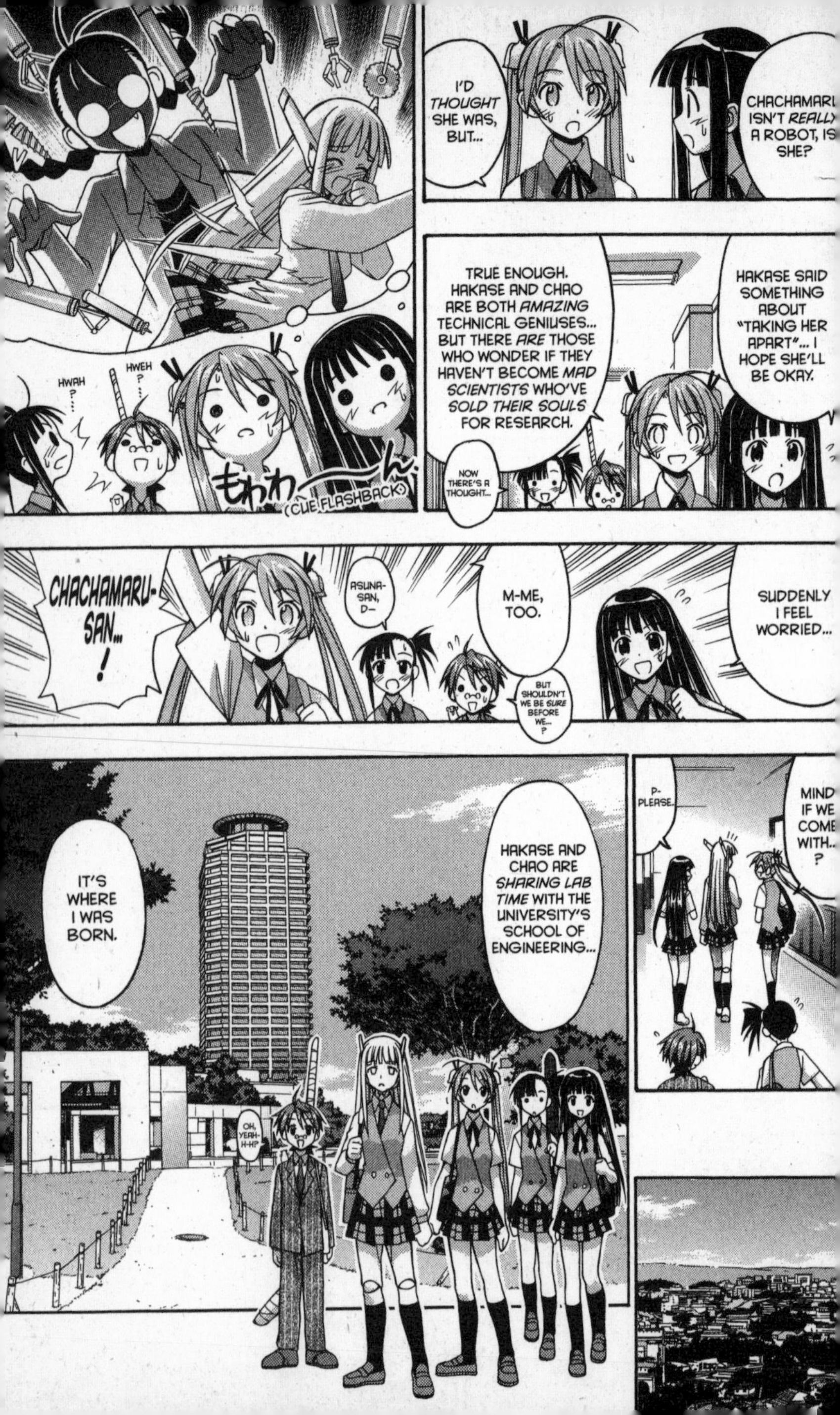

CHACHAMARU ISN'T *REALLY* A ROBOT, IS SHE?
I'D *THOUGHT* SHE WAS, BUT...
HAKASE SAID SOMETHING ABOUT "TAKING HER APART"... I HOPE SHE'LL BE OKAY.
TRUE ENOUGH. HAKASE AND CHAO ARE BOTH *AMAZING* TECHNICAL GENIUSES... BUT THERE *ARE* THOSE WHO WONDER IF THEY HAVEN'T BECOME *MAD SCIENTISTS* WHO'VE *SOLD THEIR SOULS* FOR RESEARCH.
NOW THERE'S A THOUGHT...
HWEH ?...
HWAH ?...
もわわ——ん
(CUE FLASHBACK)
SUDDENLY I FEEL WORRIED...
BUT SHOULDN'T WE BE *SURE* BEFORE WE... ?
M-ME, TOO.
ASUNA-SAN, D–
CHACHAMARU-SAN...!
MIND IF WE COME WITH... ?
P-PLEASE.
HAKASE AND CHAO ARE *SHARING LAB TIME* WITH THE UNIVERSITY'S SCHOOL OF ENGINEERING...
IT'S WHERE I WAS BORN.
OH, YEAH-H-H?

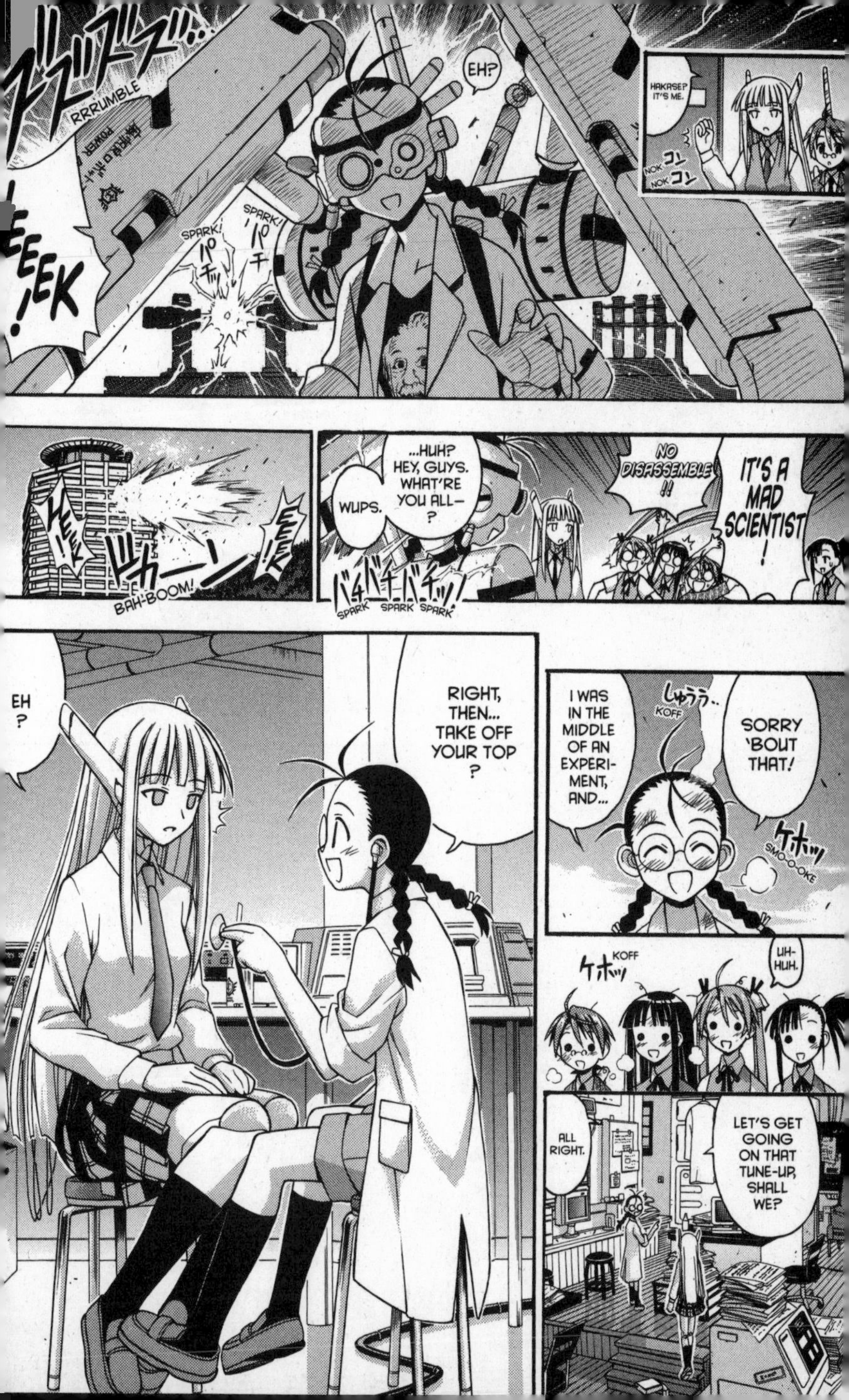
HAKASE? IT'S ME.
コン NOK
コン NOK
EH?
ズズズズ... RRRUMBLE
SPARK! パチッ
SPARK! パチ
EEEEK!
IT'S A MAD SCIENTIST!
NO DISASSEMBLE!!
...HUH? HEY, GUYS. WHAT'RE YOU ALL—?
WUPS.
バチバチバチッ! SPARK SPARK SPARK
EEEK!
HEEEK!
ドカーン BAH-BOOM!
SORRY 'BOUT THAT!
I WAS IN THE MIDDLE OF AN EXPERI-MENT, AND...
しゅううう.. KOFF
ケホッ SMO-O-OKE
UH-HUH.
ケホッ KOFF
LET'S GET GOING ON THAT TUNE-UP, SHALL WE?
ALL RIGHT.
RIGHT, THEN... TAKE OFF YOUR TOP?
EH?

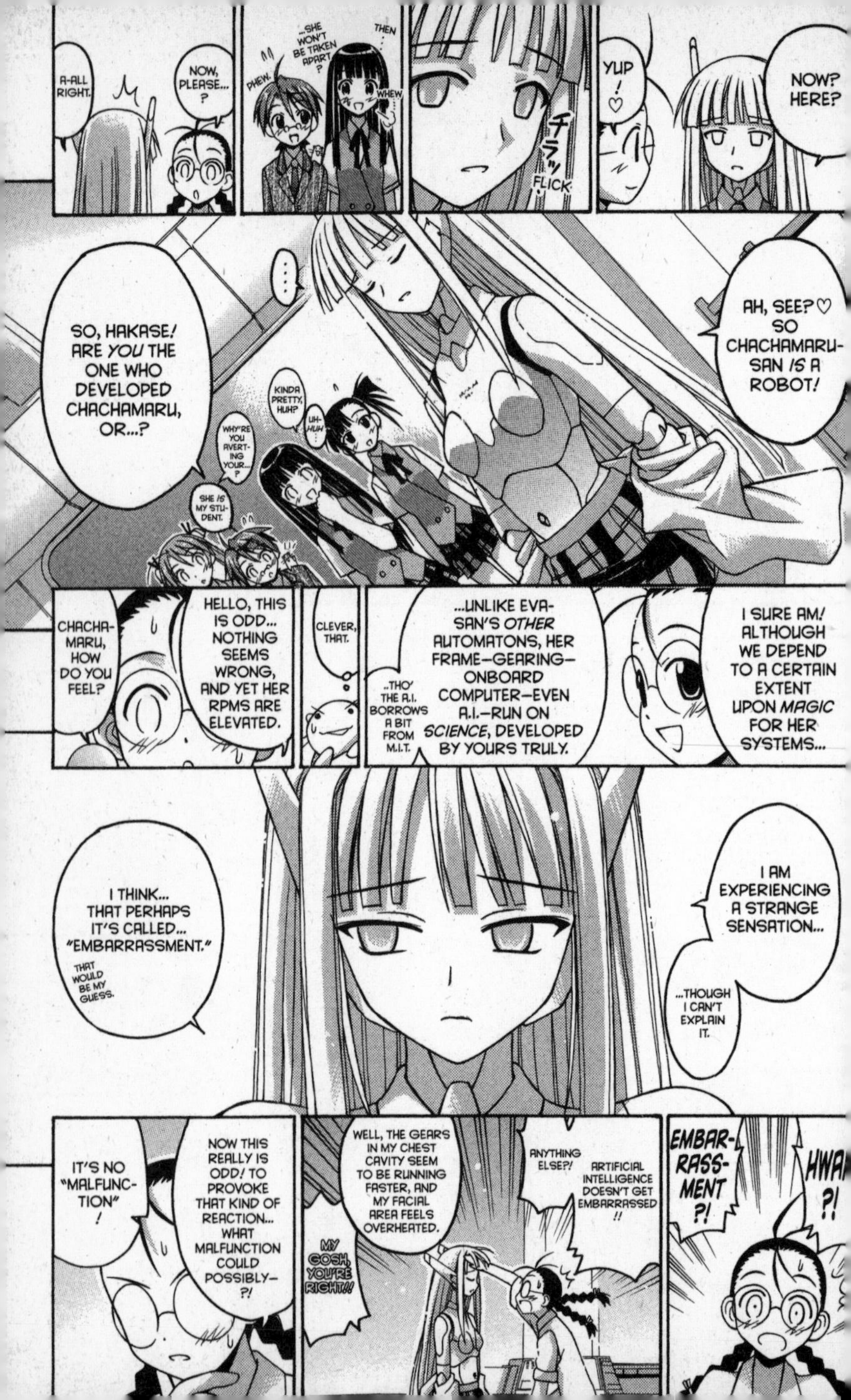
NOW? HERE?
YUP! ♡
チラッ FLICK
THEN
...SHE WON'T BE TAKEN APART?
PHEW.
WHEW
NOW, PLEASE...?
A-ALL RIGHT.
AH, SEE?♡ SO CHACHAMARU-SAN IS A ROBOT!
....
SO, HAKASE! ARE YOU THE ONE WHO DEVELOPED CHACHAMARU, OR...?
KINDA PRETTY, HUH?
UH-HUH...
WHY'RE YOU AVERTING YOUR...?
SHE IS MY STUDENT.
I SURE AM! ALTHOUGH WE DEPEND TO A CERTAIN EXTENT UPON MAGIC FOR HER SYSTEMS...
...UNLIKE EVA-SAN'S OTHER AUTOMATONS, HER FRAME—GEARING—ONBOARD COMPUTER—EVEN A.I.—RUN ON SCIENCE, DEVELOPED BY YOURS TRULY.
..THO' THE A.I. BORROWS A BIT FROM M.I.T.
CLEVER, THAT.
HELLO, THIS IS ODD... NOTHING SEEMS WRONG, AND YET HER RPMS ARE ELEVATED.
CHACHAMARU, HOW DO YOU FEEL?
I AM EXPERIENCING A STRANGE SENSATION...
...THOUGH I CAN'T EXPLAIN IT.
I THINK... THAT PERHAPS IT'S CALLED... "EMBARRASSMENT."
THAT WOULD BE MY GUESS.
HWA?!
EMBARRASSMENT?!
ARTIFICIAL INTELLIGENCE DOESN'T GET EMBARRASSED!!
ANYTHING ELSE?
WELL, THE GEARS IN MY CHEST CAVITY SEEM TO BE RUNNING FASTER, AND MY FACIAL AREA FEELS OVERHEATED.
MY GOSH, YOU'RE RIGHT!!
NOW THIS REALLY IS ODD! TO PROVOKE THAT KIND OF REACTION... WHAT MALFUNCTION COULD POSSIBLY—?!
IT'S NO "MALFUNCTION"!

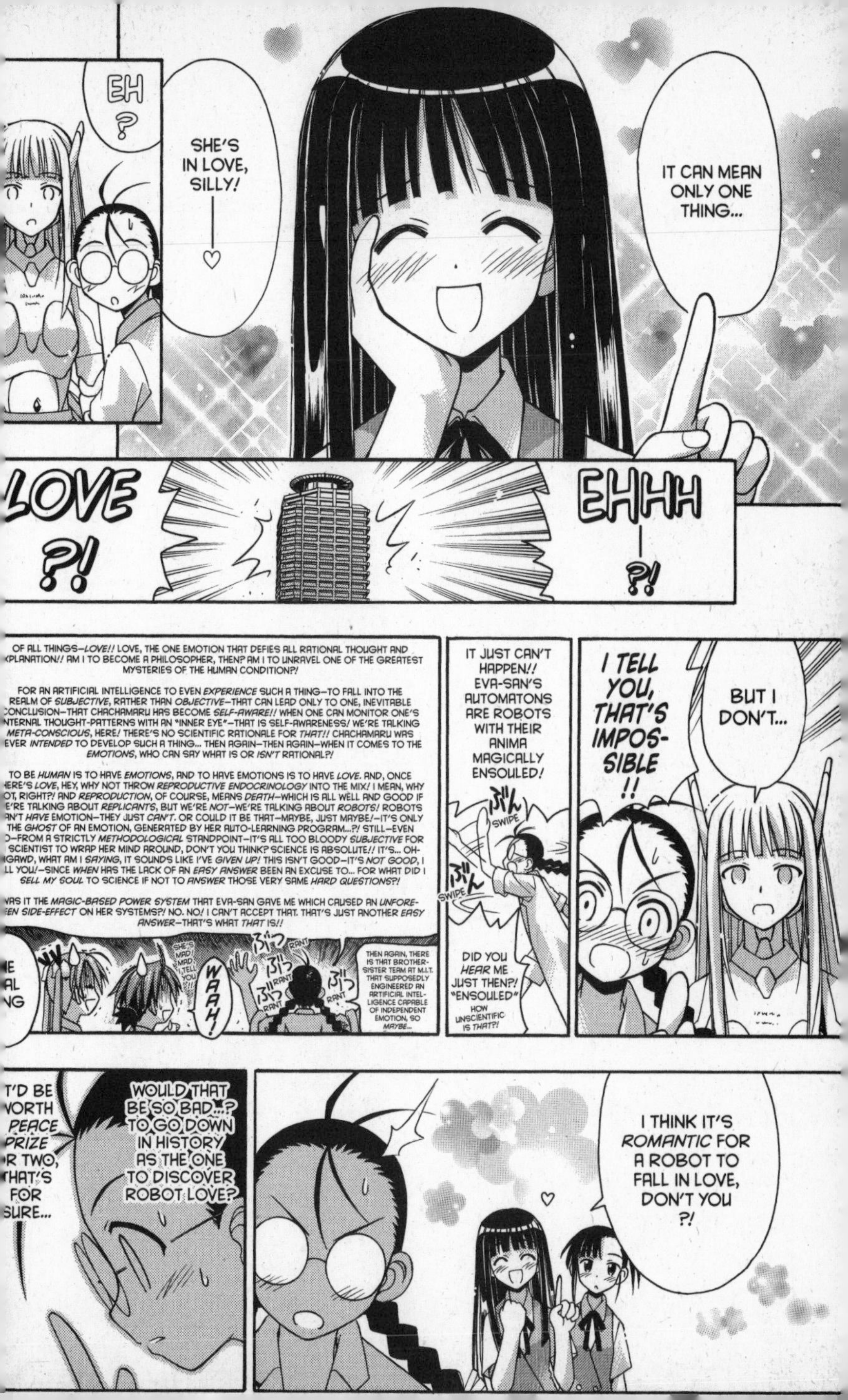
IT CAN MEAN ONLY ONE THING...
SHE'S IN LOVE, SILLY! ♡
EH?
EHHH—?!
LOVE?!
BUT I DON'T...
I TELL YOU, THAT'S IMPOSSIBLE!!
IT JUST CAN'T HAPPEN!! EVA-SAN'S AUTOMATONS ARE ROBOTS WITH THEIR ANIMA MAGICALLY ENSOULED!
ぶん SWIPE
ぶん SWIPE
DID YOU HEAR ME JUST THEN?! "ENSOULED" HOW UNSCIENTIFIC IS THAT?!
OF ALL THINGS—LOVE!! LOVE, THE ONE EMOTION THAT DEFIES ALL RATIONAL THOUGHT AND PLANATION!! AM I TO BECOME A PHILOSOPHER, THEN? AM I TO UNRAVEL ONE OF THE GREATEST MYSTERIES OF THE HUMAN CONDITION?!
FOR AN ARTIFICIAL INTELLIGENCE TO EVEN EXPERIENCE SUCH A THING—TO FALL INTO THE REALM OF SUBJECTIVE, RATHER THAN OBJECTIVE—THAT CAN LEAD ONLY TO ONE, INEVITABLE ONCLUSION—THAT CHACHAMARU HAS BECOME SELF-AWARE!! WHEN ONE CAN MONITOR ONE'S NTERNAL THOUGHT-PATTERNS WITH AN "INNER EYE"—THAT IS SELF-AWARENESS! WE'RE TALKING META-CONSCIOUS, HERE! THERE'S NO SCIENTIFIC RATIONALE FOR THAT!! CHACHAMARU WAS EVER INTENDED TO DEVELOP SUCH A THING... THEN AGAIN—THEN AGAIN—WHEN IT COMES TO THE EMOTIONS, WHO CAN SAY WHAT IS OR ISN'T RATIONAL?!
TO BE HUMAN IS TO HAVE EMOTIONS, AND TO HAVE EMOTIONS IS TO HAVE LOVE. AND, ONCE ERE'S LOVE, HEY, WHY NOT THROW REPRODUCTIVE ENDOCRINOLOGY INTO THE MIX! I MEAN, WHY OT, RIGHT?! AND REPRODUCTION, OF COURSE, MEANS DEATH—WHICH IS ALL WELL AND GOOD IF E'RE TALKING ABOUT REPLICANTS, BUT WE'RE NOT—WE'RE TALKING ABOUT ROBOTS! ROBOTS AN'T HAVE EMOTION—THEY JUST CAN'T. OR COULD IT BE THAT—MAYBE, JUST MAYBE!—IT'S ONLY THE GHOST OF AN EMOTION, GENERATED BY HER AUTO-LEARNING PROGRAM...?! STILL—EVEN —FROM A STRICTLY METHODOLOGICAL STANDPOINT—IT'S ALL TOO BLOODY SUBJECTIVE FOR SCIENTIST TO WRAP HER MIND AROUND, DON'T YOU THINK? SCIENCE IS ABSOLUTE!! IT'S... OH- GAWD, WHAT AM I SAYING, IT SOUNDS LIKE I'VE GIVEN UP! THIS ISN'T GOOD—IT'S NOT GOOD, I LL YOU!—SINCE WHEN HAS THE LACK OF AN EASY ANSWER BEEN AN EXCUSE TO... FOR WHAT DID I SELL MY SOUL TO SCIENCE IF NOT TO ANSWER THOSE VERY SAME HARD QUESTIONS?!
AS IT THE MAGIC-BASED POWER SYSTEM THAT EVA-SAN GAVE ME WHICH CAUSED AN UNFORE- EEN SIDE-EFFECT ON HER SYSTEMS?! NO. NO! I CAN'T ACCEPT THAT. THAT'S JUST ANOTHER EASY ANSWER—THAT'S WHAT THAT IS!!
THEN AGAIN, THERE IS THAT BROTHER-SISTER TEAM AT M.I.T. THAT SUPPOSEDLY ENGINEERED AN ARTIFICIAL INTELLIGENCE CAPABLE OF INDEPENDENT EMOTION, SO MAYBE...
ぶつ RANT
ぶつ RANT
ぶつ RANT
ぶつ RANT
WAAH!
SHE'S MAD! MAD! I TELL YOU!!
E
AL
NG
I THINK IT'S ROMANTIC FOR A ROBOT TO FALL IN LOVE, DON'T YOU?!
♡
WOULD THAT BE SO BAD...? TO GO DOWN IN HISTORY AS THE ONE TO DISCOVER ROBOT LOVE?
T'D BE WORTH PEACE PRIZE R TWO, THAT'S FOR SURE...

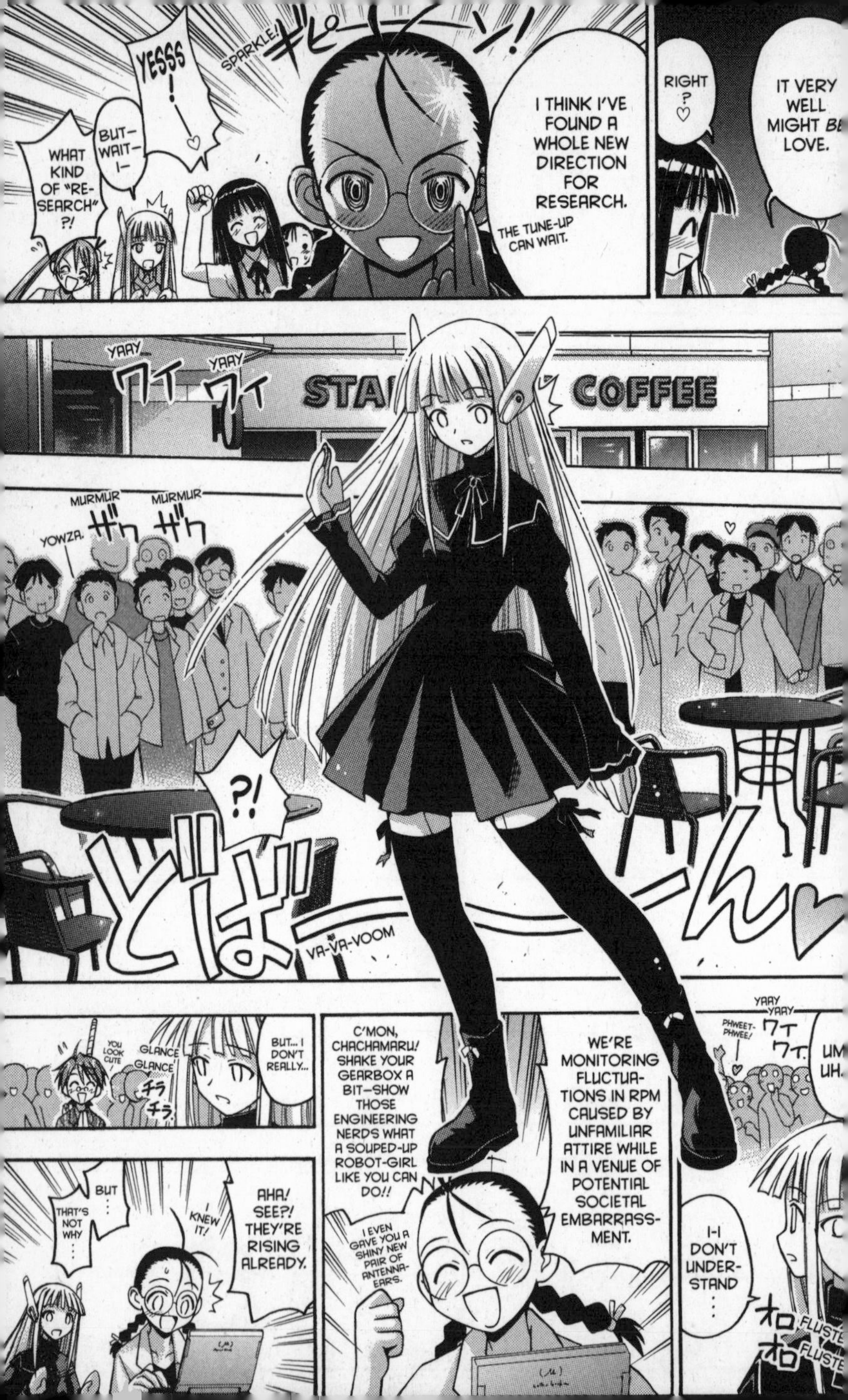
IT VERY WELL MIGHT BE LOVE.
RIGHT? ♡
SPARKLE!
I THINK I'VE FOUND A WHOLE NEW DIRECTION FOR RESEARCH.
THE TUNE-UP CAN WAIT.
YESSS! ♡
BUT— WAIT— I—
WHAT KIND OF "RE-SEARCH"?!
YAAY
YAAY
STA
COFFEE
MURMUR
MURMUR
YOWZA.
?!
VA-VA-VOOM
UM UH.
YAAY YAAY
PHWEET-PHWEE!
I-I DON'T UNDER-STAND...
FLUSTER FLUSTER
WE'RE MONITORING FLUCTUA-TIONS IN RPM CAUSED BY UNFAMILIAR ATTIRE WHILE IN A VENUE OF POTENTIAL SOCIETAL EMBARRASS-MENT.
C'MON, CHACHAMARU! SHAKE YOUR GEARBOX A BIT—SHOW THOSE ENGINEERING NERDS WHAT A SOUPED-UP ROBOT-GIRL LIKE YOU CAN DO!!
I EVEN GAVE YOU A SHINY NEW PAIR OF ANTENNA-EARS.
BUT... I DON'T REALLY...
GLANCE GLANCE
YOU LOOK CUTE!
AHA! SEE?! THEY'RE RISING ALREADY.
I KNEW IT!
BUT... THAT'S NOT WHY...

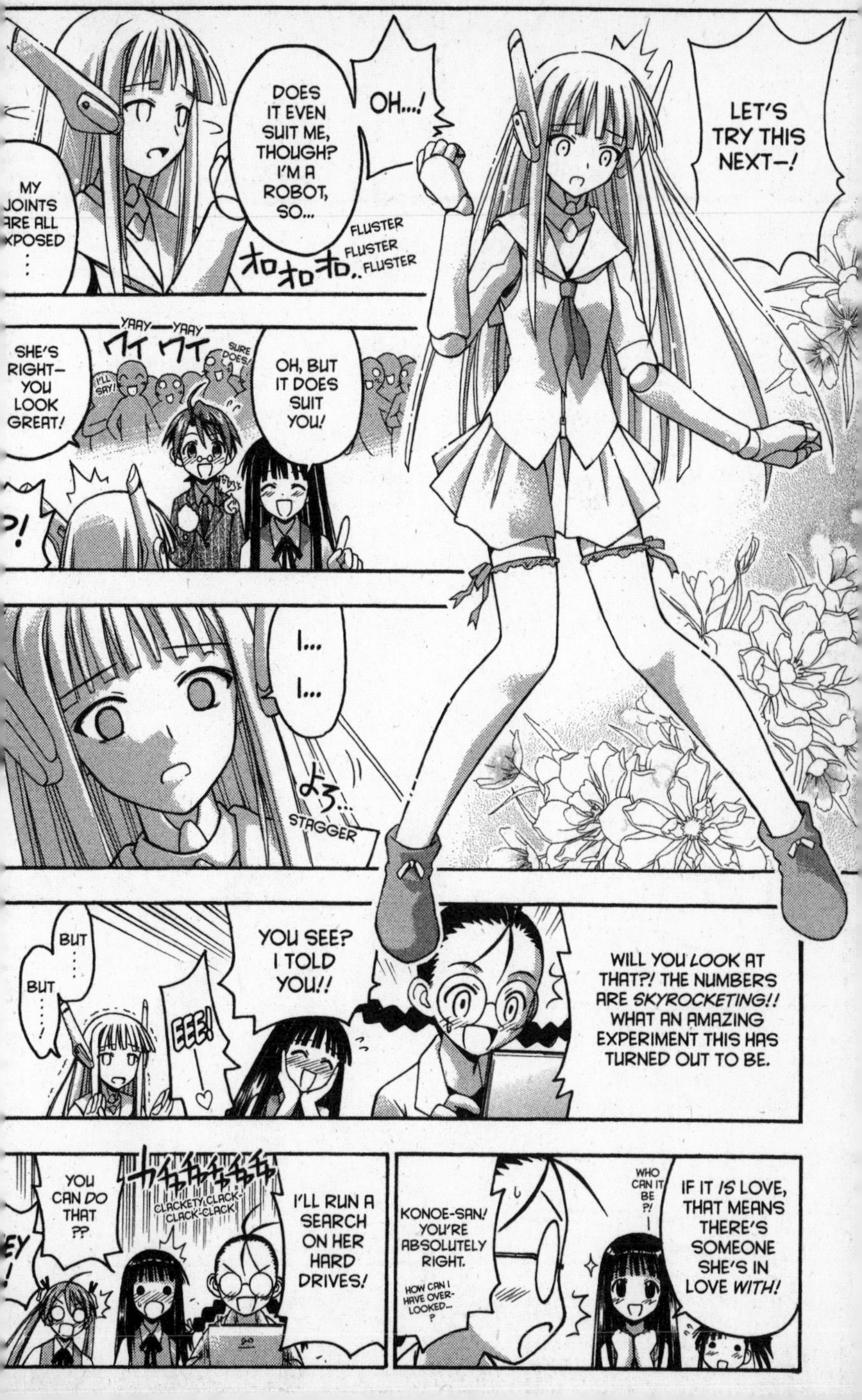
LET'S TRY THIS NEXT—!
OH...!
DOES IT EVEN SUIT ME, THOUGH? I'M A ROBOT, SO...
オロオロオロ..
FLUSTER FLUSTER FLUSTER
MY JOINTS ARE ALL XPOSED . . .
OH, BUT IT DOES SUIT YOU!
ワイ ワイ
YAAY YAAY
SURE DOES!
I'LL SAY!
SHE'S RIGHT— YOU LOOK GREAT!
?!
I... I...
よろ...
STAGGER
WILL YOU *LOOK* AT THAT?! THE NUMBERS ARE *SKYROCKETING!!* WHAT AN AMAZING EXPERIMENT THIS HAS TURNED OUT TO BE.
YOU SEE? I TOLD YOU!!
EEE!
BUT . . . . .
BUT . . . . . !
IF IT *IS* LOVE, THAT MEANS THERE'S SOMEONE SHE'S IN LOVE *WITH!*
WHO CAN IT BE ?!
KONOE-SAN! YOU'RE ABSOLUTELY RIGHT.
HOW CAN I HAVE OVER-LOOKED... ?
I'LL RUN A SEARCH ON HER HARD DRIVES!
CLACKETY-CLACK-CLACK-CLACK
YOU CAN *DO* THAT ??
EY !

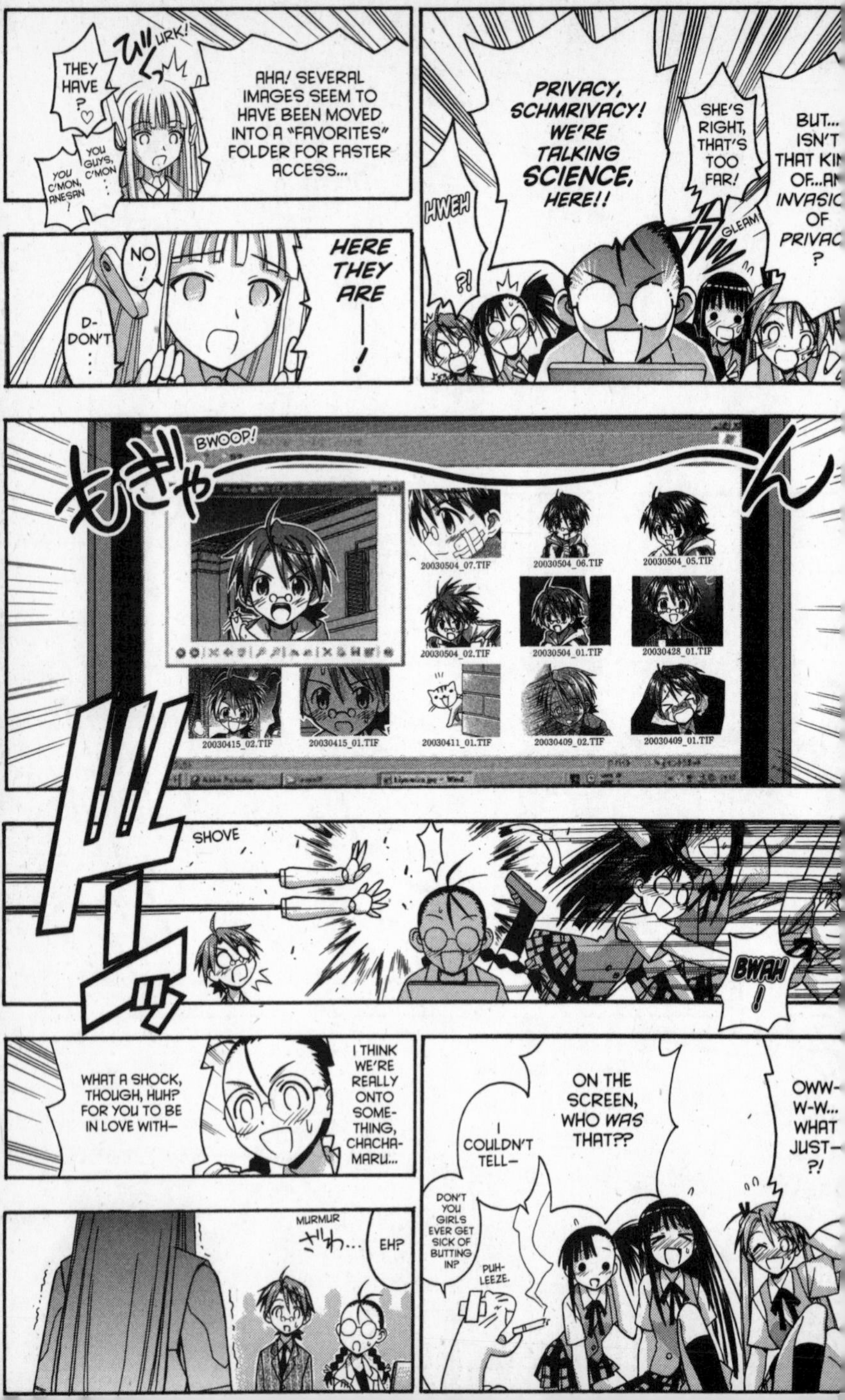
BUT... ISN'T THAT KI OF...AN INVASIO OF PRIVAC ?
SHE'S RIGHT, THAT'S TOO FAR!
GLEAM
PRIVACY, SCHMRIVACY! WE'RE TALKING SCIENCE, HERE!!
HWEH ?!
AHA! SEVERAL IMAGES SEEM TO HAVE BEEN MOVED INTO A "FAVORITES" FOLDER FOR FASTER ACCESS...
ぴくっ URK!
THEY HAVE ?♡
YOU GUYS, C'MON...
YOU C'MON, ANESAN!
HERE THEY ARE—!
NO!
D-DON'T...
もぎゃ—ん BWOOP!
20030504_07.TIF
20030504_06.TIF
20030504_05.TIF
20030504_02.TIF
20030504_01.TIF
20030428_01.TIF
20030415_02.TIF
20030415_01.TIF
20030411_01.TIF
20030409_02.TIF
20030409_01.TIF
BWAH!
SHOVE
OWW-W-W... WHAT JUST—?!
ON THE SCREEN, WHO WAS THAT??
I COULDN'T TELL—
DON'T YOU GIRLS EVER GET SICK OF BUTTING IN?
PUH-LEEZE.
I THINK WE'RE REALLY ONTO SOMETHING, CHACHAMARU...
WHAT A SHOCK, THOUGH, HUH? FOR YOU TO BE IN LOVE WITH—
EH?
MURMUR ざわ…

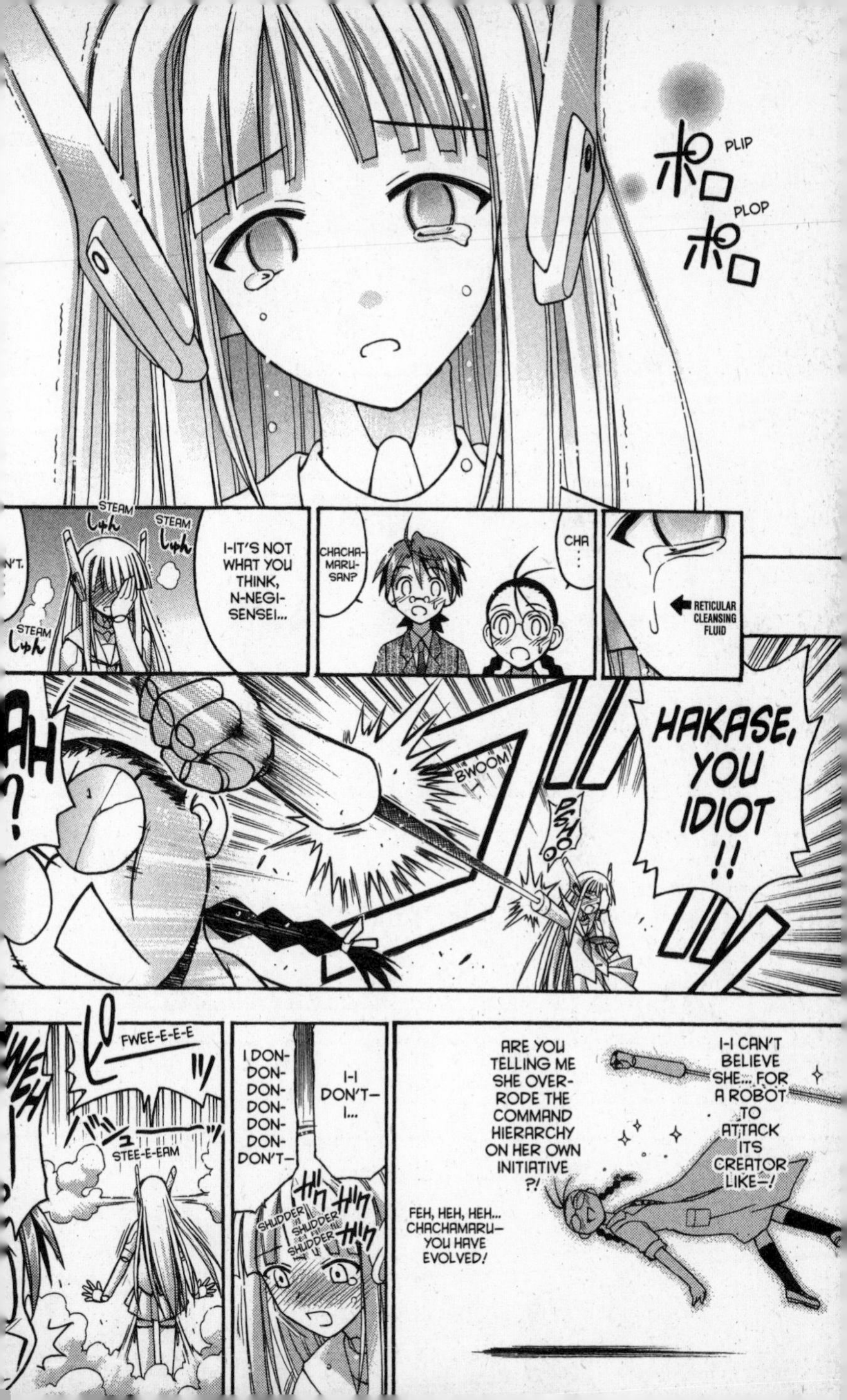

ポロ
PLIP
ポロ
PLOP
RETICULAR CLEANSING FLUID
CHA...
CHACHAMARU-SAN?
I-IT'S NOT WHAT YOU THINK, N-NEGI-SENSEI...
STEAM
STEAM
STEAM
HAKASE, YOU IDIOT!!
BWOOM
I-I CAN'T BELIEVE SHE... FOR A ROBOT TO ATTACK ITS CREATOR LIKE—!
ARE YOU TELLING ME SHE OVER-RODE THE COMMAND HIERARCHY ON HER OWN INITIATIVE?!
FEH, HEH, HEH... CHACHAMARU—YOU HAVE EVOLVED!
I-I DON'T—I...
I DON-DON-DON-DON-DON-DON-DON'T—
SHUDDER
SHUDDER
SHUDDER
FWEE-E-E-E
STEE-E-EAM

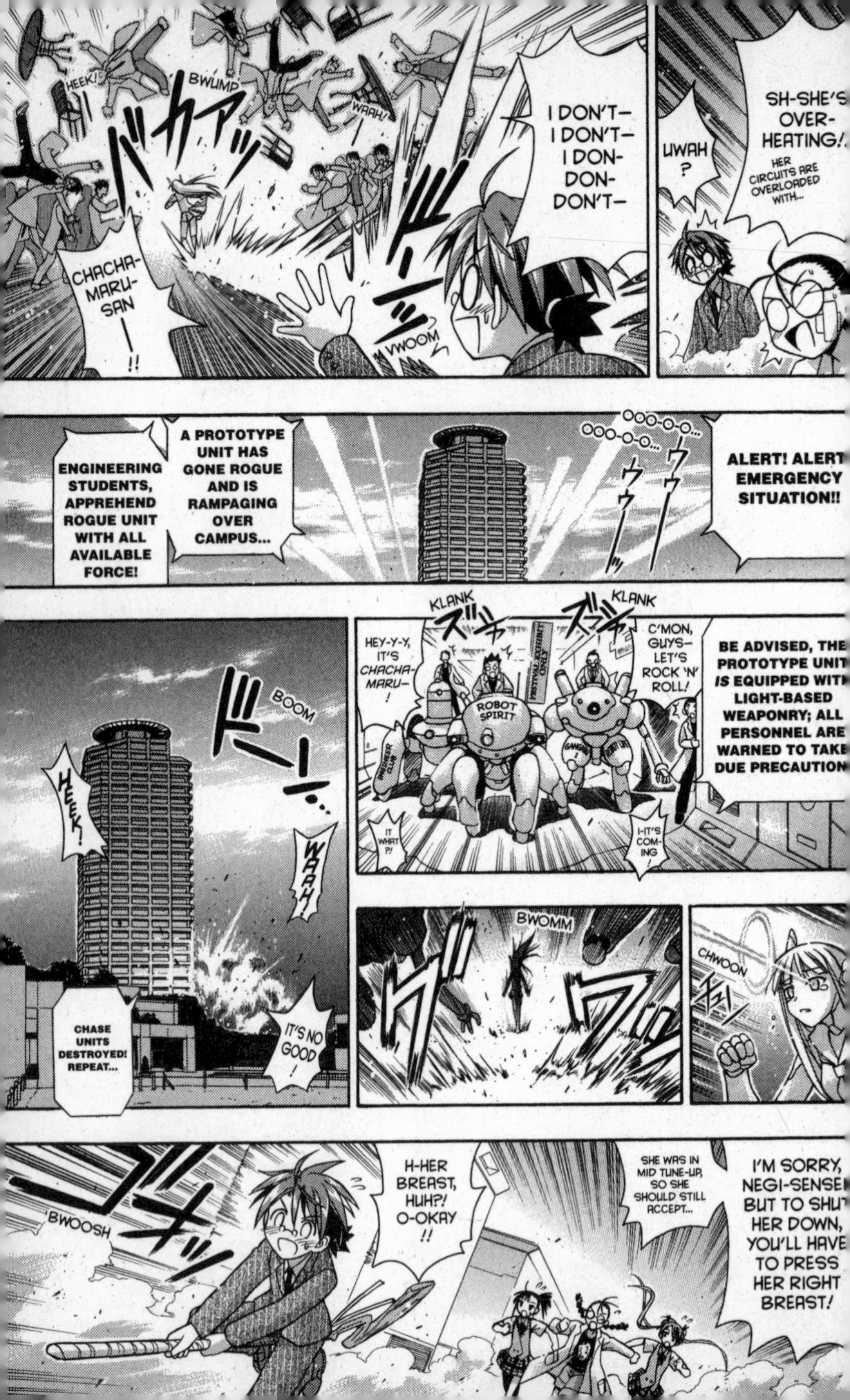
UWAH?
SH-SHE'S OVER-HEATING!.
HER CIRCUITS ARE OVERLOADED WITH...
I DON'T— I DON'T— I DON-DON-DON'T—
VWOOM
BWUMP
WAAH!
HEEK!
CHACHA-MARU-SAN—!!
ALERT! ALERT EMERGENCY SITUATION!!
OOO-O-O... OOO-O-O...
A PROTOTYPE UNIT HAS GONE ROGUE AND IS RAMPAGING OVER CAMPUS...
ENGINEERING STUDENTS, APPREHEND ROGUE UNIT WITH ALL AVAILABLE FORCE!
BE ADVISED, THE PROTOTYPE UNIT IS EQUIPPED WITH LIGHT-BASED WEAPONRY; ALL PERSONNEL ARE WARNED TO TAKE DUE PRECAUTION
KLANK
C'MON, GUYS— LET'S ROCK 'N' ROLL!
KLANK
HEY-Y-Y, IT'S CHACHAMARU!
ROBOT SPIRIT
I-IT'S COMING!
IT WHAT?!
CHWOON
BWOMM
BOOM
HEEK!
WAAAH!
IT'S NO GOOD!
CHASE UNITS DESTROYED! REPEAT...
I'M SORRY, NEGI-SENSEI BUT TO SHUT HER DOWN, YOU'LL HAVE TO PRESS HER RIGHT BREAST!
SHE WAS IN MID TUNE-UP, SO SHE SHOULD STILL ACCEPT...
H-HER BREAST, HUH?! O-OKAY!!
BWOOSH

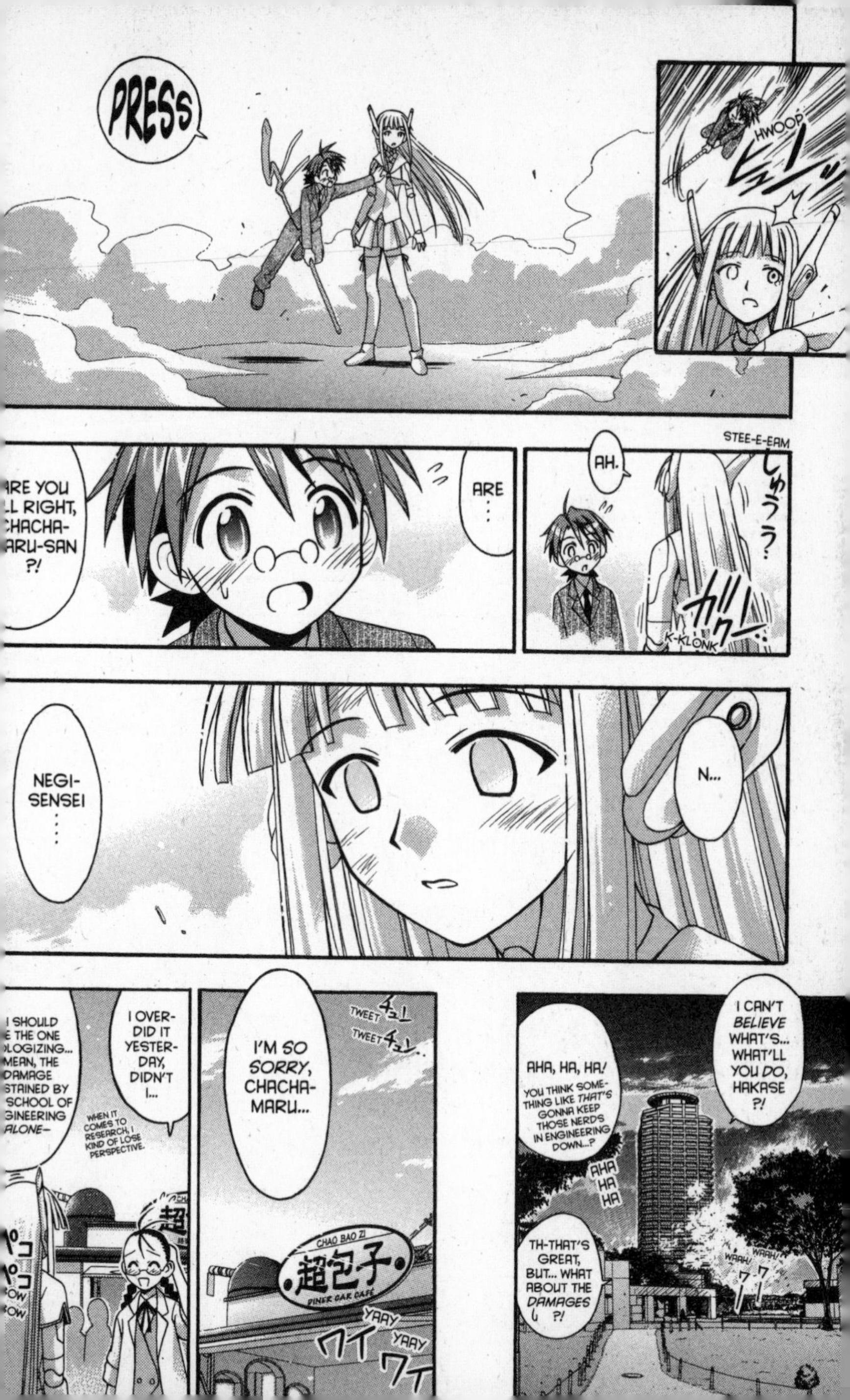
HWOOP
PRESS
STEE-E-EAM
AH.
K-KLONK
ARE ...
ARE YOU LL RIGHT, CHACHA-ARU-SAN ?!
N...
NEGI-SENSEI ....
I CAN'T *BELIEVE* WHAT'S... WHAT'LL YOU *DO*, HAKASE ?!
AHA, HA, HA!
YOU THINK SOME-THING LIKE *THAT'S* GONNA KEEP THOSE NERDS IN ENGINEERING DOWN...?
AHA HA HA
TH-THAT'S GREAT, BUT... WHAT ABOUT THE *DAMAGES* ?!
WAAH! WAAH!
TWEET TWEET
I'M *SO SORRY*, CHACHA-MARU...
CHAO BAO ZI
超包子
DINER CAR CAFÉ
YAAY YAAY
I OVER-DID IT YESTER-DAY, DIDN'T I...
WHEN IT COMES TO RESEARCH, I KIND OF LOSE PERSPECTIVE.
I SHOULD E THE ONE OLOGIZING... MEAN, THE DAMAGE STAINED BY SCHOOL OF GINEERING *ALONE*—
OW OW

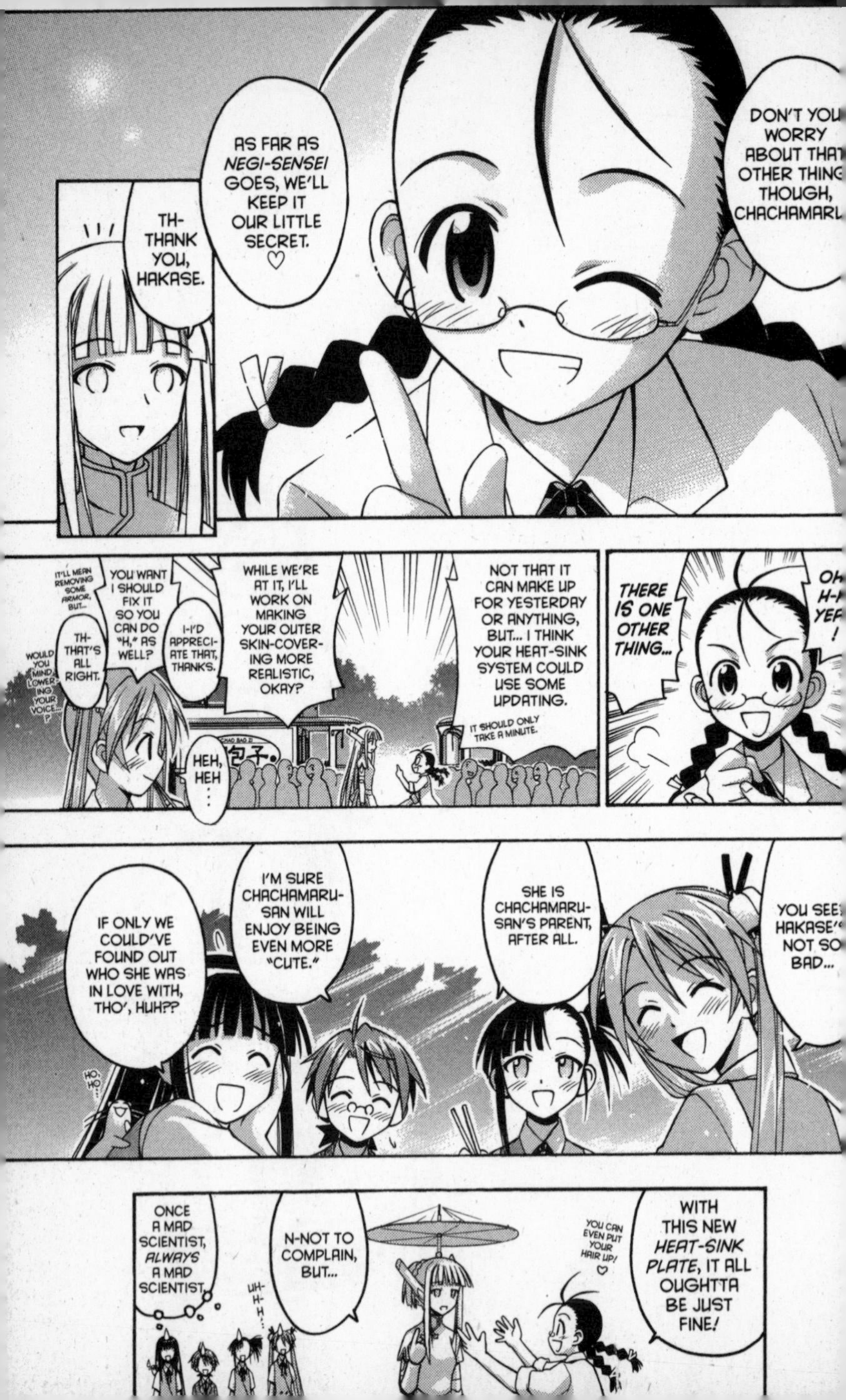
DON'T YOU WORRY ABOUT THAT OTHER THING THOUGH, CHACHAMARU.
AS FAR AS *NEGI-SENSEI* GOES, WE'LL KEEP IT OUR LITTLE SECRET. ♡
TH- THANK YOU, HAKASE.
OH H-H YEA!
THERE IS ONE OTHER THING...
NOT THAT IT CAN MAKE UP FOR YESTERDAY OR ANYTHING, BUT... I THINK YOUR HEAT-SINK SYSTEM COULD USE SOME UPDATING.
IT SHOULD ONLY TAKE A MINUTE.
WHILE WE'RE AT IT, I'LL WORK ON MAKING YOUR OUTER SKIN-COVERING MORE REALISTIC, OKAY?
I-I'D APPRECIATE THAT, THANKS.
YOU WANT I SHOULD FIX IT SO YOU CAN DO "H," AS WELL?
IT'LL MEAN REMOVING SOME ARMOR, BUT...
TH-THAT'S ALL RIGHT.
HEH, HEH...
WOULD YOU MIND LOWERING YOUR VOICE...?
YOU SEE? HAKASE'S NOT SO BAD...
SHE IS CHACHAMARU-SAN'S PARENT, AFTER ALL.
I'M SURE CHACHAMARU-SAN WILL ENJOY BEING EVEN MORE "CUTE."
IF ONLY WE COULD'VE FOUND OUT WHO SHE WAS IN LOVE WITH, THO', HUH??
HO, HO...
WITH THIS NEW *HEAT-SINK PLATE*, IT ALL OUGHTTA BE JUST FINE!
YOU CAN EVEN PUT YOUR HAIR UP! ♡
N-NOT TO COMPLAIN, BUT...
UH-H-H...
ONCE A MAD SCIENTIST, *ALWAYS* A MAD SCIENTIST.

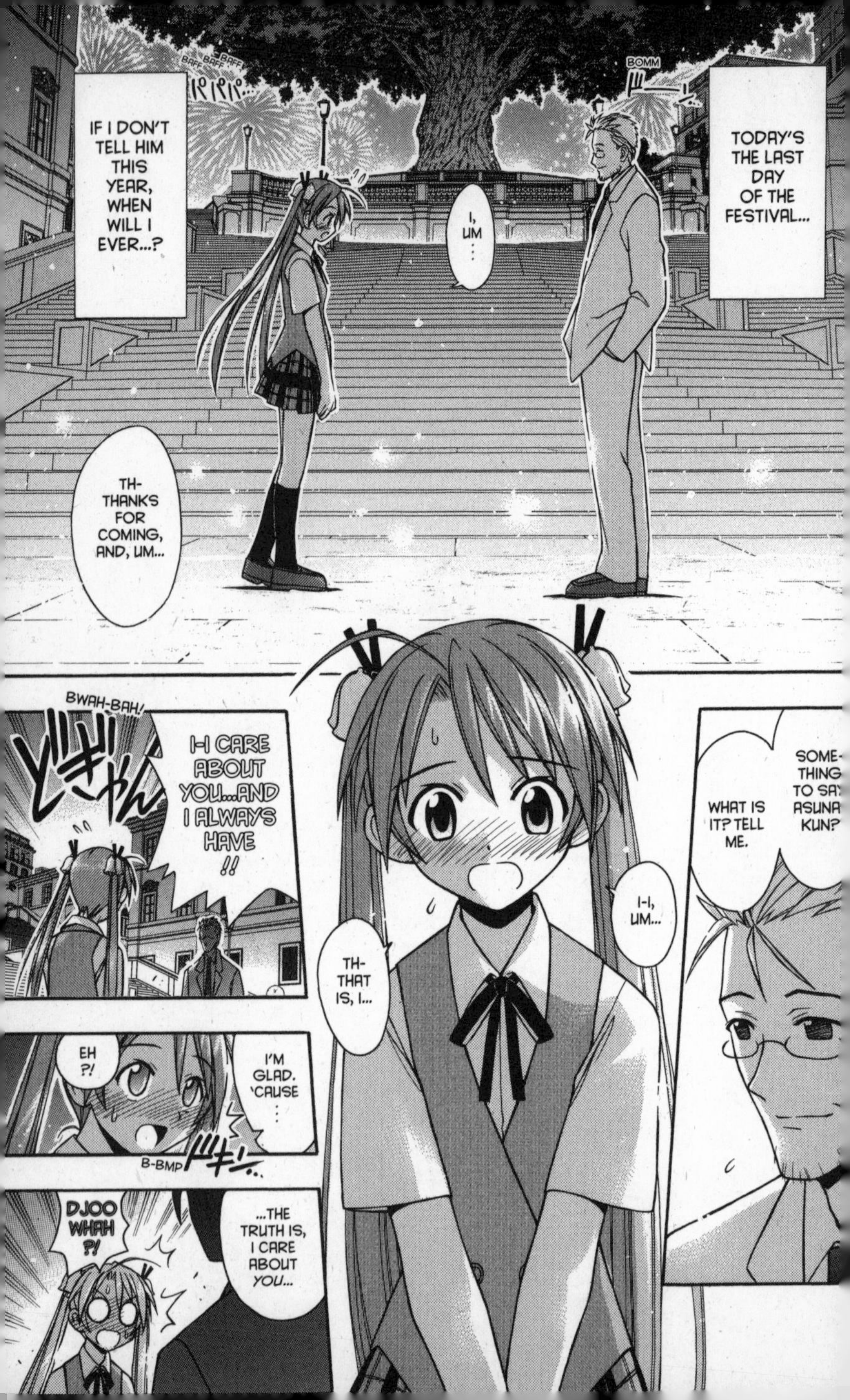
TODAY'S THE LAST DAY OF THE FESTIVAL...
BOMM
I, UM...
BAFF BAFF BAFF
パパパ...
IF I DON'T TELL HIM THIS YEAR, WHEN WILL I EVER...?
TH-THANKS FOR COMING, AND, UM...
SOME-THING TO SAY ASUNA KUN?
WHAT IS IT? TELL ME.
I-I, UM...
TH-THAT IS, I...
BWAH-BAH!
I-I CARE ABOUT YOU...AND I ALWAYS HAVE!!
I'M GLAD. 'CAUSE...
EH?!
B-BMP
...THE TRUTH IS, I CARE ABOUT YOU...
DJOO WHAH?!

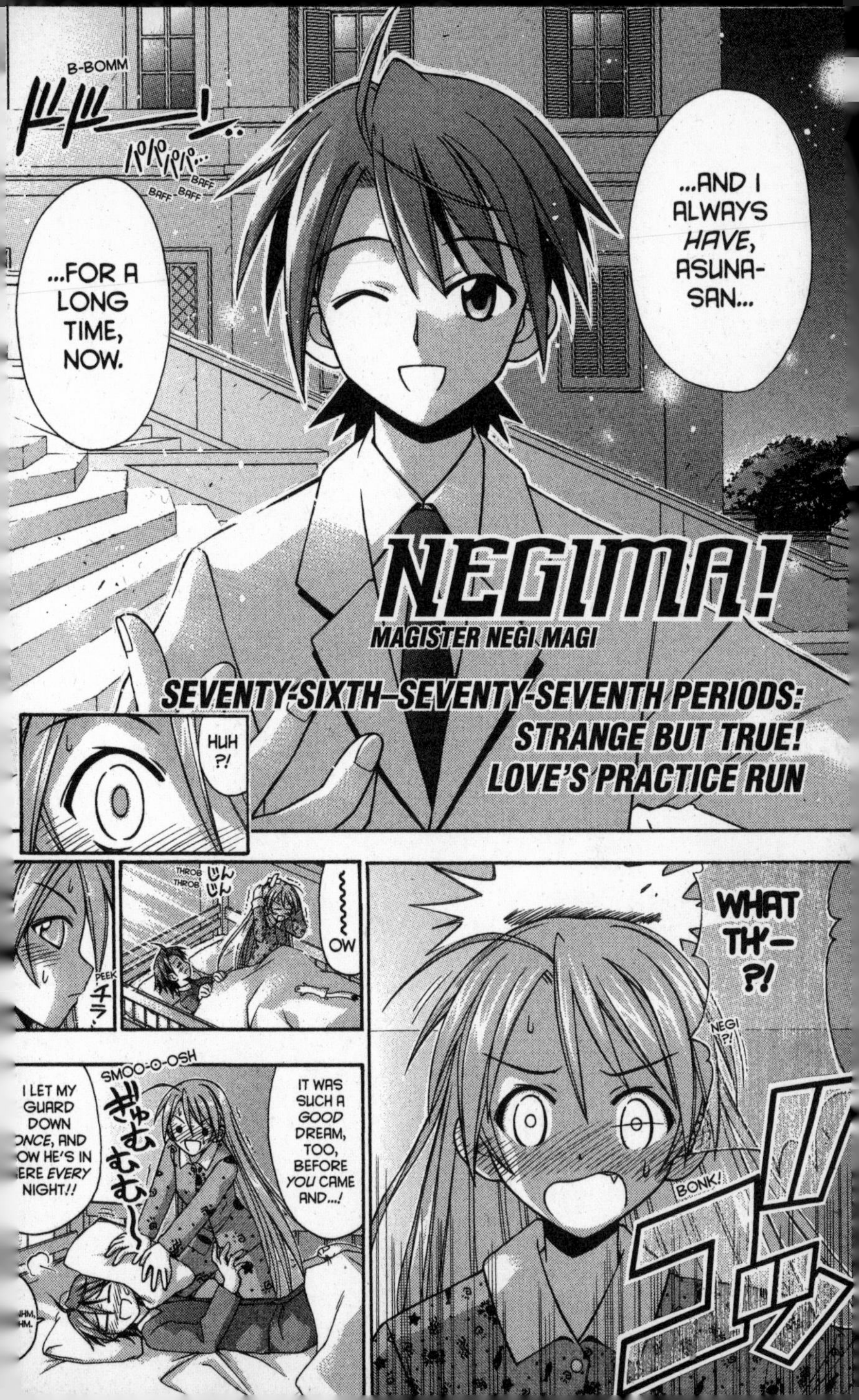
B-BOMM
BAFF BAFF BAFF
...AND I ALWAYS *HAVE*, ASUNA-SAN...
...FOR A LONG TIME, NOW.
NEGIMA!
MAGISTER NEGI MAGI
SEVENTY-SIXTH–SEVENTY-SEVENTH PERIODS:
STRANGE BUT TRUE!
LOVE'S PRACTICE RUN
HUH ?!
WHAT TH'— ?!
NEGI ?!
BONK!
THROB THROB
OW
PEEK
SMOO-O-OSH
IT WAS SUCH A *GOOD* DREAM, TOO, BEFORE *YOU* CAME AND...!
I LET MY GUARD DOWN *ONCE*, AND OW HE'S IN ERE *EVERY* NIGHT!!

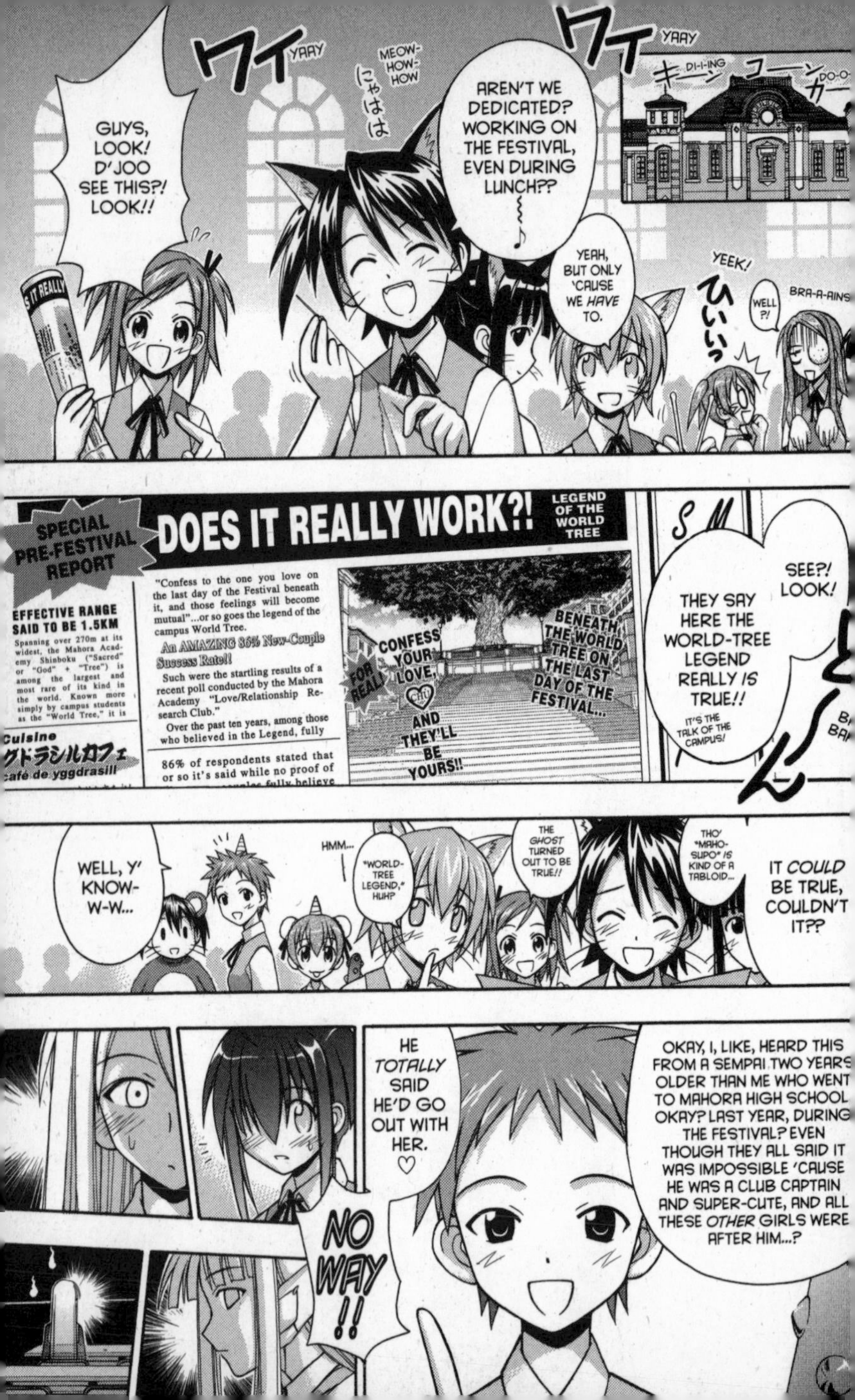
キーン DI-I-ING
コーン カー DO-O-
ワイ YAAY
AREN'T WE DEDICATED? WORKING ON THE FESTIVAL, EVEN DURING LUNCH?? ♪
にゃはは MEOW-HOW-HOW
ワイ YAAY
YEAH, BUT ONLY 'CAUSE WE HAVE TO.
BRA-A-AINS
WELL?!
YEEK! ひぃぃっ
GUYS, LOOK! D'JOO SEE THIS?! LOOK!!
S M
SEE?! LOOK!
THEY SAY HERE THE WORLD-TREE LEGEND REALLY IS TRUE!!
IT'S THE TALK OF THE CAMPUS!
どーん
SPECIAL PRE-FESTIVAL REPORT
DOES IT REALLY WORK?!
LEGEND OF THE WORLD TREE
EFFECTIVE RANGE SAID TO BE 1.5KM
Spanning over 270m at its widest, the Mahora Academy Shinboku ("Sacred" or "God" + "Tree") is among the largest and most rare of its kind in the world. Known more simply by campus students as the "World Tree," it is
Cuisine
グドラシルカフェ
café de yggdrasill
"Confess to the one you love on the last day of the Festival beneath it, and those feelings will become mutual"...or so goes the legend of the campus World Tree.
An AMAZING 86% New-Couple Success Rate!!
Such were the startling results of a recent poll conducted by the Mahora Academy "Love/Relationship Research Club."
Over the past ten years, among those who believed in the Legend, fully
86% of respondents stated that or so it's said while no proof of
FOR REAL!
CONFESS YOUR LOVE,
CHU
AND THEY'LL BE YOURS!!
BENEATH THE WORLD TREE ON THE LAST DAY OF THE FESTIVAL...
IT COULD BE TRUE, COULDN'T IT??
THO' "MAHO-SUPO" IS KIND OF A TABLOID...
THE GHOST TURNED OUT TO BE TRUE!!
"WORLD-TREE LEGEND," HUH?
HMM...
WELL, Y' KNOW-W-W...
OKAY, I, LIKE, HEARD THIS FROM A SEMPAI TWO YEARS OLDER THAN ME WHO WENT TO MAHORA HIGH SCHOOL OKAY? LAST YEAR, DURING THE FESTIVAL? EVEN THOUGH THEY ALL SAID IT WAS IMPOSSIBLE 'CAUSE HE WAS A CLUB CAPTAIN AND SUPER-CUTE, AND ALL THESE OTHER GIRLS WERE AFTER HIM...?
HE TOTALLY SAID HE'D GO OUT WITH HER. ♡
NO WAY!!

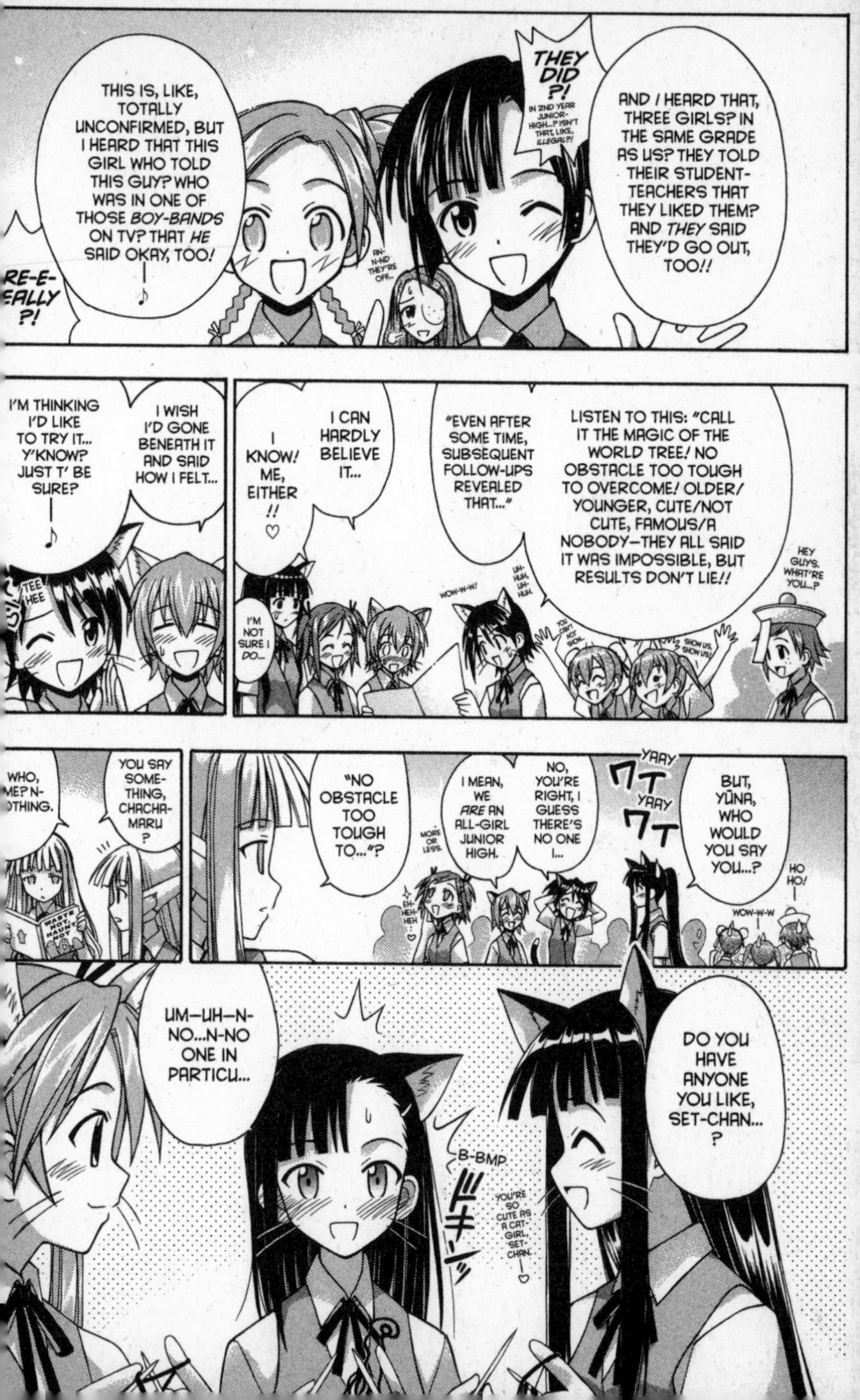
THEY DID?!
IN 2ND YEAR JUNIOR-HIGH...? ISN'T THAT, LIKE, ILLEGAL?!
AND I HEARD THAT, THREE GIRLS? IN THE SAME GRADE AS US? THEY TOLD THEIR STUDENT-TEACHERS THAT THEY LIKED THEM? AND THEY SAID THEY'D GO OUT, TOO!!
AN-N-ND THEY'RE OFF...
THIS IS, LIKE, TOTALLY UNCONFIRMED, BUT I HEARD THAT THIS GIRL WHO TOLD THIS GUY? WHO WAS IN ONE OF THOSE BOY-BANDS ON TV? THAT HE SAID OKAY, TOO! ♪
RE-E-EALLY?!
HEY GUYS. WHAT'RE YOU...?
LISTEN TO THIS: "CALL IT THE MAGIC OF THE WORLD TREE! NO OBSTACLE TOO TOUGH TO OVERCOME! OLDER/YOUNGER, CUTE/NOT CUTE, FAMOUS/A NOBODY—THEY ALL SAID IT WAS IMPOSSIBLE, BUT RESULTS DON'T LIE!!
"EVEN AFTER SOME TIME, SUBSEQUENT FOLLOW-UPS REVEALED THAT..."
SHOW US, SHOW US!
YOU CAN'T NOT SHOW.
UH-HUH, UH-HUH.
WOW-W-W!
I CAN HARDLY BELIEVE IT...
I KNOW! ME, EITHER!! ♡
I'M NOT SURE I DO...
I WISH I'D GONE BENEATH IT AND SAID HOW I FELT...
I'M THINKING I'D LIKE TO TRY IT... Y'KNOW? JUST T' BE SURE? ♪
TEE HEE
YAAY
YAAY
BUT, YŪNA, WHO WOULD YOU SAY YOU...?
HO HO!
WOW-W-W
NO, YOU'RE RIGHT, I GUESS THERE'S NO ONE I...
I MEAN, WE ARE AN ALL-GIRL JUNIOR HIGH.
EH-HEH-HEH ♡
MORE OR LESS.
"NO OBSTACLE TOO TOUGH TO..."?
YOU SAY SOME-THING, CHACHA-MARU?
WHO, ME? N-NOTHING.
WASTE NOT HAUNT NOT
DO YOU HAVE ANYONE YOU LIKE, SET-CHAN...?
YOU'RE SO CUTE AS A CAT-GIRL, SET-CHAN. ♡
B-BMP
UM—UH—N-NO...N-NO ONE IN PARTICU...

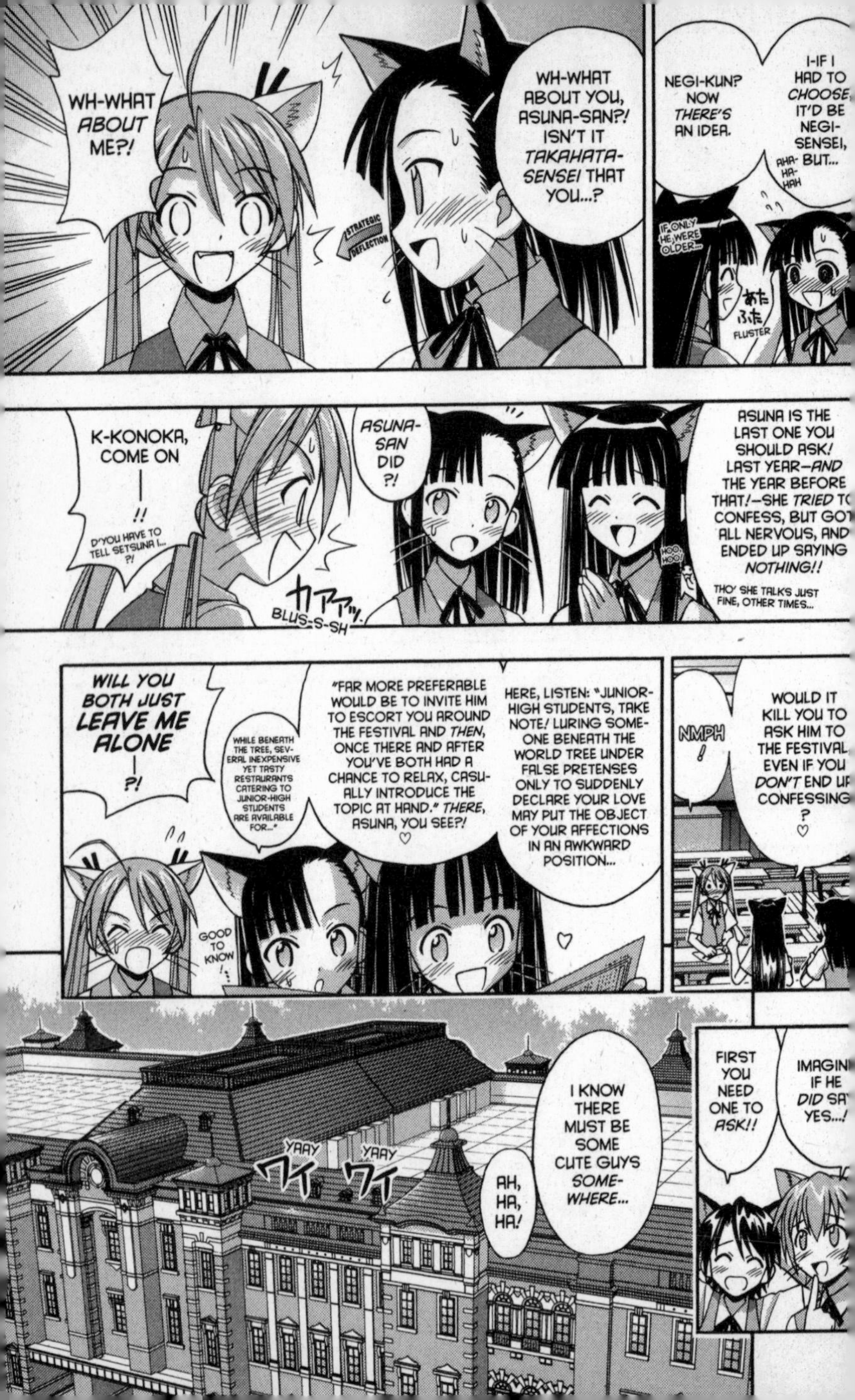
I-IF I HAD TO CHOOSE, IT'D BE NEGI-SENSEI, BUT...
AHA-HA-HAH
NEGI-KUN? NOW THERE'S AN IDEA.
IF ONLY HE WERE OLDER...
あたふた
FLUSTER
WH-WHAT ABOUT YOU, ASUNA-SAN?! ISN'T IT TAKAHATA-SENSEI THAT YOU...?
STRATEGIC DEFLECTION
WH-WHAT ABOUT ME?!
ASUNA IS THE LAST ONE YOU SHOULD ASK! LAST YEAR—AND THE YEAR BEFORE THAT!—SHE TRIED TO CONFESS, BUT GOT ALL NERVOUS, AND ENDED UP SAYING NOTHING!!
THO' SHE TALKS JUST FINE, OTHER TIMES...
HOO, HOO!
ASUNA-SAN DID?!
K-KONOKA, COME ON—!!
D'YOU HAVE TO TELL SETSUNA I...?!
カアァッ
BLUS-S-SH
WOULD IT KILL YOU TO ASK HIM TO THE FESTIVAL EVEN IF YOU DON'T END UP CONFESSING? ♡
NMPH!
HERE, LISTEN: "JUNIOR-HIGH STUDENTS, TAKE NOTE! LURING SOMEONE BENEATH THE WORLD TREE UNDER FALSE PRETENSES ONLY TO SUDDENLY DECLARE YOUR LOVE MAY PUT THE OBJECT OF YOUR AFFECTIONS IN AN AWKWARD POSITION...
"FAR MORE PREFERABLE WOULD BE TO INVITE HIM TO ESCORT YOU AROUND THE FESTIVAL AND THEN, ONCE THERE AND AFTER YOU'VE BOTH HAD A CHANCE TO RELAX, CASUALLY INTRODUCE THE TOPIC AT HAND." THERE, ASUNA, YOU SEE?! ♡
WHILE BENEATH THE TREE, SEVERAL INEXPENSIVE YET TASTY RESTRAURANTS CATERING TO JUNIOR-HIGH STUDENTS ARE AVAILABLE FOR..."
WILL YOU BOTH JUST LEAVE ME ALONE—?!
GOOD TO KNOW
IMAGIN IF HE DID SA YES...!
FIRST YOU NEED ONE TO ASK!!
I KNOW THERE MUST BE SOME CUTE GUYS SOMEWHERE...
AH, HA, HA!
ワイ
YAAY
ワイ
YAAY

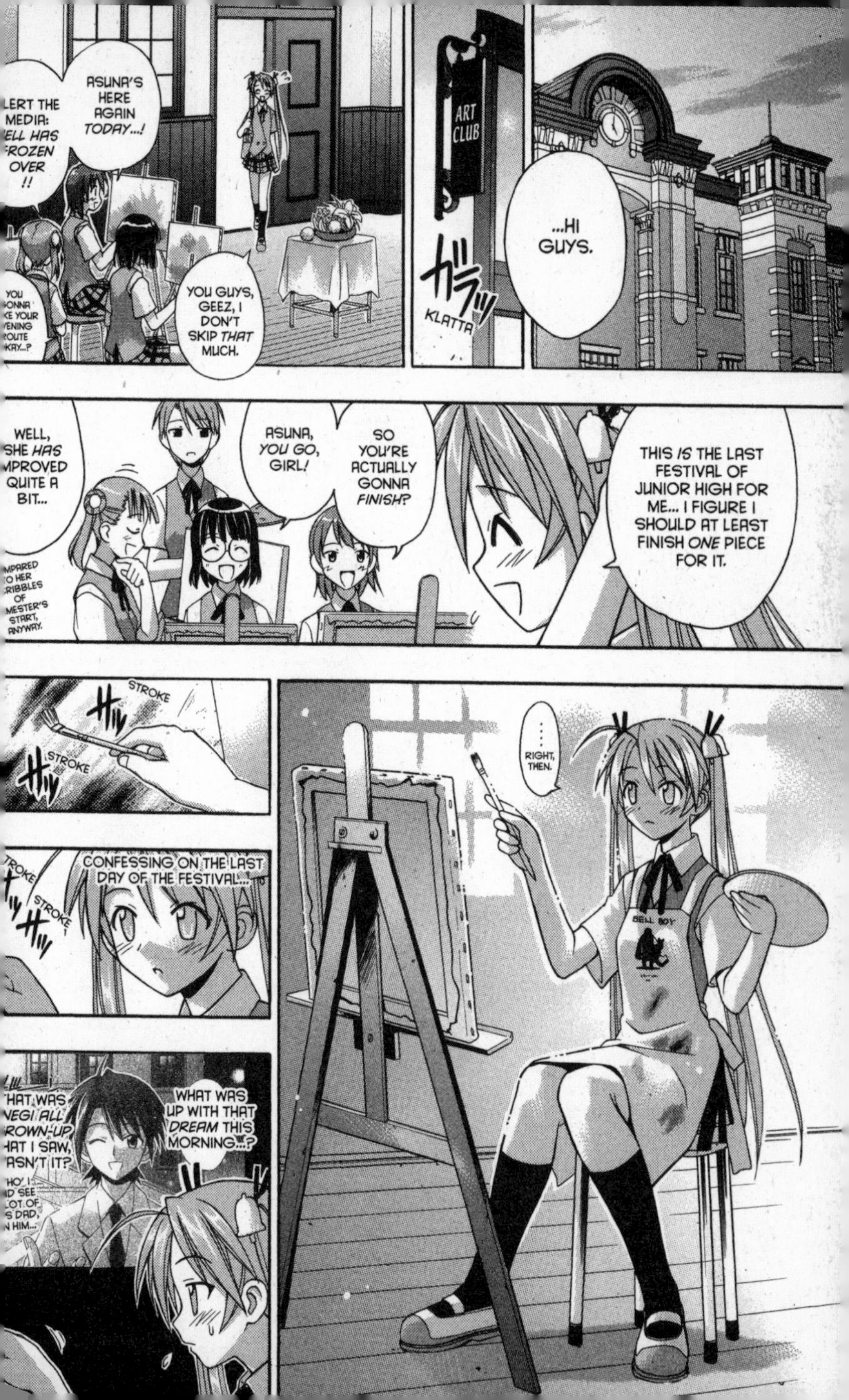
...HI GUYS.
ART CLUB
KLATTA
ASUNA'S HERE AGAIN *TODAY*...!
LERT THE MEDIA: ELL HAS FROZEN OVER !!
YOU GUYS, GEEZ, I DON'T SKIP *THAT* MUCH.
YOU ONNA KE YOUR VENING OUTE KAY...?
THIS *IS* THE LAST FESTIVAL OF JUNIOR HIGH FOR ME... I FIGURE I SHOULD AT LEAST FINISH *ONE* PIECE FOR IT.
SO YOU'RE ACTUALLY GONNA *FINISH*?
ASUNA, *YOU GO*, GIRL!
WELL, SHE *HAS* MPROVED QUITE A BIT...
MPARED TO HER CRIBBLES OF MESTER'S START, ANYWAY.
......RIGHT, THEN.
BELL BOY
STROKE
STROKE
CONFESSING ON THE LAST DAY OF THE FESTIVAL...
STROKE
STROKE
WHAT WAS UP WITH THAT *DREAM* THIS MORNING...?
THAT WAS NEGI ALL ROWN-UP HAT I SAW, ASN'T IT?

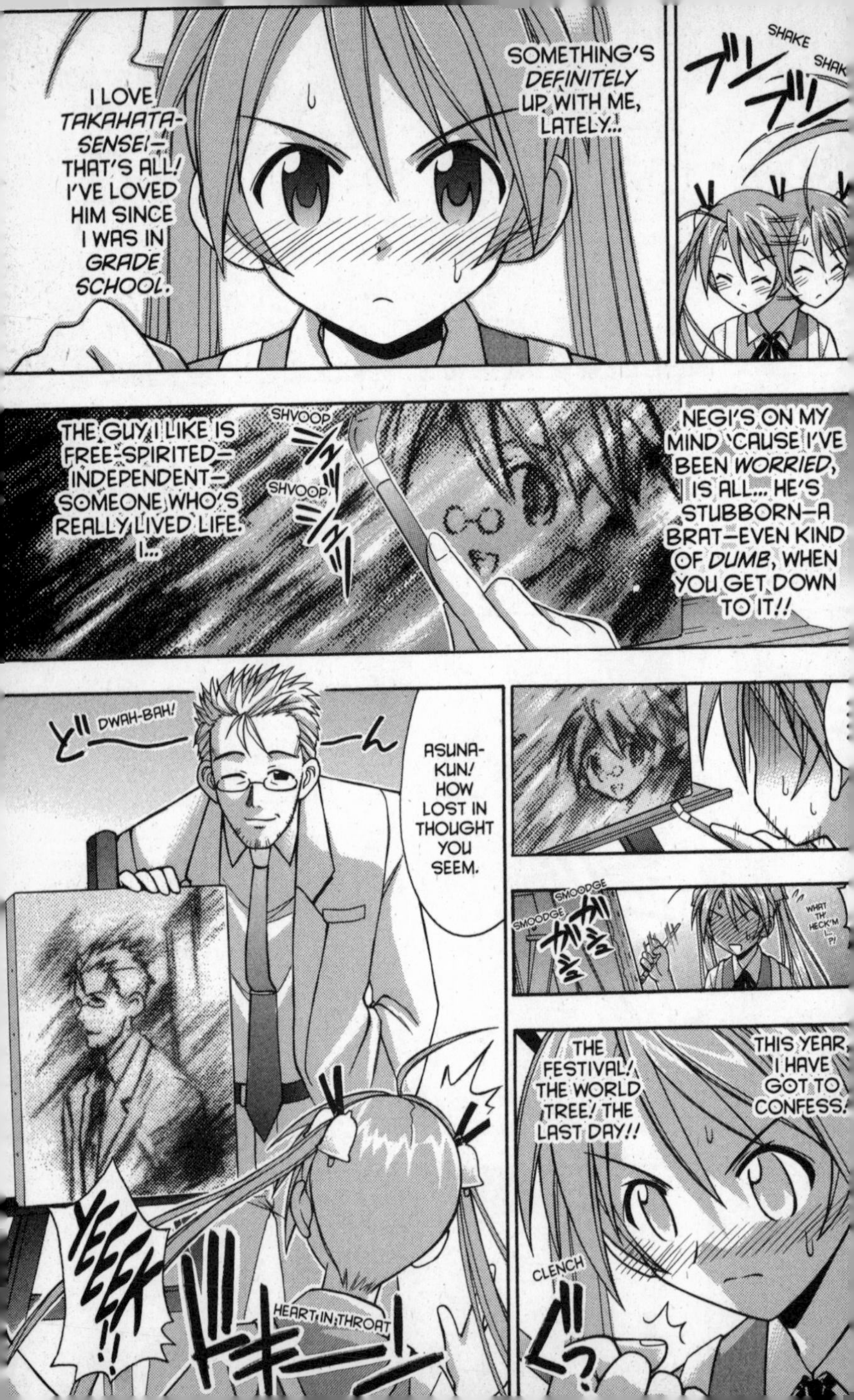
SHAKE
SHAK
SOMETHING'S *DEFINITELY* UP WITH ME, LATELY...
I LOVE *TAKAHATA-SENSEI*—THAT'S ALL! I'VE LOVED HIM SINCE I WAS IN *GRADE SCHOOL*.
NEGI'S ON MY MIND 'CAUSE I'VE BEEN *WORRIED*, IS ALL... HE'S STUBBORN—A BRAT—EVEN KIND OF *DUMB*, WHEN YOU GET DOWN TO IT!!
SHVOOP
SHVOOP
THE GUY I LIKE IS FREE-SPIRITED—INDEPENDENT—SOMEONE WHO'S REALLY LIVED LIFE. I...
SMOODGE
SMOODGE
WHAT TH' HECK'M I...?!
THIS YEAR, I HAVE GOT TO CONFESS.
THE FESTIVAL! THE WORLD TREE! THE LAST DAY!!
CLENCH
DWAH-BAH!
ASUNA-KUN! HOW LOST IN THOUGHT YOU SEEM.
YEEEK!!
HEART IN THROAT

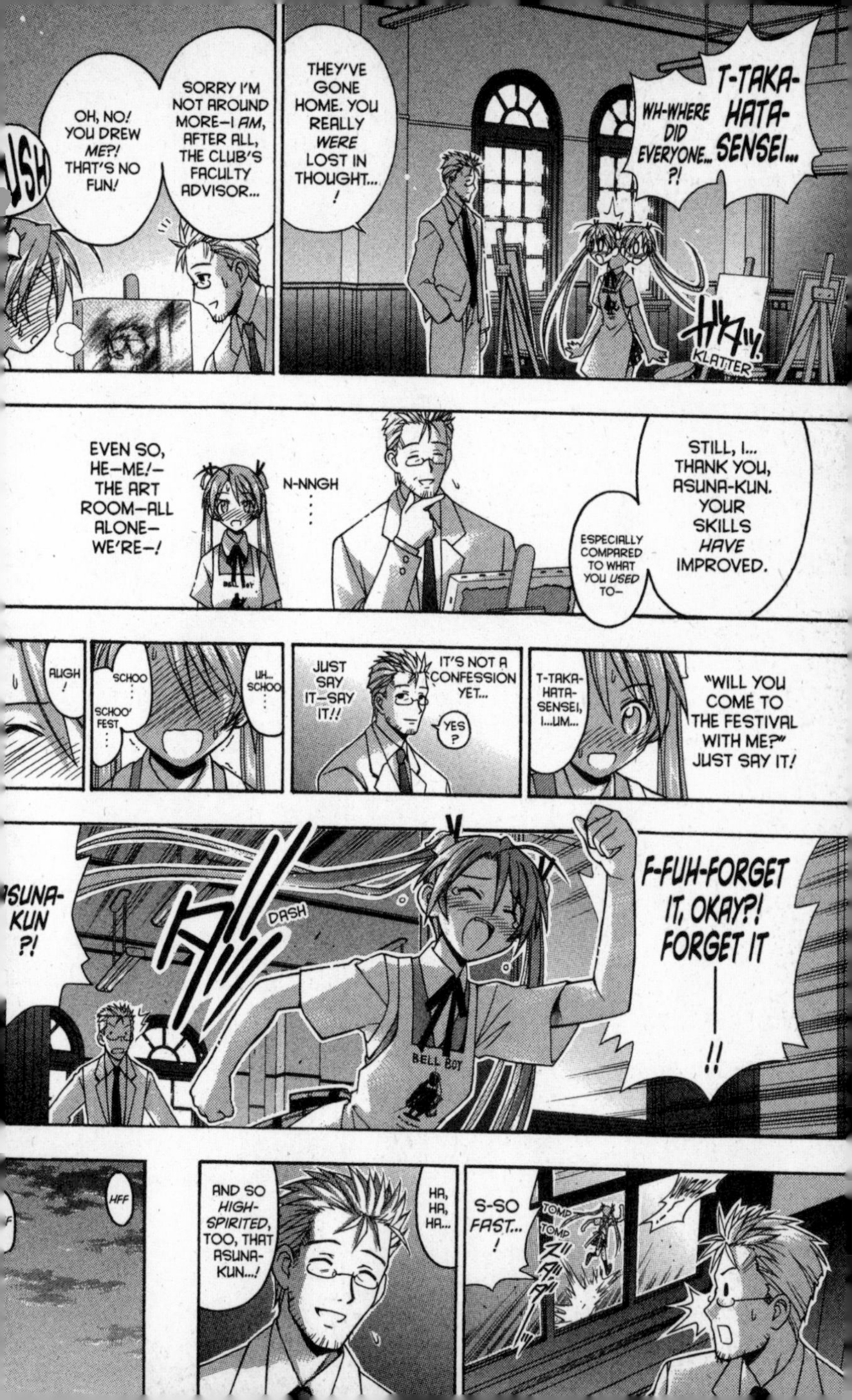
T-TAKA-HATA-SENSEI...
WH-WHERE DID EVERYONE...?!
KLATTER
THEY'VE GONE HOME. YOU REALLY WERE LOST IN THOUGHT...!
SORRY I'M NOT AROUND MORE—I AM, AFTER ALL, THE CLUB'S FACULTY ADVISOR...
OH, NO! YOU DREW ME?! THAT'S NO FUN!
STILL, I... THANK YOU, ASUNA-KUN. YOUR SKILLS HAVE IMPROVED.
ESPECIALLY COMPARED TO WHAT YOU USED TO—
N-NNGH...
EVEN SO, HE—ME!—THE ART ROOM—ALL ALONE—WE'RE—!
"WILL YOU COME TO THE FESTIVAL WITH ME?" JUST SAY IT!
T-TAKA-HATA-SENSEI, I...UM...
IT'S NOT A CONFESSION YET...
JUST SAY IT—SAY IT!!
YES?
UH... SCHOO...
SCHOO...
SCHOO' FEST...
AUGH!
F-FUH-FORGET IT, OKAY?! FORGET IT—!!
DASH
SUNA-KUN ?!
S-SO FAST...!
TOMP
TOMP
HA, HA, HA...
AND SO HIGH-SPIRITED, TOO, THAT ASUNA-KUN...!
HFF

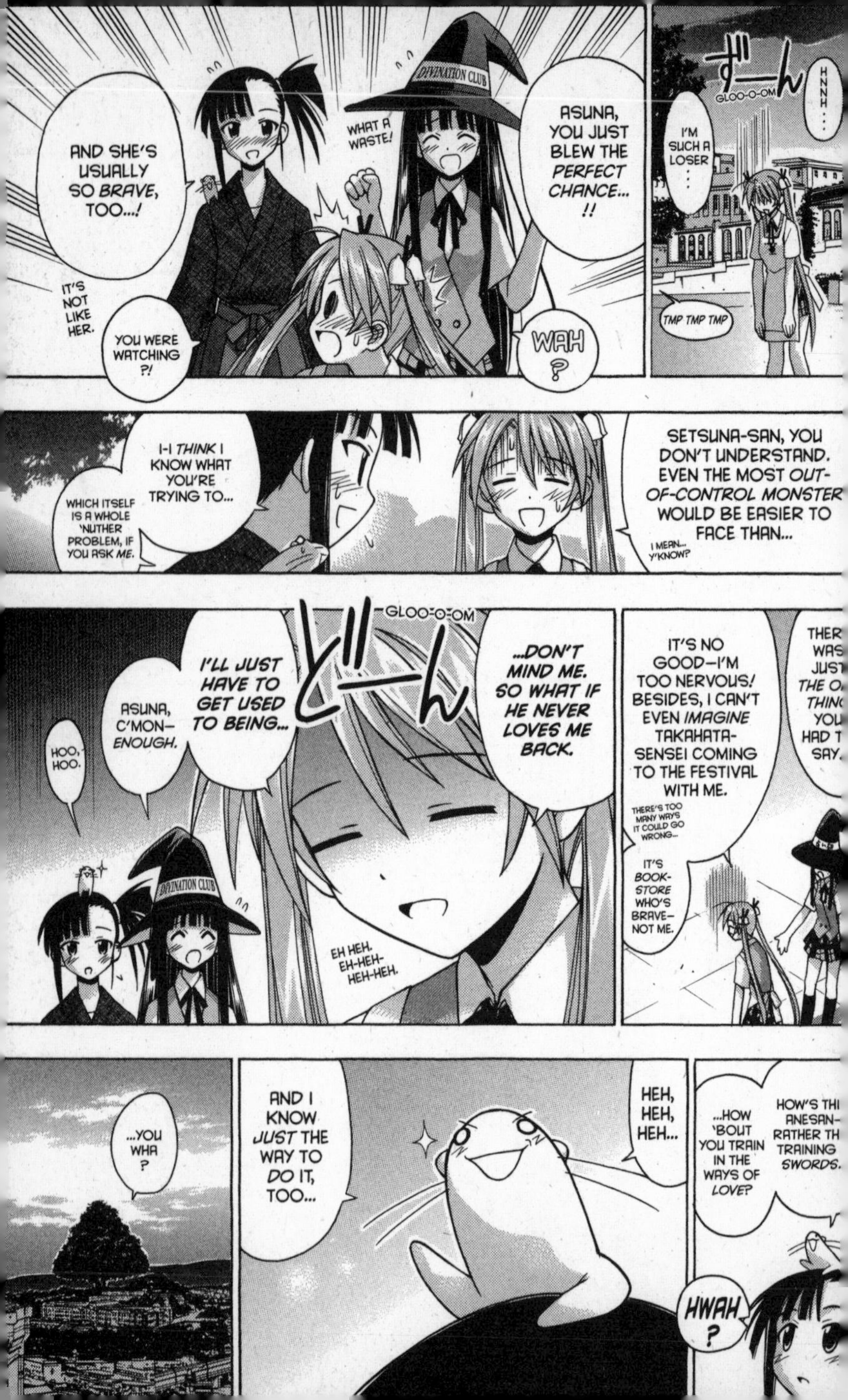

ずーん GLOO-O-OM
HNNH...
I'M SUCH A LOSER...
TMP TMP TMP
ASUNA, YOU JUST BLEW THE *PERFECT CHANCE*...!!
WHAT A WASTE!
AND SHE'S USUALLY SO *BRAVE*, TOO...!
WAH?
YOU WERE WATCHING?!
IT'S NOT LIKE HER.
SETSUNA-SAN, YOU DON'T UNDERSTAND. EVEN THE MOST *OUT-OF-CONTROL MONSTER* WOULD BE EASIER TO FACE THAN...
I MEAN... Y'KNOW?
I-I *THINK* I KNOW WHAT YOU'RE TRYING TO...
WHICH ITSELF IS A WHOLE 'NUTHER PROBLEM, IF YOU ASK *ME*.
THER WAS JUST *THE O THING* YOU HAD T SAY.
IT'S NO GOOD—I'M TOO NERVOUS! BESIDES, I CAN'T EVEN *IMAGINE* TAKAHATA-SENSEI COMING TO THE FESTIVAL WITH ME.
THERE'S TOO MANY WAYS IT COULD GO WRONG...
IT'S *BOOKSTORE* WHO'S BRAVE—NOT ME.
...DON'T MIND ME. SO WHAT IF HE NEVER LOVES ME BACK.
どーん GLOO-O-OM
I'LL JUST HAVE TO GET USED TO BEING...
ASUNA, C'MON—*ENOUGH*.
HOO, HOO.
EH HEH. EH-HEH-HEH-HEH.
HOW'S THI ANESAN- RATHER TH TRAINING *SWORDS*.
...HOW 'BOUT YOU TRAIN IN THE WAYS OF *LOVE*?
HWAH?
HEH, HEH, HEH...
AND I KNOW *JUST* THE WAY TO *DO* IT, TOO...
...YOU WHA?

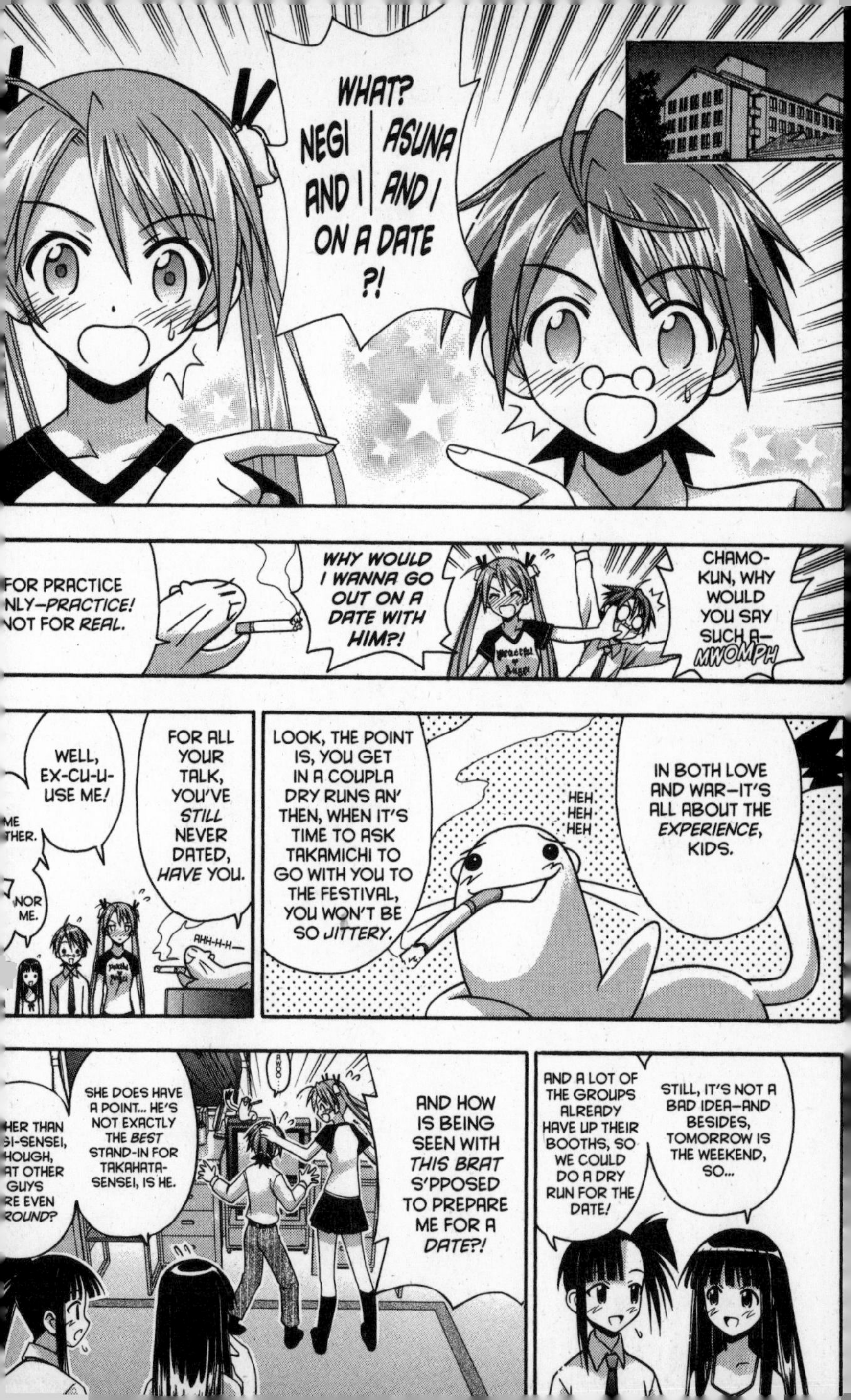
WHAT? NEGI AND I ON A DATE ?!
ASUNA AND I
CHAMO-KUN, WHY WOULD YOU SAY SUCH A— MWOMPH
WHY WOULD I WANNA GO OUT ON A DATE WITH HIM?!
FOR PRACTICE NLY—PRACTICE! NOT FOR REAL.
IN BOTH LOVE AND WAR—IT'S ALL ABOUT THE EXPERIENCE, KIDS.
HEH. HEH HEH
LOOK, THE POINT IS, YOU GET IN A COUPLA DRY RUNS AN' THEN, WHEN IT'S TIME TO ASK TAKAMICHI TO GO WITH YOU TO THE FESTIVAL, YOU WON'T BE SO JITTERY.
FOR ALL YOUR TALK, YOU'VE STILL NEVER DATED, HAVE YOU.
AHH-H-H—
WELL, EX-CU-U-USE ME!
ME THER.
NOR ME.
STILL, IT'S NOT A BAD IDEA—AND BESIDES, TOMORROW IS THE WEEKEND, SO...
AND A LOT OF THE GROUPS ALREADY HAVE UP THEIR BOOTHS, SO WE COULD DO A DRY RUN FOR THE DATE!
AND HOW IS BEING SEEN WITH THIS BRAT S'PPOSED TO PREPARE ME FOR A DATE?!
SHE DOES HAVE A POINT... HE'S NOT EXACTLY THE BEST STAND-IN FOR TAKAHATA-SENSEI, IS HE.
HER THAN GI-SENSEI, HOUGH, AT OTHER GUYS RE EVEN ROUND?

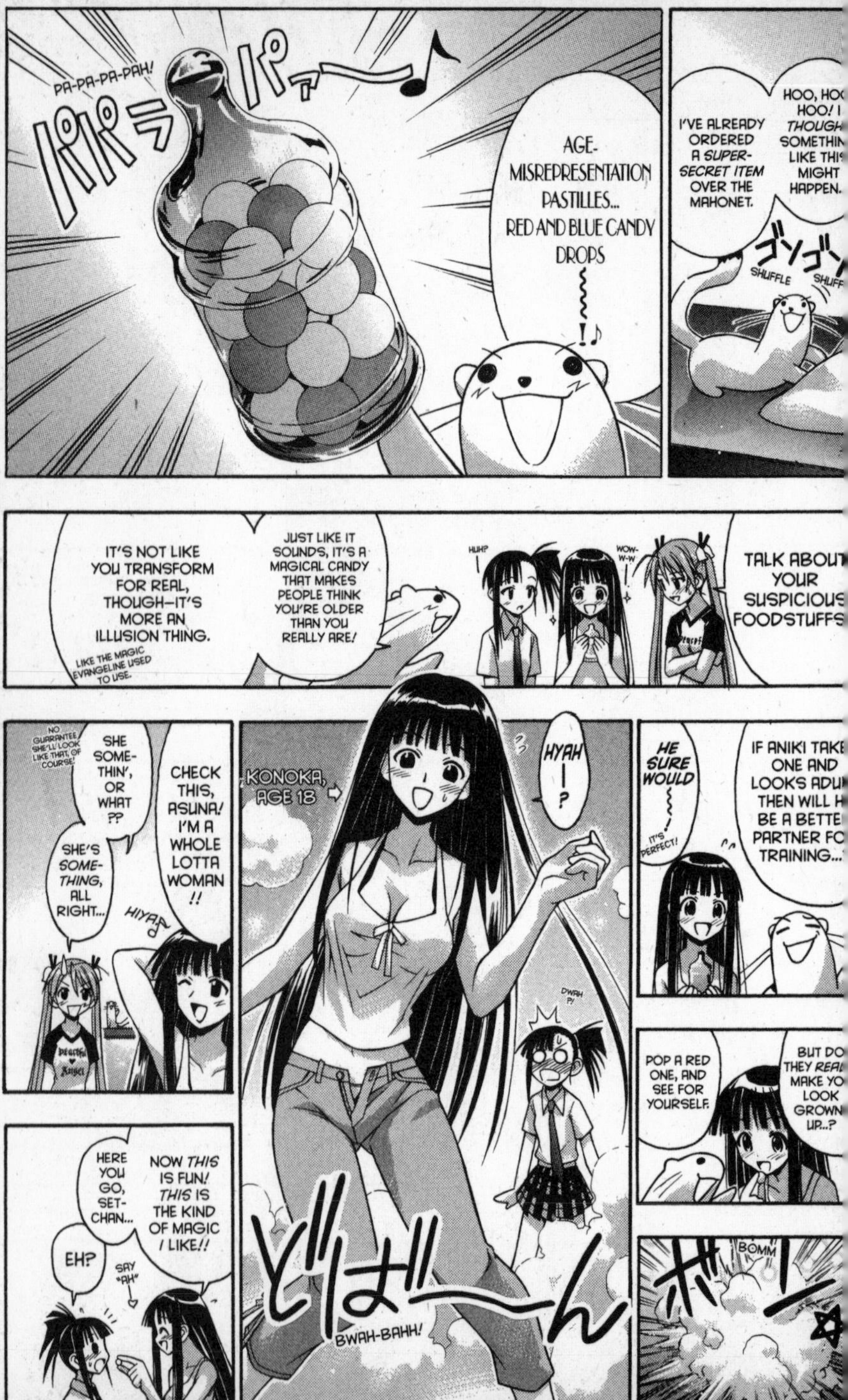
HOO, HOO HOO! I THOUGH SOMETHIN LIKE THIS MIGHT HAPPEN.
I'VE ALREADY ORDERED A SUPER-SECRET ITEM OVER THE MAHONET.
SHUFFLE SHUFF
PA-PA-PA-PAH!
AGE-MISREPRESENTATION PASTILLES... RED AND BLUE CANDY DROPS~~~!♪
TALK ABOUT YOUR SUSPICIOUS FOODSTUFFS
WOW-W-W!
HUH?!
JUST LIKE IT SOUNDS, IT'S A MAGICAL CANDY THAT MAKES PEOPLE THINK YOU'RE OLDER THAN YOU REALLY ARE!
IT'S NOT LIKE YOU TRANSFORM FOR REAL, THOUGH—IT'S MORE AN ILLUSION THING.
LIKE THE MAGIC EVANGELINE USED TO USE.
IF ANIKI TAKE ONE AND LOOKS ADU THEN WILL H BE A BETTE PARTNER FO TRAINING...
HE SURE WOULD~~!
IT'S PERFECT!
BUT DO THEY REAL MAKE YO LOOK GROWN UP...?
POP A RED ONE, AND SEE FOR YOURSELF.
BOMM
HYAH—?
KONOKA, AGE 18
DWAH?!
BWAH-BAHH!
CHECK THIS, ASUNA! I'M A WHOLE LOTTA WOMAN!!
SHE SOMETHIN', OR WHAT??
NO GUARANTEE SHE'LL LOOK LIKE THAT, OF COURSE!
SHE'S SOMETHING, ALL RIGHT...
HIYAA
NOW THIS IS FUN! THIS IS THE KIND OF MAGIC I LIKE!!
HERE YOU GO, SET-CHAN...
EH?
SAY "AH"♡

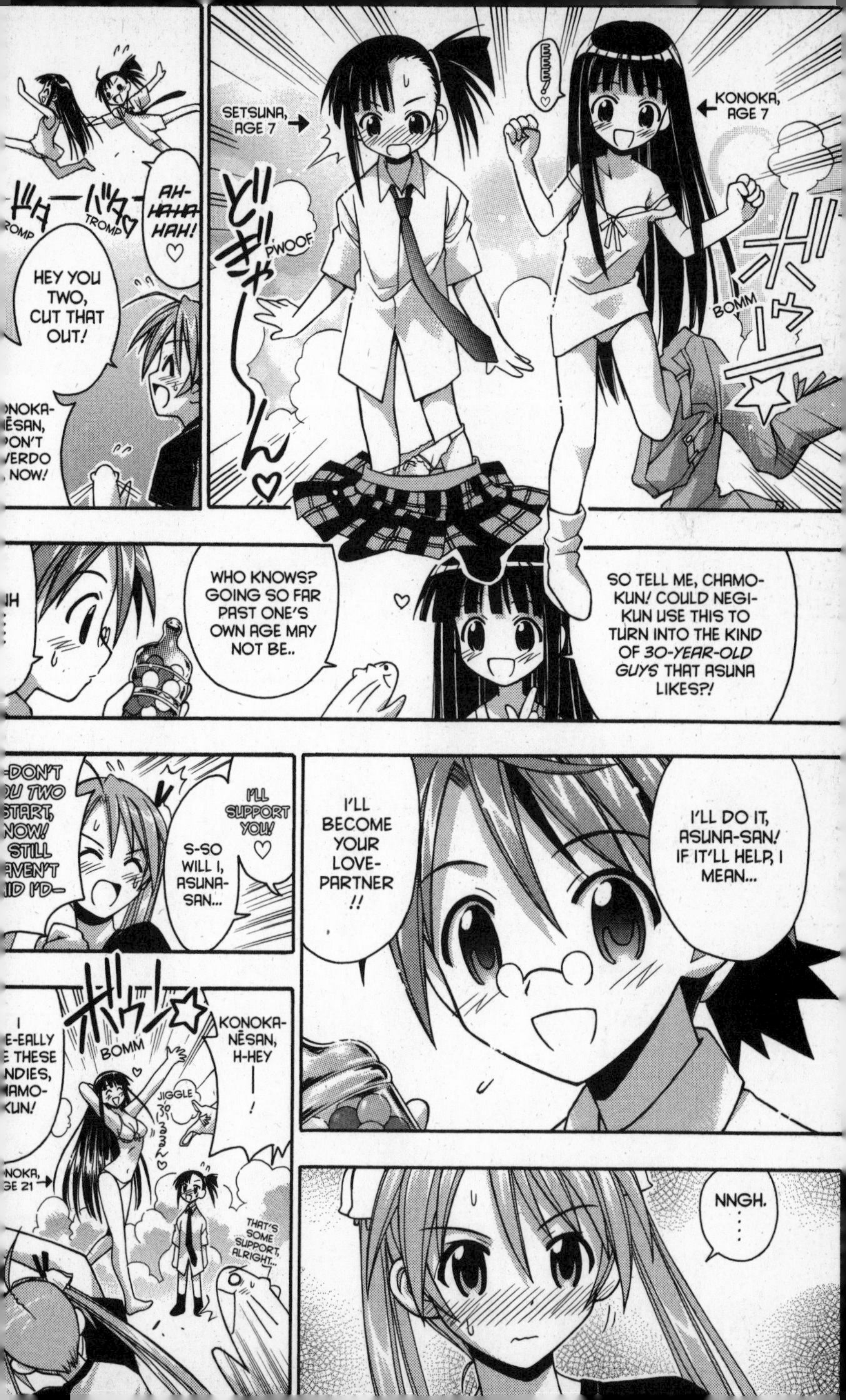
EEEE!♡
SETSUNA, AGE 7 →
← KONOKA, AGE 7
PWOOF
BOMM
TROMP
AH-HAHAHA HAH! ♡
ROMP
HEY YOU TWO, CUT THAT OUT!
ONOKA-NĒSAN, DON'T VERDO NOW!
SO TELL ME, CHAMO-KUN! COULD NEGI-KUN USE THIS TO TURN INTO THE KIND OF *30-YEAR-OLD GUYS* THAT ASUNA LIKES?!
WHO KNOWS? GOING SO FAR PAST ONE'S OWN AGE MAY NOT BE..
NH
I'LL DO IT, ASUNA-SAN! IF IT'LL HELP, I MEAN...
I'LL BECOME YOUR LOVE-PARTNER!!
NNGH. ....
I'LL SUPPORT YOU! ♡
S-SO WILL I, ASUNA-SAN...
-DON'T OU TWO START, NOW! STILL AVEN'T AID I'D-
BOMM
KONOKA-NĒSAN, H-HEY!
I E-EALLY E THESE NDIES, AMO-KUN!
JIGGLE
NOKA, GE 21 →
THAT'S SOME SUPPORT, ALRIGHT...

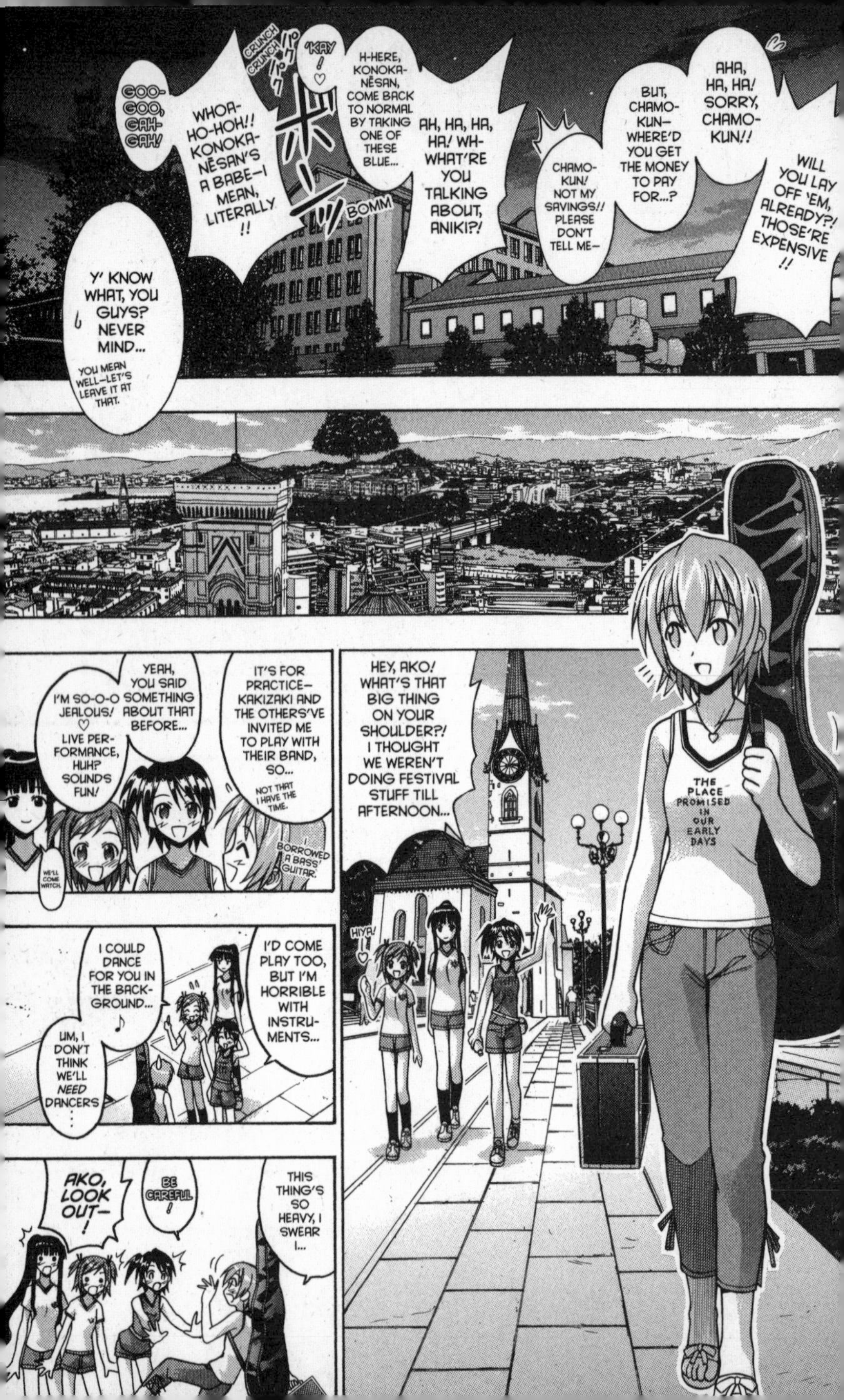

AHA, HA, HA! SORRY, CHAMO-KUN!!
WILL YOU LAY OFF 'EM, ALREADY?! THOSE'RE EXPENSIVE!!
BUT, CHAMO-KUN— WHERE'D YOU GET THE MONEY TO PAY FOR...?
CHAMO-KUN! NOT MY SAVINGS!! PLEASE DON'T TELL ME—
AH, HA, HA, HA! WH-WHAT'RE YOU TALKING ABOUT, ANIKI?!
H-HERE, KONOKA-NĒSAN, COME BACK TO NORMAL BY TAKING ONE OF THESE BLUE...
'KAY! ♡
CRUNCH CRUNCH
BOMM
WHOA-HO-HOH!! KONOKA-NĒSAN'S A BABE—I MEAN, LITERALLY!!
GOO-GOO, GAH-GAH!
Y' KNOW WHAT, YOU GUYS? NEVER MIND...
YOU MEAN WELL—LET'S LEAVE IT AT THAT.
HEY, AKO! WHAT'S THAT BIG THING ON YOUR SHOULDER?! I THOUGHT WE WEREN'T DOING FESTIVAL STUFF TILL AFTERNOON...
HIYA! ♡
THE PLACE PROMISED IN OUR EARLY DAYS
IT'S FOR PRACTICE— KAKIZAKI AND THE OTHERS'VE INVITED ME TO PLAY WITH THEIR BAND, SO...
NOT THAT I HAVE THE TIME.
I BORROWED A BASS GUITAR.
YEAH, YOU SAID SOMETHING ABOUT THAT BEFORE...
I'M SO-O-O JEALOUS! ♡ LIVE PERFORMANCE, HUH? SOUNDS FUN!
WE'LL COME WATCH.
I'D COME PLAY TOO, BUT I'M HORRIBLE WITH INSTRUMENTS...
I COULD DANCE FOR YOU IN THE BACK-GROUND... ♪
UM, I DON'T THINK WE'LL NEED DANCERS...
THIS THING'S SO HEAVY, I SWEAR I...
BE CAREFUL!
AKO, LOOK OUT—!

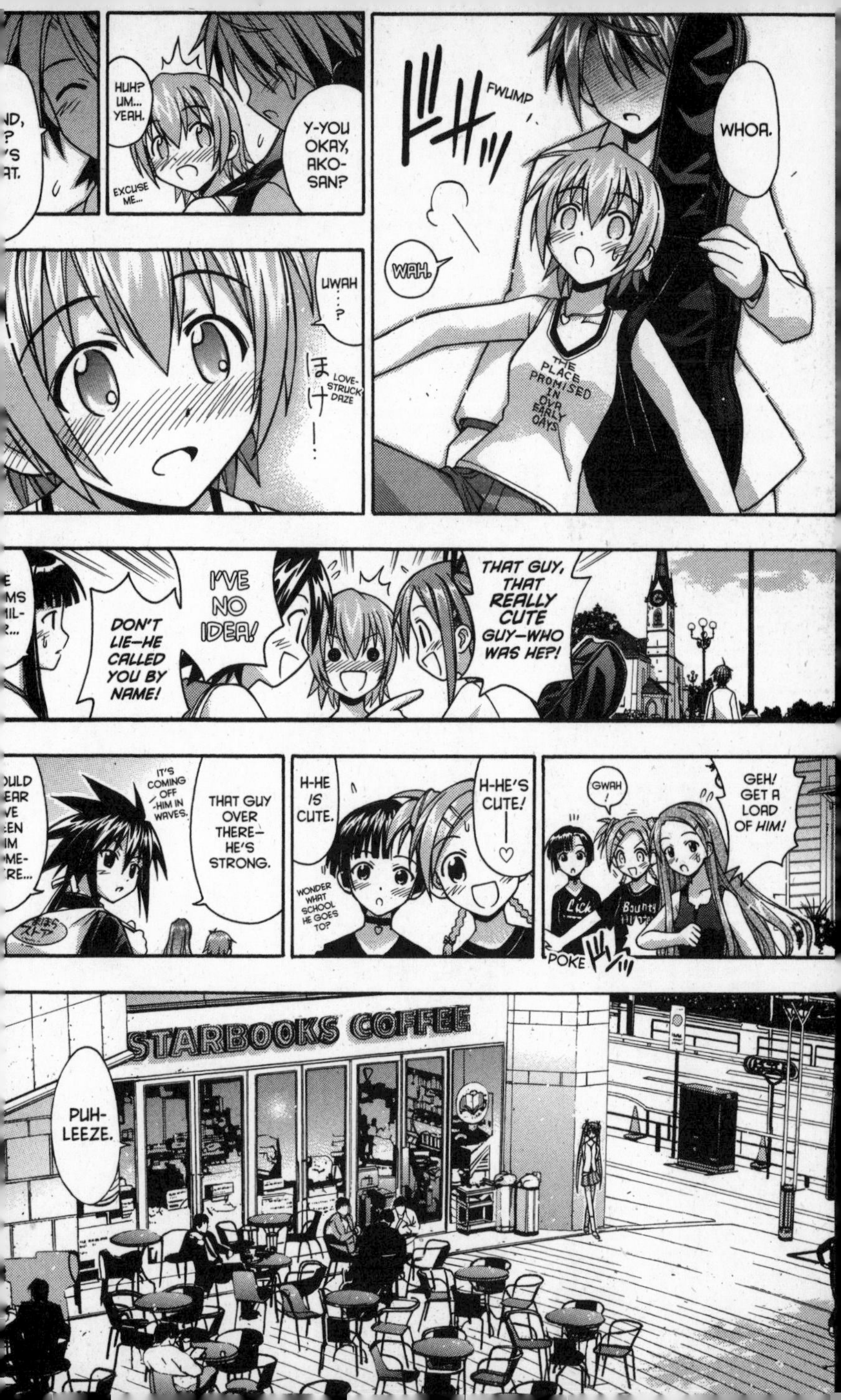
ドサッ
FWUMP
WHOA.
WAH.
Y-YOU OKAY, AKO-SAN?
HUH? UM... YEAH.
EXCUSE ME...
UWAH...?
ほけ!!
LOVE-STRUCK DAZE
THE PLACE PROMISED IN OUR EARLY DAYS
THAT GUY, THAT REALLY CUTE GUY—WHO WAS HE?!
I'VE NO IDEA!
DON'T LIE—HE CALLED YOU BY NAME!
GEH! GET A LOAD OF HIM!
GWAH!
POKE
H-HE'S CUTE! ♡
H-HE IS CUTE.
WONDER WHAT SCHOOL HE GOES TO?
THAT GUY OVER THERE—HE'S STRONG.
IT'S COMING OFF HIM IN WAVES.
STARBOOKS COFFEE
PUH-LEEZE.

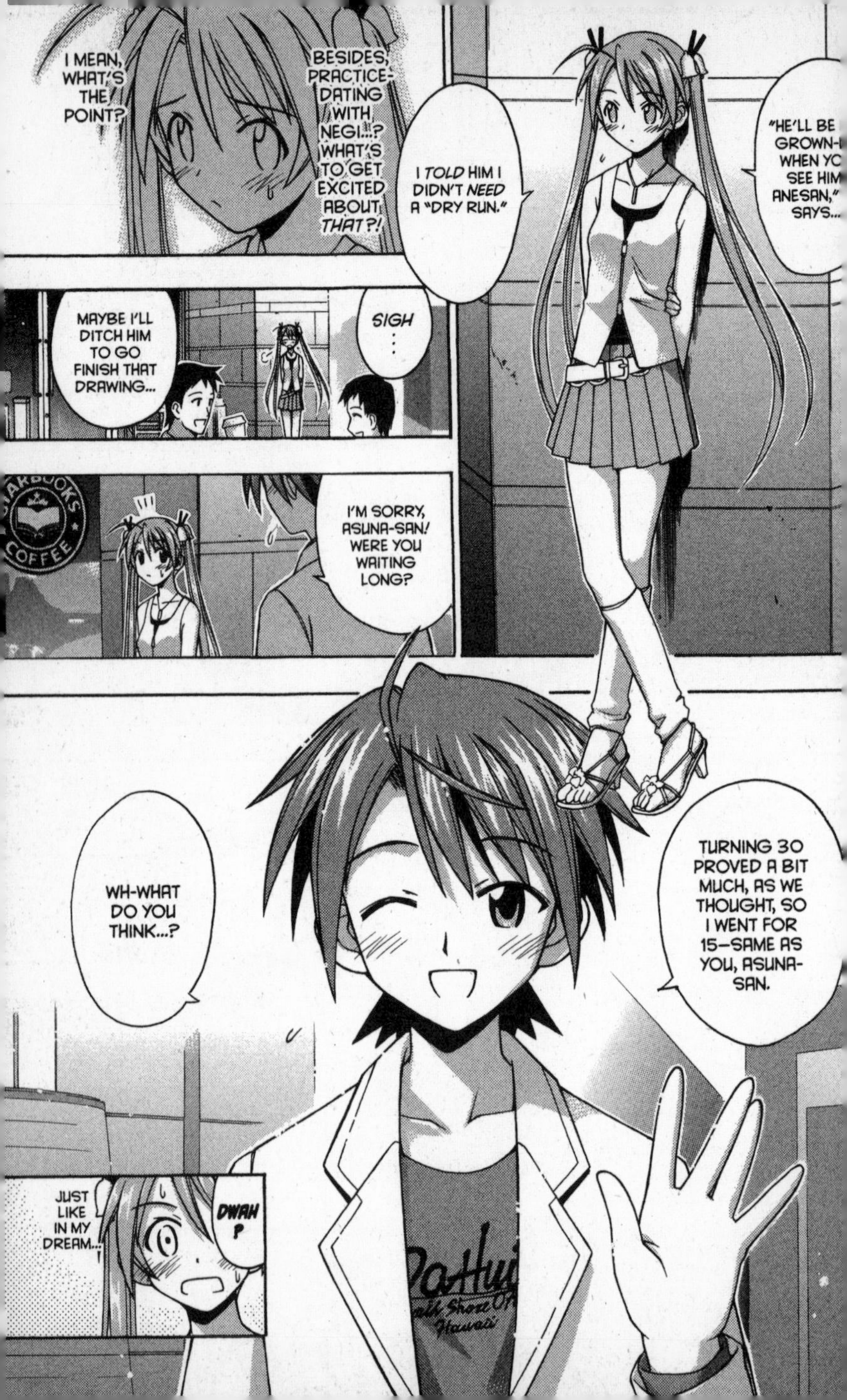
"HE'LL BE GROWN- WHEN YO SEE HIM ANESAN," SAYS...
I TOLD HIM I DIDN'T NEED A "DRY RUN."
BESIDES, PRACTICE-DATING WITH NEGI...? WHAT'S TO GET EXCITED ABOUT THAT?!
I MEAN, WHAT'S THE POINT?
SIGH . . .
MAYBE I'LL DITCH HIM TO GO FINISH THAT DRAWING...
I'M SORRY, ASUNA-SAN! WERE YOU WAITING LONG?
TURNING 30 PROVED A BIT MUCH, AS WE THOUGHT, SO I WENT FOR 15—SAME AS YOU, ASUNA-SAN.
WH-WHAT DO YOU THINK...?
DWAH?
JUST LIKE IN MY DREAM...

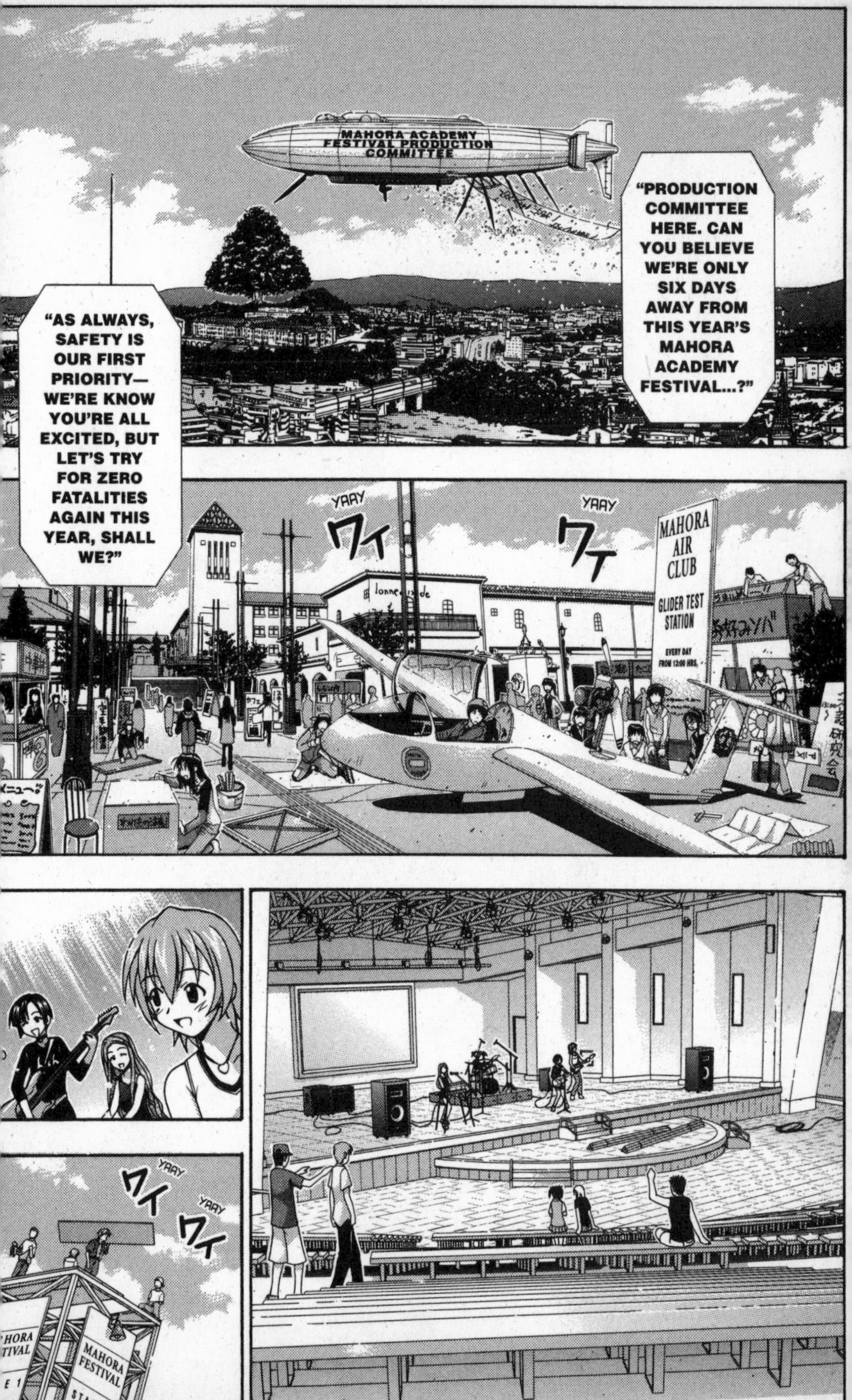
MAHORA ACADEMY FESTIVAL PRODUCTION COMMITTEE
"PRODUCTION COMMITTEE HERE. CAN YOU BELIEVE WE'RE ONLY SIX DAYS AWAY FROM THIS YEAR'S MAHORA ACADEMY FESTIVAL...?"
"AS ALWAYS, SAFETY IS OUR FIRST PRIORITY—WE'RE KNOW YOU'RE ALL EXCITED, BUT LET'S TRY FOR ZERO FATALITIES AGAIN THIS YEAR, SHALL WE?"
MAHORA AIR CLUB
GLIDER TEST STATION
EVERY DAY FROM 13:00 HRS.
YAAY
ワイ
YAAY
ワイ
YAAY
ワイ
YAAY
ワイ
MAHORA FESTIVAL

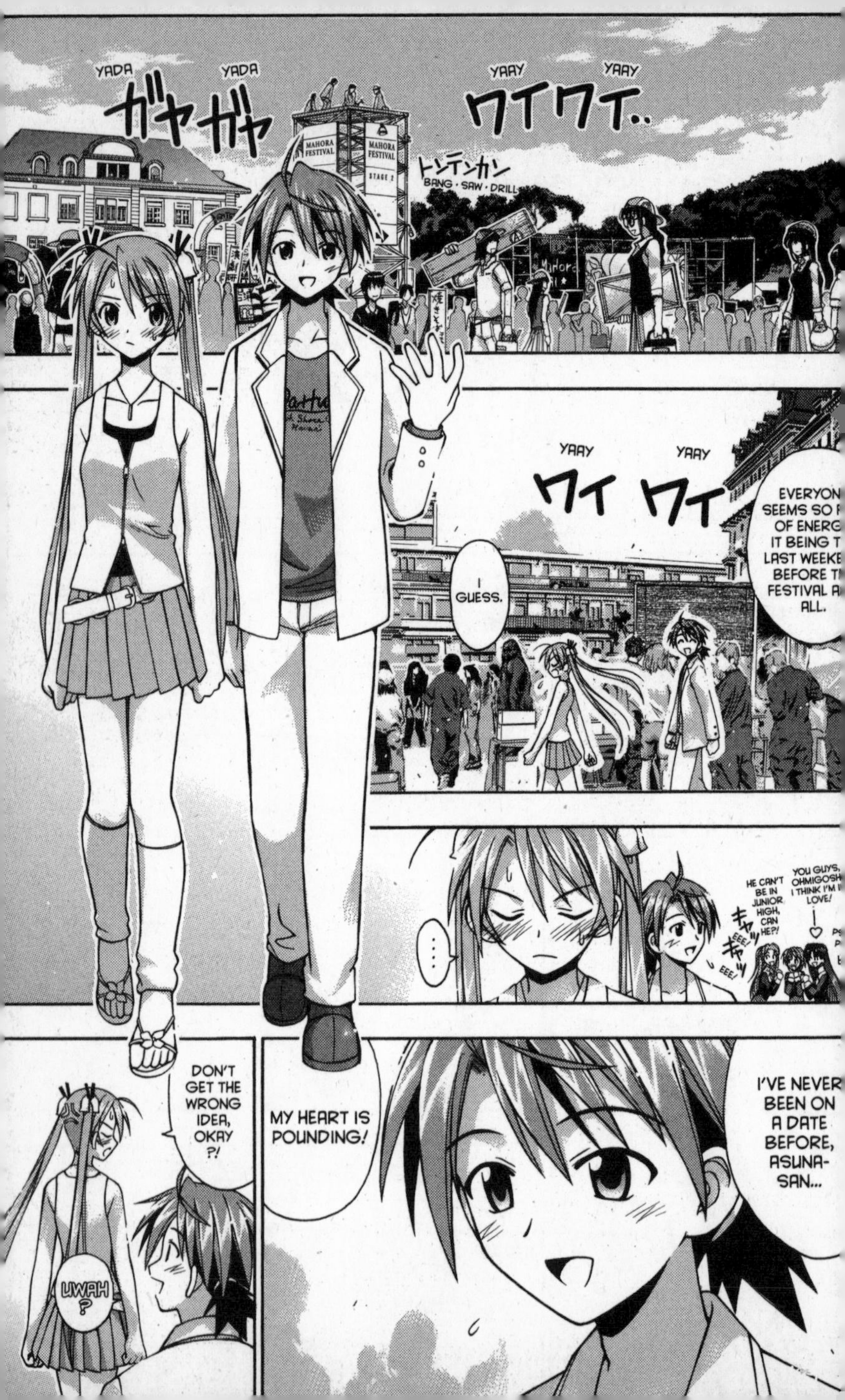
YAAY YAAY
ワイワイ..
トンテンカン
BANG・SAW・DRILL
YADA YADA
ガヤガヤ
MAHORA FESTIVAL
MAHORA FESTIVAL STAGE 2
YAAY YAAY
ワイ ワイ
EVERYON SEEMS SO F OF ENERG IT BEING T LAST WEEKE BEFORE T FESTIVAL A ALL.
I GUESS.
YOU GUYS, OHMIGOSH I THINK I'M IN LOVE!
HE CAN'T BE IN JUNIOR HIGH, CAN HE?!
キャッ EEE!
キャッ EEE!
....
I'VE NEVER BEEN ON A DATE BEFORE, ASUNA-SAN...
MY HEART IS POUNDING!
DON'T GET THE WRONG IDEA, OKAY ?!
UWAH ?

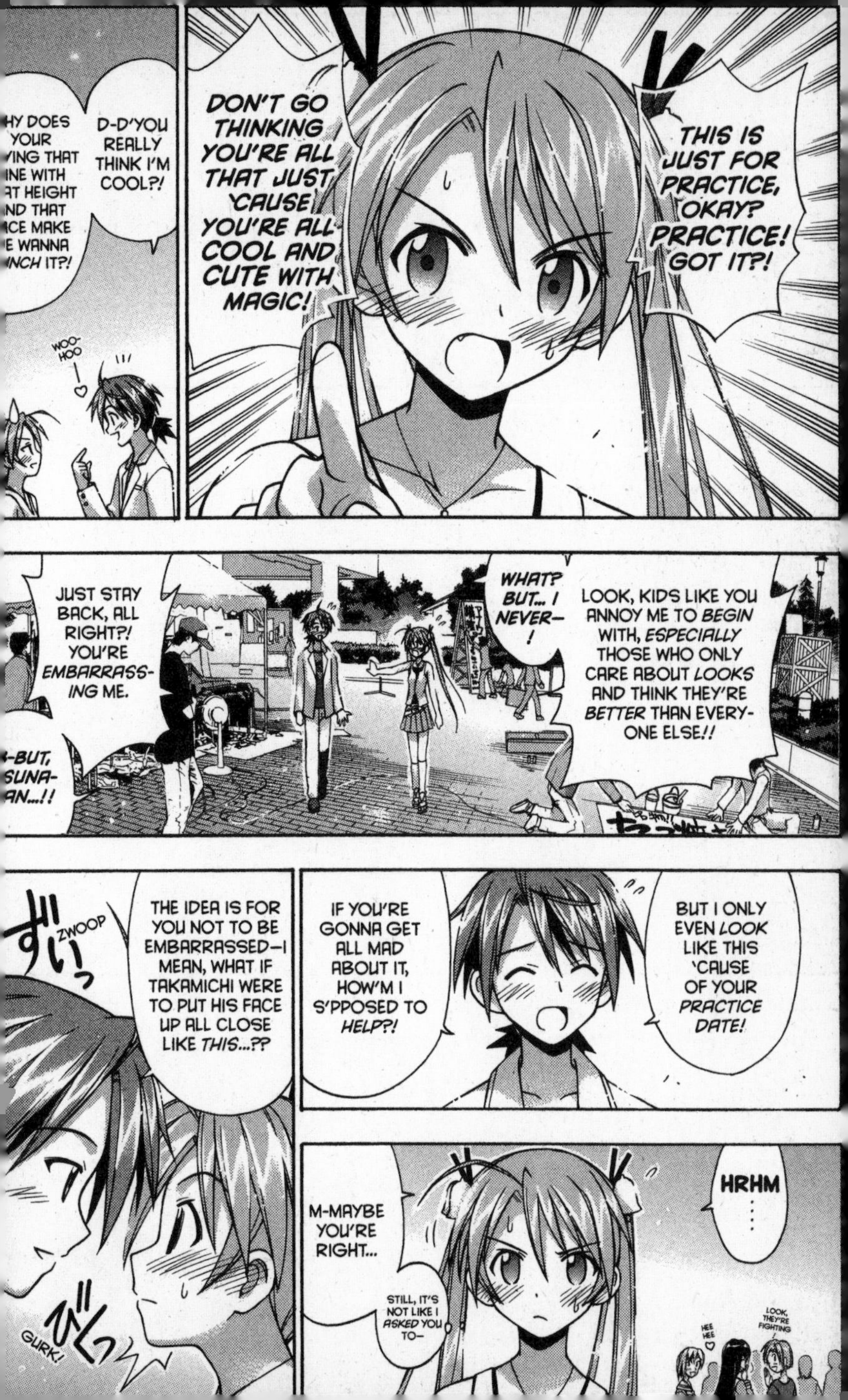
THIS IS JUST FOR PRACTICE, OKAY? PRACTICE! GOT IT?!
DON'T GO THINKING YOU'RE ALL THAT JUST 'CAUSE YOU'RE ALL COOL AND CUTE WITH MAGIC!
D-D'YOU REALLY THINK I'M COOL?!
HY DOES YOUR YING THAT INE WITH AT HEIGHT ND THAT ACE MAKE E WANNA NCH IT?!
WOO-HOO
LOOK, KIDS LIKE YOU ANNOY ME TO BEGIN WITH, ESPECIALLY THOSE WHO ONLY CARE ABOUT LOOKS AND THINK THEY'RE BETTER THAN EVERY-ONE ELSE!!
WHAT? BUT... I NEVER—!
JUST STAY BACK, ALL RIGHT?! YOU'RE EMBARRASS-ING ME.
-BUT, SUNA-AN...!!
BUT I ONLY EVEN LOOK LIKE THIS 'CAUSE OF YOUR PRACTICE DATE!
IF YOU'RE GONNA GET ALL MAD ABOUT IT, HOW'M I S'PPOSED TO HELP?!
HRHM ....
M-MAYBE YOU'RE RIGHT...
STILL, IT'S NOT LIKE I ASKED YOU TO—
LOOK, THEY'RE FIGHTING
HEE HEE
ずいっ ZWOOP
THE IDEA IS FOR YOU NOT TO BE EMBARRASSED—I MEAN, WHAT IF TAKAMICHI WERE TO PUT HIS FACE UP ALL CLOSE LIKE THIS...??
びくっ GURK!

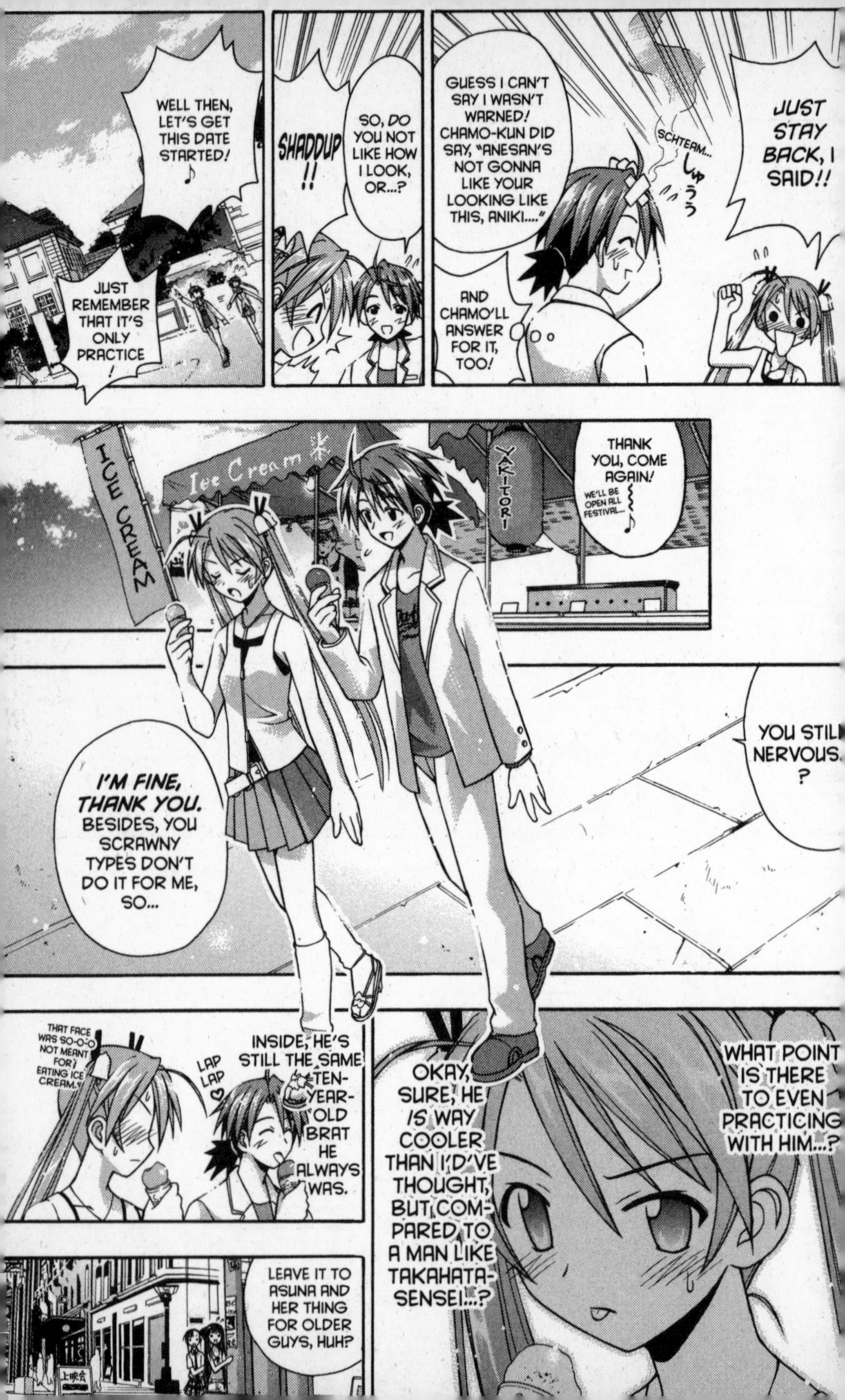
JUST STAY BACK, I SAID!!
SCHTEAM...
しゅうう
GUESS I CAN'T SAY I WASN'T WARNED! CHAMO-KUN DID SAY, "ANESAN'S NOT GONNA LIKE YOUR LOOKING LIKE THIS, ANIKI...."
AND CHAMO'LL ANSWER FOR IT, TOO!
SO, DO YOU NOT LIKE HOW I LOOK, OR...?
SHADDUP!!
WELL THEN, LET'S GET THIS DATE STARTED! ♪
JUST REMEMBER THAT IT'S ONLY PRACTICE!
THANK YOU, COME AGAIN!
WE'LL BE OPEN ALL FESTIVAL... ♪
YAKITORI
Ice Cream
ICE CREAM
YOU STIL NERVOUS. ?
I'M FINE, THANK YOU. BESIDES, YOU SCRAWNY TYPES DON'T DO IT FOR ME, SO...
WHAT POINT IS THERE TO EVEN PRACTICING WITH HIM...?
OKAY, SURE, HE IS WAY COOLER THAN I'D'VE THOUGHT, BUT COMPARED TO A MAN LIKE TAKAHATA-SENSEI...?
INSIDE, HE'S STILL THE SAME TEN-YEAR-OLD BRAT HE ALWAYS WAS.
LAP LAP ♡
THAT FACE WAS SO-O-O NOT MEANT FOR EATING ICE CREAM.
LEAVE IT TO ASUNA AND HER THING FOR OLDER GUYS, HUH?
上映会

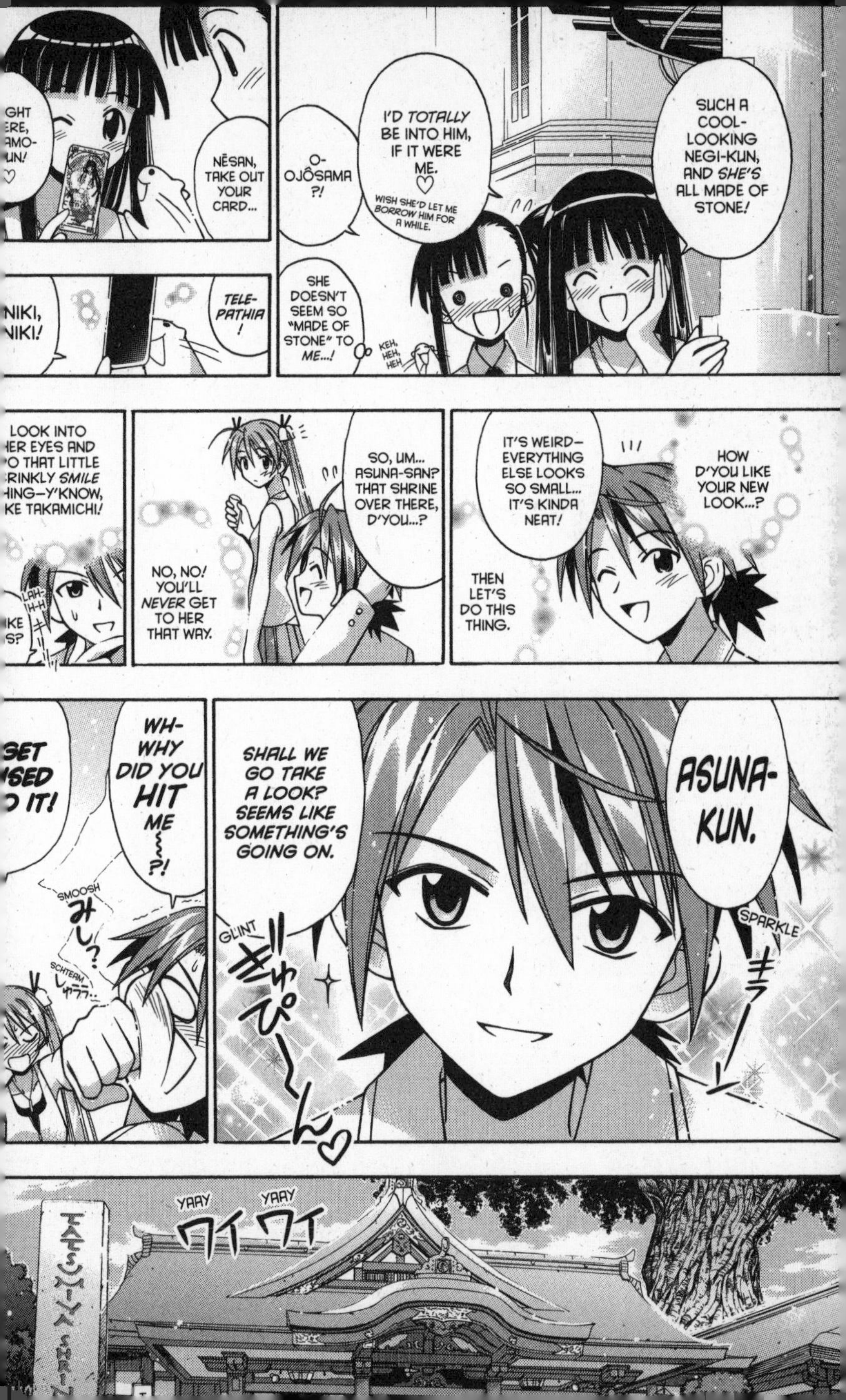

SUCH A COOL-LOOKING NEGI-KUN, AND SHE'S ALL MADE OF STONE!
I'D TOTALLY BE INTO HIM, IF IT WERE ME. ♡
WISH SHE'D LET ME BORROW HIM FOR A WHILE.
O-OJÔSAMA?!
SHE DOESN'T SEEM SO "MADE OF STONE" TO ME...!
KEH, HEH, HEH
NĒSAN, TAKE OUT YOUR CARD...
TELE-PATHIA!
HOW D'YOU LIKE YOUR NEW LOOK...?
IT'S WEIRD—EVERYTHING ELSE LOOKS SO SMALL... IT'S KINDA NEAT!
THEN LET'S DO THIS THING.
SO, UM... ASUNA-SAN? THAT SHRINE OVER THERE, D'YOU...?
NO, NO! YOU'LL NEVER GET TO HER THAT WAY.
LAH-H-H
ASUNA-KUN.
SPARKLE
SHALL WE GO TAKE A LOOK? SEEMS LIKE SOMETHING'S GOING ON.
GLINT
WH-WHY DID YOU HIT ME~~?!
SMOOSH
SCHTERM
YAAY
YAAY

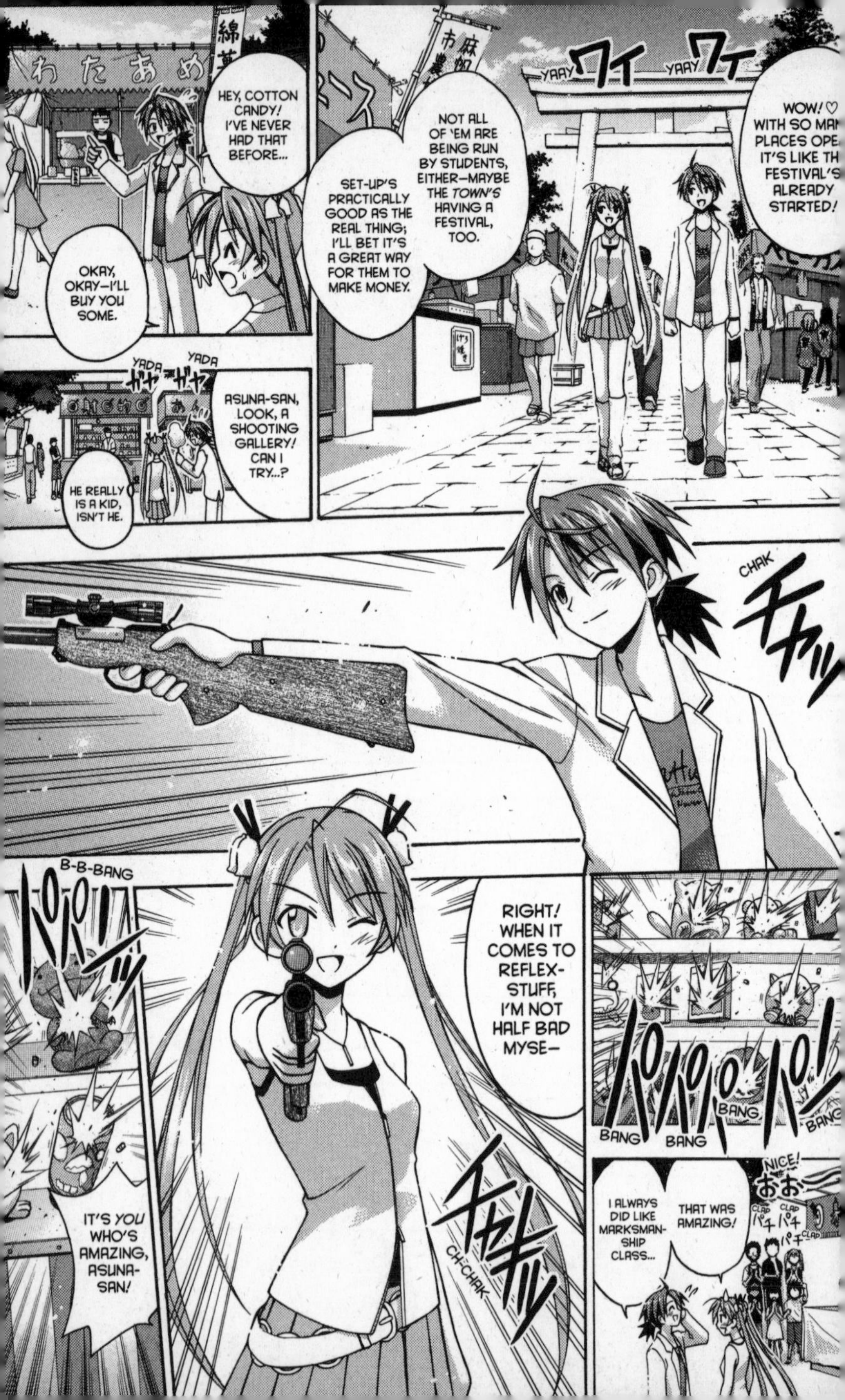
YAAY ワイ YAAY ワイ
WOW! ♡ WITH SO MAN PLACES OPE IT'S LIKE TH FESTIVAL'S ALREADY STARTED!
NOT ALL OF 'EM ARE BEING RUN BY STUDENTS, EITHER—MAYBE THE *TOWN'S* HAVING A FESTIVAL, TOO.
SET-UP'S PRACTICALLY GOOD AS THE REAL THING; I'LL BET IT'S A GREAT WAY FOR THEM TO MAKE MONEY.
わたあめ
HEY, COTTON CANDY! I'VE NEVER HAD THAT BEFORE...
OKAY, OKAY—I'LL BUY YOU SOME.
YADA ガヤ YADA ガヤ
ASUNA-SAN, LOOK, A SHOOTING GALLERY! CAN I TRY...?
HE REALLY IS A KID, ISN'T HE.
CHAK
BANG BANG BANG BANG
NICE! おお
CLAP パチ CLAP パチ パチ CLAP
THAT WAS AMAZING!
I ALWAYS DID LIKE MARKSMANSHIP CLASS...
RIGHT! WHEN IT COMES TO REFLEX-STUFF, I'M NOT HALF BAD MYSE—
CH-CHAK
B-B-BANG
IT'S *YOU* WHO'S AMAZING, ASUNA-SAN!

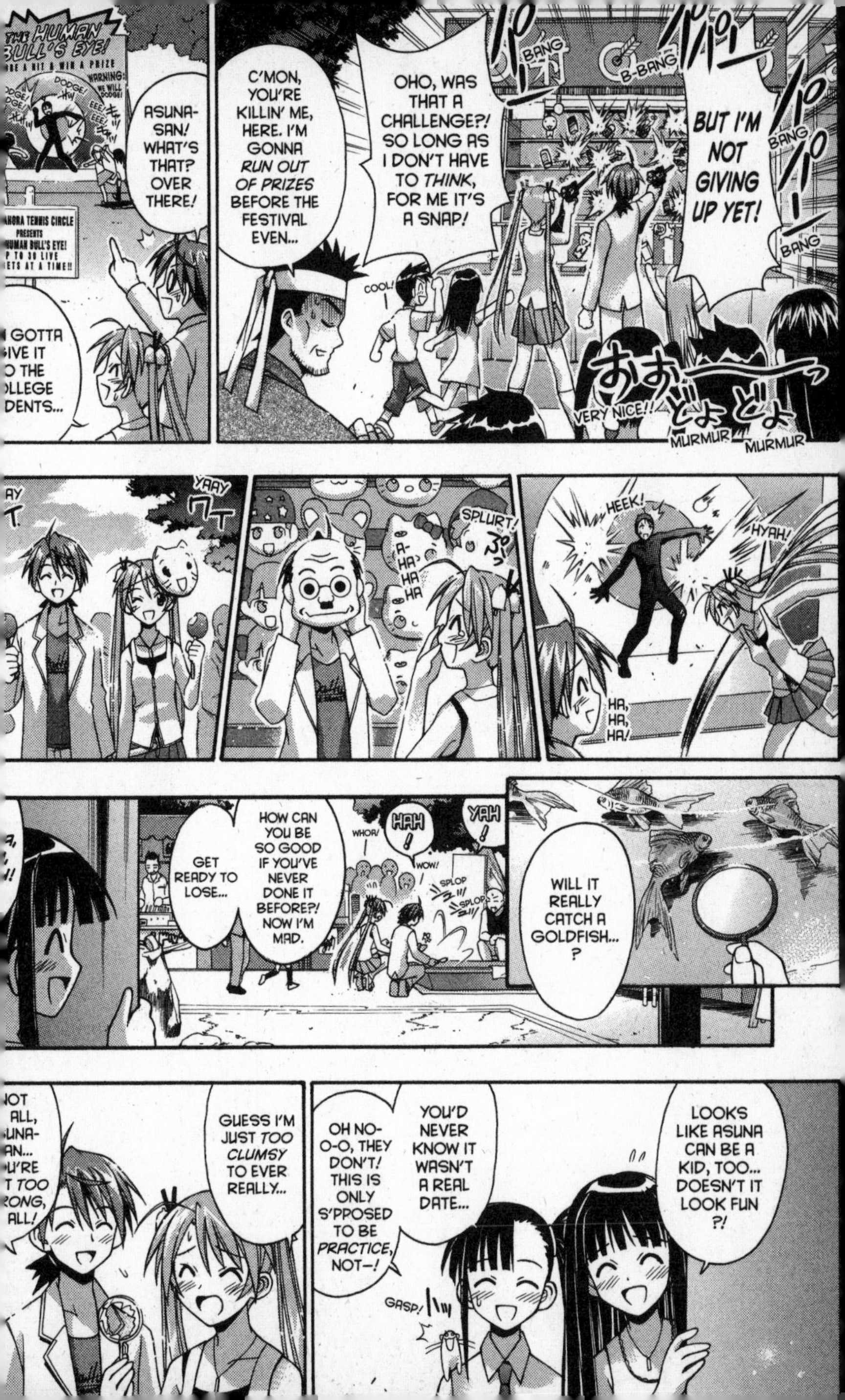
BANG
BUT I'M NOT GIVING UP YET!
B-BANG
BANG
OHO, WAS THAT A CHALLENGE?! SO LONG AS I DON'T HAVE TO *THINK*, FOR ME IT'S A SNAP!
C'MON, YOU'RE KILLIN' ME, HERE. I'M GONNA *RUN OUT OF PRIZES* BEFORE THE FESTIVAL EVEN...
COOL!
おお――っ
VERY NICE!!
どよどよ
MURMUR MURMUR
THE HUMAN BULL'S EYE!
WARNING:
ASUNA-SAN! WHAT'S THAT? OVER THERE!
HEEK!
HYAH!
HA, HA, HA!
SPLURT!
A-HA HA HA
YAAY
WILL IT REALLY CATCH A GOLDFISH...?
YAH!
HAH!
WHOA!
WOW!
SPLOP
SPLOP
HOW CAN YOU BE SO GOOD IF YOU'VE NEVER DONE IT BEFORE?! NOW I'M MAD.
GET READY TO LOSE...
LOOKS LIKE ASUNA CAN BE A KID, TOO... DOESN'T IT LOOK FUN?!
YOU'D NEVER KNOW IT WASN'T A REAL DATE...
OH NO-O-O, THEY DON'T! THIS IS ONLY S'PPOSED TO BE *PRACTICE*, NOT–!
GASP!
GUESS I'M JUST *TOO CLUMSY* TO EVER REALLY...

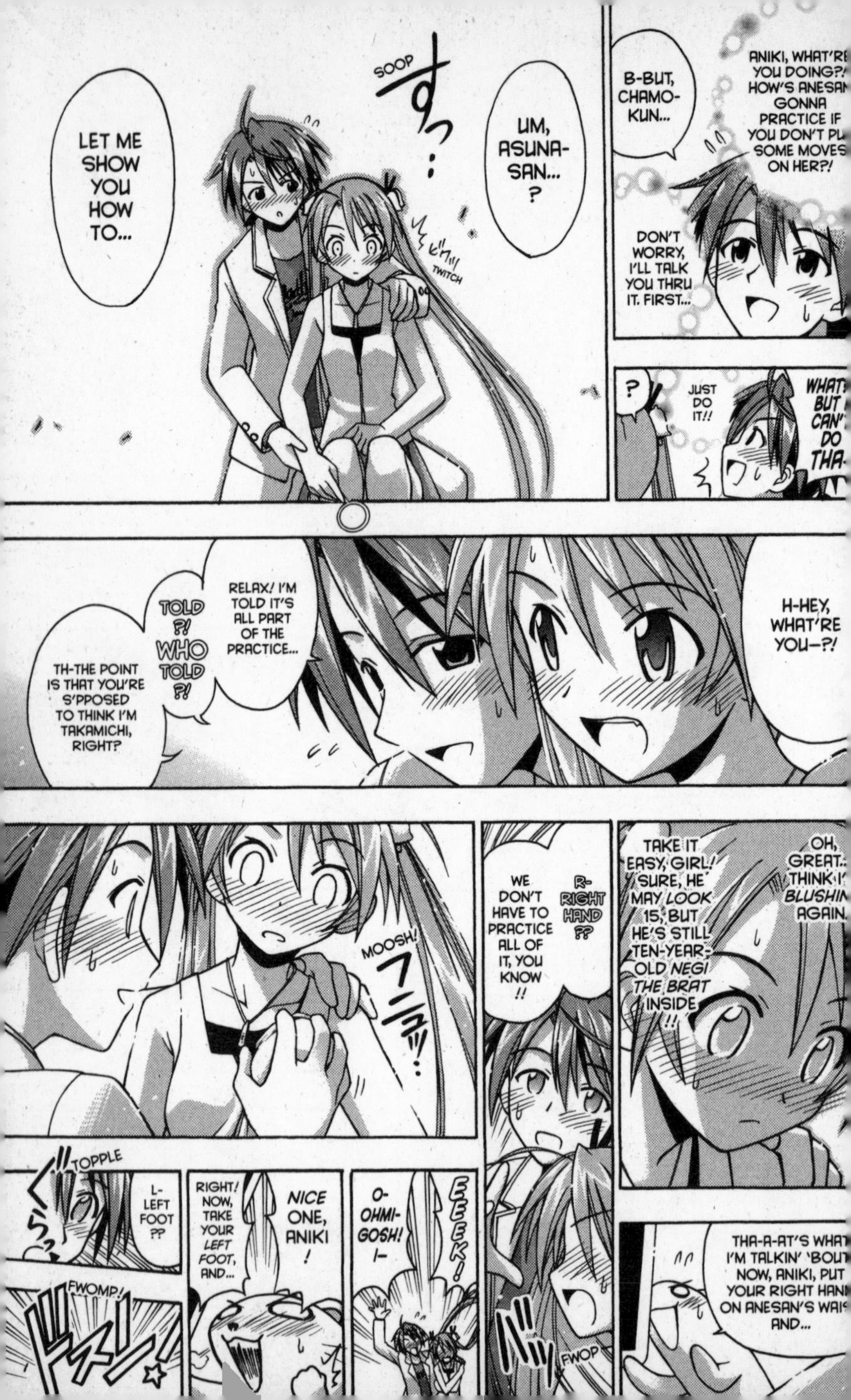
ANIKI, WHAT'RE YOU DOING?! HOW'S ANESAN GONNA PRACTICE IF YOU DON'T PU SOME MOVES ON HER?!
B-BUT, CHAMO-KUN...
DON'T WORRY, I'LL TALK YOU THRU IT. FIRST...
WHAT BUT CAN' DO THA-
JUST DO IT!!
?
SOOP
UM, ASUNA-SAN...?
TWITCH
LET ME SHOW YOU HOW TO...
H-HEY, WHAT'RE YOU-?!
RELAX! I'M TOLD IT'S ALL PART OF THE PRACTICE...
TOLD?! WHO TOLD?!
TH-THE POINT IS THAT YOU'RE S'PPOSED TO THINK I'M TAKAMICHI, RIGHT?
OH, GREAT... THINK I BLUSHIN AGAIN
TAKE IT EASY, GIRL! SURE, HE MAY *LOOK* 15, BUT HE'S STILL TEN-YEAR-OLD *NEGI THE BRAT* INSIDE!!
R-RIGHT HAND??
WE DON'T HAVE TO PRACTICE ALL OF IT, YOU KNOW!!
MOOSH!
THA-A-AT'S WHAT I'M TALKIN' 'BOUT NOW, ANIKI, PUT YOUR RIGHT HAN ON ANESAN'S WAIS AND...
FWOP
EEEEK!
O-OHMI-GOSH! I-
NICE ONE, ANIKI!
RIGHT! NOW, TAKE YOUR *LEFT FOOT*, AND...
L-LEFT FOOT??
TOPPLE
FWOMP!

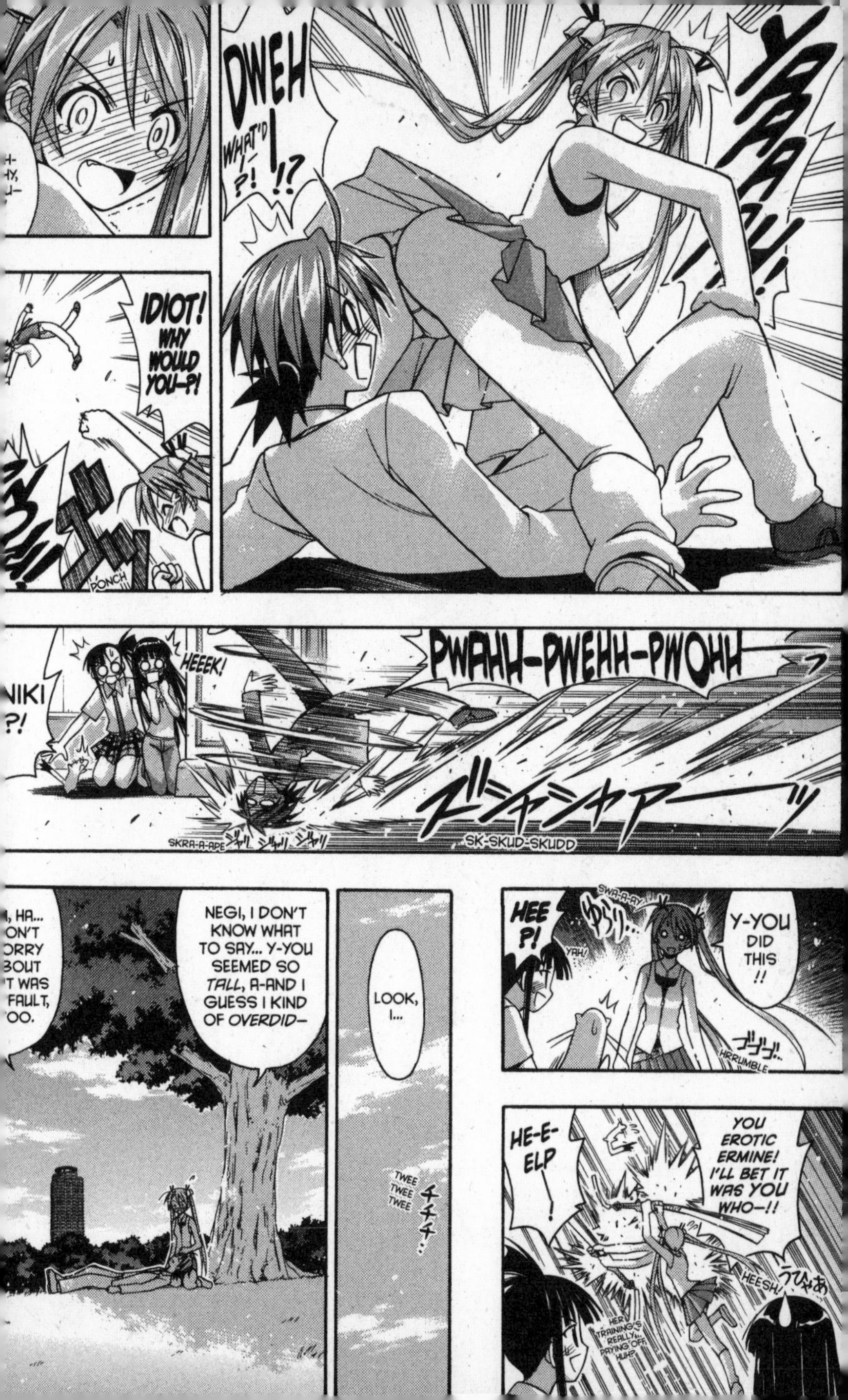
YAAAAH!!
DWEH
WHAT'D I—?!
!!?
IDIOT! WHY WOULD YOU—?!
PONCH
PWAHH-PWEHH-PWOHH
HEEEK!
NIKI ?!
SK-SKUD-SKUDD
SKRA-A-APE
SWA-A-AY
HEE ?!
YAH!
Y-YOU DID THIS !!
HRRUMBLE
YOU EROTIC ERMINE! I'LL BET IT WAS YOU WHO—!!
HE-E-ELP !
HEESH!
HER TRAINING'S REALLY... PAYING OFF, HUH?
LOOK, I...
TWEE TWEE TWEE
NEGI, I DON'T KNOW WHAT TO SAY... Y-YOU SEEMED SO TALL, A-AND I GUESS I KIND OF OVERDID—

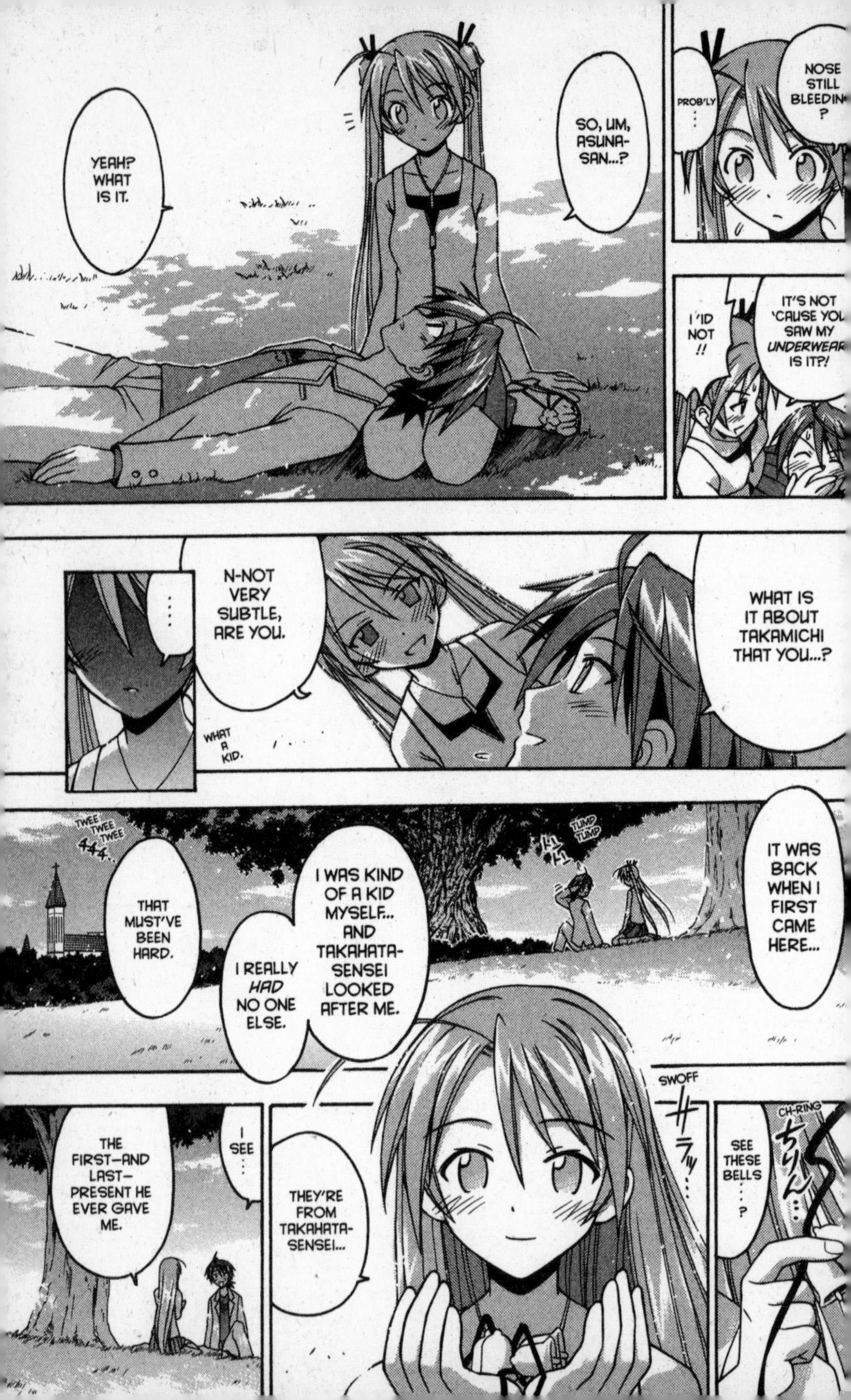
NOSE STILL BLEEDIN ?
PROB'LY ...
IT'S NOT 'CAUSE YOU SAW MY *UNDERWEAR* IS IT?!
I'ID NOT !!
SO, UM, ASUNA-SAN...?
YEAH? WHAT IS IT.
WHAT IS IT ABOUT TAKAMICHI THAT YOU...?
N-NOT VERY SUBTLE, ARE YOU.
WHAT A KID.
....
IT WAS BACK WHEN I FIRST CAME HERE...
TUMP TUMP
I WAS KIND OF A KID MYSELF... AND TAKAHATA-SENSEI LOOKED AFTER ME.
I REALLY *HAD* NO ONE ELSE.
THAT MUST'VE BEEN HARD.
TWEE TWEE TWEE
CH-RING
SEE THESE BELLS ...?
SWOFF
THEY'RE FROM TAKAHATA-SENSEI...
I SEE ...
THE FIRST—AND LAST—PRESENT HE EVER GAVE ME.

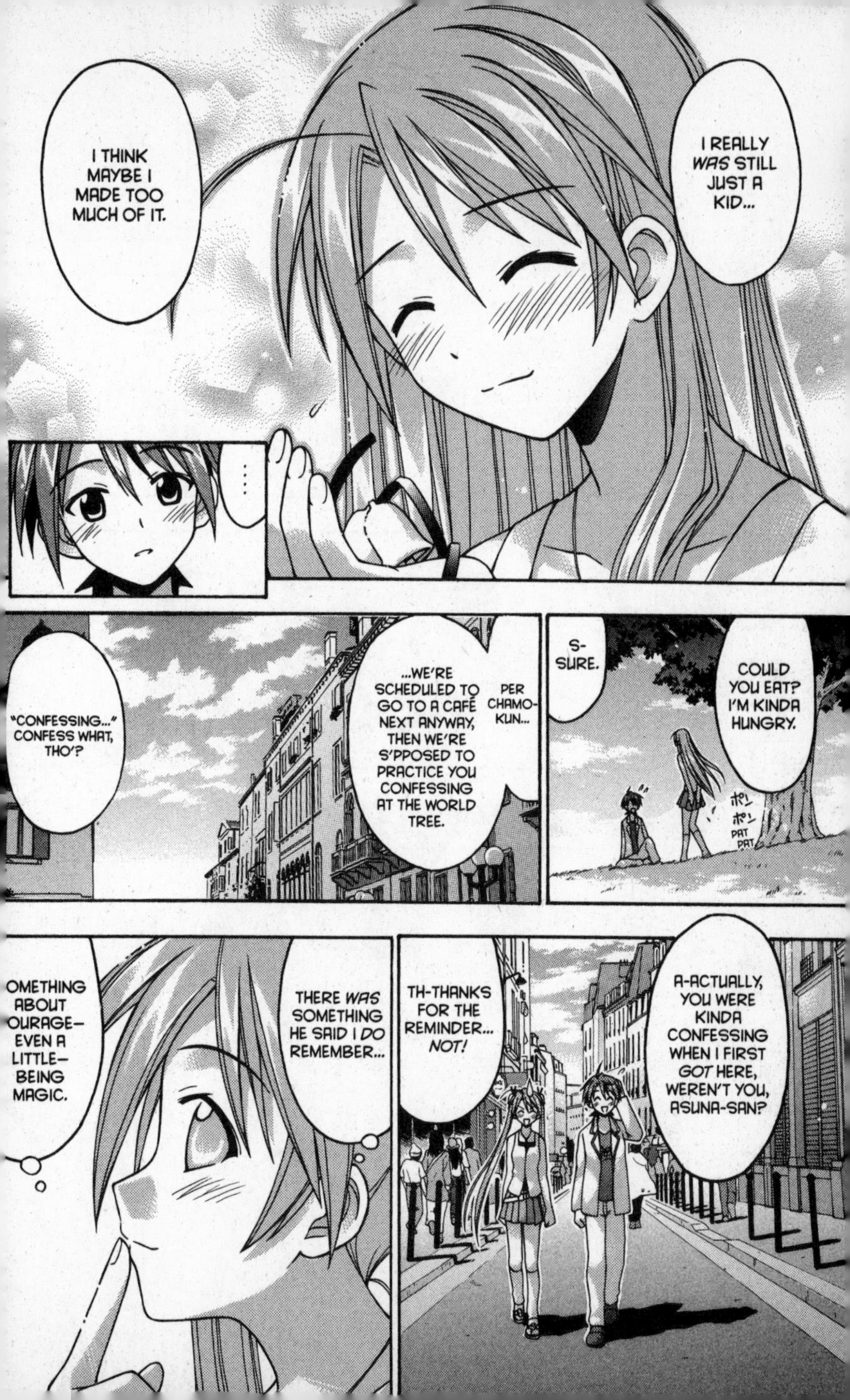
I REALLY *WAS* STILL JUST A KID...
I THINK MAYBE I MADE TOO MUCH OF IT.
...
COULD YOU EAT? I'M KINDA HUNGRY.
S-SURE.
ポン ポン
PAT PAT
PER CHAMO-KUN...
...WE'RE SCHEDULED TO GO TO A CAFÉ NEXT ANYWAY, THEN WE'RE S'PPOSED TO PRACTICE YOU CONFESSING AT THE WORLD TREE.
"CONFESSING..." CONFESS WHAT, THO'?
A-ACTUALLY, YOU WERE KINDA CONFESSING WHEN I FIRST *GOT* HERE, WEREN'T YOU, ASUNA-SAN?
TH-THANKS FOR THE REMINDER... *NOT!*
THERE *WAS* SOMETHING HE SAID I *DO* REMEMBER...
OMETHING ABOUT OURAGE— EVEN A LITTLE— BEING MAGIC.

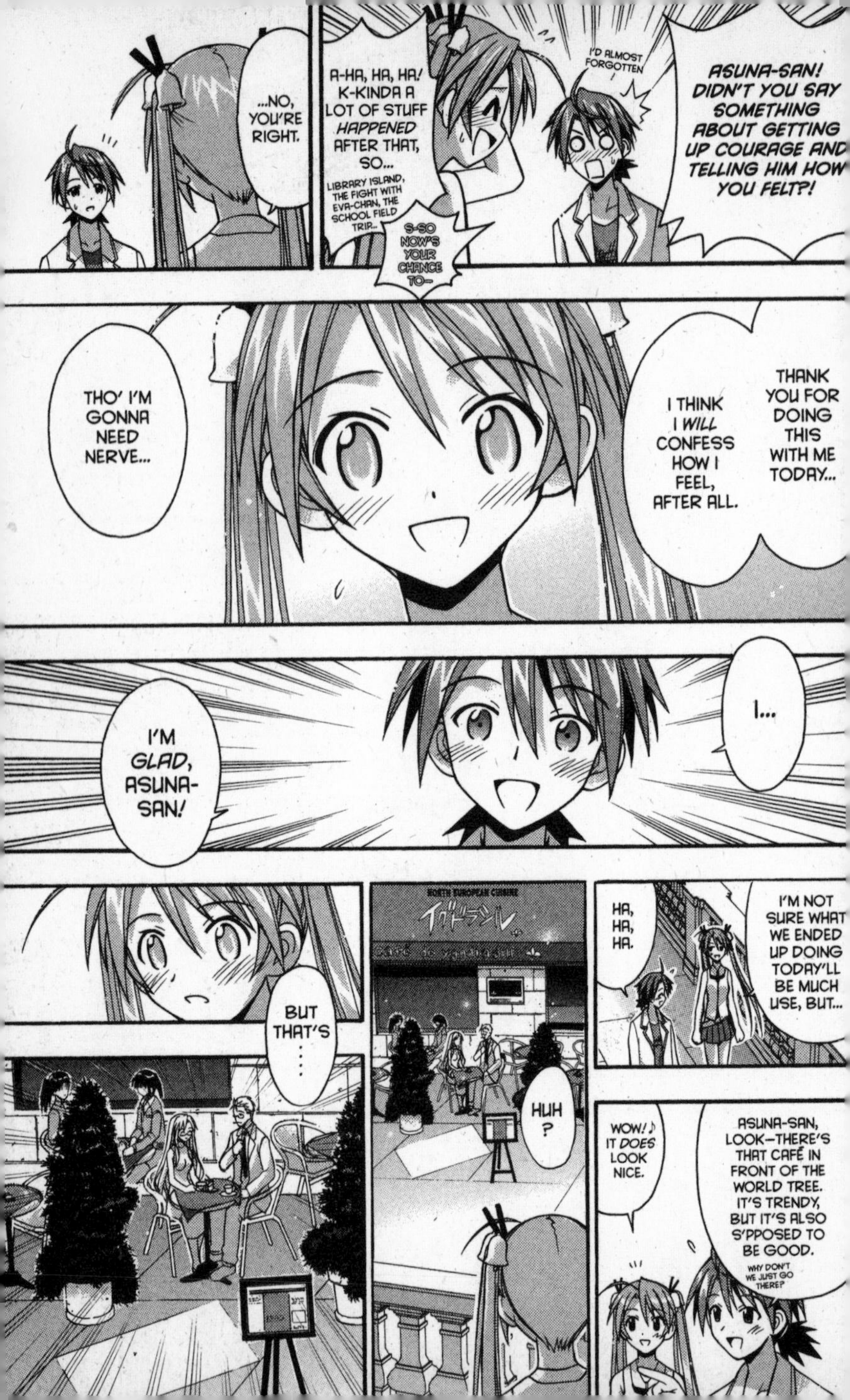
ASUNA-SAN! DIDN'T YOU SAY SOMETHING ABOUT GETTING UP COURAGE AND TELLING HIM HOW YOU FELT?!
I'D ALMOST FORGOTTEN
A-HA, HA, HA! K-KINDA A LOT OF STUFF *HAPPENED* AFTER THAT, SO...
LIBRARY ISLAND, THE FIGHT WITH EVA-CHAN, THE SCHOOL FIELD TRIP...
S-SO NOW'S YOUR CHANCE TO—
...NO, YOU'RE RIGHT.
THANK YOU FOR DOING THIS WITH ME TODAY...
I THINK I *WILL* CONFESS HOW I FEEL, AFTER ALL.
THO' I'M GONNA NEED NERVE...
I...
I'M *GLAD*, ASUNA-SAN!
I'M NOT SURE WHAT WE ENDED UP DOING TODAY'LL BE MUCH USE, BUT...
HA, HA, HA.
ASUNA-SAN, LOOK—THERE'S THAT CAFÉ IN FRONT OF THE WORLD TREE. IT'S TRENDY, BUT IT'S ALSO S'PPOSED TO BE GOOD.
WHY DON'T WE JUST GO THERE?
WOW!♪ IT *DOES* LOOK NICE.
NORTH EUROPEAN CUISINE
HUH?
BUT THAT'S ......

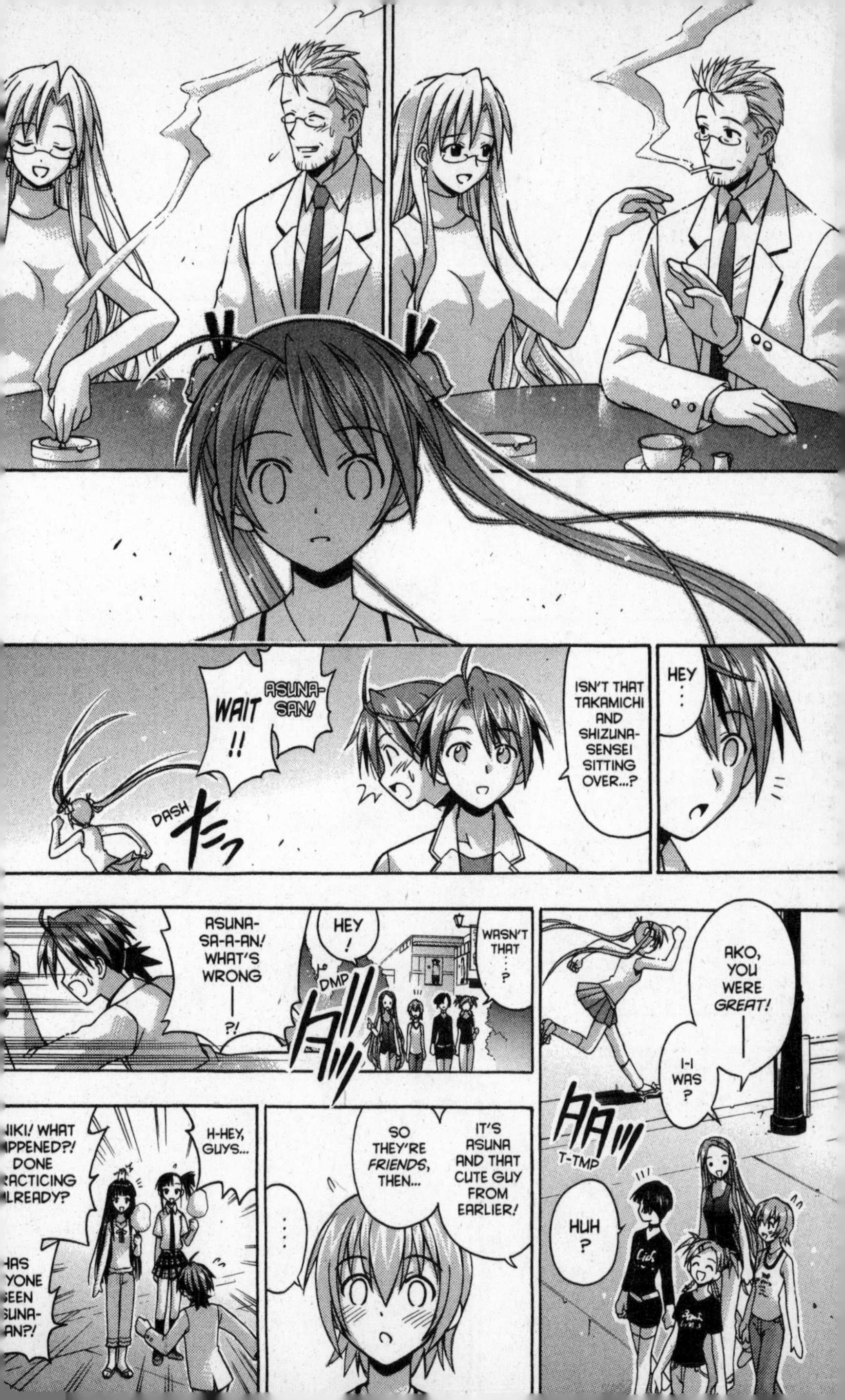
HEY...
ISN'T THAT TAKAMICHI AND SHIZUNA-SENSEI SITTING OVER...?
WAIT!! ASUNA-SAN!
DASH
AKO, YOU WERE GREAT! —
I-I WAS?
T-TMP
HUH?
WASN'T THAT...?
HEY!
DMP
ASUNA-SA-A-AN! WHAT'S WRONG—?!
IT'S ASUNA AND THAT CUTE GUY FROM EARLIER!
SO THEY'RE FRIENDS, THEN...
...
H-HEY, GUYS...
NIKI! WHAT APPENED?! DONE RACTICING LREADY?
HAS YONE EEN SUNA-AN?!

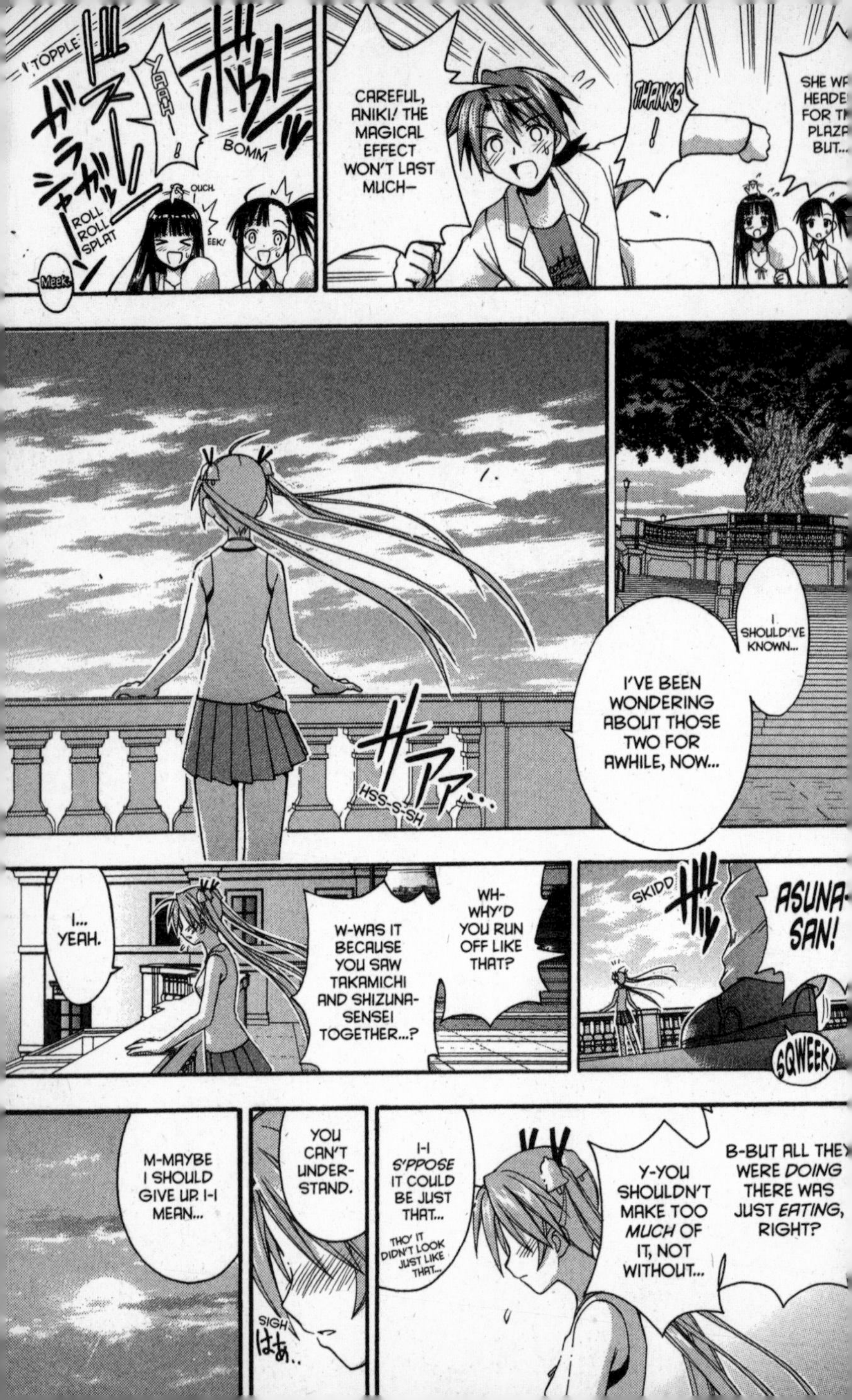

SHE WA HEADE FOR TH PLAZA BUT...
THANKS!
CAREFUL, ANIKI! THE MAGICAL EFFECT WON'T LAST MUCH—
TOPPLE
YAAAH!
BOMM
OUCH!
EEK!
ROLL ROLL SPLAT
Meek.
I SHOULD'VE KNOWN...
I'VE BEEN WONDERING ABOUT THOSE TWO FOR AWHILE, NOW...
HSS-S-SH
ASUNA-SAN!
SKIDD
SQWEEK!
WH-WHY'D YOU RUN OFF LIKE THAT?
W-WAS IT BECAUSE YOU SAW TAKAMICHI AND SHIZUNA-SENSEI TOGETHER...?
I... YEAH.
B-BUT ALL THEY WERE *DOING* THERE WAS JUST *EATING*, RIGHT?
Y-YOU SHOULDN'T MAKE TOO *MUCH* OF IT, NOT WITHOUT...
I-I *S'POSE* IT COULD BE JUST THAT...
THO' IT DIDN'T LOOK JUST LIKE THAT...
YOU CAN'T UNDER-STAND.
SIGH
はぁ..
M-MAYBE I SHOULD GIVE UP. I-I MEAN...

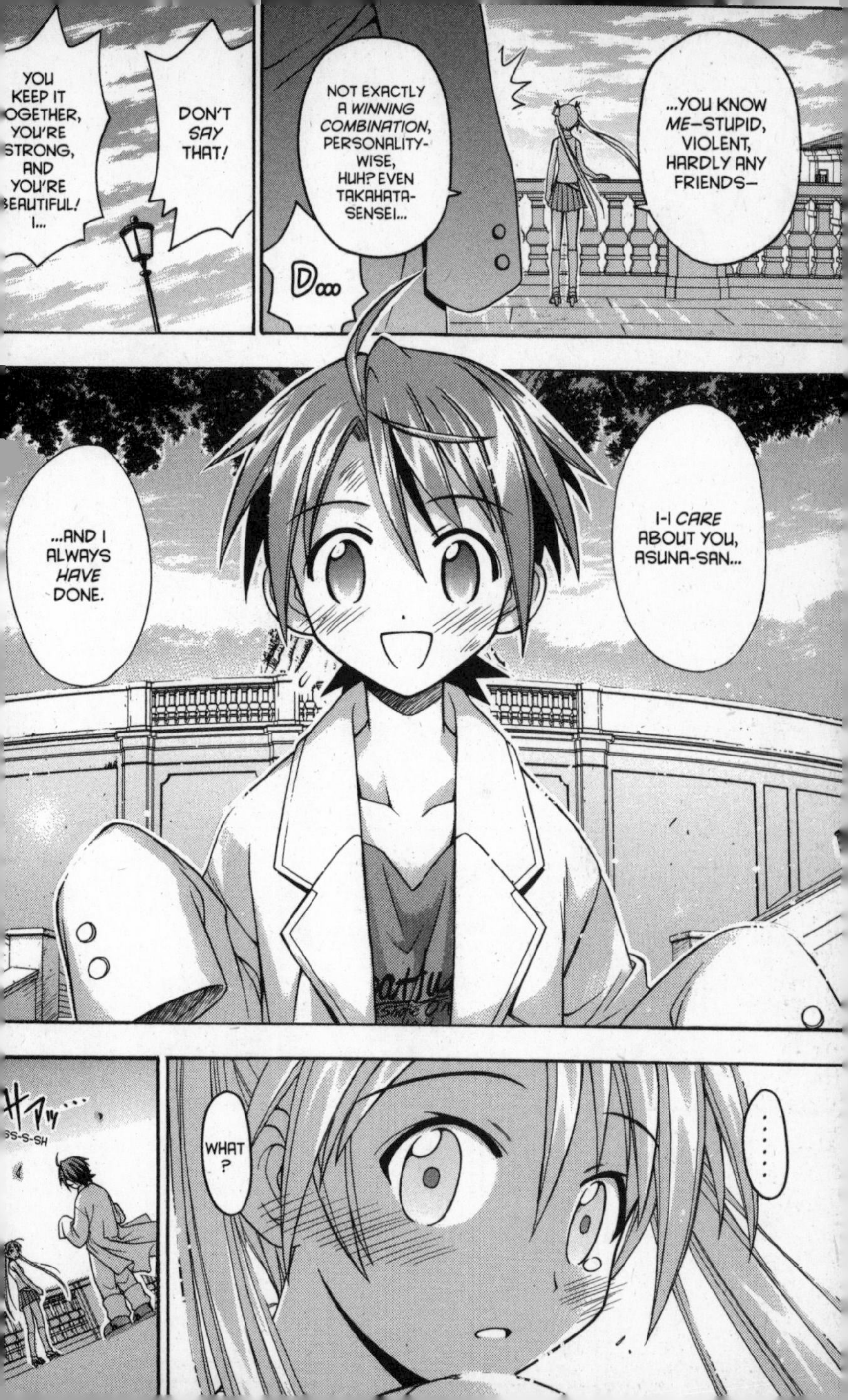
...YOU KNOW *ME*—STUPID, VIOLENT, HARDLY ANY FRIENDS—
NOT EXACTLY A *WINNING COMBINATION*, PERSONALITY-WISE, HUH? EVEN TAKAHATA-SENSEI...
Dooo
DON'T *SAY* THAT!
YOU KEEP IT OGETHER, YOU'RE STRONG, AND YOU'RE BEAUTIFUL! I...
I-I *CARE* ABOUT YOU, ASUNA-SAN...
...AND I ALWAYS *HAVE* DONE.
......
WHAT ?
SS-S-SH

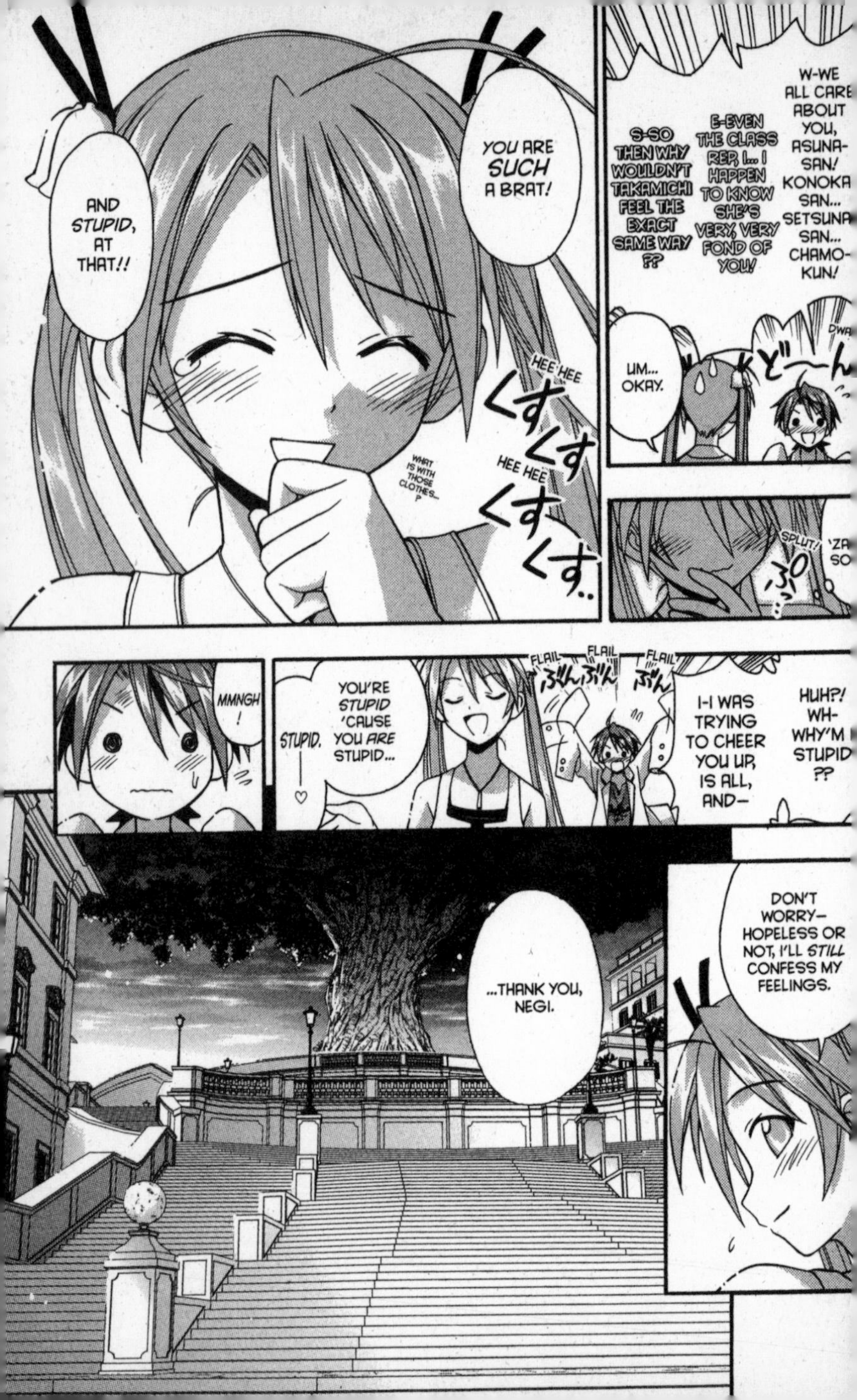
W-WE ALL CARE ABOUT YOU, ASUNA-SAN! KONOKA-SAN... SETSUNA-SAN... CHAMO-KUN!
E-EVEN THE CLASS REP, I... I HAPPEN TO KNOW SHE'S VERY, VERY FOND OF YOU!
S-SO THEN WHY WOULDN'T TAKAMICHI FEEL THE EXACT SAME WAY??
DWA
どーん
UM... OKAY.
'ZA SO
SPLUT!
ぷっ
YOU ARE SUCH A BRAT!
AND STUPID, AT THAT!!
HEE HEE
くすくす
HEE HEE
くすくす..
WHAT IS WITH THOSE CLOTHES...?
HUH?! WH-WHY'M I STUPID??
I-I WAS TRYING TO CHEER YOU UP, IS ALL, AND—
FLAIL FLAIL FLAIL
ぶんぶんぶん
YOU'RE STUPID 'CAUSE YOU ARE STUPID...
STUPID. ♡
MMNGH!
DON'T WORRY—HOPELESS OR NOT, I'LL STILL CONFESS MY FEELINGS.
...THANK YOU, NEGI.

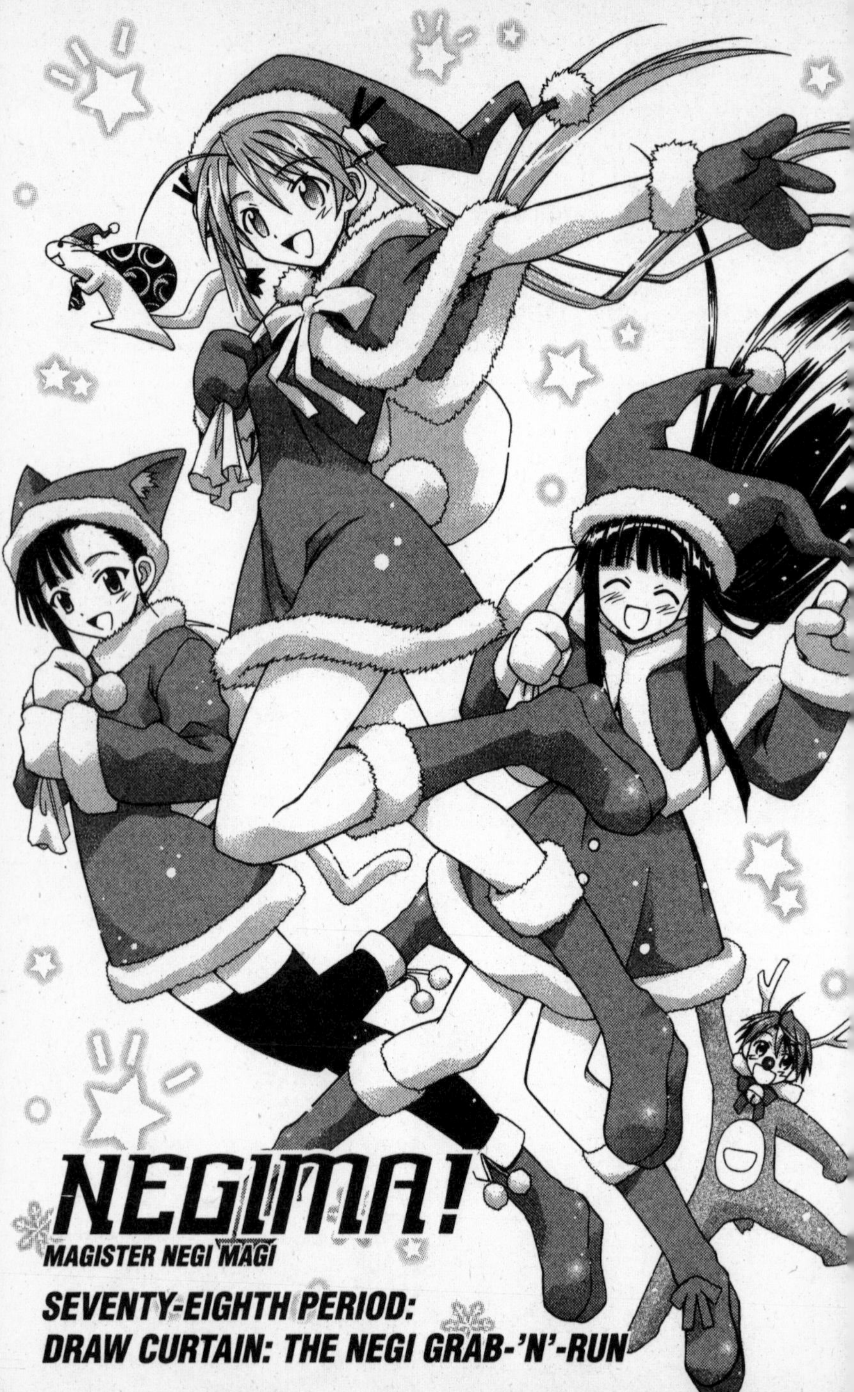

NEGIMA!
MAGISTER NEGI MAGI

SEVENTY-EIGHTH PERIOD: DRAW CURTAIN: THE NEGI GRAB-'N'-RUN

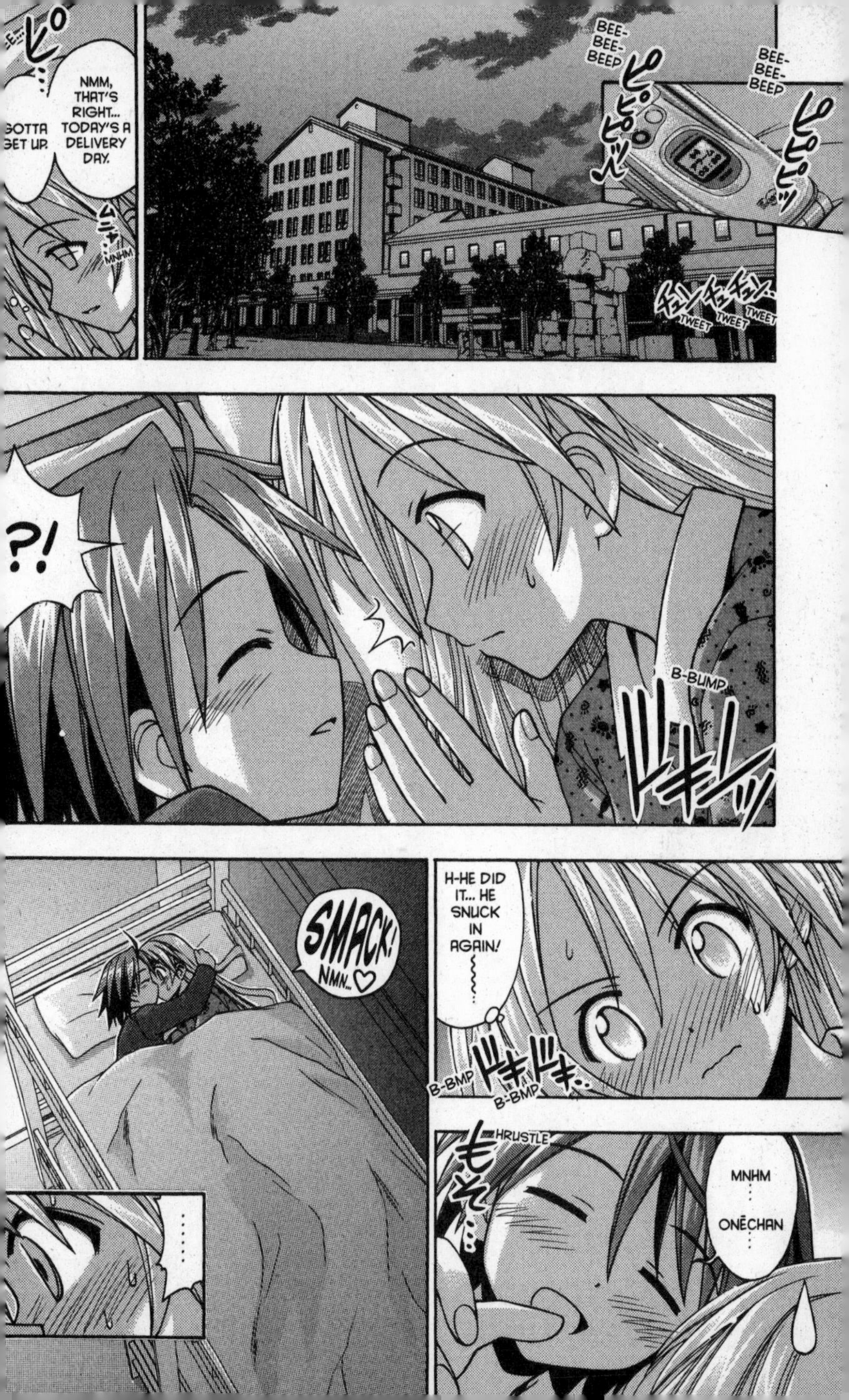

BEE-BEE-BEEP
BEE-BEE-BEEP
TWEET TWEET TWEET
NMM, THAT'S RIGHT... TODAY'S A DELIVERY DAY.
GOTTA GET UP.
MNHM
?!
B-BUMP
H-HE DID IT... HE SNUCK IN AGAIN!
B-BMP B-BMP
HRUSTLE
MNHM... ONĒCHAN...
SMACK!
NMN...♡
......

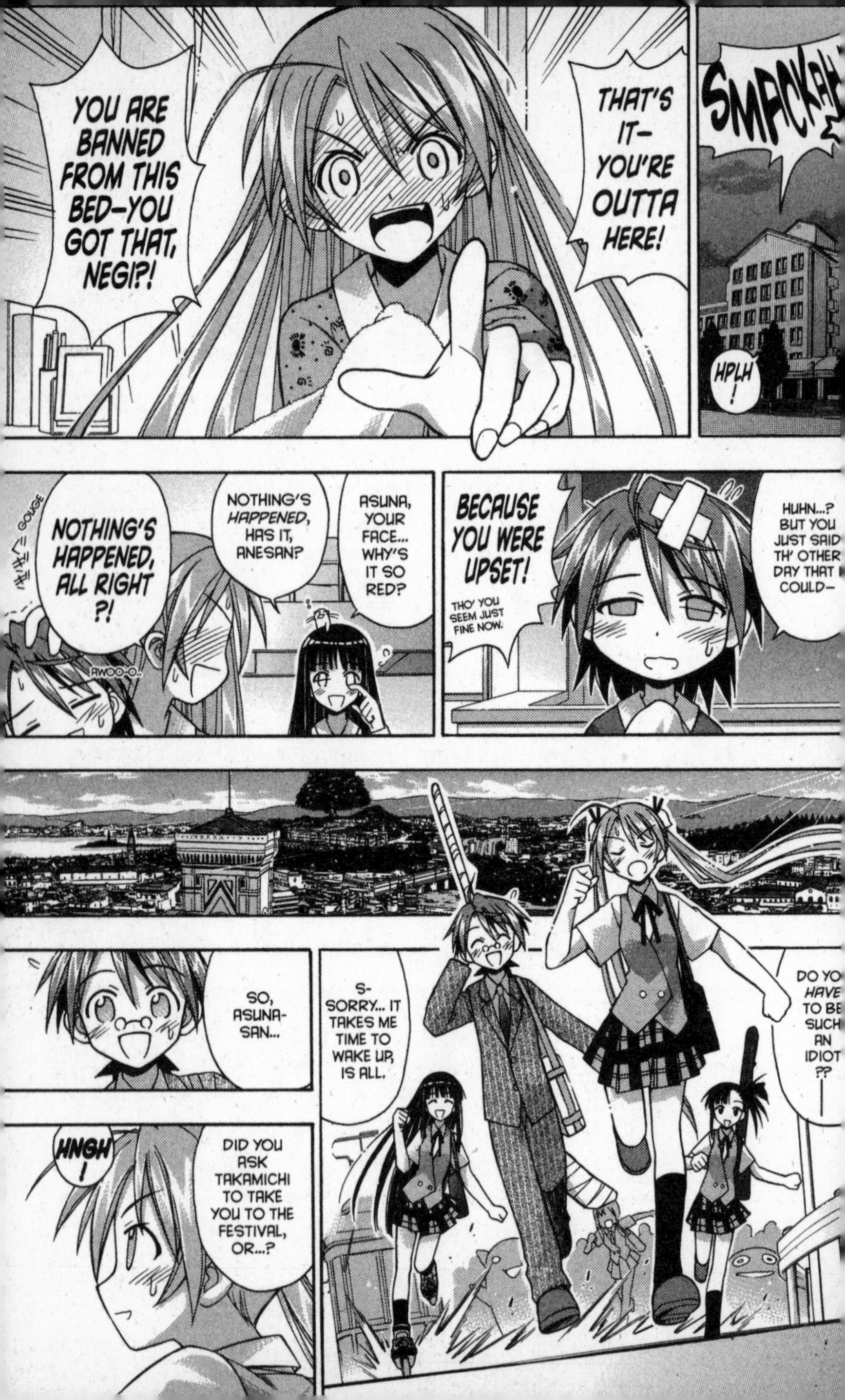
SMACKAH
HPLH!
THAT'S IT— YOU'RE OUTTA HERE!
YOU ARE BANNED FROM THIS BED—YOU GOT THAT, NEGI?!
HUHN...? BUT YOU JUST SAID TH' OTHER DAY THAT I COULD—
BECAUSE YOU WERE UPSET!
THO' YOU SEEM JUST FINE NOW.
ASUNA, YOUR FACE... WHY'S IT SO RED?
NOTHING'S HAPPENED, HAS IT, ANESAN?
NOTHING'S HAPPENED, ALL RIGHT?!
AWOO-O..
GOUGE
DO YO HAVE TO BE SUCH AN IDIOT??
S-SORRY... IT TAKES ME TIME TO WAKE UP, IS ALL.
SO, ASUNA-SAN...
HNGH!
DID YOU ASK TAKAMICHI TO TAKE YOU TO THE FESTIVAL, OR...?

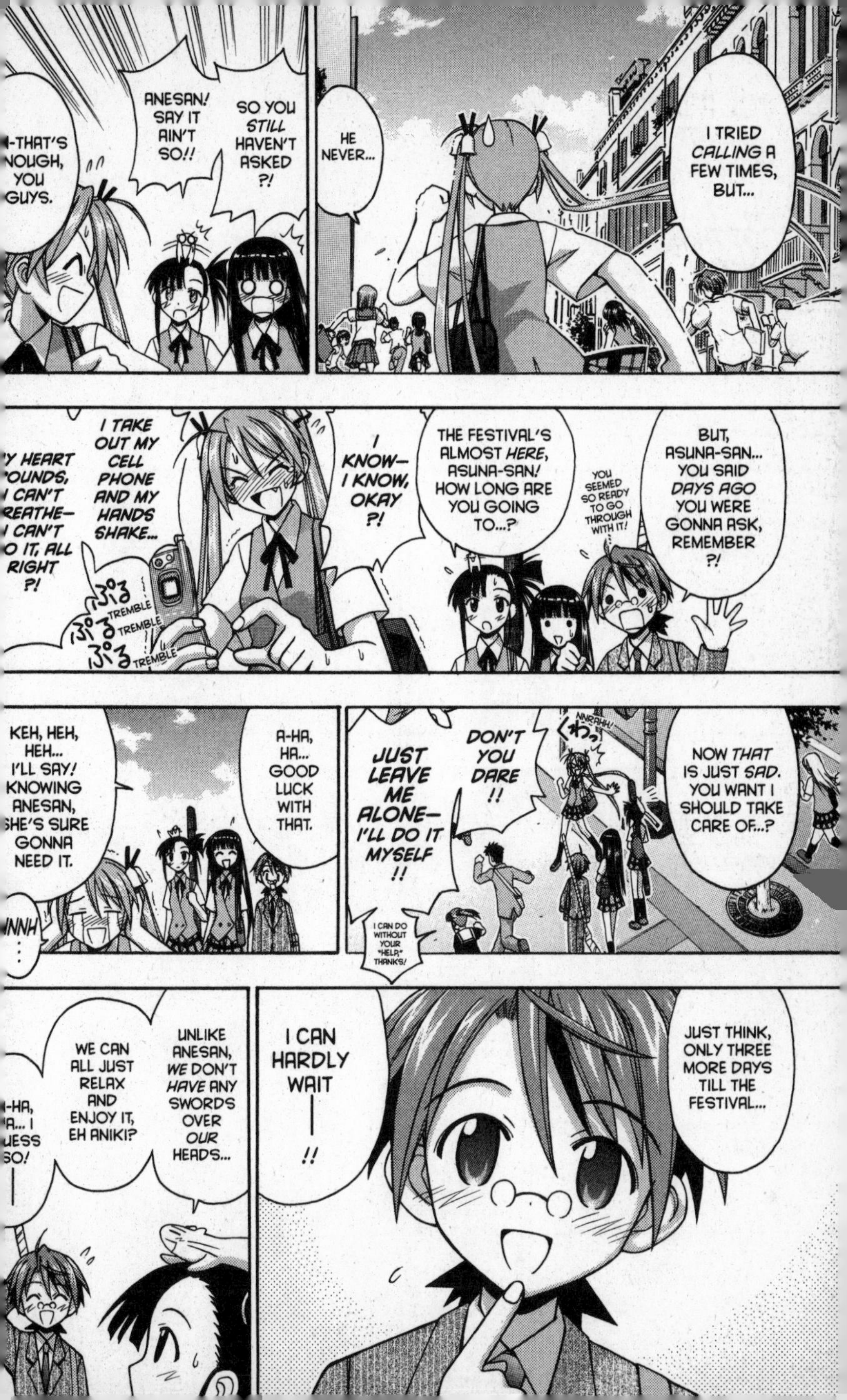
I TRIED CALLING A FEW TIMES, BUT...
HE NEVER...
SO YOU STILL HAVEN'T ASKED ?!
ANESAN! SAY IT AIN'T SO!!
-THAT'S NOUGH, YOU GUYS.
BUT, ASUNA-SAN... YOU SAID DAYS AGO YOU WERE GONNA ASK, REMEMBER ?!
YOU SEEMED SO READY TO GO THROUGH WITH IT!
THE FESTIVAL'S ALMOST HERE, ASUNA-SAN! HOW LONG ARE YOU GOING TO...?
I KNOW— I KNOW, OKAY ?!
I TAKE OUT MY CELL PHONE AND MY HANDS SHAKE...
Y HEART OUNDS, I CAN'T REATHE— I CAN'T O IT, ALL RIGHT ?!
ぷる TREMBLE
ぷる TREMBLE
ぷる TREMBLE
NOW THAT IS JUST SAD. YOU WANT I SHOULD TAKE CARE OF...?
くわっ NNRAHH!
DON'T YOU DARE !!
JUST LEAVE ME ALONE— I'LL DO IT MYSELF !!
I CAN DO WITHOUT YOUR "HELP," THANKS!
A-HA, HA... GOOD LUCK WITH THAT.
KEH, HEH, HEH... I'LL SAY! KNOWING ANESAN, HE'S SURE GONNA NEED IT.
NNH ...
JUST THINK, ONLY THREE MORE DAYS TILL THE FESTIVAL...
I CAN HARDLY WAIT — !!
UNLIKE ANESAN, WE DON'T HAVE ANY SWORDS OVER OUR HEADS...
WE CAN ALL JUST RELAX AND ENJOY IT, EH ANIKI?
-HA, A... I UESS SO! —

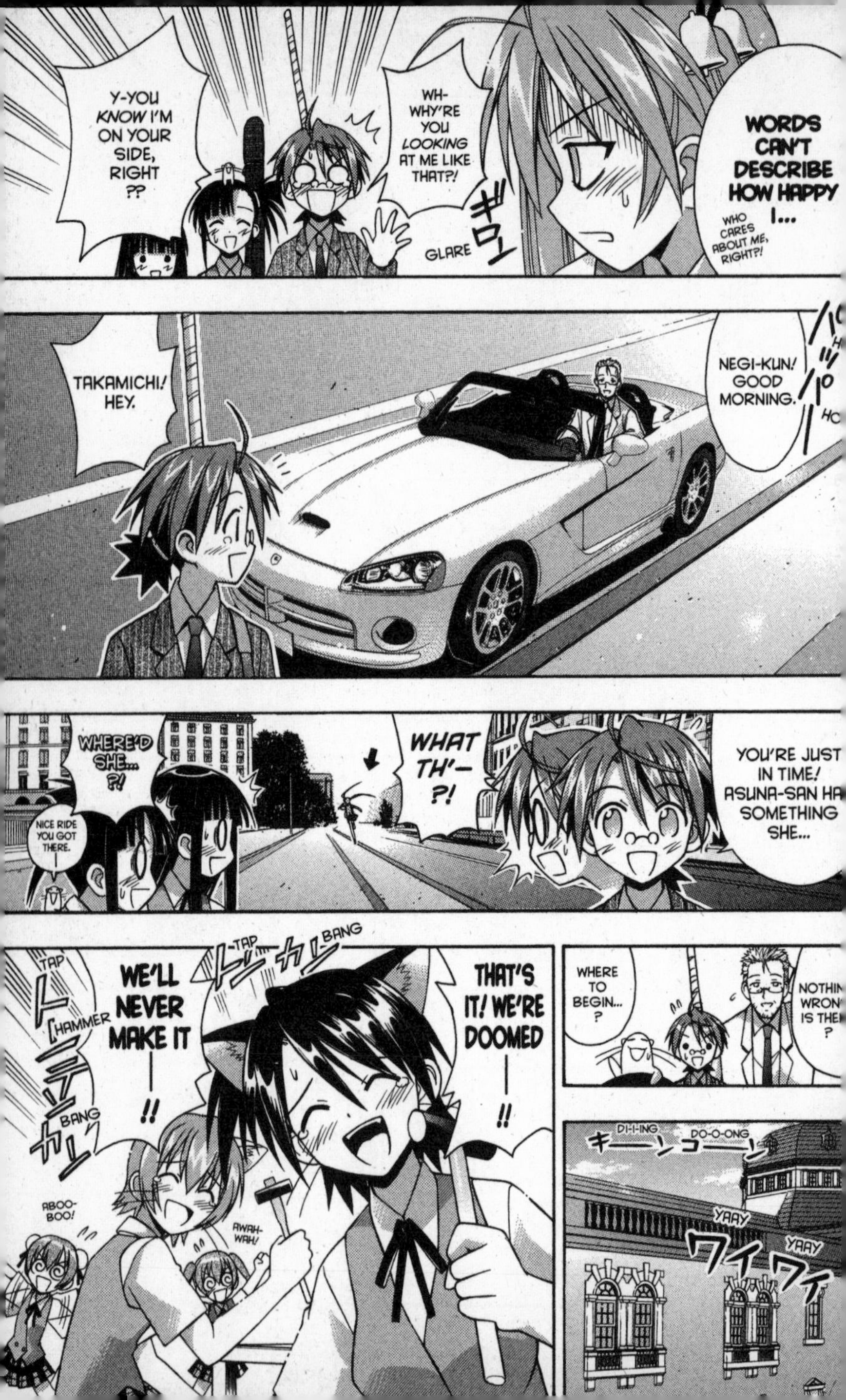
WORDS CAN'T DESCRIBE HOW HAPPY I...
WHO CARES ABOUT ME, RIGHT?!
GLARE
WH- WHY'RE YOU LOOKING AT ME LIKE THAT?!
Y-YOU KNOW I'M ON YOUR SIDE, RIGHT ??
HA HA HO
NEGI-KUN! GOOD MORNING.
TAKAMICHI! HEY.
YOU'RE JUST IN TIME! ASUNA-SAN HA SOMETHING SHE...
WHAT TH'— ?!
WHERE'D SHE... ?!
NICE RIDE YOU GOT THERE.
NOTHIN WRON IS THE ?
WHERE TO BEGIN... ?
DI-I-ING DO-O-ONG
YAAY
YAAY
TAP BANG
THAT'S IT! WE'RE DOOMED —!!
WE'LL NEVER MAKE IT —!!
TAP HAMMER BANG
AWAH-WAH!
ABOO-BOO!

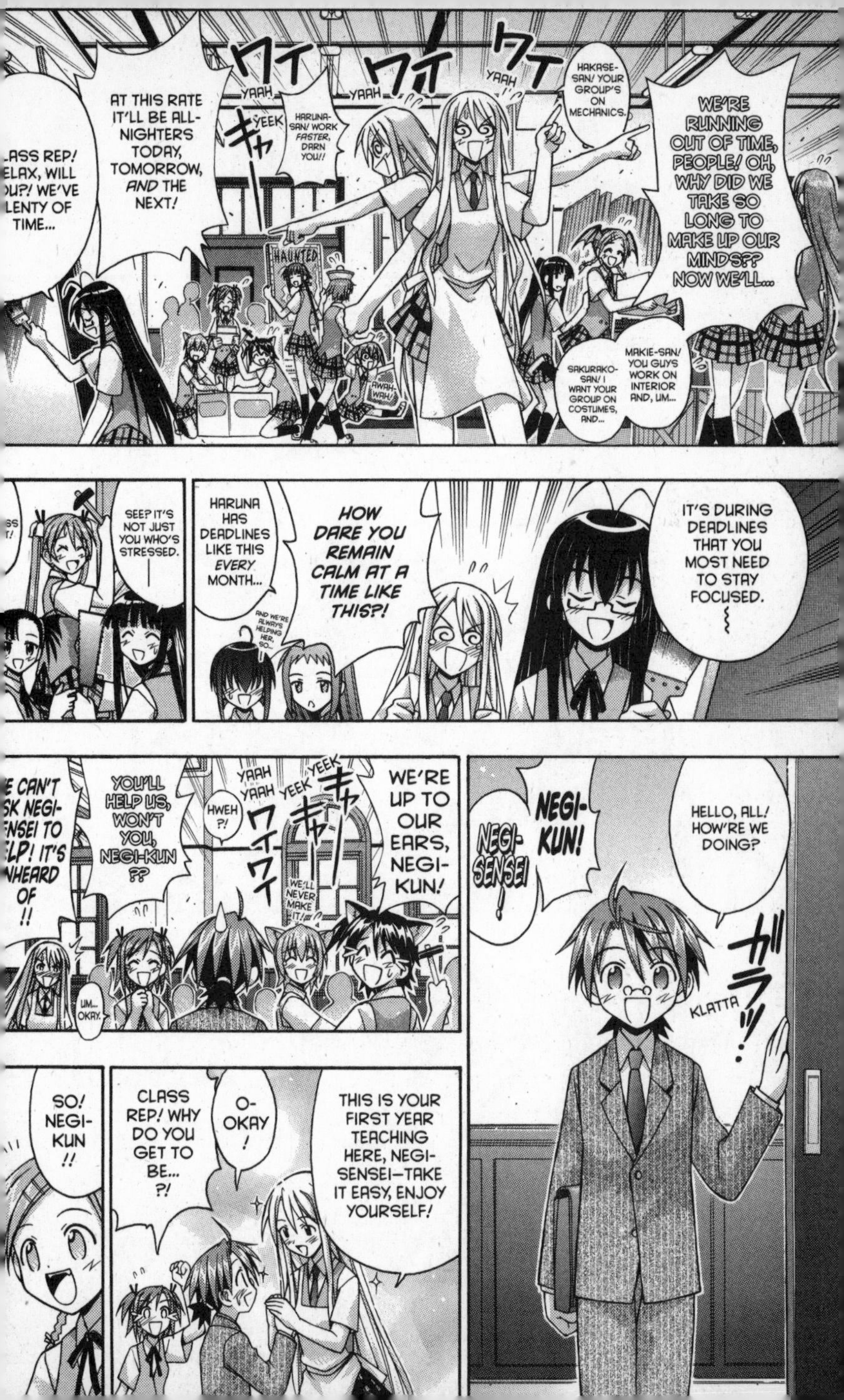
WE'RE RUNNING OUT OF TIME, PEOPLE! OH, WHY DID WE TAKE SO LONG TO MAKE UP OUR MINDS?? NOW WE'LL...
HAKASE-SAN! YOUR GROUP'S ON MECHANICS.
MAKIE-SAN! YOU GUYS WORK ON INTERIOR AND, UM...
SAKURAKO-SAN! I WANT YOUR GROUP ON COSTUMES, AND...
YAAH
YAAH
YAAH
YEEK
HARUNA-SAN! WORK FASTER, DARN YOU!!
HAUNTED
AWAH-WAH!
AT THIS RATE IT'LL BE ALL-NIGHTERS TODAY, TOMORROW, AND THE NEXT!
LASS REP! ELAX, WILL OU?! WE'VE LENTY OF TIME...
IT'S DURING DEADLINES THAT YOU MOST NEED TO STAY FOCUSED.
HOW DARE YOU REMAIN CALM AT A TIME LIKE THIS?!
HARUNA HAS DEADLINES LIKE THIS EVERY MONTH...
AND WE'RE ALWAYS HELPING HER, SO...
SEE? IT'S NOT JUST YOU WHO'S STRESSED.
HELLO, ALL! HOW'RE WE DOING?
KLATTA
NEGI-KUN!
NEGI-SENSEI!
WE'RE UP TO OUR EARS, NEGI-KUN!
YEEK YEEK
YAAH YAAH
WE'LL NEVER MAKE IT!
HWEH?!
YOU'LL HELP US, WON'T YOU, NEGI-KUN??
E CAN'T SK NEGI-NSEI TO ELP! IT'S NHEARD OF!!
UM... OKAY.
THIS IS YOUR FIRST YEAR TEACHING HERE, NEGI-SENSEI—TAKE IT EASY, ENJOY YOURSELF!
O-OKAY!
CLASS REP! WHY DO YOU GET TO BE...?!
SO! NEGI-KUN!!

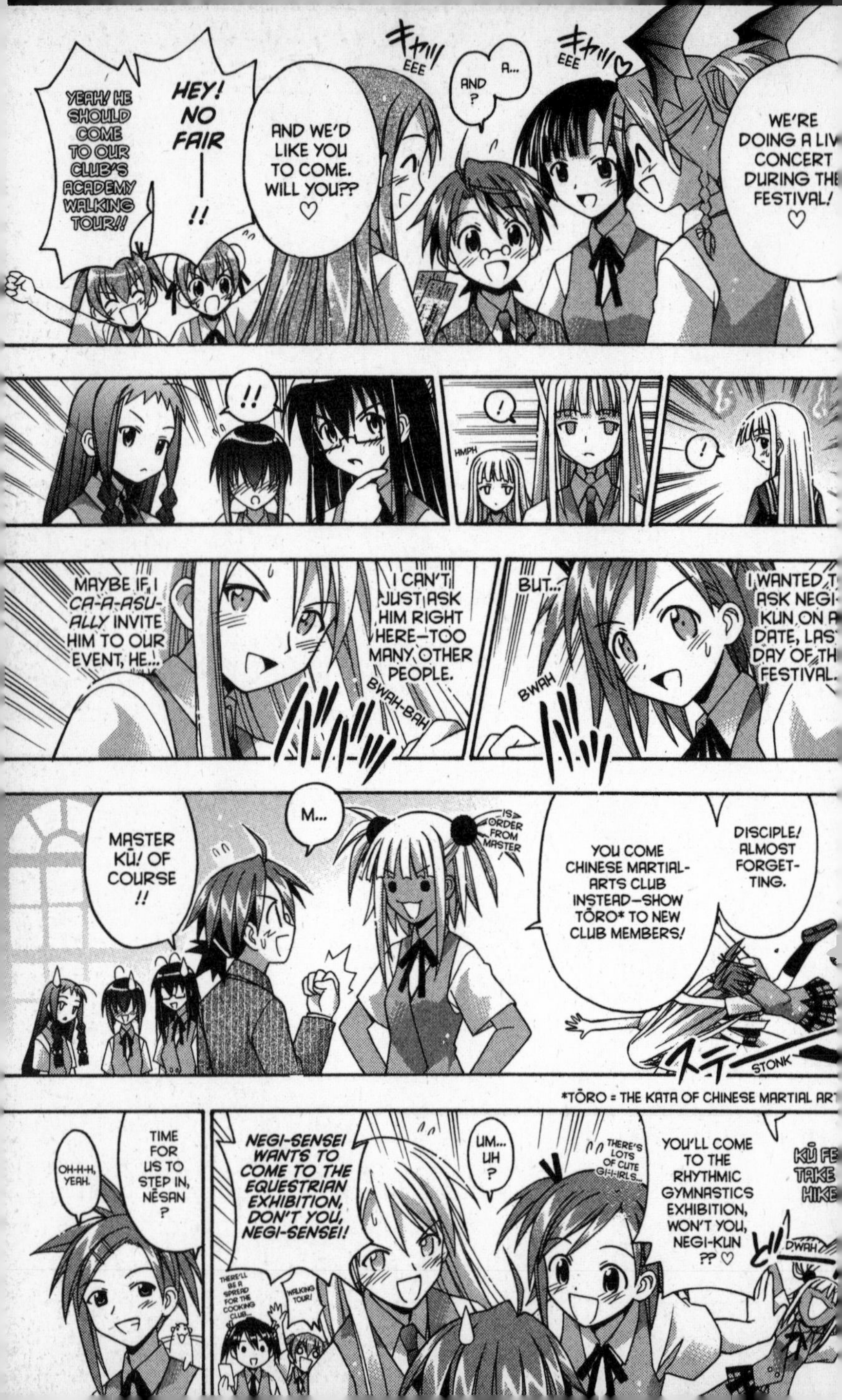
WE'RE DOING A LIV CONCERT DURING THE FESTIVAL! ♡
EEE
A...
AND ?
EEE
AND WE'D LIKE YOU TO COME. WILL YOU?? ♡
HEY! NO FAIR!!
YEAH! HE SHOULD COME TO OUR CLUB'S ACADEMY WALKING TOUR!!
!
HMPH
!
!!
I WANTED T ASK NEGI-KUN ON A DATE, LAS DAY OF TH FESTIVAL.
BUT...
BWAH
I CAN'T JUST ASK HIM RIGHT HERE—TOO MANY OTHER PEOPLE.
BWAH-BAH
MAYBE IF I CA-A-ASU-ALLY INVITE HIM TO OUR EVENT, HE...
DISCIPLE! ALMOST FORGET-TING.
YOU COME CHINESE MARTIAL-ARTS CLUB INSTEAD—SHOW TŌRO* TO NEW CLUB MEMBERS!
STONK
—IS ORDER FROM MASTER!
M...
MASTER KŪ! OF COURSE!!
*TŌRO = THE KATA OF CHINESE MARTIAL AR
KŪ FE TAKE HIKE
DWAH
YOU'LL COME TO THE RHYTHMIC GYMNASTICS EXHIBITION, WON'T YOU, NEGI-KUN ?? ♡
THERE'S LOTS OF CUTE GI-I-IRLS...
UM... UH ?
NEGI-SENSEI WANTS TO COME TO THE EQUESTRIAN EXHIBITION, DON'T YOU, NEGI-SENSEI!
WALKING TOUR!
THERE'LL BE A SPREAD FOR THE COOKING CLUB...
TIME FOR US TO STEP IN, NĒSAN ?
OH-H-H, YEAH.

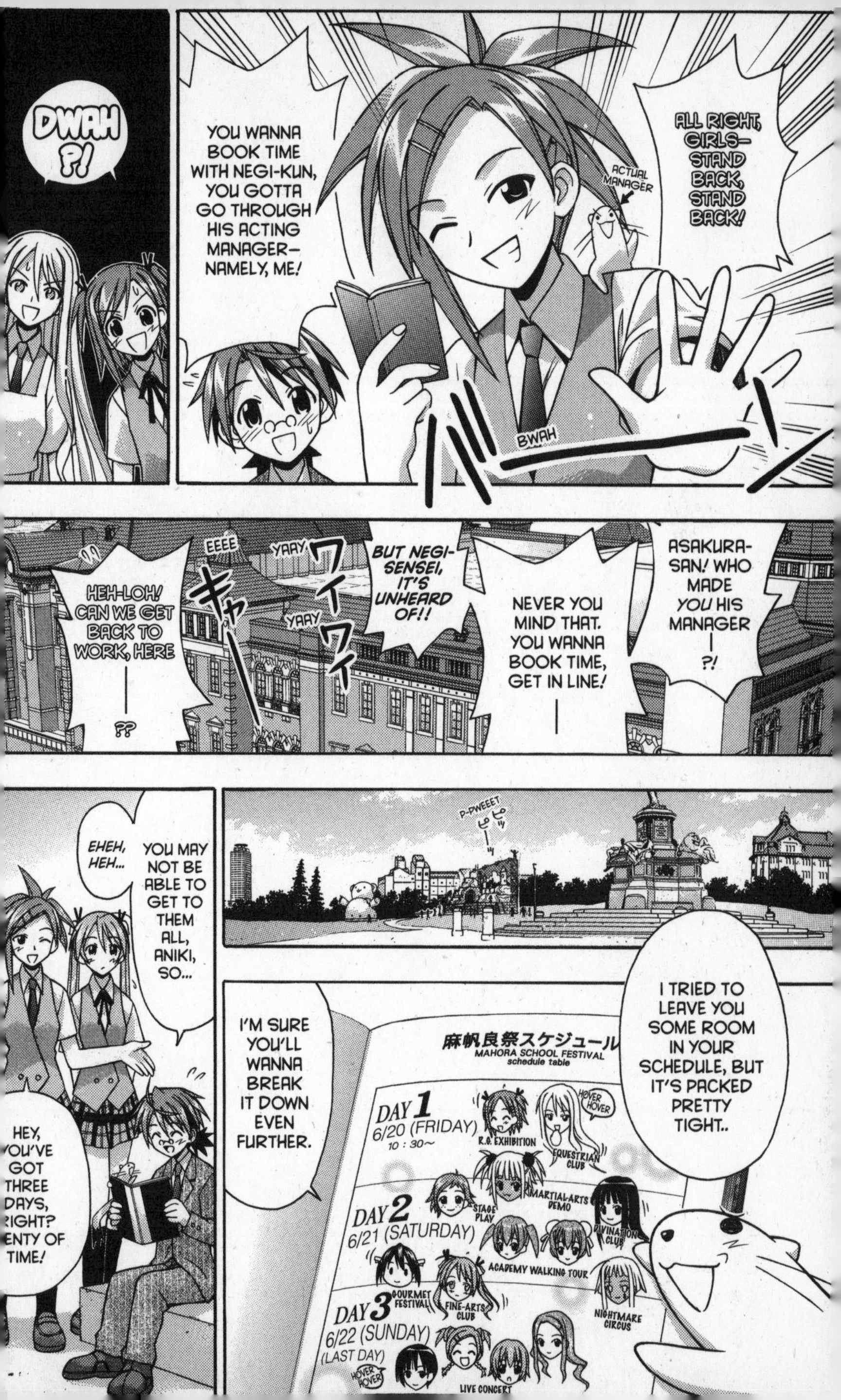
ALL RIGHT, GIRLS— STAND BACK, STAND BACK!
ACTUAL MANAGER
YOU WANNA BOOK TIME WITH NEGI-KUN, YOU GOTTA GO THROUGH HIS ACTING MANAGER— NAMELY, ME!
BWAH
DWAH ?!
ASAKURA-SAN! WHO MADE YOU HIS MANAGER —?!
NEVER YOU MIND THAT. YOU WANNA BOOK TIME, GET IN LINE! —
BUT NEGI-SENSEI, IT'S UNHEARD OF!!
YAAY ワイワイ YAAY
EEEE キャー
HEH-LOH! CAN WE GET BACK TO WORK, HERE —??
P-PWEEET ピッピーッ
I TRIED TO LEAVE YOU SOME ROOM IN YOUR SCHEDULE, BUT IT'S PACKED PRETTY TIGHT..
麻帆良祭スケジュール
MAHORA SCHOOL FESTIVAL schedule table
DAY 1 6/20 (FRIDAY) 10：30～
R.C. EXHIBITION
HOVER HOVER
EQUESTRIAN CLUB
MARTIAL-ARTS DEMO
DAY 2 6/21 (SATURDAY)
STAGE PLAY
DIVINATION CLUB
ACADEMY WALKING TOUR
GOURMET FESTIVAL
FINE-ARTS CLUB
NIGHTMARE CIRCUS
DAY 3 6/22 (SUNDAY) (LAST DAY)
HOVER HOVER
LIVE CONCERT
I'M SURE YOU'LL WANNA BREAK IT DOWN EVEN FURTHER.
YOU MAY NOT BE ABLE TO GET TO THEM ALL, ANIKI, SO...
EHEH, HEH...
HEY, OU'VE GOT THREE DAYS, RIGHT? ENTY OF TIME!

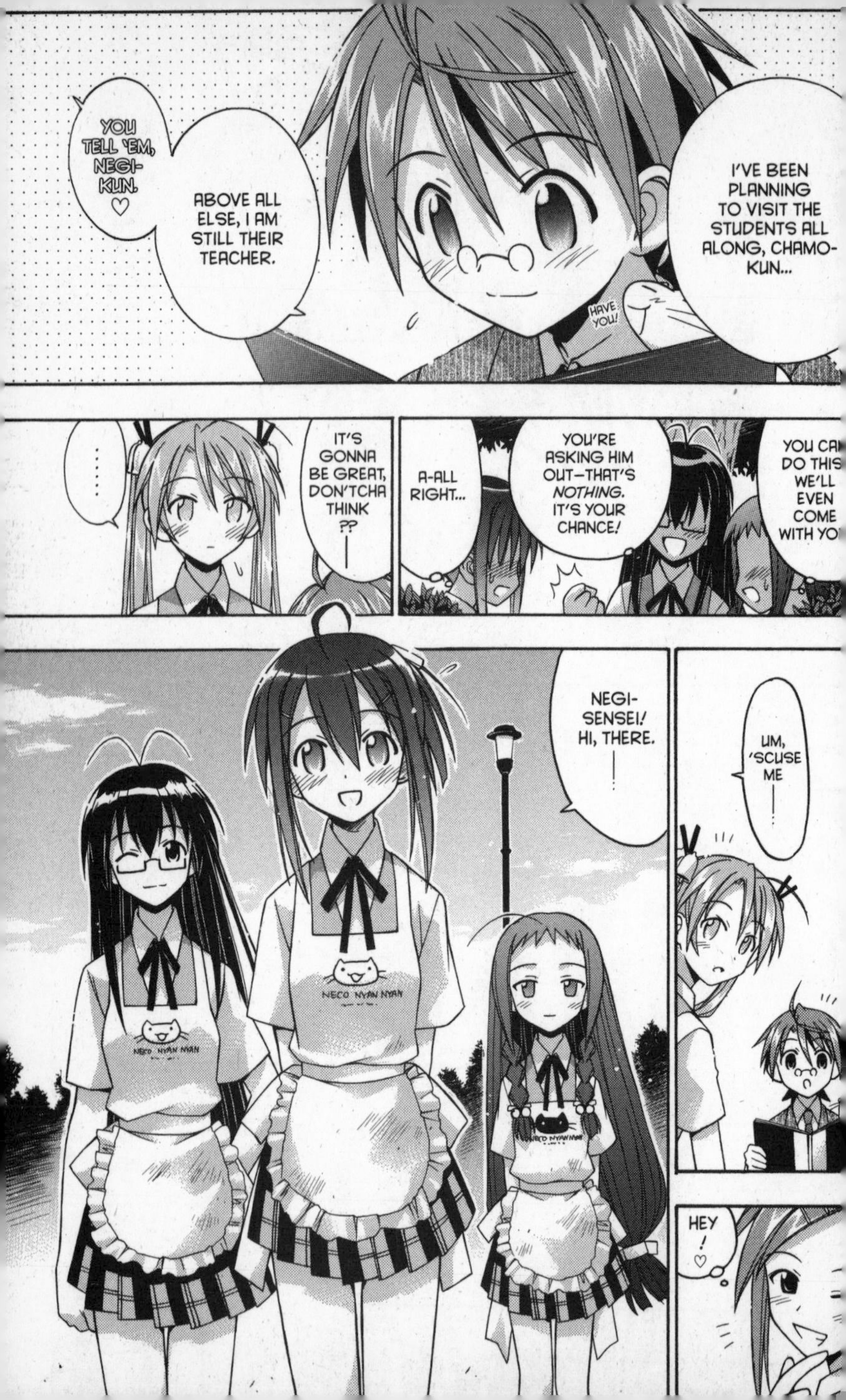
I'VE BEEN PLANNING TO VISIT THE STUDENTS ALL ALONG, CHAMO-KUN...
HAVE YOU!
ABOVE ALL ELSE, I AM STILL THEIR TEACHER.
YOU TELL 'EM, NEGI-KUN. ♡
YOU CA DO THIS WE'LL EVEN COME WITH YO
YOU'RE ASKING HIM OUT—THAT'S NOTHING. IT'S YOUR CHANCE!
A-ALL RIGHT...
IT'S GONNA BE GREAT, DON'TCHA THINK ??
......
UM, 'SCUSE ME
HEY! ♡
NEGI-SENSEI! HI, THERE.
NECO NYAN NYAN
NECO NYAN NYAN

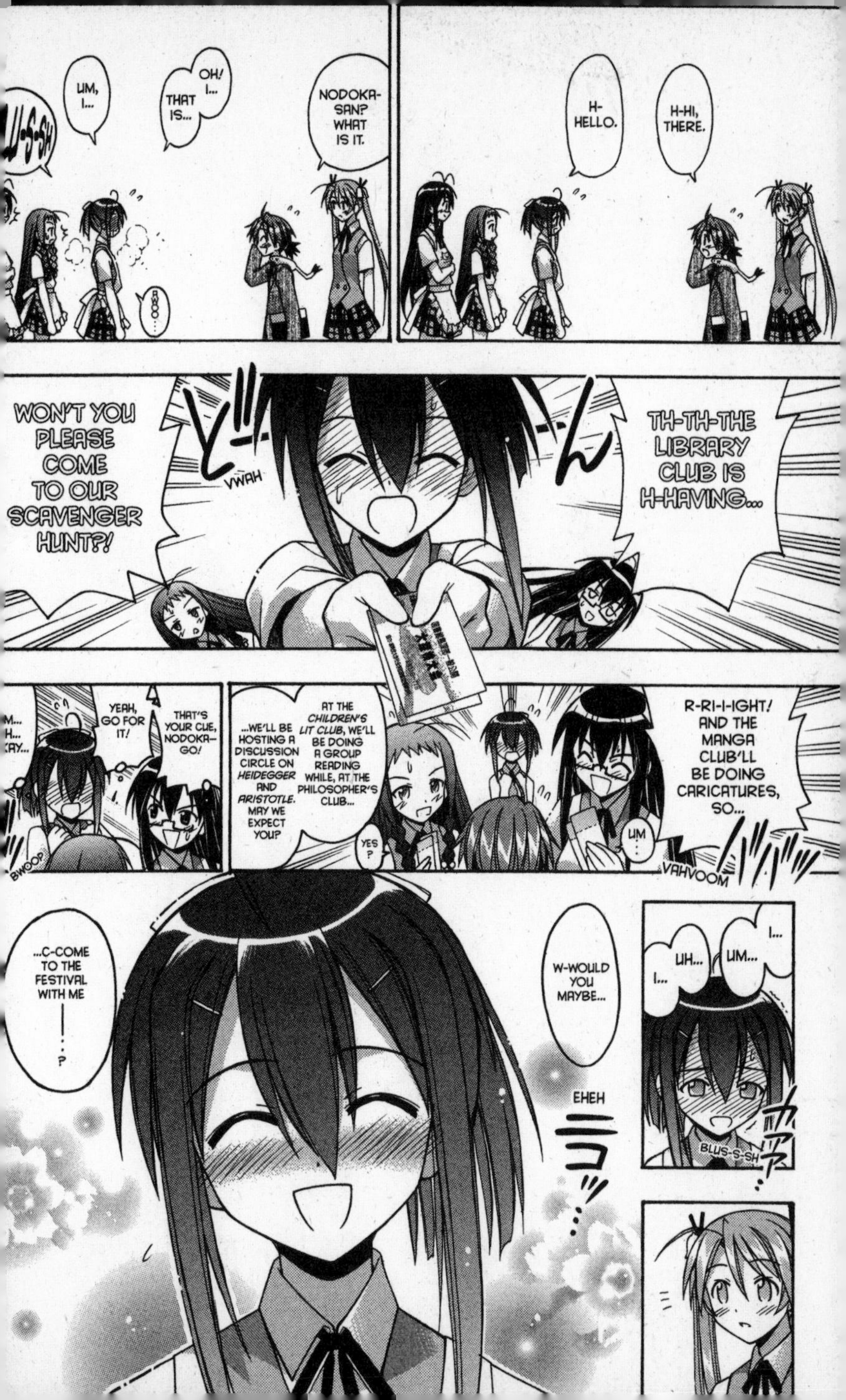

H-HI, THERE.
H-HELLO.
NODOKA-SAN? WHAT IS IT.
OH! I... THAT IS...
UM, I...
AWOO...
TH-TH-THE LIBRARY CLUB IS H-HAVING...
WON'T YOU PLEASE COME TO OUR SCAVENGER HUNT?!
VWAH
R-RI-I-IGHT! AND THE MANGA CLUB'LL BE DOING CARICATURES, SO...
UM...
VAHVOOM
AT THE CHILDREN'S LIT CLUB, WE'LL BE DOING A GROUP READING WHILE, AT THE PHILOSOPHER'S CLUB...
...WE'LL BE HOSTING A DISCUSSION CIRCLE ON HEIDEGGER AND ARISTOTLE. MAY WE EXPECT YOU?
YES?
THAT'S YOUR CUE, NODOKA—GO!
YEAH, GO FOR IT!
BWOOP
I... UM...
UH... I...
BLUS-S-SH
W-WOULD YOU MAYBE...
...C-COME TO THE FESTIVAL WITH ME...?
EHEH

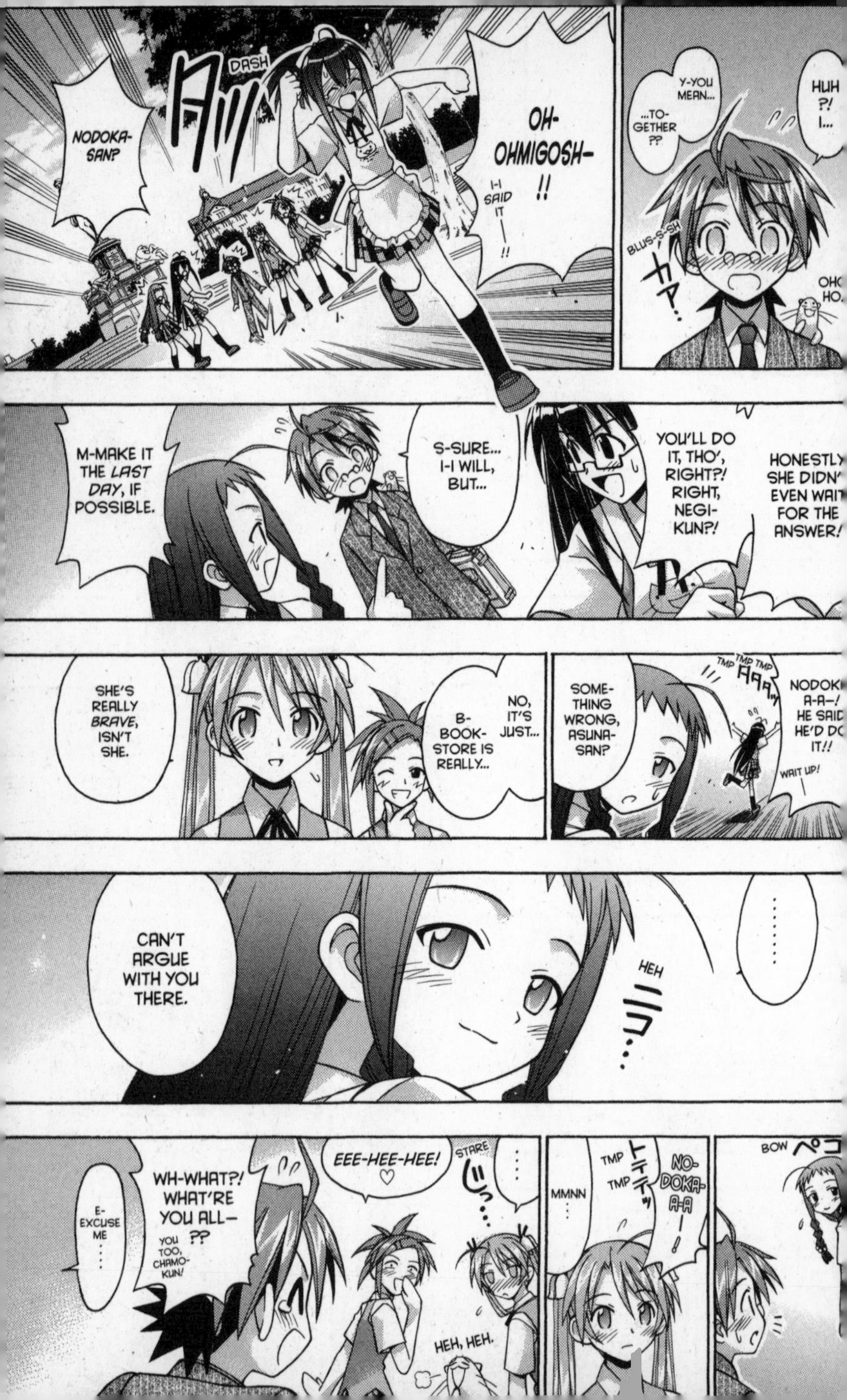

HUH ?! I...
Y-YOU MEAN... ...TO-GETHER ??
BLUS-S-SH
OHO HO.
OH-OHMIGOSH-!!
I-I SAID IT—!!
DASH
NODOKA-SAN?
HONESTLY SHE DIDN' EVEN WAIT FOR THE ANSWER!
YOU'LL DO IT, THO', RIGHT?! RIGHT, NEGI-KUN?!
S-SURE... I-I WILL, BUT...
M-MAKE IT THE *LAST DAY*, IF POSSIBLE.
NODOK A-A-! HE SAID HE'D DO IT!!
WAIT UP!
TMP TMP TMP
SOME-THING WRONG, ASUNA-SAN?
NO, IT'S JUST...
B-BOOK-STORE IS REALLY...
SHE'S REALLY *BRAVE*, ISN'T SHE.
......
HEH
CAN'T ARGUE WITH YOU THERE.
BOW
NO-DOKA-A-A!
TMP TMP
MMNN...
...
STARE
EEE-HEE-HEE! ♡
WH-WHAT?! WHAT'RE YOU ALL—??
YOU TOO, CHAMO-KUN!
E-EXCUSE ME ....
HEH, HEH.

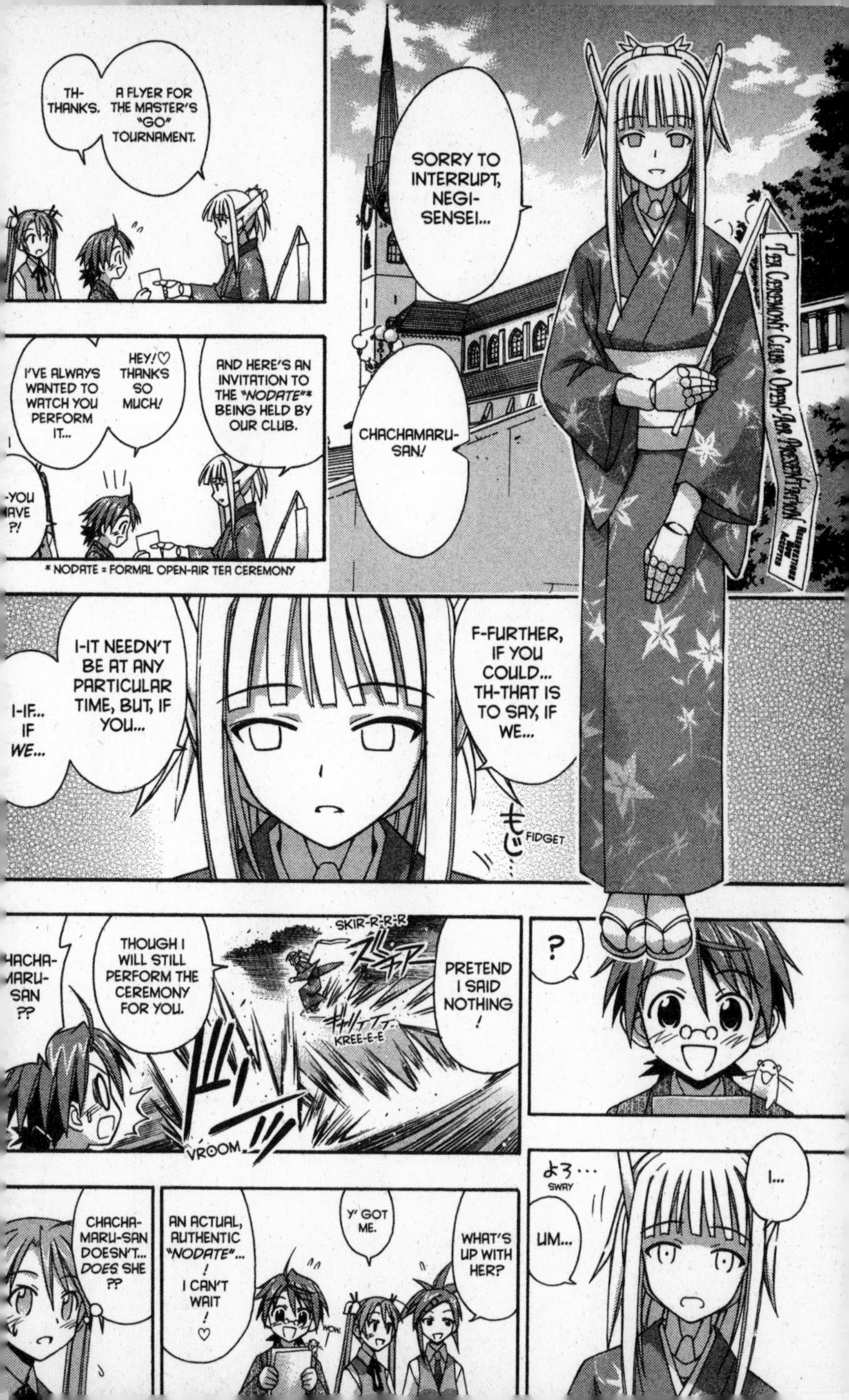
SORRY TO INTERRUPT, NEGI-SENSEI...
CHACHAMARU-SAN!
TEA CEREMONY CLUB ♦ OPEN-AIR PRESENTATION
RESERVATIONS NOT ACCEPTED
A FLYER FOR THE MASTER'S "GO" TOURNAMENT.
TH- THANKS.
AND HERE'S AN INVITATION TO THE "NODATE"* BEING HELD BY OUR CLUB.
HEY!♡ THANKS SO MUCH!
I'VE ALWAYS WANTED TO WATCH YOU PERFORM IT...
-YOU HAVE ?!
* NODATE = FORMAL OPEN-AIR TEA CEREMONY
F-FURTHER, IF YOU COULD... TH-THAT IS TO SAY, IF WE...
もじ FIDGET
I-IT NEEDN'T BE AT ANY PARTICULAR TIME, BUT, IF YOU...
I-IF... IF WE...
?
PRETEND I SAID NOTHING!
SKIR-R-R-R
THOUGH I WILL STILL PERFORM THE CEREMONY FOR YOU.
KREE-E-E
VROOM
CHACHA-MARU-SAN ??
I...
よろ… SWAY
UM...
WHAT'S UP WITH HER?
Y' GOT ME.
AN ACTUAL, AUTHENTIC "NODATE"...! I CAN'T WAIT! ♡
WOW.
CHACHA-MARU-SAN DOESN'T... DOES SHE ??

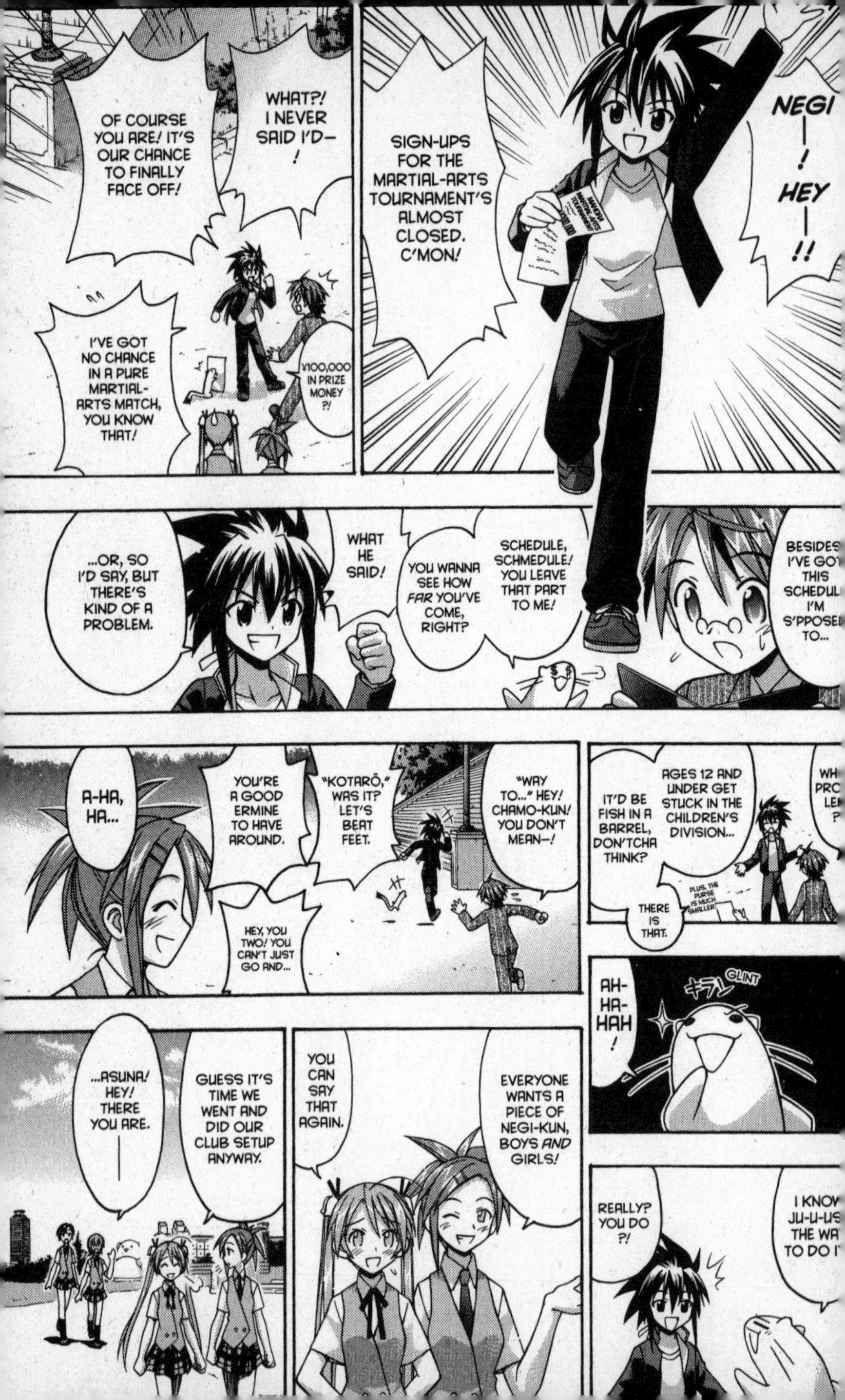
NEGI—! HEY—!!
SIGN-UPS FOR THE MARTIAL-ARTS TOURNAMENT'S ALMOST CLOSED. C'MON!
WHAT?! I NEVER SAID I'D—!
OF COURSE YOU ARE! IT'S OUR CHANCE TO FINALLY FACE OFF!
¥100,000 IN PRIZE MONEY?!
I'VE GOT NO CHANCE IN A PURE MARTIAL-ARTS MATCH, YOU KNOW THAT!
BESIDES I'VE GOT THIS SCHEDUL I'M S'PPOSE TO...
SCHEDULE, SCHMEDULE! YOU LEAVE THAT PART TO ME!
YOU WANNA SEE HOW *FAR* YOU'VE COME, RIGHT?
WHAT HE SAID!
...OR, SO I'D SAY, BUT THERE'S KIND OF A PROBLEM.
AGES 12 AND UNDER GET STUCK IN THE CHILDREN'S DIVISION...
IT'D BE FISH IN A BARREL, DON'TCHA THINK?
PLUS, THE PURSE IS MUCH SMALLER!
THERE IS THAT.
GLINT
AH-HA-HAH!
REALLY? YOU DO?!
"WAY TO..." HEY! CHAMO-KUN! YOU DON'T MEAN—!
"KOTARŌ," WAS IT? LET'S BEAT FEET.
HEY, YOU TWO! YOU CAN'T JUST GO AND...
YOU'RE A GOOD ERMINE TO HAVE AROUND.
A-HA, HA...
EVERYONE WANTS A PIECE OF NEGI-KUN, BOYS *AND* GIRLS!
YOU CAN SAY THAT AGAIN.
GUESS IT'S TIME WE WENT AND DID OUR CLUB SETUP ANYWAY.
...ASUNA! HEY! THERE YOU ARE.

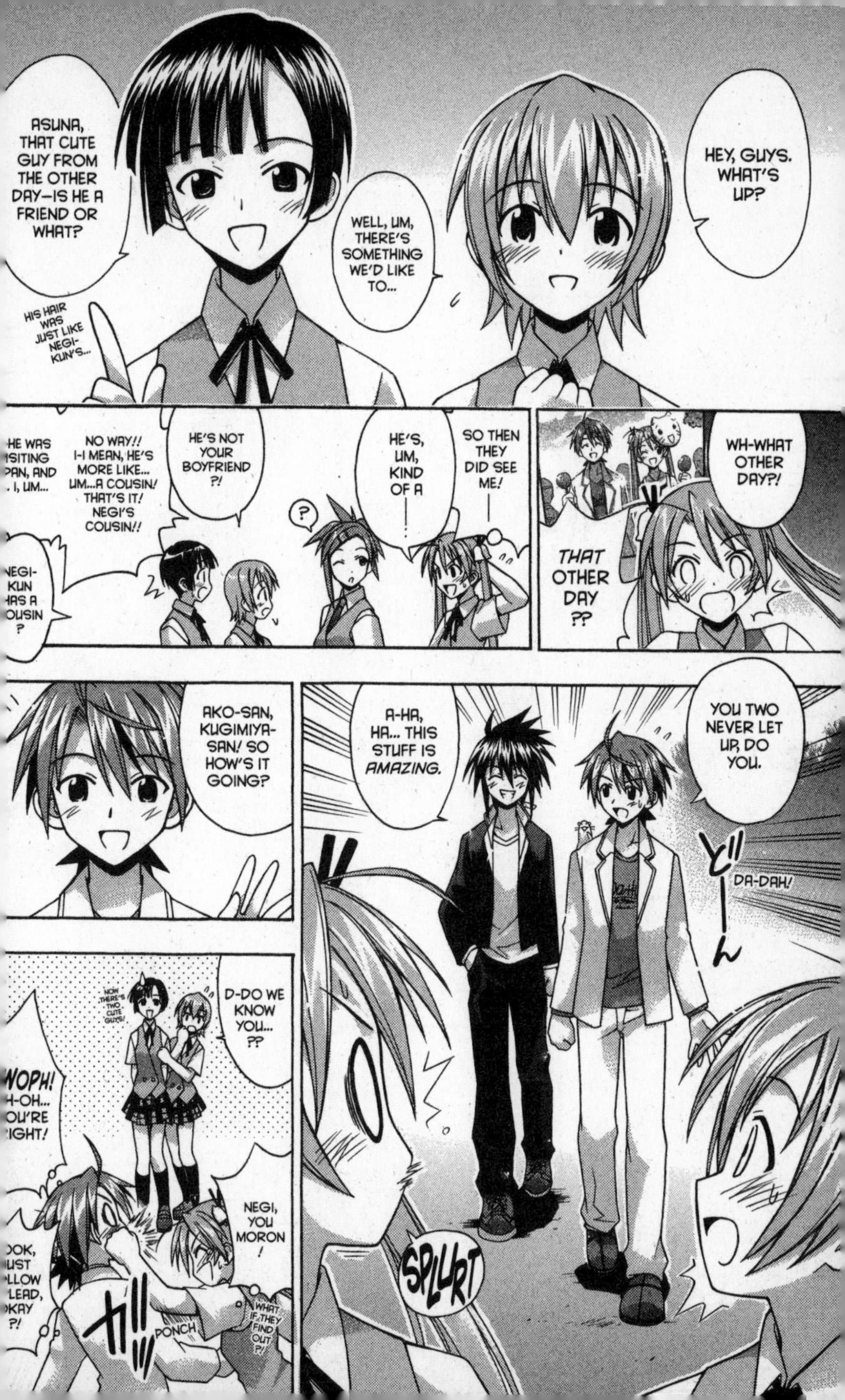
HEY, GUYS. WHAT'S UP?
WELL, UM, THERE'S SOMETHING WE'D LIKE TO...
ASUNA, THAT CUTE GUY FROM THE OTHER DAY—IS HE A FRIEND OR WHAT?
HIS HAIR WAS JUST LIKE NEGI-KUN'S...
WH-WHAT OTHER DAY?!
THAT OTHER DAY ??
SO THEN THEY DID SEE ME!
HE'S, UM, KIND OF A
?
HE'S NOT YOUR BOYFRIEND ?!
NO WAY!! I-I MEAN, HE'S MORE LIKE... UM...A COUSIN! THAT'S IT! NEGI'S COUSIN!!
HE WAS ISITING PAN, AND . I, UM...
NEGI-KUN HAS A OUSIN ?
YOU TWO NEVER LET UP, DO YOU.
DA-DAH!
A-HA, HA... THIS STUFF IS *AMAZING.*
SPLURT
AKO-SAN, KUGIMIYA-SAN! SO HOW'S IT GOING?
D-DO WE KNOW YOU... ??
NOW THERE'S TWO CUTE GUYS!
WOPH! H-OH... OU'RE IGHT!
NEGI, YOU MORON !
OOK, UST LLOW LEAD, OKAY ?!
WHAT IF THEY FIND OUT?!
PONCH

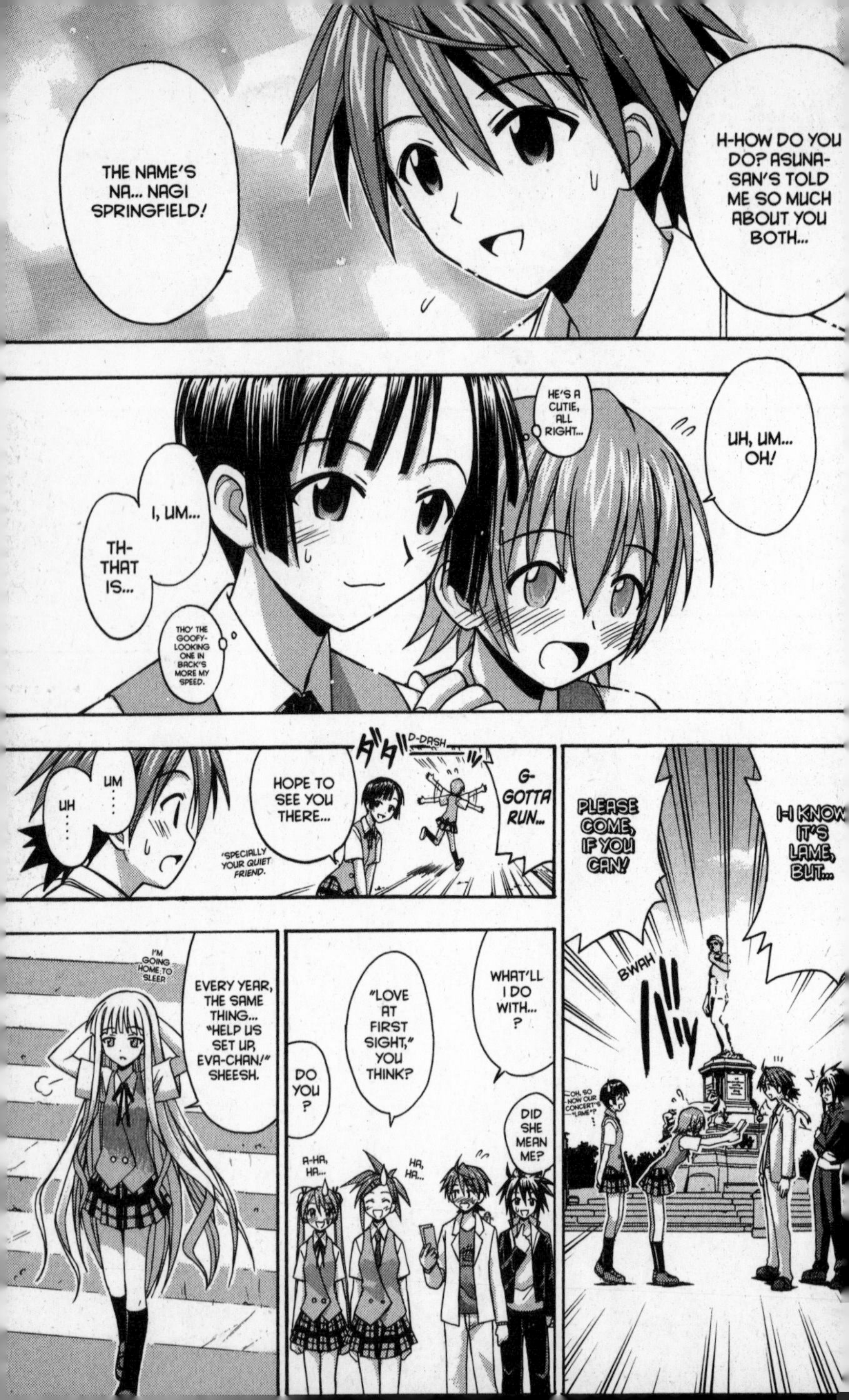
H-HOW DO YOU DO? ASUNA-SAN'S TOLD ME SO MUCH ABOUT YOU BOTH...
THE NAME'S NA... NAGI SPRINGFIELD!
UH, UM... OH!
HE'S A CUTIE, ALL RIGHT...
I, UM...
TH-THAT IS...
THO' THE GOOFY-LOOKING ONE IN BACK'S MORE MY SPEED.
I-I KNOW IT'S LAME, BUT...
PLEASE COME, IF YOU CAN!
G-GOTTA RUN...
D-DASH
HOPE TO SEE YOU THERE...
'SPECIALLY YOUR QUIET FRIEND.
UM...
UH...
BWAH
OH, SO NOW OUR CONCERT'S "LAME"?
WHAT'LL I DO WITH... ?
DID SHE MEAN ME?
"LOVE AT FIRST SIGHT," YOU THINK?
DO YOU?
HA, HA...
A-HA, HA...
I'M GOING HOME TO SLEEP
EVERY YEAR, THE SAME THING... "HELP US SET UP, EVA-CHAN!" SHEESH.

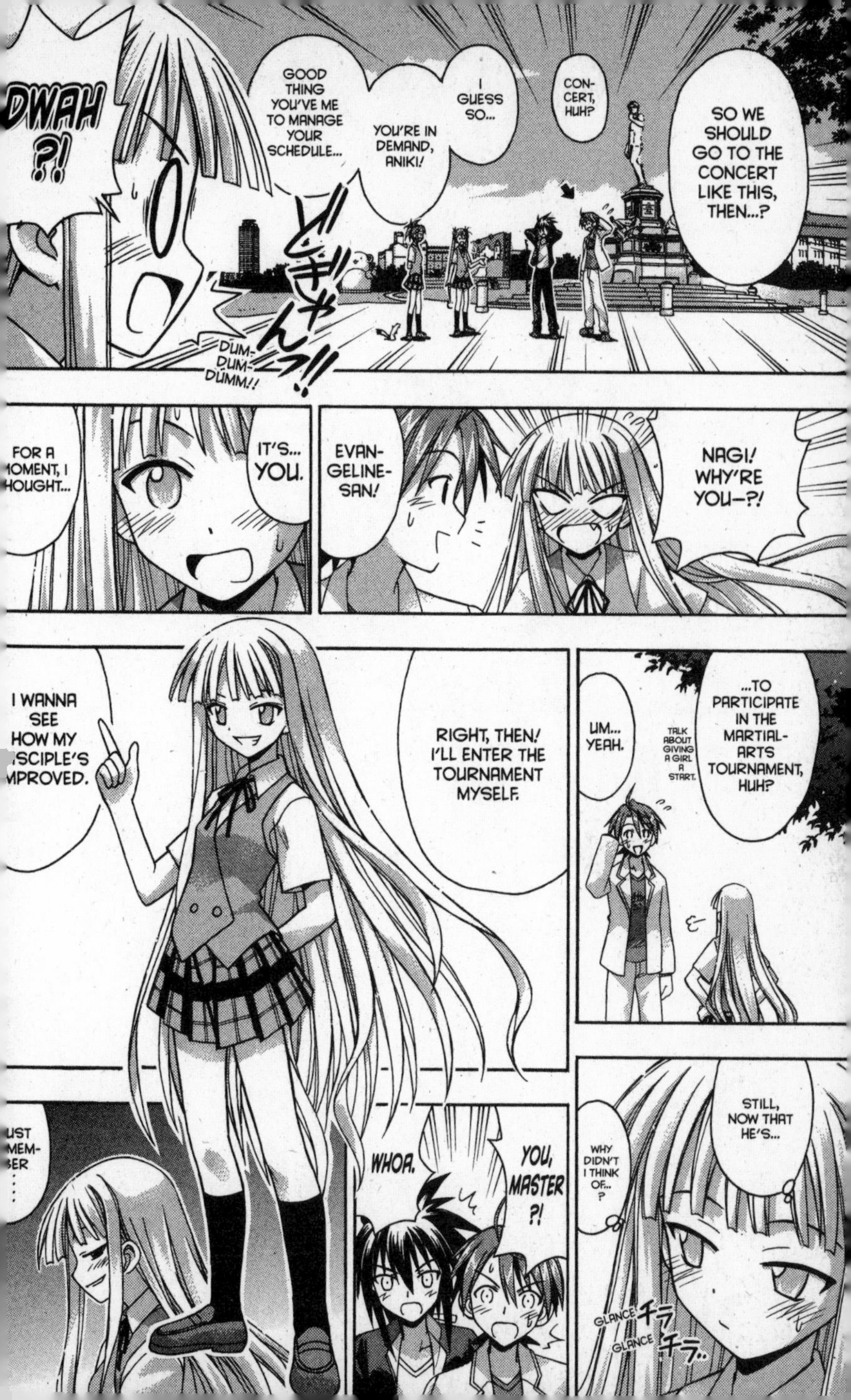
SO WE SHOULD GO TO THE CONCERT LIKE THIS, THEN...?
CON-CERT, HUH?
I GUESS SO...
YOU'RE IN DEMAND, ANIKI!
GOOD THING YOU'VE ME TO MANAGE YOUR SCHEDULE...
DUM-DUM-DUMM!!
DWAH?!
NAGI! WHY'RE YOU—?!
EVAN-GELINE-SAN!
IT'S... YOU.
FOR A OMENT, I HOUGHT...
...TO PARTICIPATE IN THE MARTIAL-ARTS TOURNAMENT, HUH?
TALK ABOUT GIVING A GIRL A START.
UM... YEAH.
RIGHT, THEN! I'LL ENTER THE TOURNAMENT MYSELF.
I WANNA SEE HOW MY ISCIPLE'S MPROVED.
STILL, NOW THAT HE'S...
WHY DIDN'T I THINK OF...?
GLANCE
GLANCE
YOU, MASTER?!
WHOA.
UST MEM-BER....

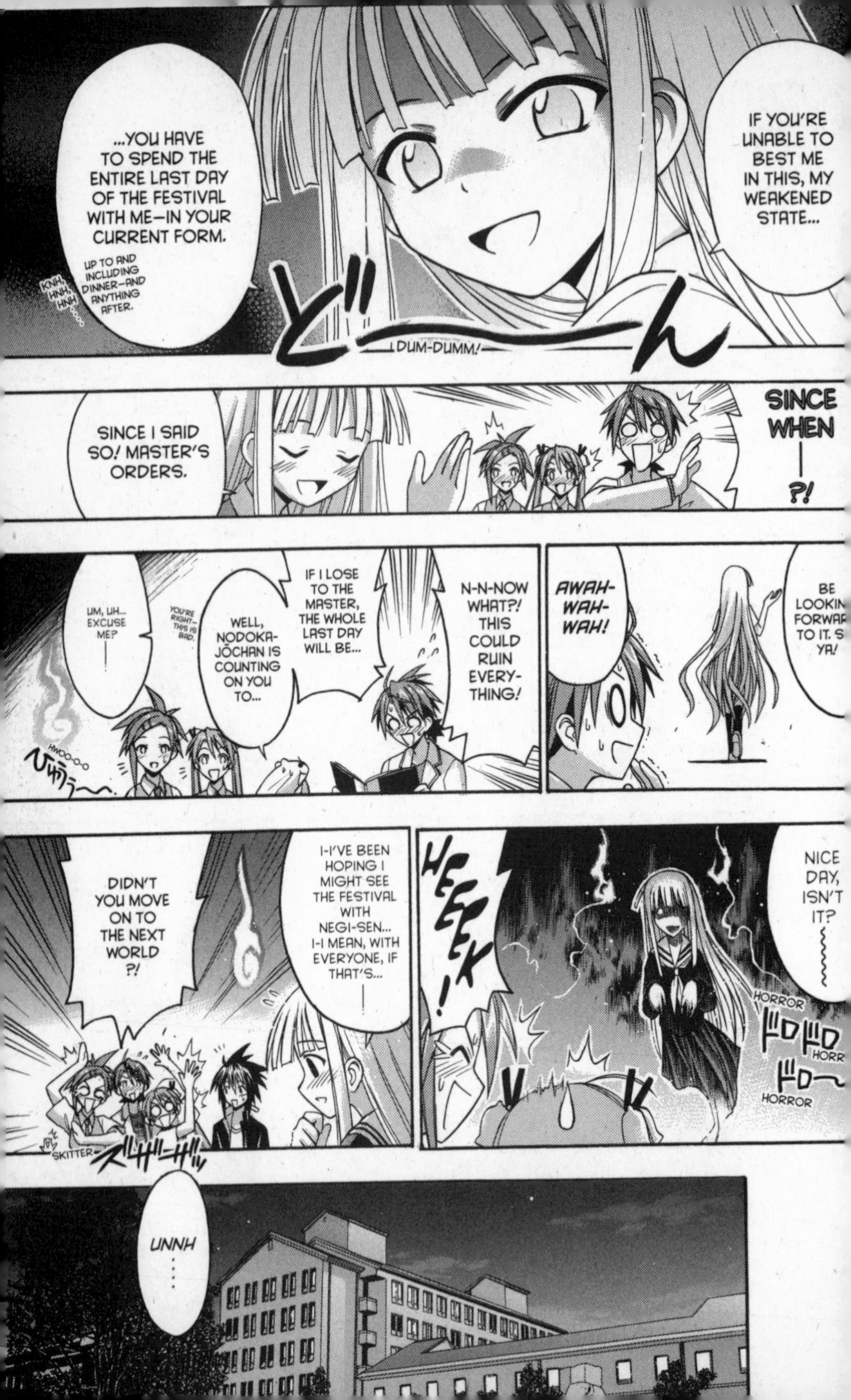

IF YOU'RE UNABLE TO BEST ME IN THIS, MY WEAKENED STATE...
...YOU HAVE TO SPEND THE ENTIRE LAST DAY OF THE FESTIVAL WITH ME—IN YOUR CURRENT FORM.
UP TO AND INCLUDING DINNER—AND ANYTHING AFTER.
KNH, HNH, HNH...
DUM-DUMM!
SINCE WHEN—?!
SINCE I SAID SO! MASTER'S ORDERS.
BE LOOKIN FORWAR TO IT. S YA!
AWAH-WAH-WAH!
N-N-NOW WHAT?! THIS COULD RUIN EVERYTHING!
IF I LOSE TO THE MASTER, THE WHOLE LAST DAY WILL BE...
WELL, NODOKA-JŌCHAN IS COUNTING ON YOU TO...
YOU'RE RIGHT—THIS IS BAD.
UM, UH... EXCUSE ME?—
HWOO-O-O
NICE DAY, ISN'T IT?~
HORROR
HORR
HORROR
HEEEK!
I-I'VE BEEN HOPING I MIGHT SEE THE FESTIVAL WITH NEGI-SEN... I-I MEAN, WITH EVERYONE, IF THAT'S...—
DIDN'T YOU MOVE ON TO THE NEXT WORLD?!
SKITTER
UNNH...

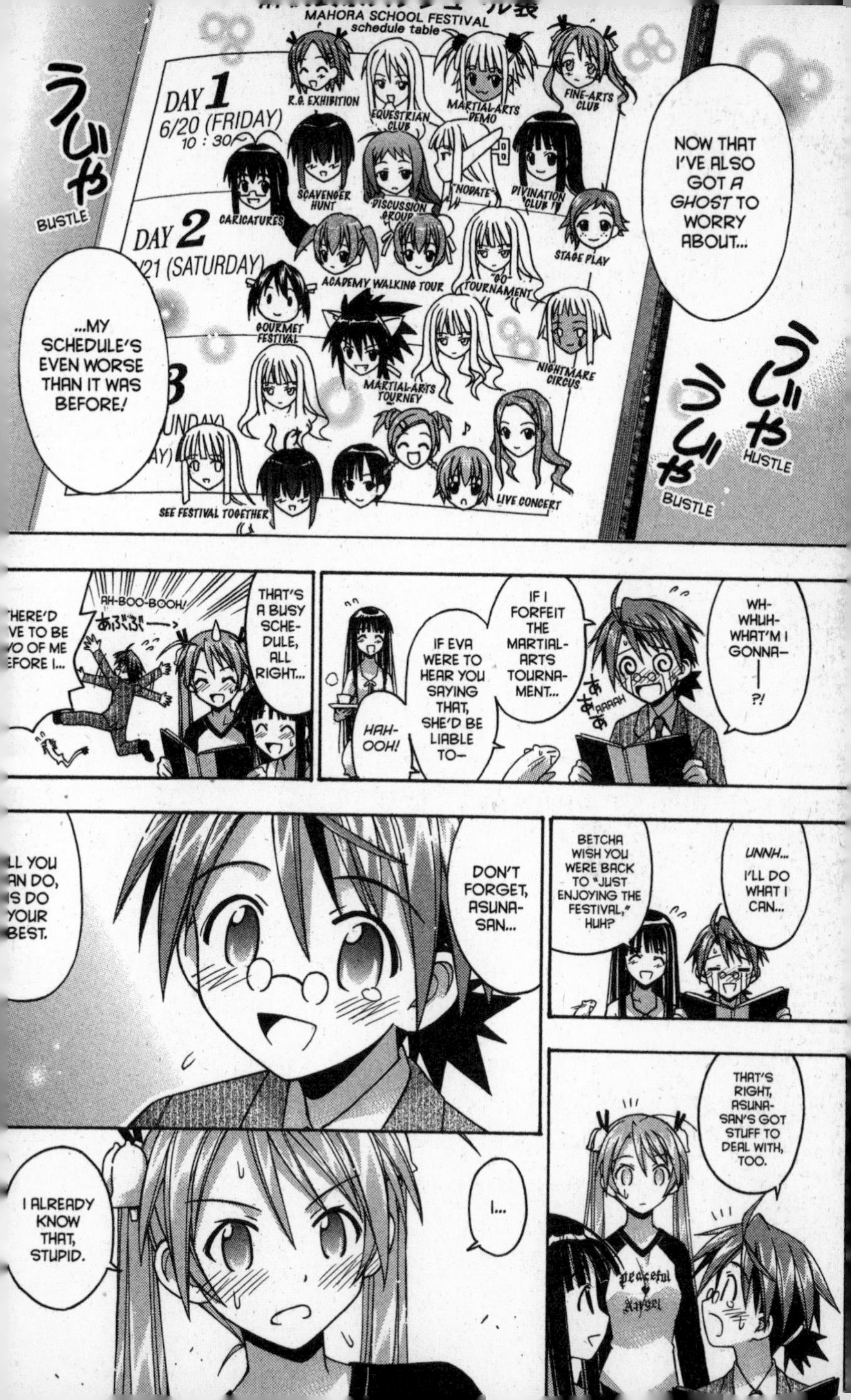
NOW THAT I'VE ALSO GOT A GHOST TO WORRY ABOUT...
うじゃ HUSTLE
うじゃ BUSTLE
MAHORA SCHOOL FESTIVAL schedule table
DAY 1
6/20 (FRIDAY)
10 : 30~
R.G. EXHIBITION
EQUESTRIAN CLUB
MARTIAL-ARTS DEMO
FINE-ARTS CLUB
CARICATURES
SCAVENGER HUNT
DISCUSSION GROUP
"NODATE"
DIVINATION CLUB
DAY 2
/21 (SATURDAY)
STAGE PLAY
ACADEMY WALKING TOUR
"GO" TOURNAMENT
GOURMET FESTIVAL
MARTIAL-ARTS TOURNEY
NIGHTMARE CIRCUS
LIVE CONCERT
SEE FESTIVAL TOGETHER
...MY SCHEDULE'S EVEN WORSE THAN IT WAS BEFORE!
うじゃ BUSTLE
WH-WHUH-WHAT'M I GONNA— —?!
IF I FORFEIT THE MARTIAL-ARTS TOURNAMENT...
あああ AAAAH
IF EVA WERE TO HEAR YOU SAYING THAT, SHE'D BE LIABLE TO—
HAH-OOH!
THAT'S A BUSY SCHEDULE, ALL RIGHT...
AH-BOO-BOOH! あぶぶ
UNNH... I'LL DO WHAT I CAN...
BETCHA WISH YOU WERE BACK TO "JUST ENJOYING THE FESTIVAL," HUH?
DON'T FORGET, ASUNA-SAN...
THAT'S RIGHT, ASUNA-SAN'S GOT STUFF TO DEAL WITH, TOO.
I...
I ALREADY KNOW THAT, STUPID.

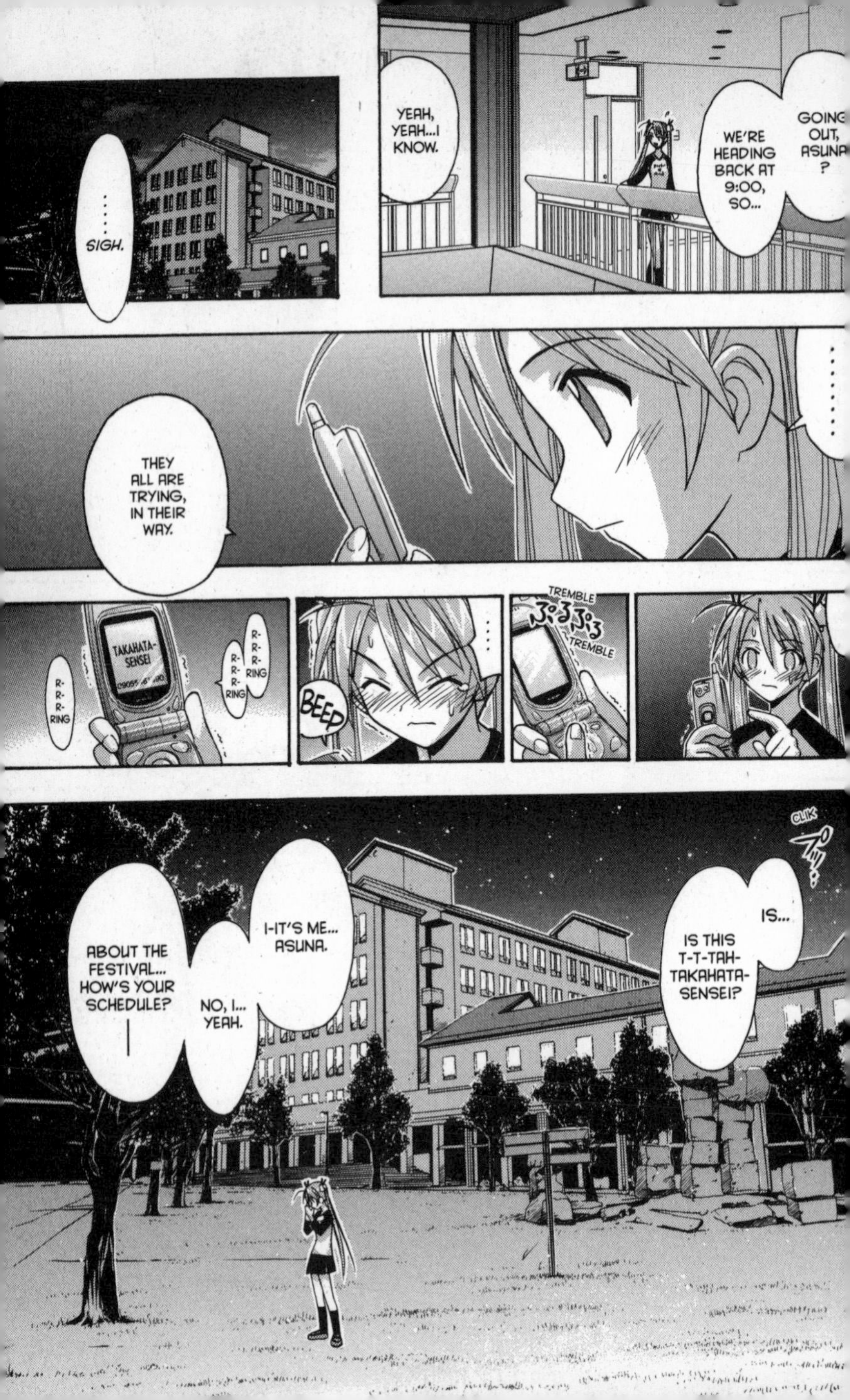
GOING OUT, ASUNA?
WE'RE HEADING BACK AT 9:00, SO...
YEAH, YEAH...I KNOW.
...SIGH.
......
THEY ALL ARE TRYING, IN THEIR WAY.
TREMBLE ぷるぷる TREMBLE
...
BEEP
R-R-R-RING
R-R-R-RING
TAKAHATA-SENSEI
R-R-R-RING
CLIK
IS...
IS THIS T-T-TAH-TAKAHATA-SENSEI?
I-IT'S ME... ASUNA.
NO, I... YEAH.
ABOUT THE FESTIVAL... HOW'S YOUR SCHEDULE?

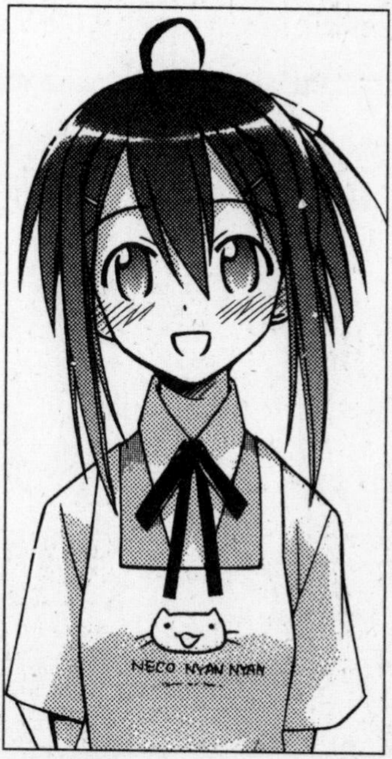
NECO NYAN NYAN

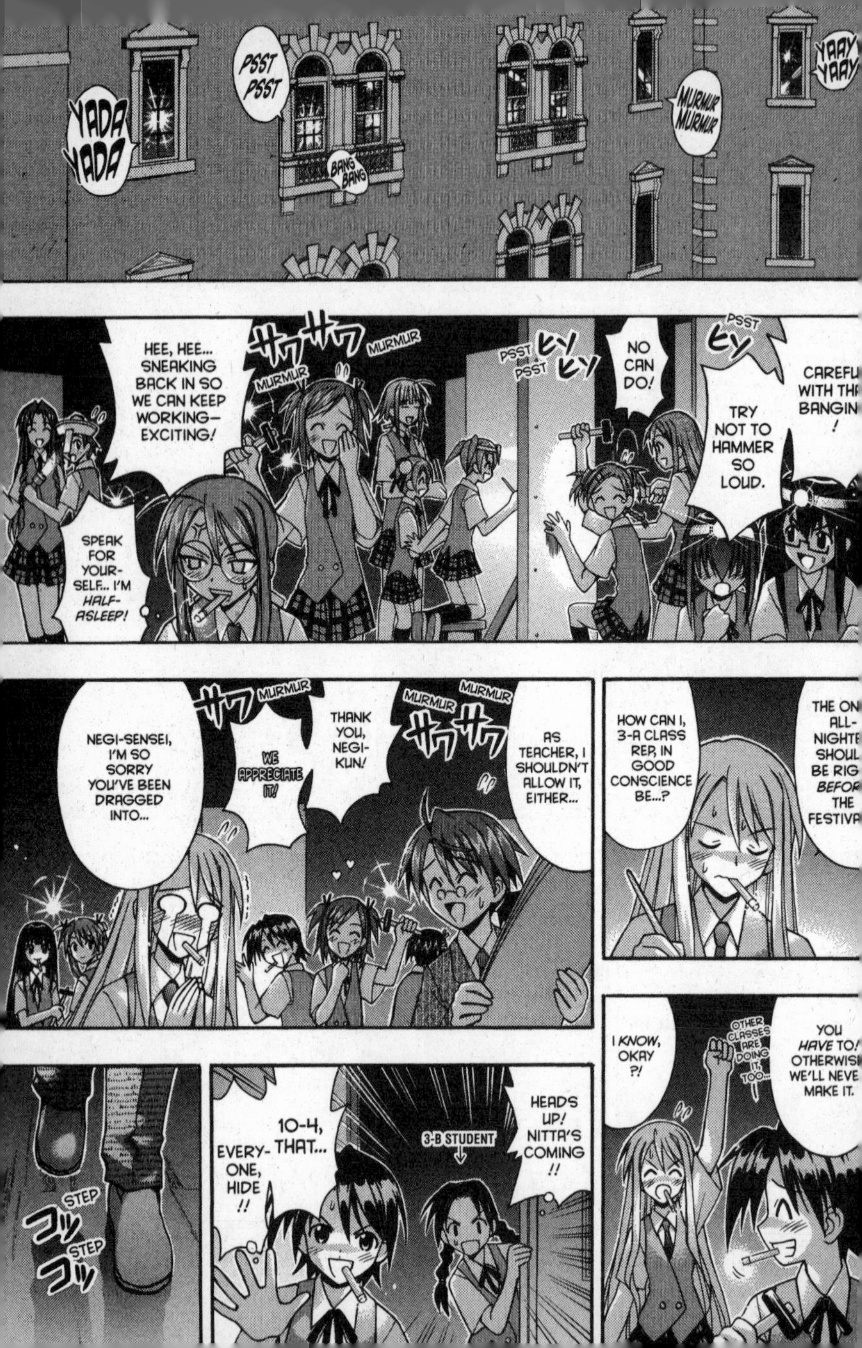

YAAY YAAY
MURMUR MURMUR
PSST PSST
BANG BANG
YADA YADA
CAREFU WITH TH BANGIN !
PSST ヒソ
TRY NOT TO HAMMER SO LOUD.
NO CAN DO!
PSST ヒソ PSST ヒソ
サワサワ MURMUR MURMUR
HEE, HEE... SNEAKING BACK IN SO WE CAN KEEP WORKING— EXCITING!
SPEAK FOR YOUR-SELF... I'M HALF-ASLEEP!
THE ON ALL-NIGHTE SHOUL BE RIG BEFOR THE FESTIVA
HOW CAN I, 3-A CLASS REP, IN GOOD CONSCIENCE BE...?
AS TEACHER, I SHOULDN'T ALLOW IT, EITHER...
MURMUR MURMUR サワサワ
THANK YOU, NEGI-KUN!
WE APPRECIATE IT!
サワ MURMUR
NEGI-SENSEI, I'M SO SORRY YOU'VE BEEN DRAGGED INTO...
YOU HAVE TO! OTHERWIS WE'LL NEVE MAKE IT.
OTHER CLASSES ARE DOING IT, TOO...
I KNOW, OKAY ?!
HEADS UP! NITTA'S COMING !!
3-B STUDENT
10-4, THAT...
EVERY-ONE, HIDE !!
STEP コツ
STEP コツ

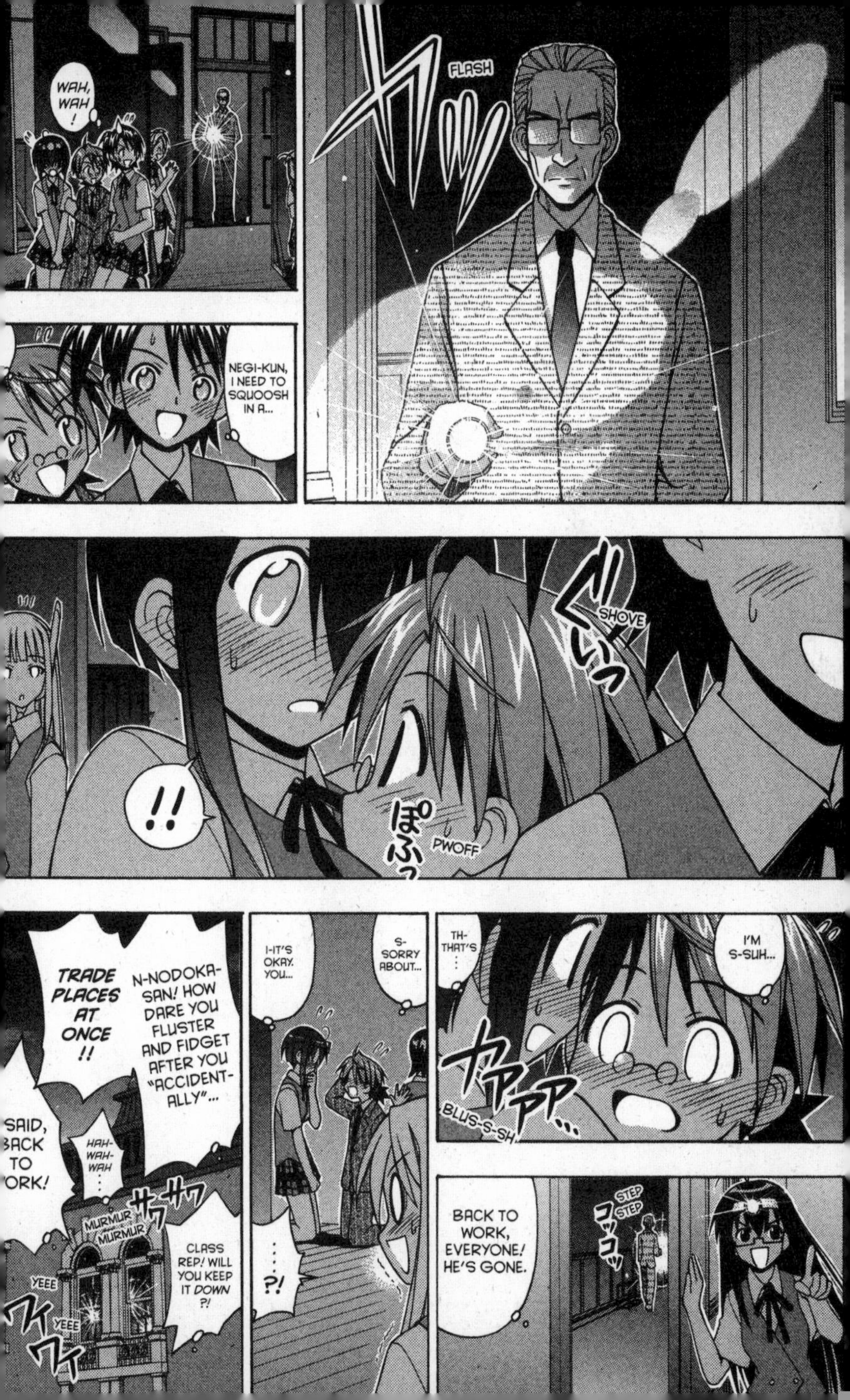
FLASH
WAH, WAH!
NEGI-KUN, I NEED TO SQUOOSH IN A...
SHOVE
PWOFF
!!
I'M S-SUH...
TH-THAT'S...
BLUS-S-SH
STEP STEP
BACK TO WORK, EVERYONE! HE'S GONE.
S-SORRY ABOUT...
I-IT'S OKAY. YOU...
...?!
N-NODOKA-SAN! HOW DARE YOU FLUSTER AND FIDGET AFTER YOU "ACCIDENT-ALLY"...
TRADE PLACES AT ONCE !!
SAID, BACK TO WORK!
HAH-WAH-WAH...
MURMUR MURMUR
CLASS REP! WILL YOU KEEP IT DOWN ?!
YEEE
YEEE

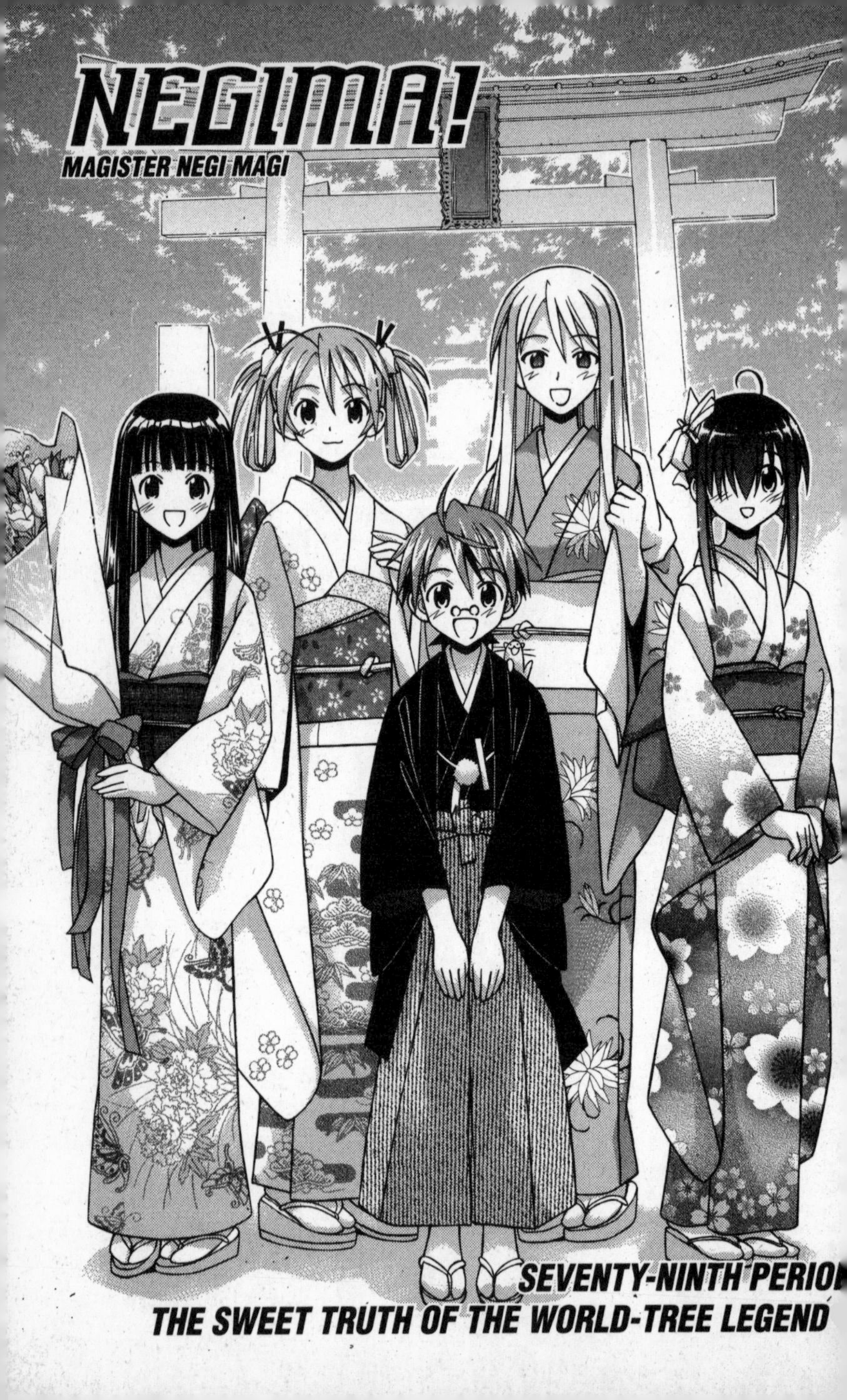
NEGIMA!
MAGISTER NEGI MAGI
SEVENTY-NINTH PERIOD
THE SWEET TRUTH OF THE WORLD-TREE LEGEND

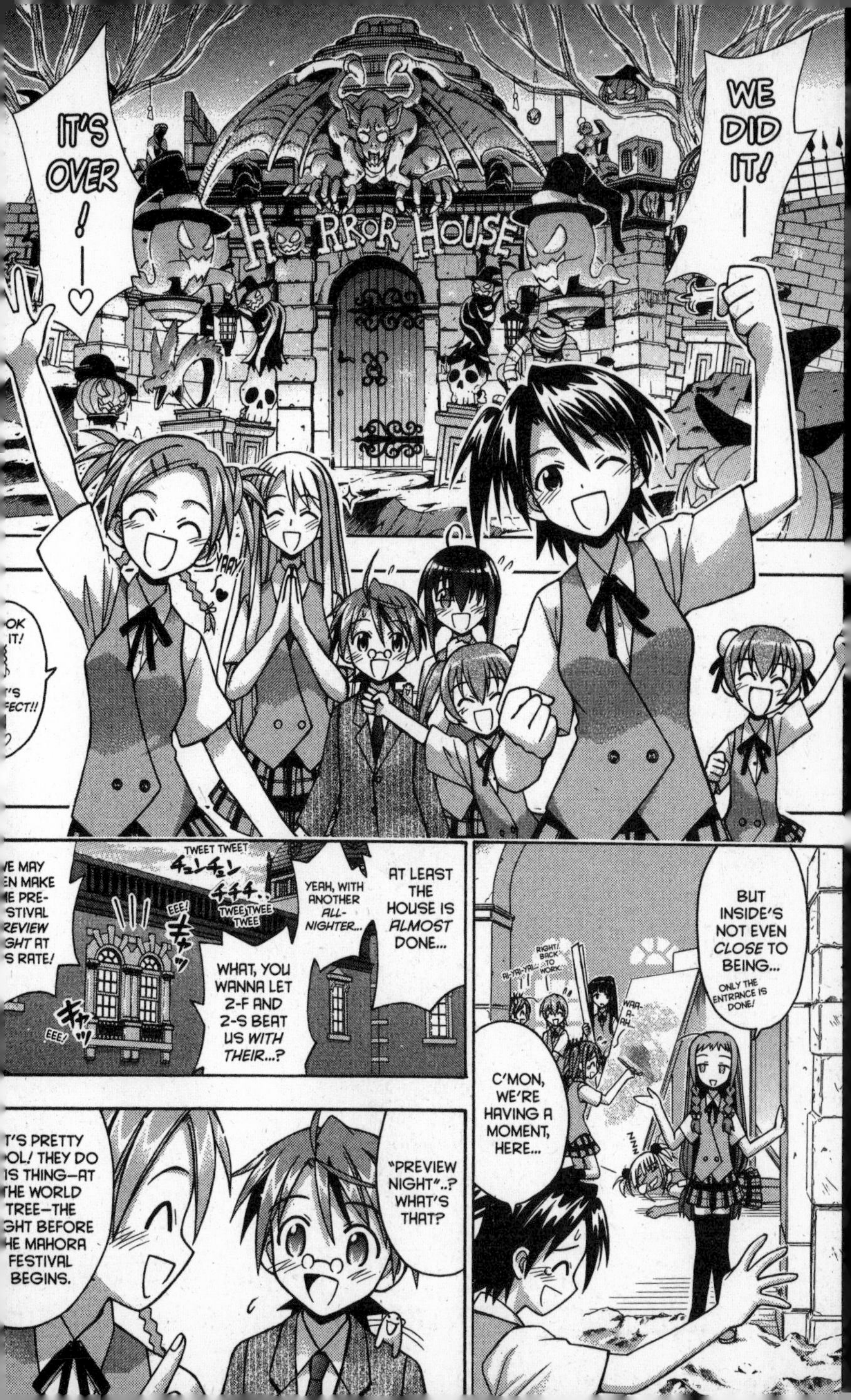
WE DID IT!
IT'S OVER! ♡
YAAY! ♡
OK IT!
'S FECT!!
BUT INSIDE'S NOT EVEN CLOSE TO BEING...
ONLY THE ENTRANCE IS DONE!
RIGHT! BACK TO WORK!
AI-YAI-YAI...
WAA-A-AH...
C'MON, WE'RE HAVING A MOMENT, HERE...
ZZZ
TWEET TWEET
TWEE TWEE TWEE
AT LEAST THE HOUSE IS ALMOST DONE...
YEAH, WITH ANOTHER ALL-NIGHTER...
WHAT, YOU WANNA LET 2-F AND 2-S BEAT US WITH THEIR...?
E MAY EN MAKE E PRE-FESTIVAL REVIEW GHT AT S RATE!
EEE!
EEE!
"PREVIEW NIGHT"..? WHAT'S THAT?
T'S PRETTY OL! THEY DO IS THING—AT THE WORLD TREE—THE GHT BEFORE HE MAHORA FESTIVAL BEGINS.

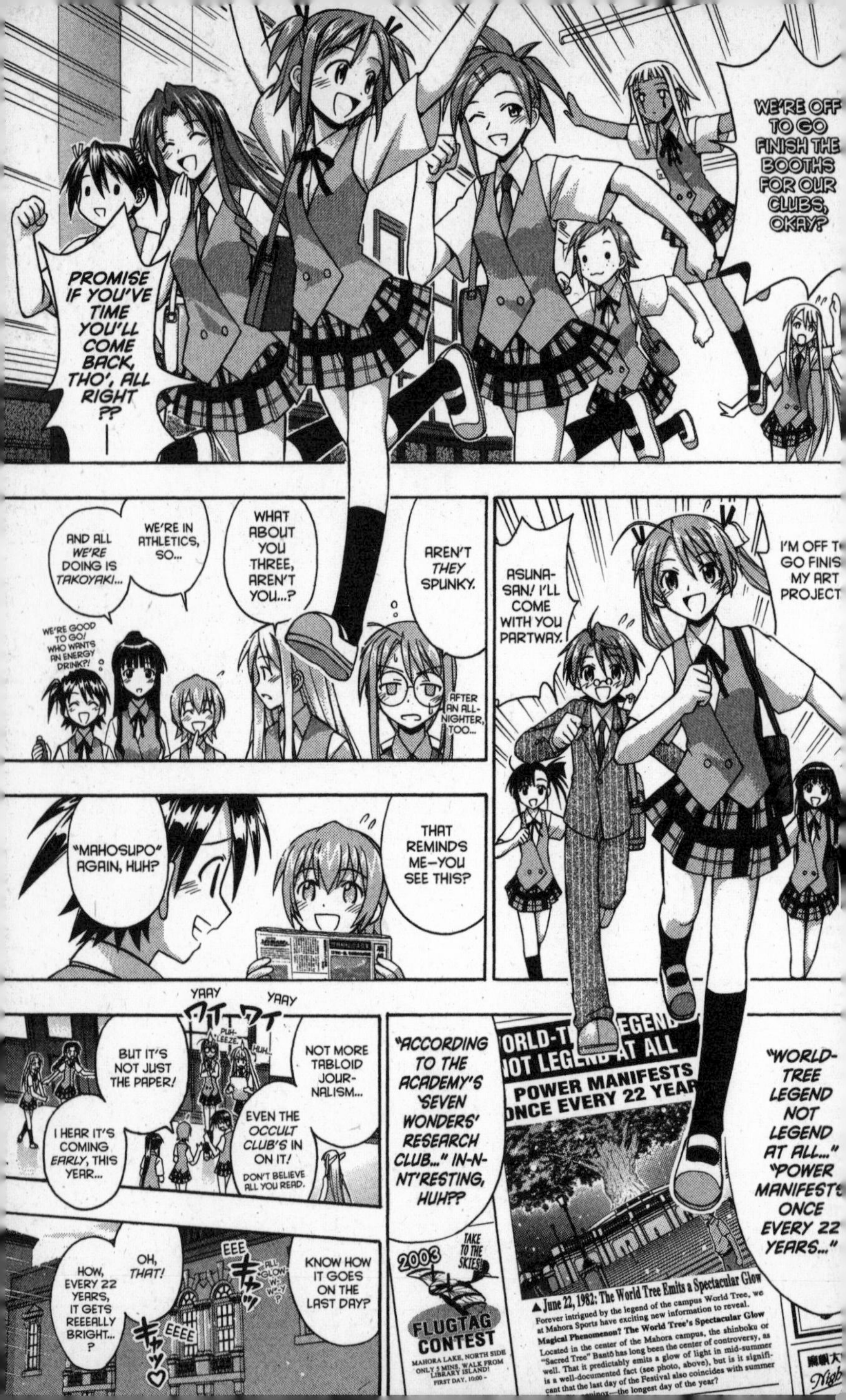
WE'RE OFF TO GO FINISH THE BOOTHS FOR OUR CLUBS, OKAY?
PROMISE IF YOU'VE TIME YOU'LL COME BACK, THO', ALL RIGHT??
I'M OFF T GO FINIS MY ART PROJECT
ASUNA-SAN! I'LL COME WITH YOU PARTWAY.
AREN'T THEY SPUNKY.
AFTER AN ALL-NIGHTER, TOO...
WHAT ABOUT YOU THREE, AREN'T YOU...?
WE'RE IN ATHLETICS, SO...
AND ALL WE'RE DOING IS TAKOYAKI...
WE'RE GOOD TO GO! WHO WANTS AN ENERGY DRINK?!
THAT REMINDS ME—YOU SEE THIS?
"MAHOSUPO" AGAIN, HUH?
"WORLD-TREE LEGEND NOT LEGEND AT ALL..." "POWER MANIFESTS ONCE EVERY 22 YEARS..."
POWER MANIFESTS
ONCE EVERY 22 YEAR
▲June 22, 1982: The World Tree Emits a Spectacular Glow
Forever intrigued by the legend of the campus World Tree, we at Mahora Sports have exciting new information to reveal.
Magical Phenomenon? The World Tree's Spectacular Glow
Located in the center of the Mahora campus, the shinboku or "Sacred Tree" Bantō has long been the center of controversy, as well. That it predictably emits a glow of light in mid-summer is a well-documented fact (see photo, above), but is it significant that the last day of the Festival also coincides with summer
—the longest day of the year?
"ACCORDING TO THE ACADEMY'S 'SEVEN WONDERS' RESEARCH CLUB..." IN-N-NT'RESTING, HUH??
2003
TAKE TO THE SKIES!
FLUGTAG CONTEST
MAHORA LAKE, NORTH SIDE
ONLY 5 MINS. WALK FROM LIBRARY ISLAND!
FIRST DAY, 10:00 ~
YAAY
YAAY
NOT MORE TABLOID JOURNALISM...
HUH!
PUH-LEEZE.
BUT IT'S NOT JUST THE PAPER!
EVEN THE OCCULT CLUB'S IN ON IT!
DON'T BELIEVE ALL YOU READ.
I HEAR IT'S COMING EARLY, THIS YEAR...
KNOW HOW IT GOES ON THE LAST DAY?
ALL GLOW-W-W-Y?
EEE
OH, THAT!
HOW, EVERY 22 YEARS, IT GETS REEEALLY BRIGHT...?
EEEE

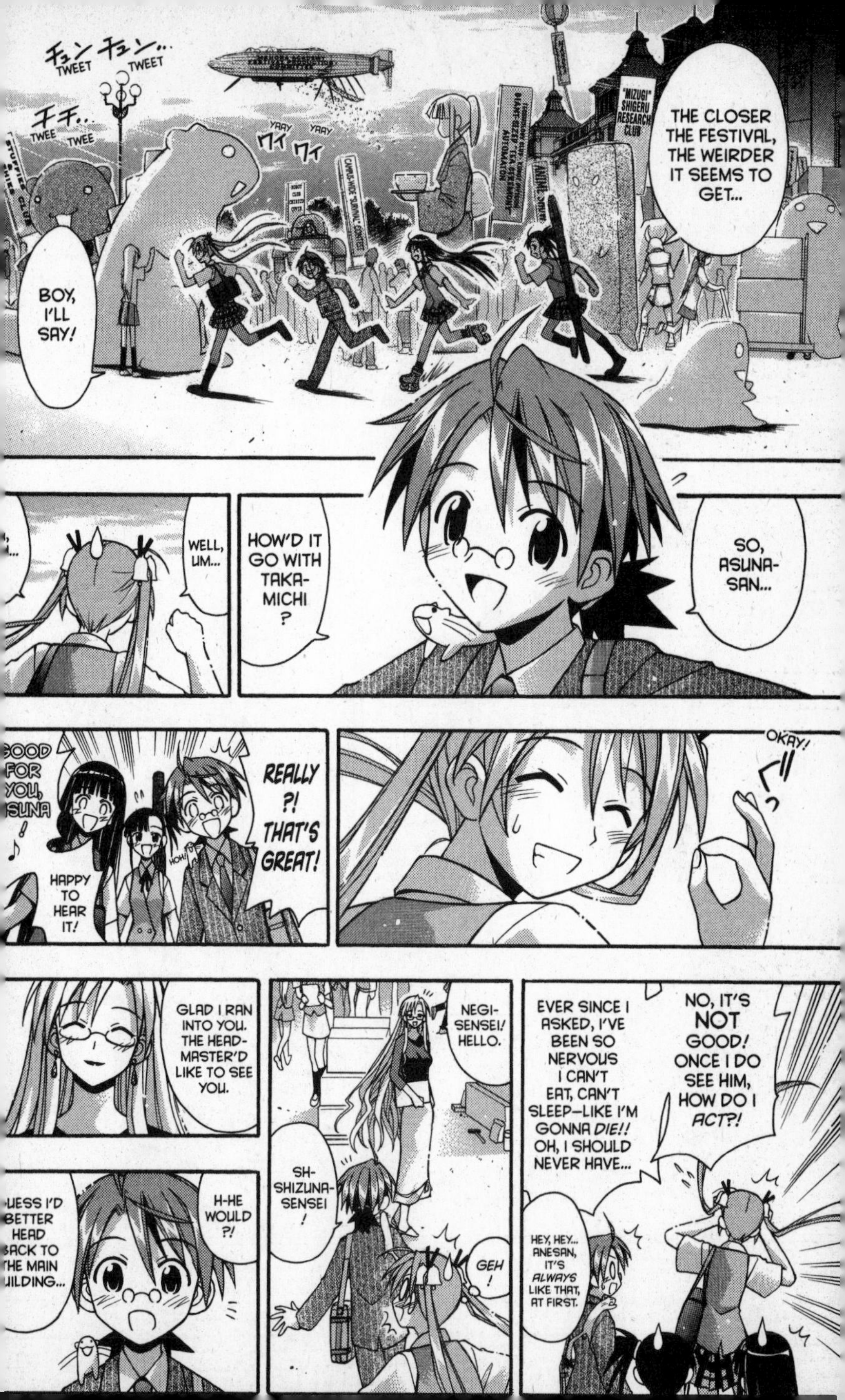
チュン チュン…
TWEET TWEET
チチ…
TWEE TWEE
"MIZUGI" SHIGERU RESEARCH CLUB
ANIME
CAMPUS-WIDE "SURVIVAL" CONTEST
YAAY YAAY
ワイ ワイ
THE CLOSER THE FESTIVAL, THE WEIRDER IT SEEMS TO GET...
BOY, I'LL SAY!
SO, ASUNA-SAN...
HOW'D IT GO WITH TAKA-MICHI?
WELL, UM...
OKAY!
REALLY?! THAT'S GREAT!
HOH!
GOOD FOR YOU, ASUNA!
HAPPY TO HEAR IT!
NO, IT'S NOT GOOD! ONCE I DO SEE HIM, HOW DO I ACT?!
EVER SINCE I ASKED, I'VE BEEN SO NERVOUS I CAN'T EAT, CAN'T SLEEP—LIKE I'M GONNA DIE!! OH, I SHOULD NEVER HAVE...
HEY, HEY... ANESAN, IT'S ALWAYS LIKE THAT, AT FIRST.
NEGI-SENSEI! HELLO.
SH-SHIZUNA-SENSEI!
GEH!
GLAD I RAN INTO YOU. THE HEAD-MASTER'D LIKE TO SEE YOU.
H-HE WOULD?!
GUESS I'D BETTER HEAD BACK TO THE MAIN BUILDING...

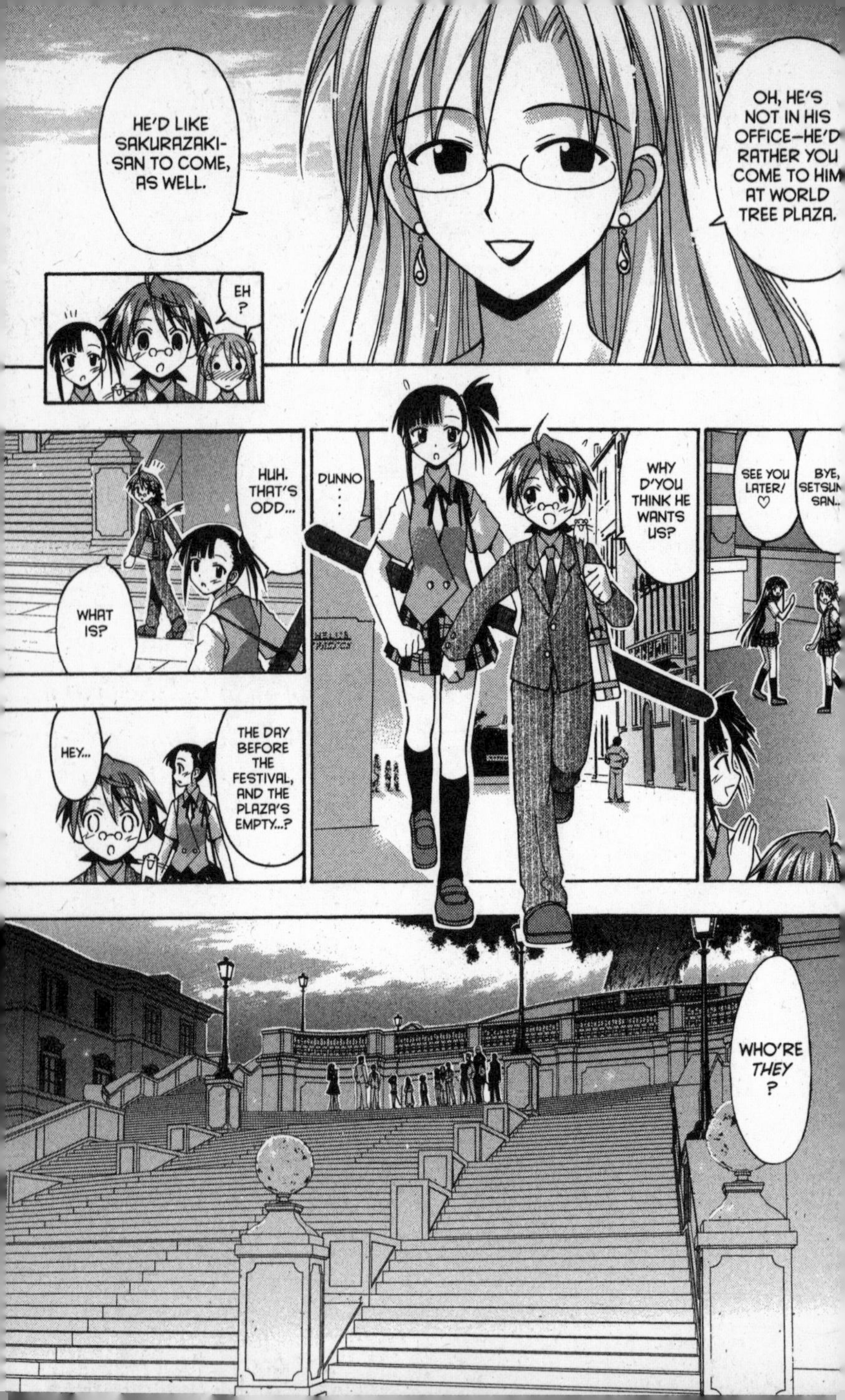
OH, HE'S NOT IN HIS OFFICE—HE'D RATHER YOU COME TO HIM AT WORLD TREE PLAZA.
HE'D LIKE SAKURAZAKI-SAN TO COME, AS WELL.
EH?
BYE, SETSUN SAN...
SEE YOU LATER! ♡
WHY D'YOU THINK HE WANTS US?
DUNNO ....
HUH. THAT'S ODD...
WHAT IS?
THE DAY BEFORE THE FESTIVAL, AND THE PLAZA'S EMPTY...?
HEY...
WHO'RE *THEY*?

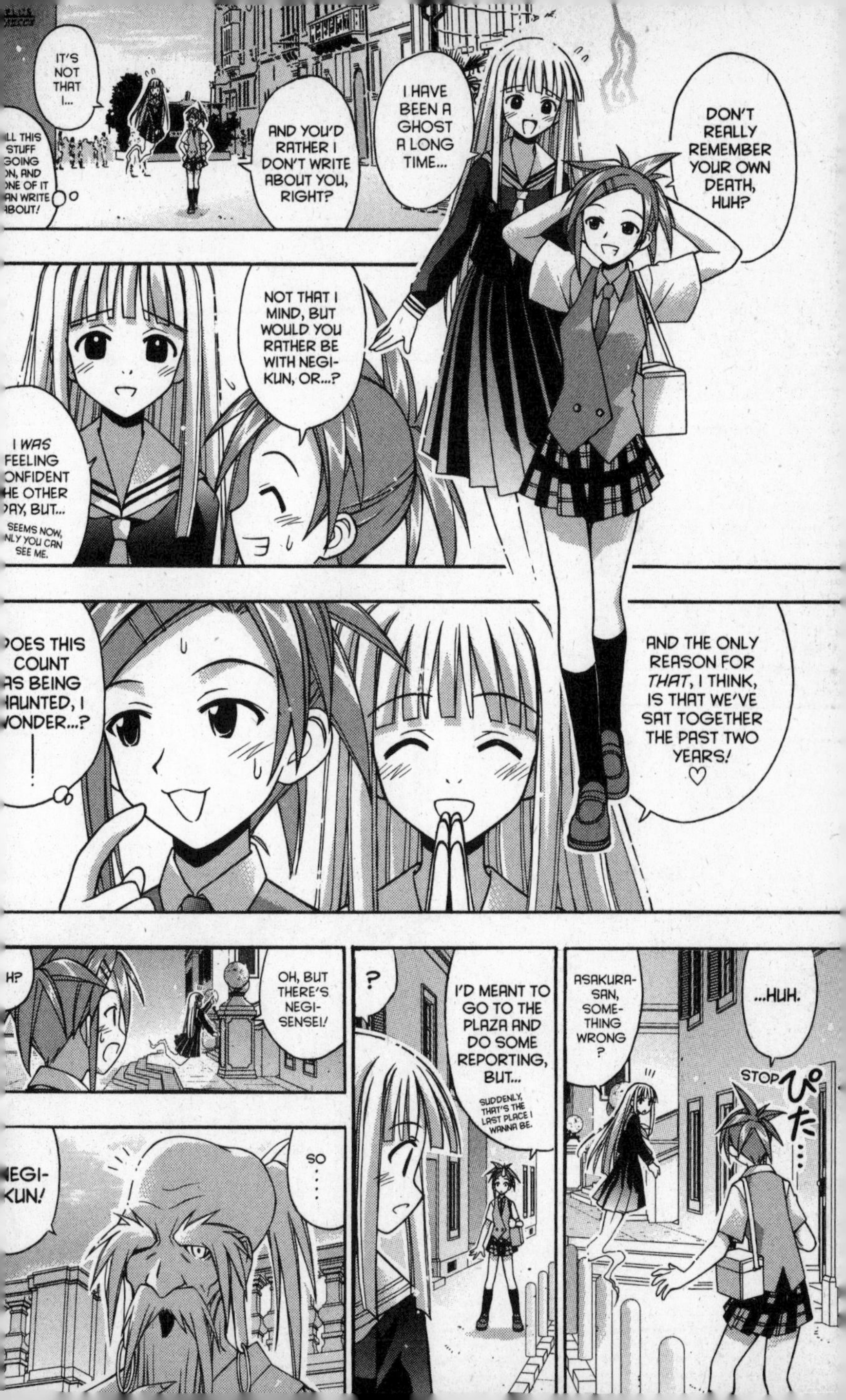
DON'T REALLY REMEMBER YOUR OWN DEATH, HUH?
I HAVE BEEN A GHOST A LONG TIME...
AND YOU'D RATHER I DON'T WRITE ABOUT YOU, RIGHT?
IT'S NOT THAT I...
LL THIS STUFF GOING ON, AND ONE OF IT AN WRITE ABOUT!
NOT THAT I MIND, BUT WOULD YOU RATHER BE WITH NEGI-KUN, OR...?
I WAS FEELING ONFIDENT HE OTHER AY, BUT...
SEEMS NOW, NLY YOU CAN SEE ME.
AND THE ONLY REASON FOR THAT, I THINK, IS THAT WE'VE SAT TOGETHER THE PAST TWO YEARS! ♡
OES THIS COUNT AS BEING AUNTED, I ONDER...?
!
...HUH.
STOP
ぴた...
ASAKURA-SAN, SOME-THING WRONG?
I'D MEANT TO GO TO THE PLAZA AND DO SOME REPORTING, BUT...
SUDDENLY, THAT'S THE LAST PLACE I WANNA BE.
?
OH, BUT THERE'S NEGI-SENSEI!
H?
SO....
EGI-KUN!

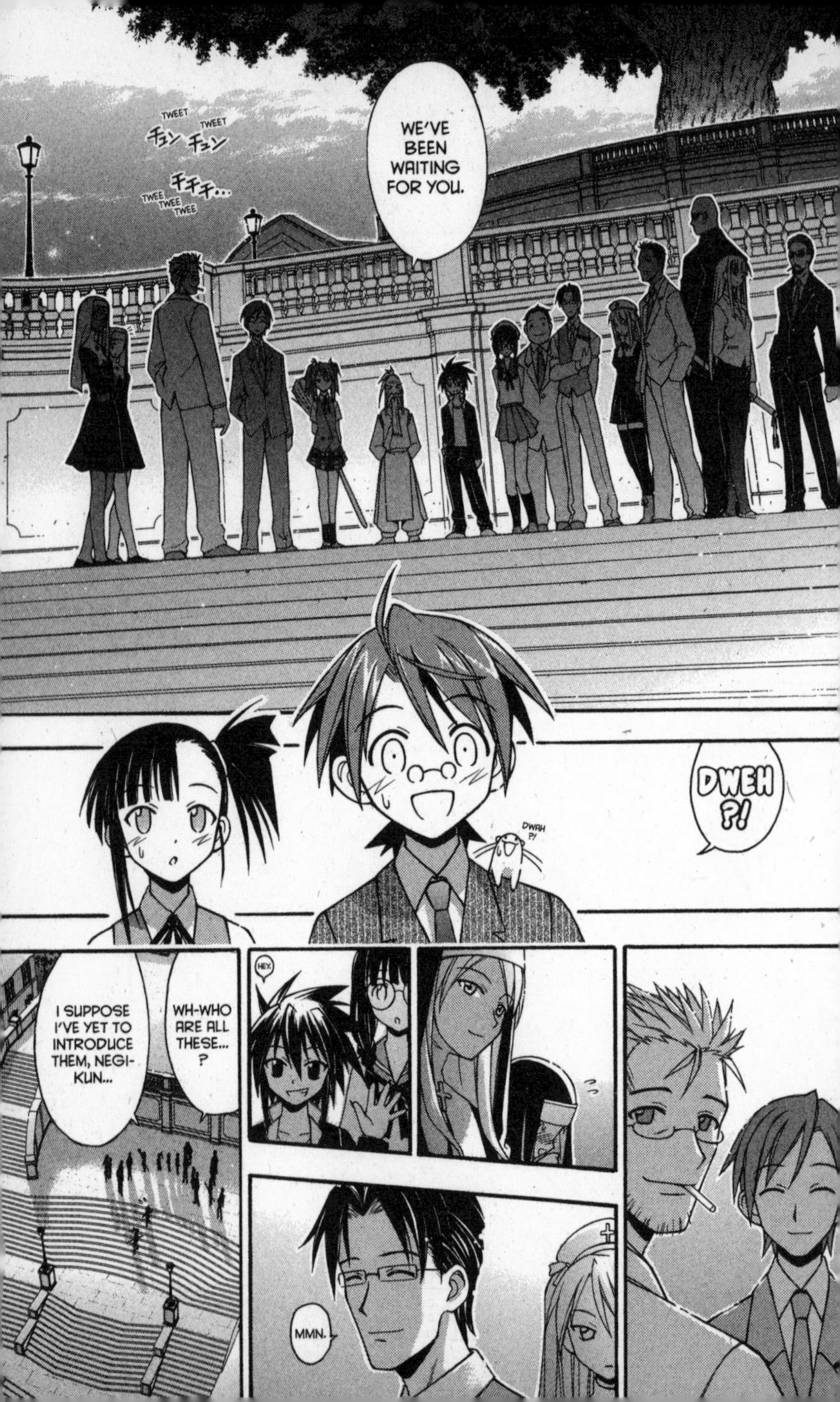
WE'VE BEEN WAITING FOR YOU.
TWEET
チュン
TWEET
チュン
チチチ…
TWEE TWEE TWEE
DWEH ?!
DWAH ?!
HEY.
MMN.
WH-WHO ARE ALL THESE... ?
I SUPPOSE I'VE YET TO INTRODUCE THEM, NEGI-KUN...

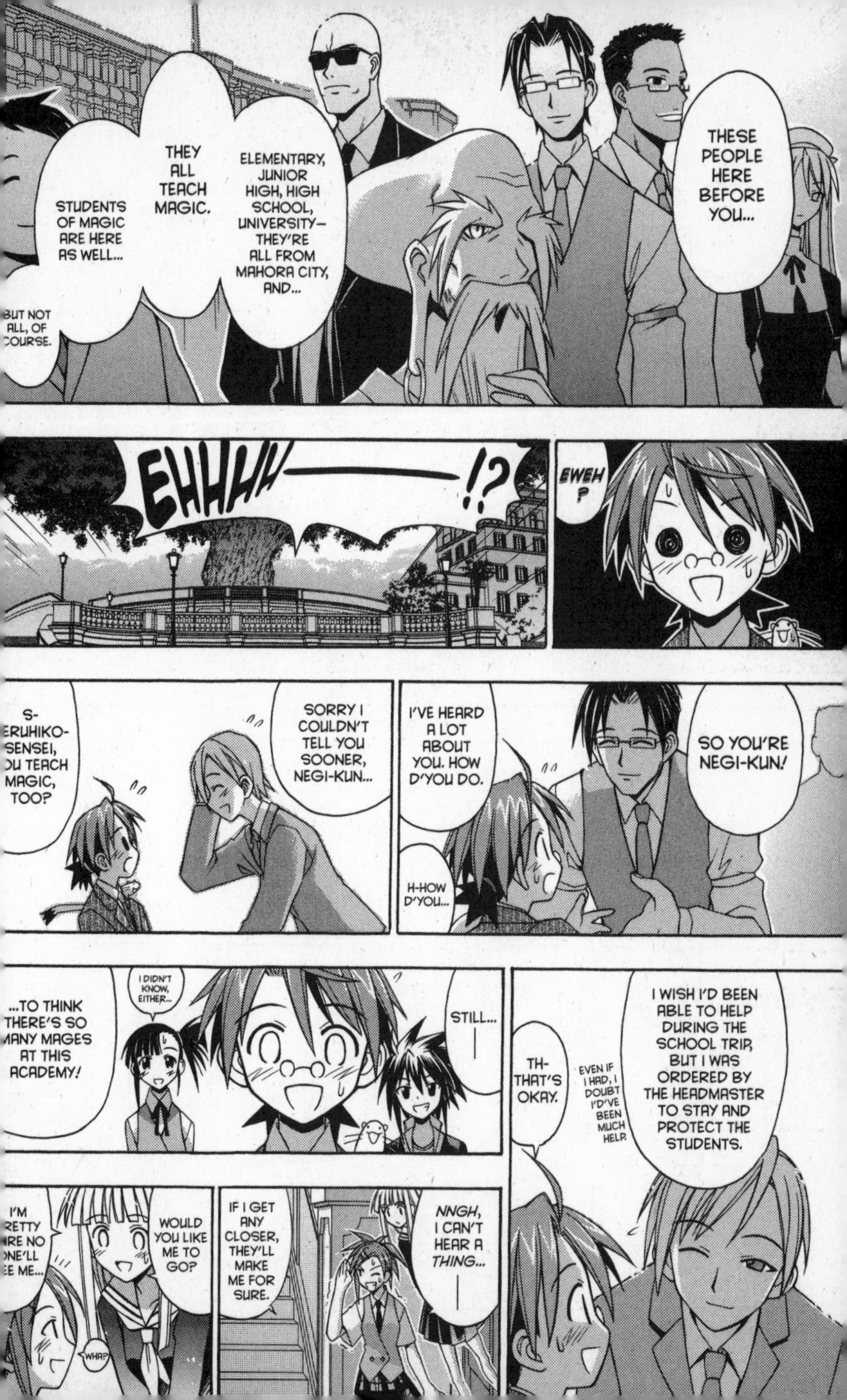
THESE PEOPLE HERE BEFORE YOU...
ELEMENTARY, JUNIOR HIGH, HIGH SCHOOL, UNIVERSITY— THEY'RE ALL FROM MAHORA CITY, AND...
THEY ALL TEACH MAGIC.
STUDENTS OF MAGIC ARE HERE AS WELL...
BUT NOT ALL, OF COURSE.
EWEH?
EHHHH———!?
SO YOU'RE NEGI-KUN!
I'VE HEARD A LOT ABOUT YOU. HOW D'YOU DO.
H-HOW D'YOU...
SORRY I COULDN'T TELL YOU SOONER, NEGI-KUN...
S- ERUHIKO-SENSEI, OU TEACH MAGIC, TOO?
I WISH I'D BEEN ABLE TO HELP DURING THE SCHOOL TRIP, BUT I WAS ORDERED BY THE HEADMASTER TO STAY AND PROTECT THE STUDENTS.
EVEN IF I HAD, I DOUBT I'D'VE BEEN MUCH HELP.
TH-THAT'S OKAY.
STILL...
I DIDN'T KNOW, EITHER...
...TO THINK THERE'S SO MANY MAGES AT THIS ACADEMY!
NNGH, I CAN'T HEAR A THING...
IF I GET ANY CLOSER, THEY'LL MAKE ME FOR SURE.
WOULD YOU LIKE ME TO GO?
I'M RETTY RE NO NE'LL EE ME...
WHAP

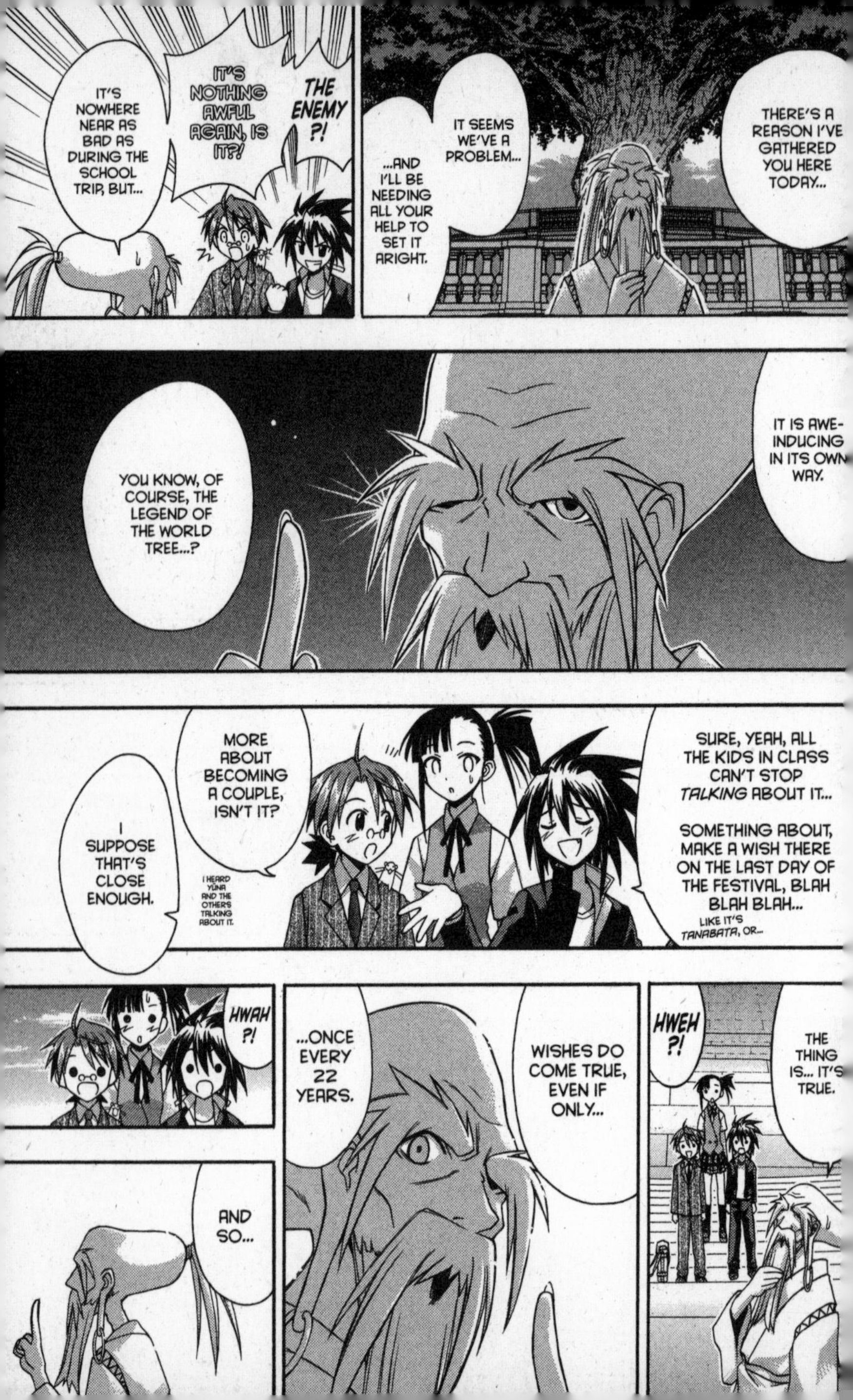
THERE'S A REASON I'VE GATHERED YOU HERE TODAY...
IT SEEMS WE'VE A PROBLEM...
...AND I'LL BE NEEDING ALL YOUR HELP TO SET IT ARIGHT.
THE ENEMY ?!
IT'S NOTHING AWFUL AGAIN, IS IT?!
IT'S NOWHERE NEAR AS BAD AS DURING THE SCHOOL TRIP, BUT...
IT IS AWE-INDUCING IN ITS OWN WAY.
YOU KNOW, OF COURSE, THE LEGEND OF THE WORLD TREE...?
SURE, YEAH, ALL THE KIDS IN CLASS CAN'T STOP *TALKING* ABOUT IT...
SOMETHING ABOUT, MAKE A WISH THERE ON THE LAST DAY OF THE FESTIVAL, BLAH BLAH BLAH...
LIKE IT'S *TANABATA*, OR...
MORE ABOUT BECOMING A COUPLE, ISN'T IT?
I HEARD YUNA AND THE OTHERS TALKING ABOUT IT.
I SUPPOSE THAT'S CLOSE ENOUGH.
THE THING IS... IT'S TRUE.
HWEH ?!
WISHES DO COME TRUE, EVEN IF ONLY...
...ONCE EVERY 22 YEARS.
HWAH ?!
AND SO...

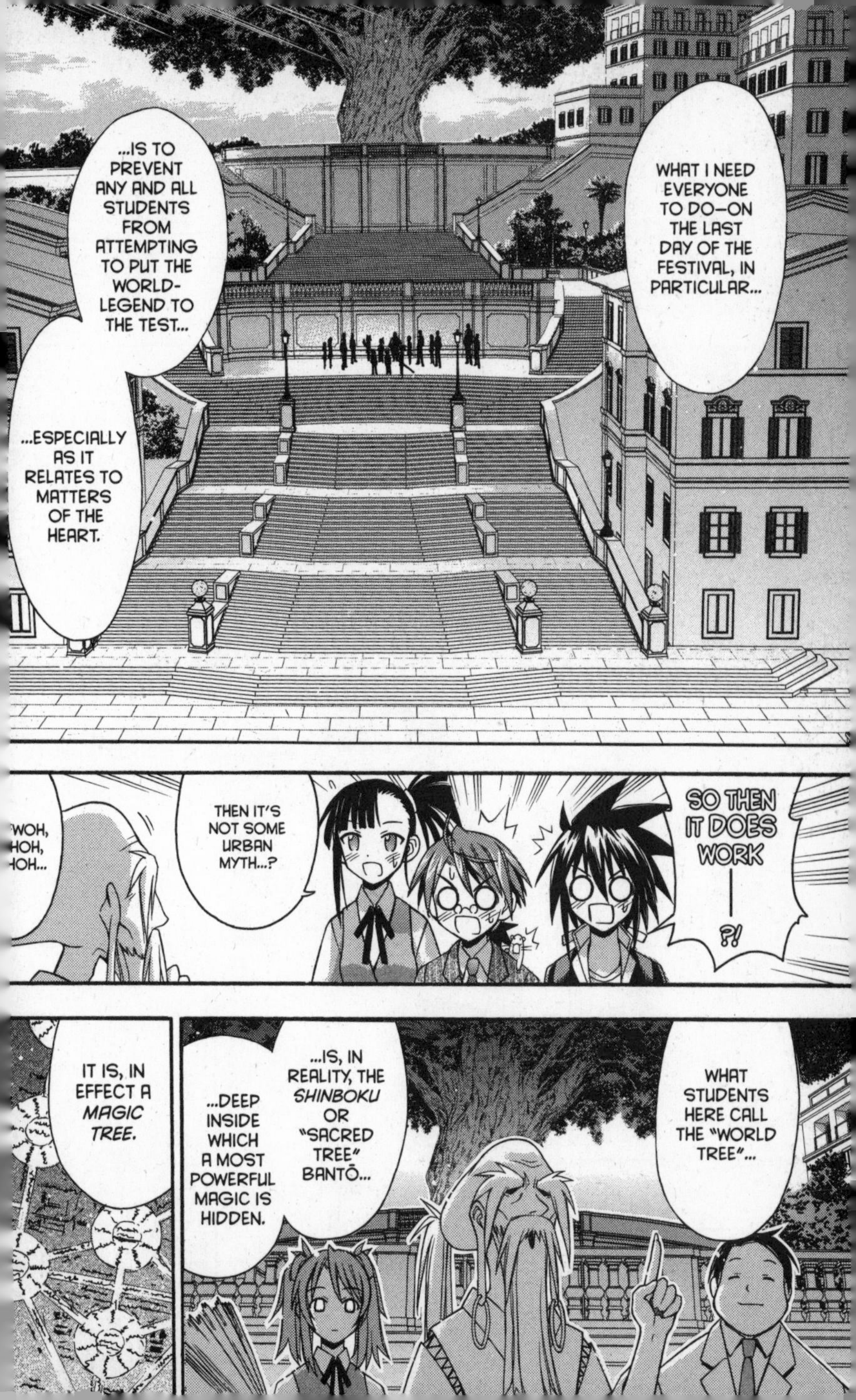
WHAT I NEED EVERYONE TO DO—ON THE LAST DAY OF THE FESTIVAL, IN PARTICULAR...
...IS TO PREVENT ANY AND ALL STUDENTS FROM ATTEMPTING TO PUT THE WORLD-LEGEND TO THE TEST...
...ESPECIALLY AS IT RELATES TO MATTERS OF THE HEART.
SO THEN IT DOES WORK—?!
THEN IT'S NOT SOME URBAN MYTH...?
WOH, HOH, HOH...
WHAT STUDENTS HERE CALL THE "WORLD TREE"...
...IS, IN REALITY, THE *SHINBOKU* OR "SACRED TREE" BANTŌ...
...DEEP INSIDE WHICH A MOST POWERFUL MAGIC IS HIDDEN.
IT IS, IN EFFECT A *MAGIC TREE.*

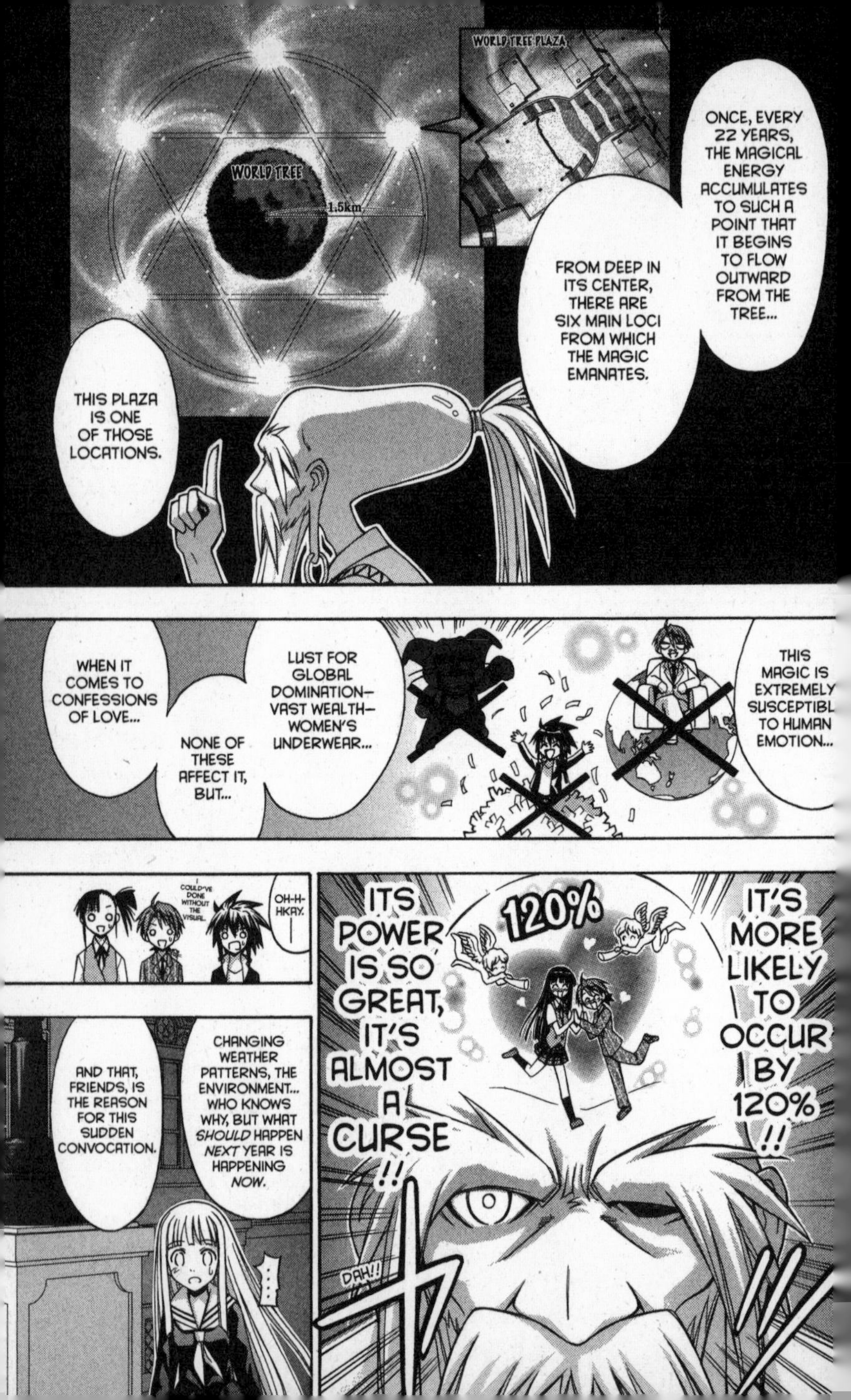
WORLD TREE PLAZA
WORLD TREE
1.5km
ONCE, EVERY 22 YEARS, THE MAGICAL ENERGY ACCUMULATES TO SUCH A POINT THAT IT BEGINS TO FLOW OUTWARD FROM THE TREE...
FROM DEEP IN ITS CENTER, THERE ARE SIX MAIN LOCI FROM WHICH THE MAGIC EMANATES.
THIS PLAZA IS ONE OF THOSE LOCATIONS.
THIS MAGIC IS EXTREMELY SUSCEPTIBL TO HUMAN EMOTION...
LUST FOR GLOBAL DOMINATION— VAST WEALTH— WOMEN'S UNDERWEAR...
NONE OF THESE AFFECT IT, BUT...
WHEN IT COMES TO CONFESSIONS OF LOVE...
IT'S MORE LIKELY TO OCCUR BY 120% !!
120%
ITS POWER IS SO GREAT, IT'S ALMOST A CURSE !!
DAH!!
OH-H-HKAY.
I COULD'VE DONE WITHOUT THE VISUAL.
CHANGING WEATHER PATTERNS, THE ENVIRONMENT... WHO KNOWS WHY, BUT WHAT *SHOULD* HAPPEN *NEXT* YEAR IS HAPPENING *NOW*.
AND THAT, FRIENDS, IS THE REASON FOR THIS SUDDEN CONVOCATION.
....

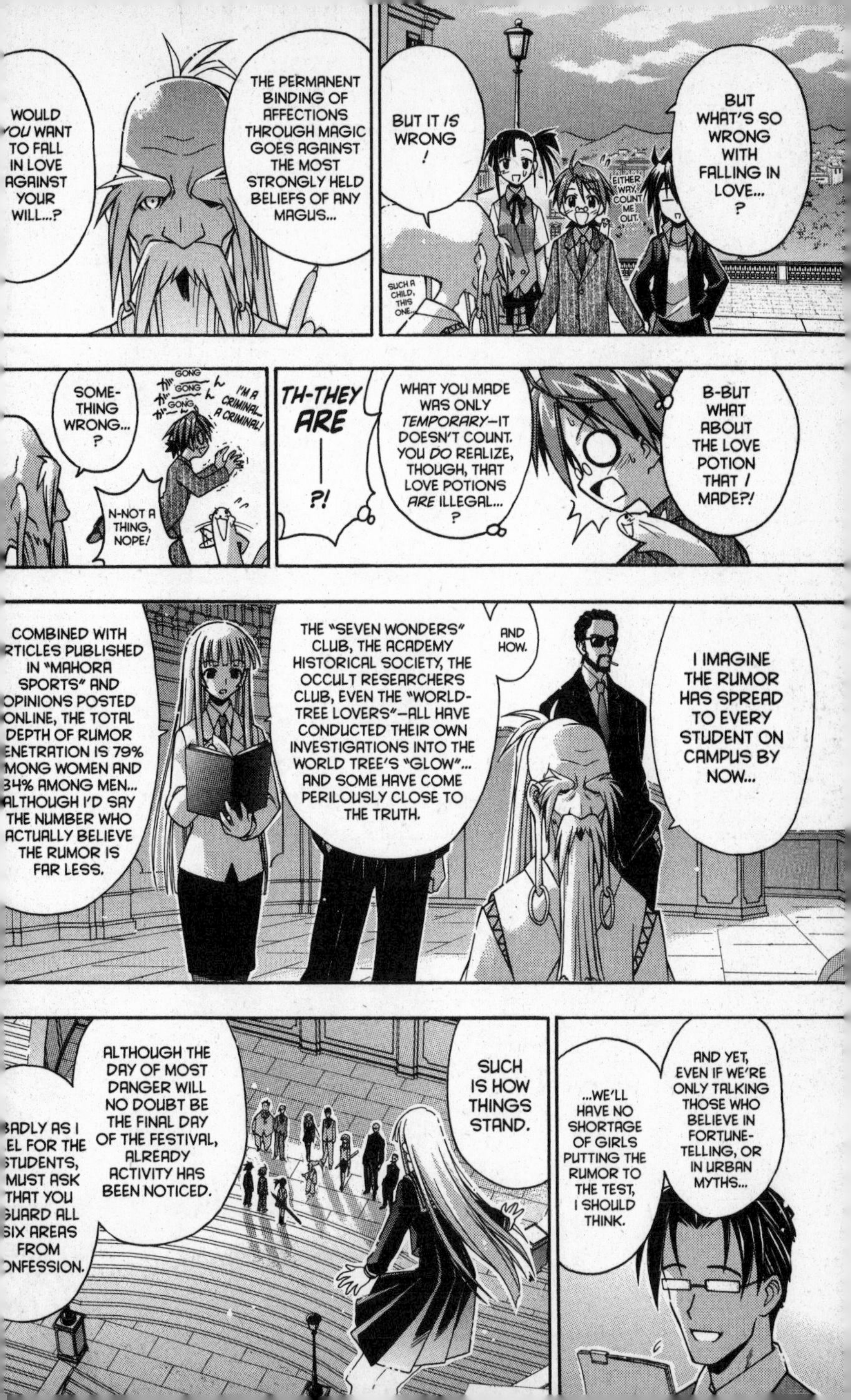
BUT WHAT'S SO WRONG WITH FALLING IN LOVE...?
EITHER WAY, COUNT ME OUT.
BUT IT *IS* WRONG!
SUCH A CHILD, THIS ONE...
THE PERMANENT BINDING OF AFFECTIONS THROUGH MAGIC GOES AGAINST THE MOST STRONGLY HELD BELIEFS OF ANY MAGUS...
WOULD *YOU* WANT TO FALL IN LOVE AGAINST YOUR WILL...?
B-BUT WHAT ABOUT THE LOVE POTION THAT *I* MADE?!
WHAT YOU MADE WAS ONLY *TEMPORARY*—IT DOESN'T COUNT. YOU *DO* REALIZE, THOUGH, THAT LOVE POTIONS *ARE* ILLEGAL...?
TH-THEY ARE—?!
SOMETHING WRONG...?
GONG GONG GONG
I'M A CRIMINAL... A CRIMINAL!
N-NOT A THING, NOPE!
I IMAGINE THE RUMOR HAS SPREAD TO EVERY STUDENT ON CAMPUS BY NOW...
AND HOW.
THE "SEVEN WONDERS" CLUB, THE ACADEMY HISTORICAL SOCIETY, THE OCCULT RESEARCHERS CLUB, EVEN THE "WORLD-TREE LOVERS"—ALL HAVE CONDUCTED THEIR OWN INVESTIGATIONS INTO THE WORLD TREE'S "GLOW"... AND SOME HAVE COME PERILOUSLY CLOSE TO THE TRUTH.
COMBINED WITH RTICLES PUBLISHED IN "MAHORA SPORTS" AND OPINIONS POSTED ONLINE, THE TOTAL DEPTH OF RUMOR ENETRATION IS 79% MONG WOMEN AND 34% AMONG MEN... ALTHOUGH I'D SAY THE NUMBER WHO ACTUALLY BELIEVE THE RUMOR IS FAR LESS.
AND YET, EVEN IF WE'RE ONLY TALKING THOSE WHO BELIEVE IN FORTUNE-TELLING, OR IN URBAN MYTHS...
...WE'LL HAVE NO SHORTAGE OF GIRLS PUTTING THE RUMOR TO THE TEST, I SHOULD THINK.
SUCH IS HOW THINGS STAND.
ALTHOUGH THE DAY OF MOST DANGER WILL NO DOUBT BE THE FINAL DAY OF THE FESTIVAL, ALREADY ACTIVITY HAS BEEN NOTICED.
BADLY AS I EL FOR THE STUDENTS, MUST ASK THAT YOU GUARD ALL SIX AREAS FROM ONFESSION.

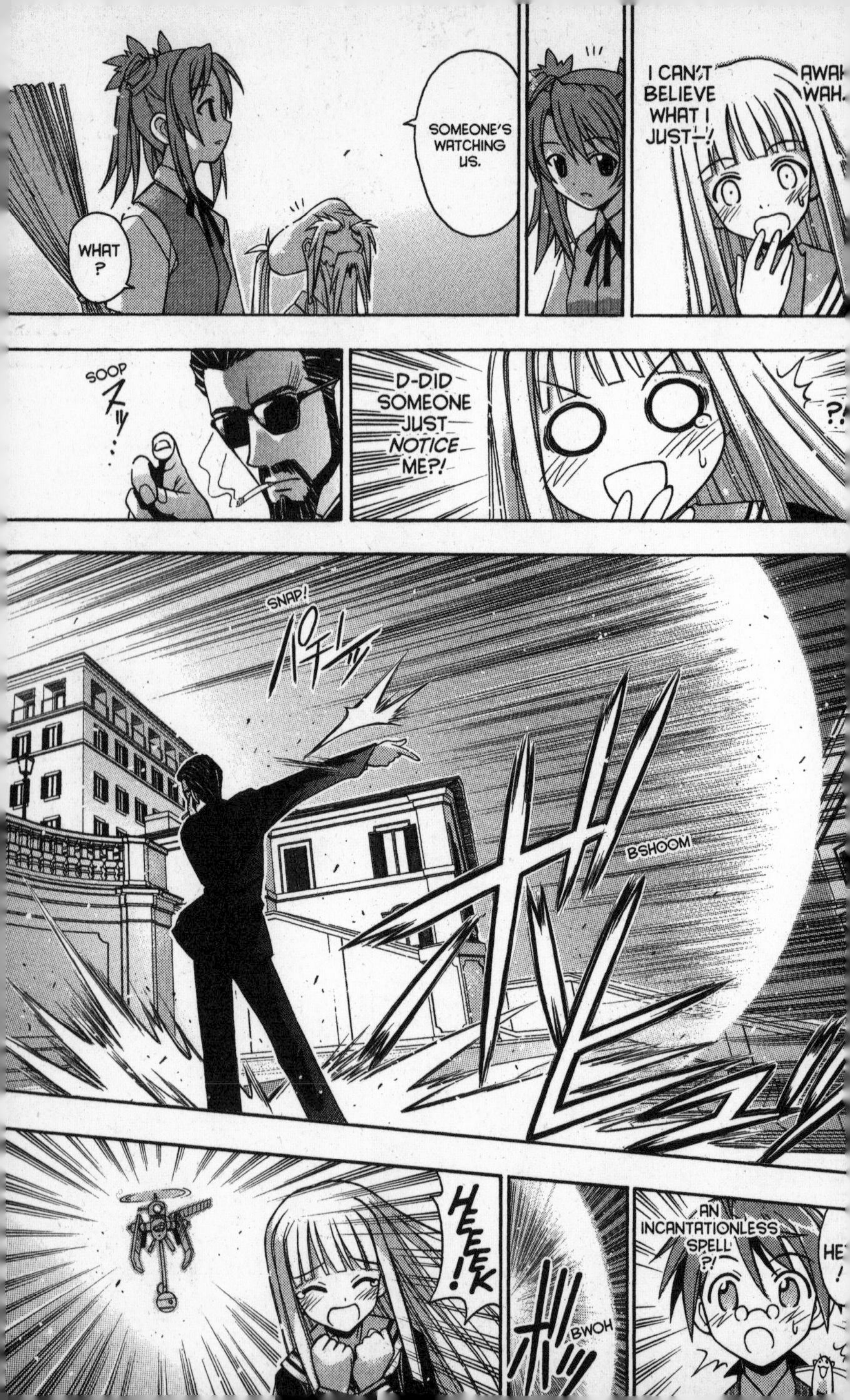

AWAH WAH.
I CAN'T BELIEVE WHAT I JUST—!
SOMEONE'S WATCHING US.
WHAT?
?!
D-DID SOMEONE JUST NOTICE ME?!
SOOP
SNAP!
BSHOOM
HE
AN INCANTATIONLESS SPELL?!
BWOH
HEEEK!

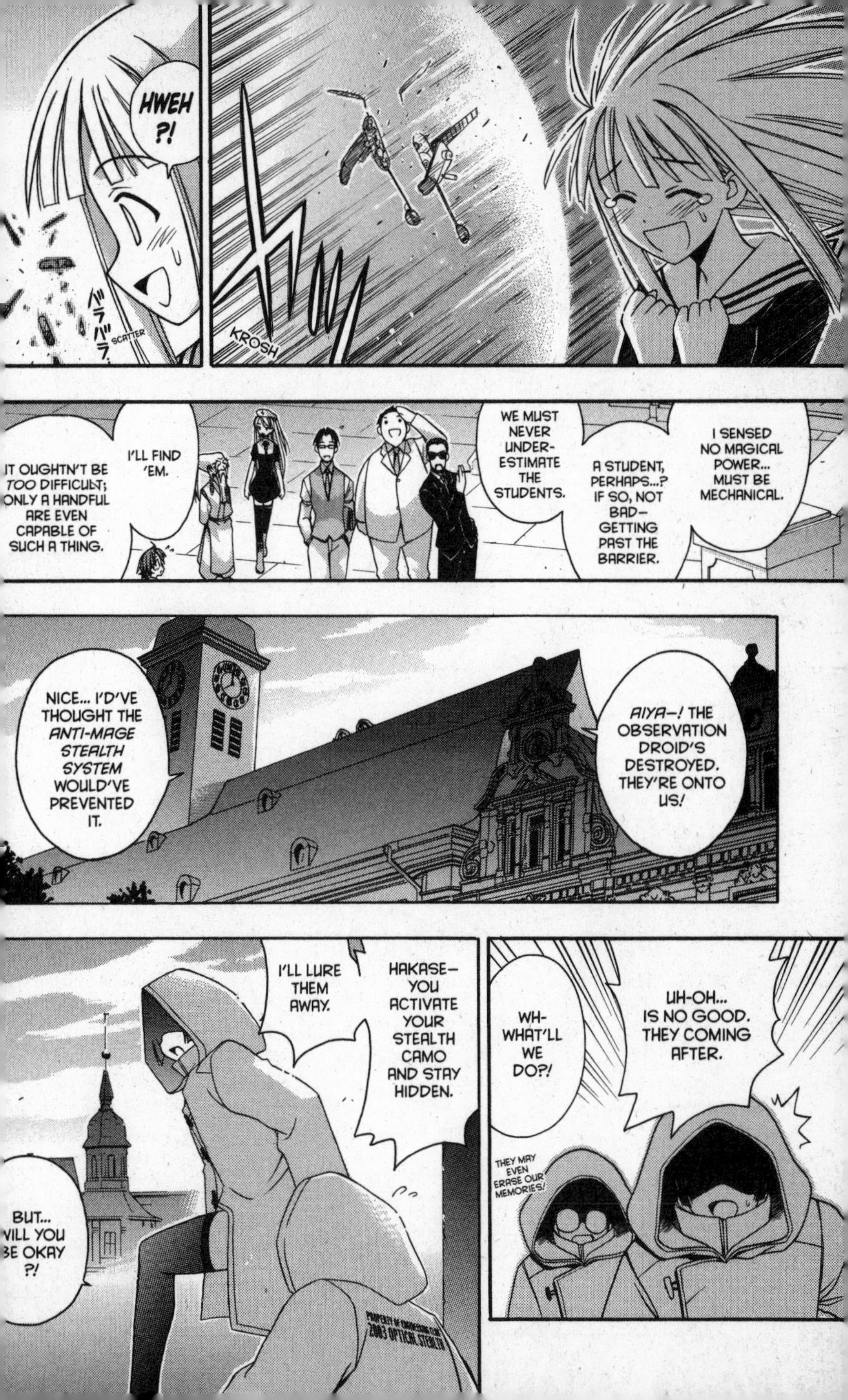
KROSH
HWEH ?!
バラバラ
SCATTER
I SENSED NO MAGICAL POWER... MUST BE MECHANICAL.
A STUDENT, PERHAPS...? IF SO, NOT BAD—GETTING PAST THE BARRIER.
WE MUST NEVER UNDER-ESTIMATE THE STUDENTS.
I'LL FIND 'EM.
IT OUGHTN'T BE TOO DIFFICULT; ONLY A HANDFUL ARE EVEN CAPABLE OF SUCH A THING.
AIYA—! THE OBSERVATION DROID'S DESTROYED. THEY'RE ONTO US!
NICE... I'D'VE THOUGHT THE ANTI-MAGE STEALTH SYSTEM WOULD'VE PREVENTED IT.
UH-OH... IS NO GOOD. THEY COMING AFTER.
WH-WHAT'LL WE DO?!
THEY MAY EVEN ERASE OUR MEMORIES!
HAKASE—YOU ACTIVATE YOUR STEALTH CAMO AND STAY HIDDEN.
I'LL LURE THEM AWAY.
BUT... WILL YOU BE OKAY?!
2003 OPTICAL STEALTH

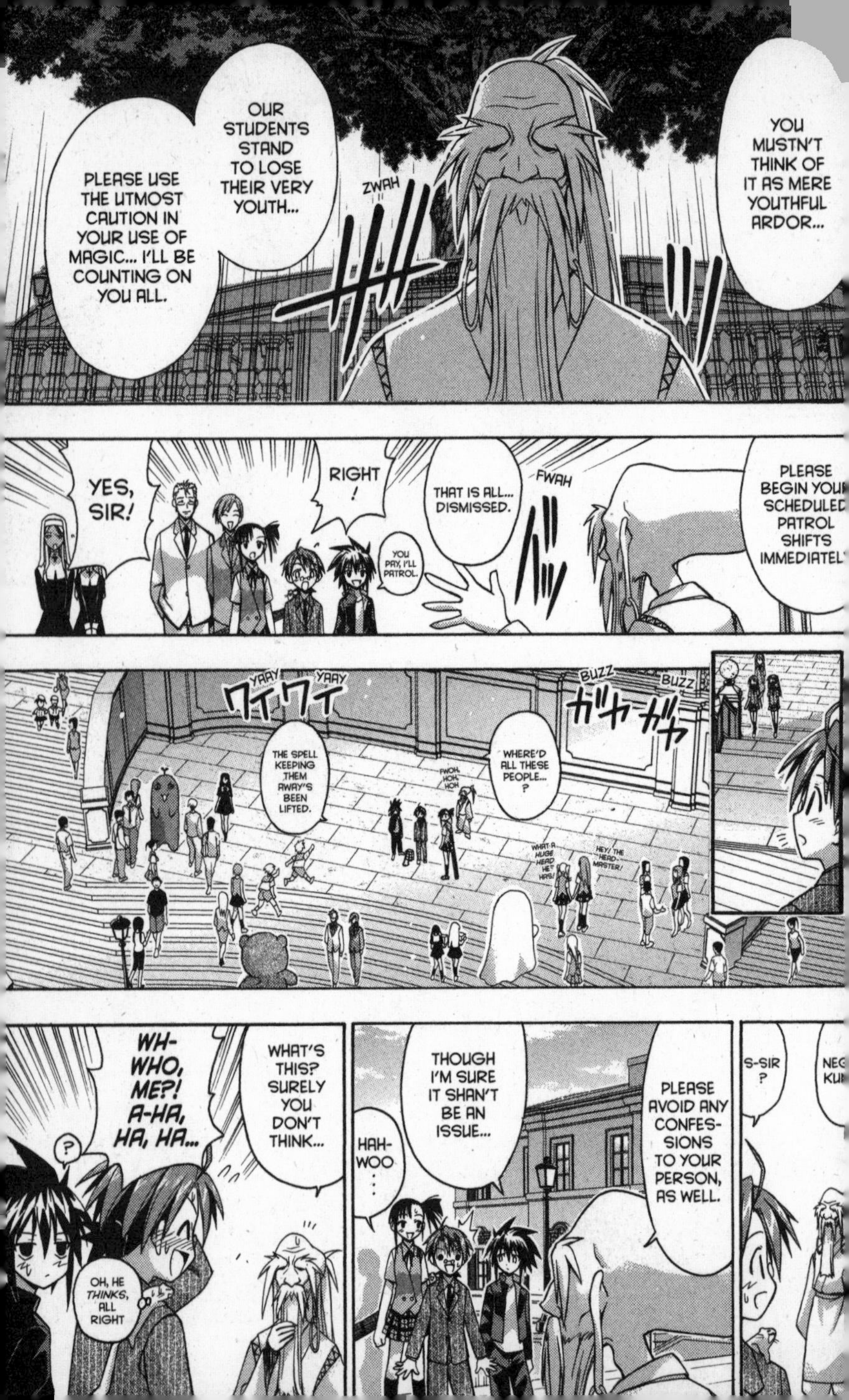
YOU MUSTN'T THINK OF IT AS MERE YOUTHFUL ARDOR...
ZWAH
OUR STUDENTS STAND TO LOSE THEIR VERY YOUTH...
PLEASE USE THE UTMOST CAUTION IN YOUR USE OF MAGIC... I'LL BE COUNTING ON YOU ALL.
PLEASE BEGIN YOUR SCHEDULED PATROL SHIFTS IMMEDIATEL
FWAH
THAT IS ALL... DISMISSED.
YOU PAY, I'LL PATROL.
RIGHT!
YES, SIR!
BUZZ BUZZ
WHERE'D ALL THESE PEOPLE...?
HEY! THE HEAD-MASTER!
WHAT A HUGE HEAD HE HAS!
FWOH, HOH, HOH
THE SPELL KEEPING THEM AWAY'S BEEN LIFTED.
YAAY YAAY
NEG KU
S-SIR?
PLEASE AVOID ANY CONFES-SIONS TO YOUR PERSON, AS WELL.
THOUGH I'M SURE IT SHAN'T BE AN ISSUE...
HAH-WOO...
WHAT'S THIS? SURELY YOU DON'T THINK...
WH-WHO, ME?! A-HA, HA, HA...
?
OH, HE THINKS, ALL RIGHT

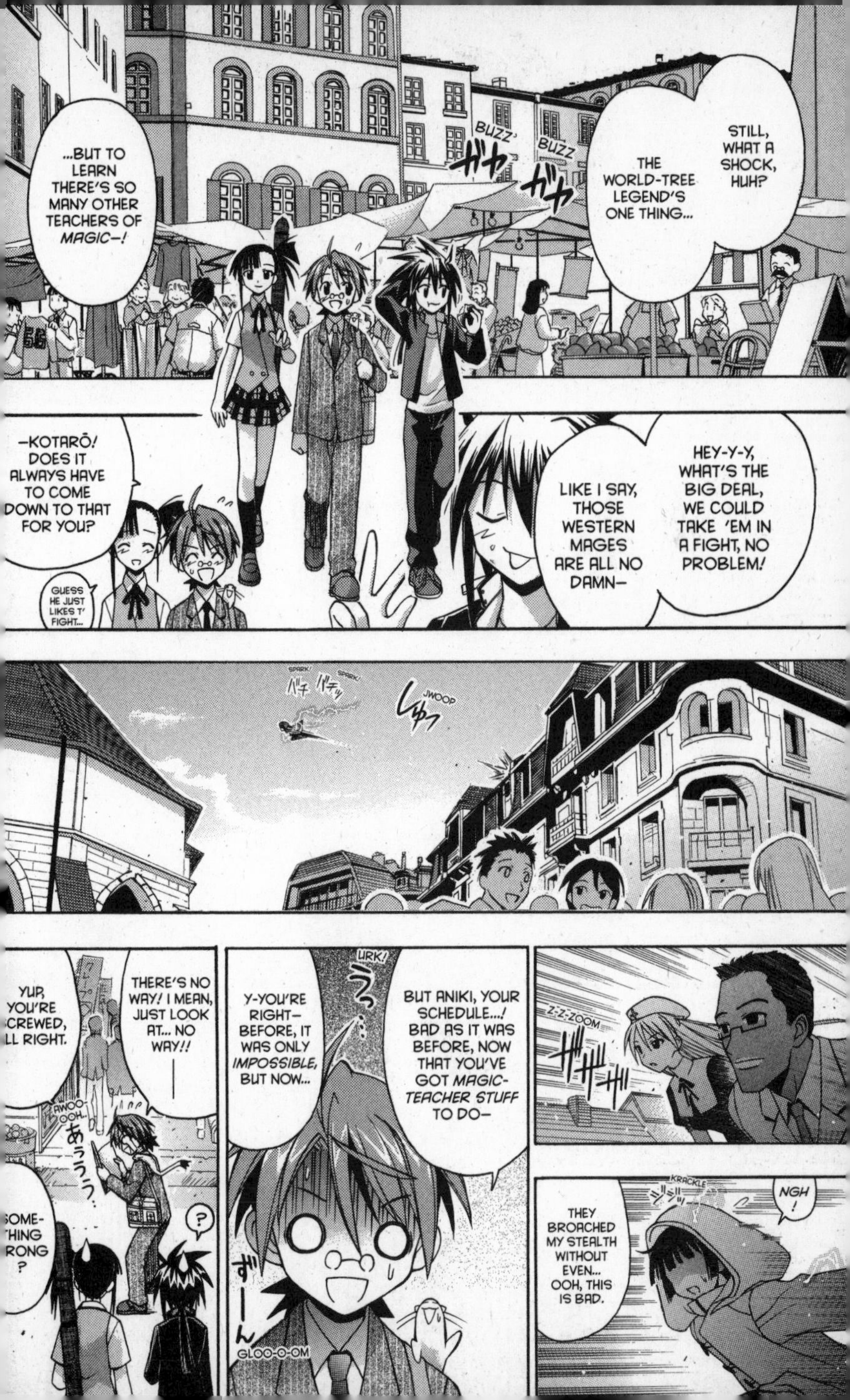
STILL, WHAT A SHOCK, HUH?
THE WORLD-TREE LEGEND'S ONE THING...
BUZZ BUZZ
...BUT TO LEARN THERE'S SO MANY OTHER TEACHERS OF *MAGIC*—!
HEY-Y-Y, WHAT'S THE BIG DEAL, WE COULD TAKE 'EM IN A FIGHT, NO PROBLEM!
LIKE I SAY, THOSE WESTERN MAGES ARE ALL NO DAMN—
—KOTARŌ! DOES IT ALWAYS HAVE TO COME DOWN TO THAT FOR YOU?
GUESS HE JUST LIKES T' FIGHT...
JWOOP
SPARK SPARK
Z-Z-ZOOM
KRACKLE
NGH!
THEY BROACHED MY STEALTH WITHOUT EVEN... OOH, THIS IS BAD.
BUT ANIKI, YOUR SCHEDULE...! BAD AS IT WAS BEFORE, NOW THAT YOU'VE GOT *MAGIC-TEACHER STUFF* TO DO—
URK!
Y-YOU'RE RIGHT— BEFORE, IT WAS ONLY *IMPOSSIBLE*, BUT NOW...
GLOO-O-OM
THERE'S NO WAY! I MEAN, JUST LOOK AT... NO WAY!!
YUP, YOU'RE CREWED, LL RIGHT.
AWOO-OOH.
OME-THING RONG?
?

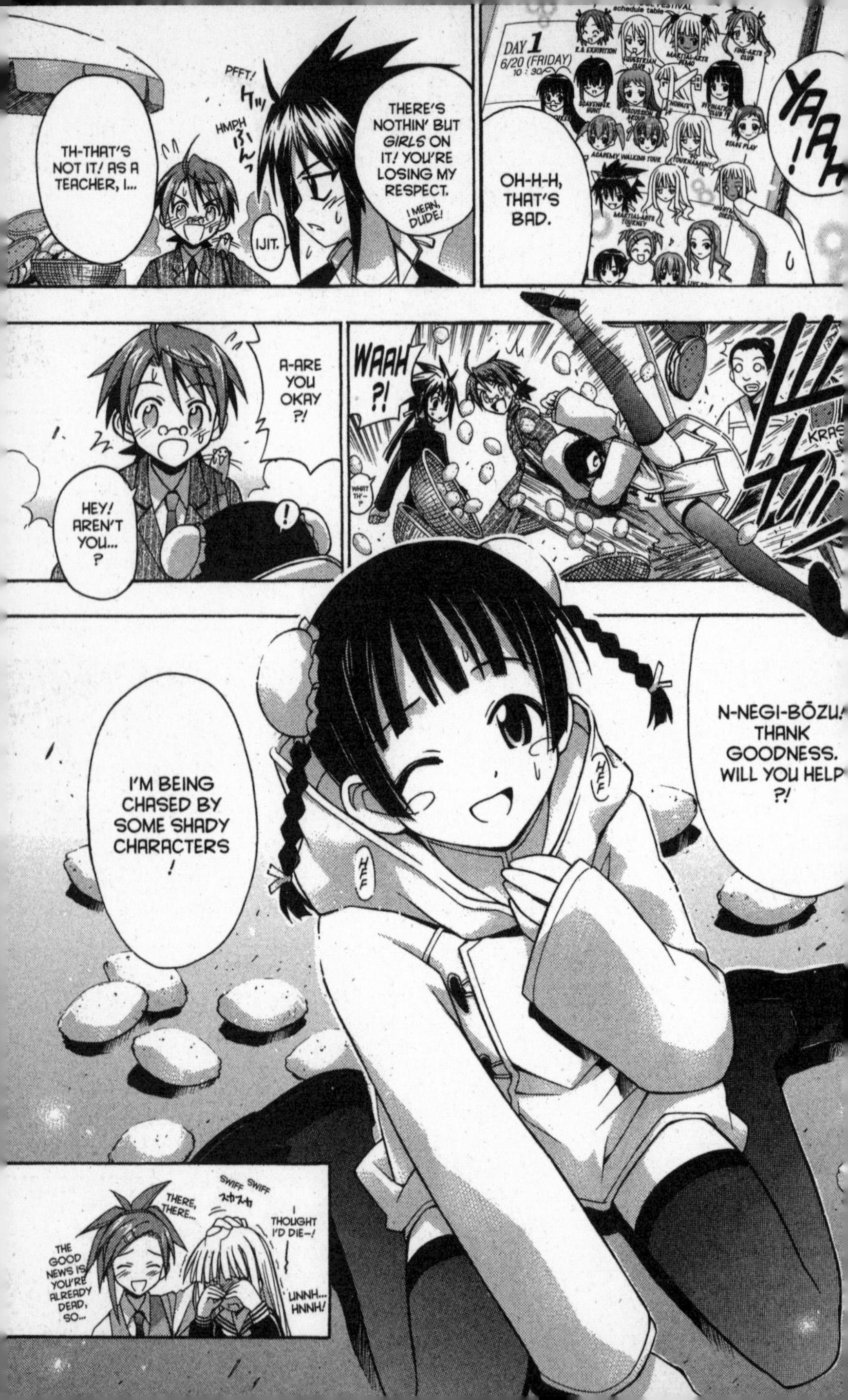
schedule table
DAY 1
6/20 (FRIDAY)
10:30
FINE-ARTS CLUB
MARTIAL-ARTS DEMO
EQUESTRIAN CLUB
SCAVENGER HUNT
PERCUSSION GROUP
STAGE PLAY
ACADEMY WALKING TOUR
MARTIAL-ARTS TOURNEY
YAAAH!
OH-H-H, THAT'S BAD.
THERE'S NOTHIN' BUT GIRLS ON IT! YOU'RE LOSING MY RESPECT.
I MEAN, DUDE!
PFFT!
HMPH
IJIT.
TH-THAT'S NOT IT! AS A TEACHER, I...
KRASH
WAAH?!
WHAT TH-?
A-ARE YOU OKAY?!
HEY! AREN'T YOU...?
!
N-NEGI-BŌZU! THANK GOODNESS. WILL YOU HELP?!
HFF
HFF
I'M BEING CHASED BY SOME SHADY CHARACTERS!
THERE, THERE...
SWIFF SWIFF
I THOUGHT I'D DIE-!
UNNH... HNNH!
THE GOOD NEWS IS YOU'RE ALREADY DEAD, SO...

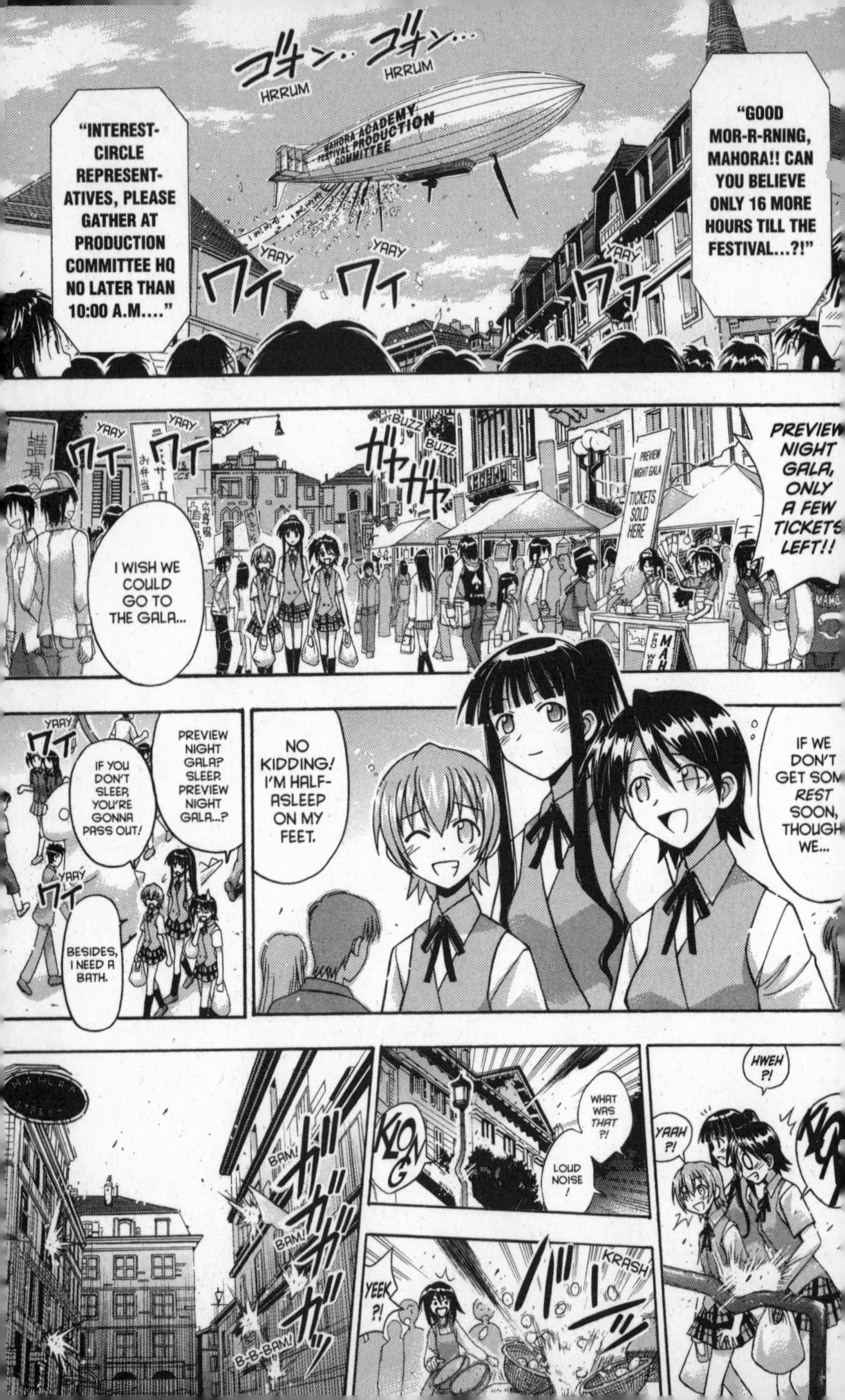
ゴオン… ゴオン…
HRRUM
HRRUM
MAHORA ACADEMY FESTIVAL PRODUCTION COMMITTEE
"GOOD MOR-R-RNING, MAHORA!! CAN YOU BELIEVE ONLY 16 MORE HOURS TILL THE FESTIVAL...?!"
"INTEREST-CIRCLE REPRESENT-ATIVES, PLEASE GATHER AT PRODUCTION COMMITTEE HQ NO LATER THAN 10:00 A.M...."
YAAY ワイ
YAAY ワイ
YAAY ワイ
PREVIEW NIGHT GALA, ONLY A FEW TICKETS LEFT!!
PREVIEW NIGHT GALA TICKETS SOLD HERE
BUZZ ガヤ
BUZZ ガヤ
YAAY ワイ
YAAY ワイ
I WISH WE COULD GO TO THE GALA...
IF WE DON'T GET SOM REST SOON, THOUGH WE...
NO KIDDING! I'M HALF-ASLEEP ON MY FEET.
PREVIEW NIGHT GALA? SLEEP. PREVIEW NIGHT GALA...?
IF YOU DON'T SLEEP, YOU'RE GONNA PASS OUT!
YAAY ワイ
YAAY ワイ
BESIDES, I NEED A BATH.
HWEH ?!
YAAH ?!
WHAT WAS THAT ?!
LOUD NOISE !
KLONG
KRASH
YEEK ?!
BAM!
BAM!
B-B-BAM!

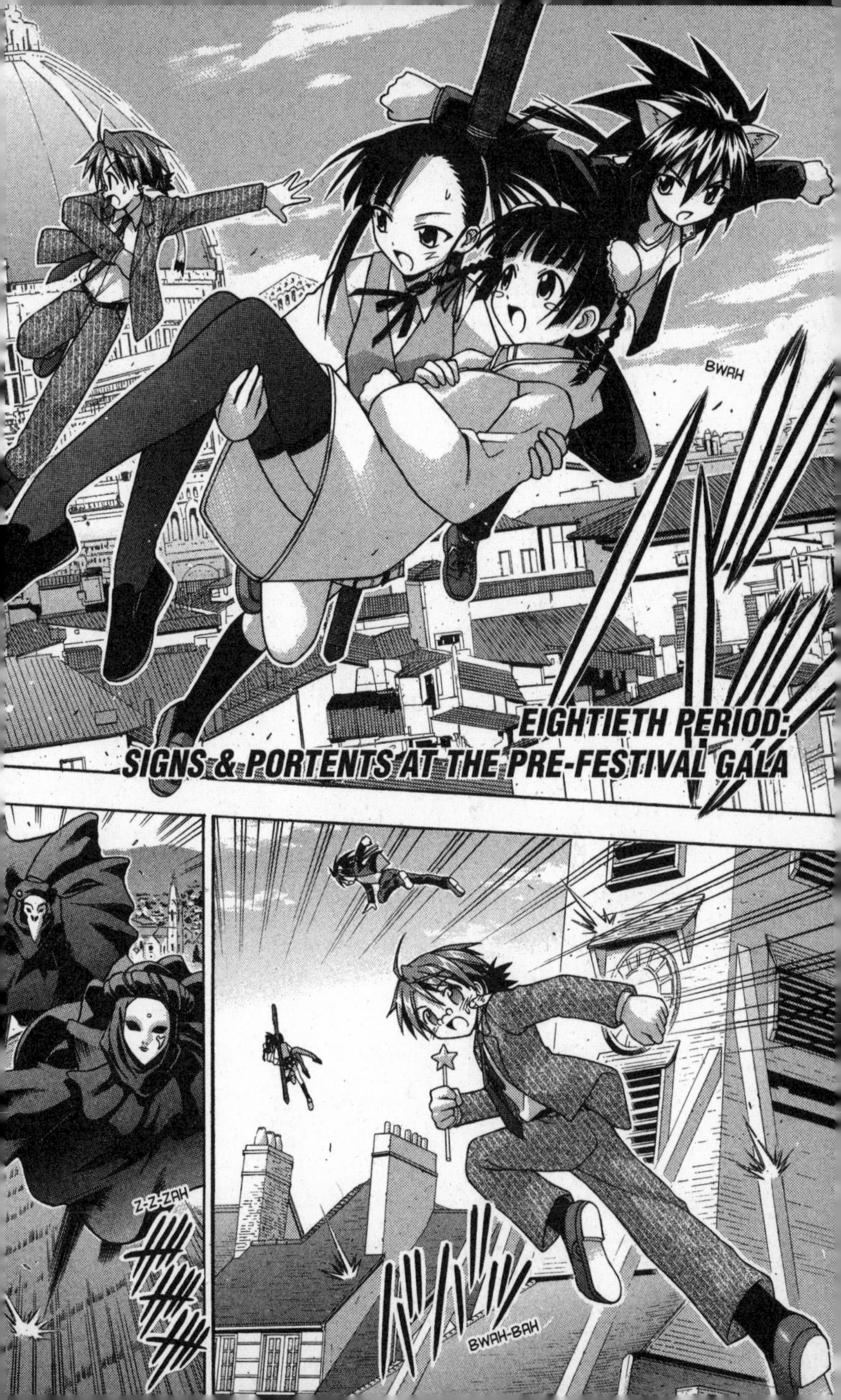
BWAH
EIGHTIETH PERIOD:
SIGNS & PORTENTS AT THE PRE-FESTIVAL GALA
BWAH-BAH
Z-Z-ZAH

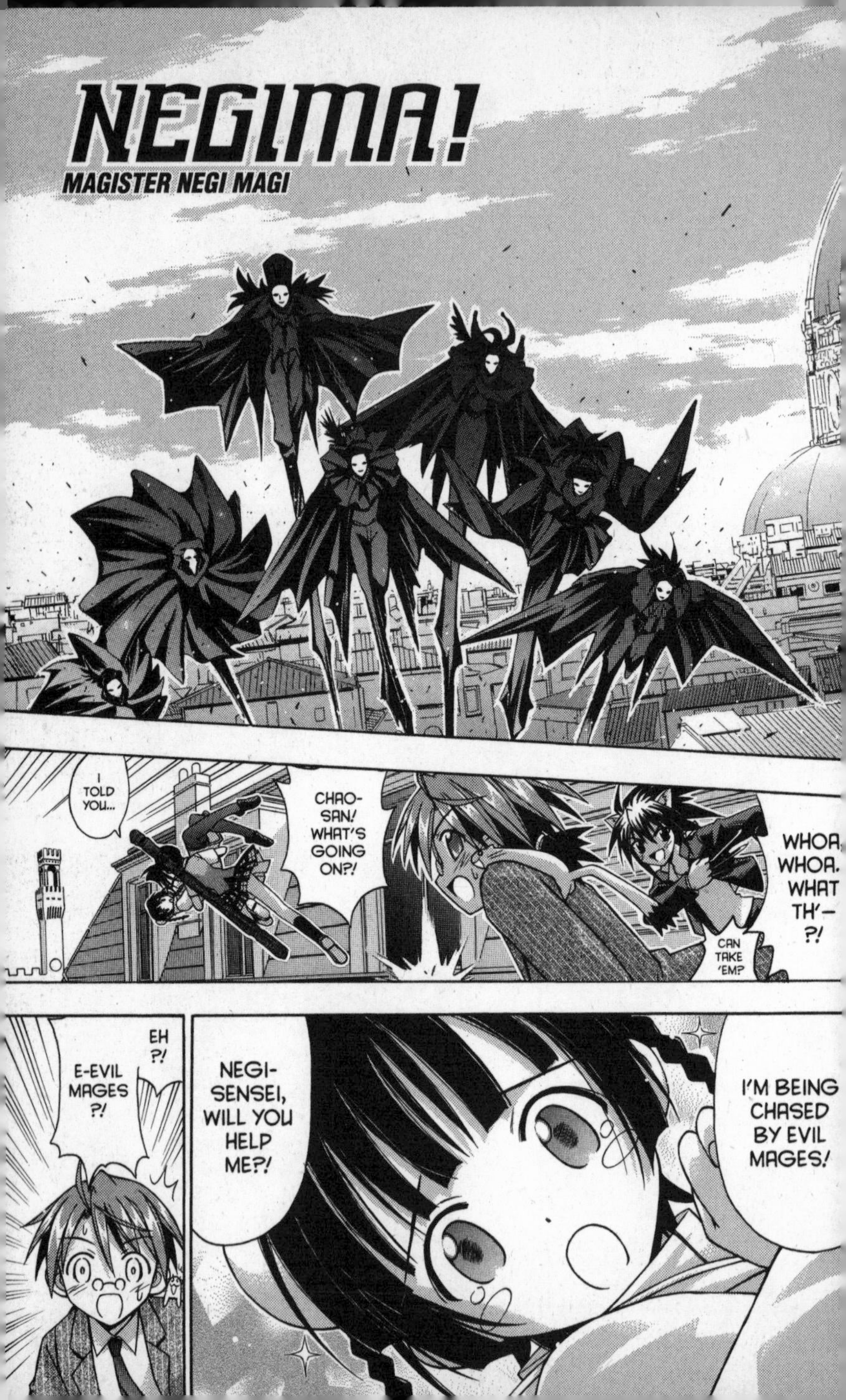
NEGIMA!
MAGISTER NEGI MAGI
WHOA. WHOA. WHAT TH'—?!
CAN TAKE 'EM?
CHAO-SAN! WHAT'S GOING ON?!
I TOLD YOU...
I'M BEING CHASED BY EVIL MAGES!
NEGI-SENSEI, WILL YOU HELP ME?!
EH?!
E-EVIL MAGES?!

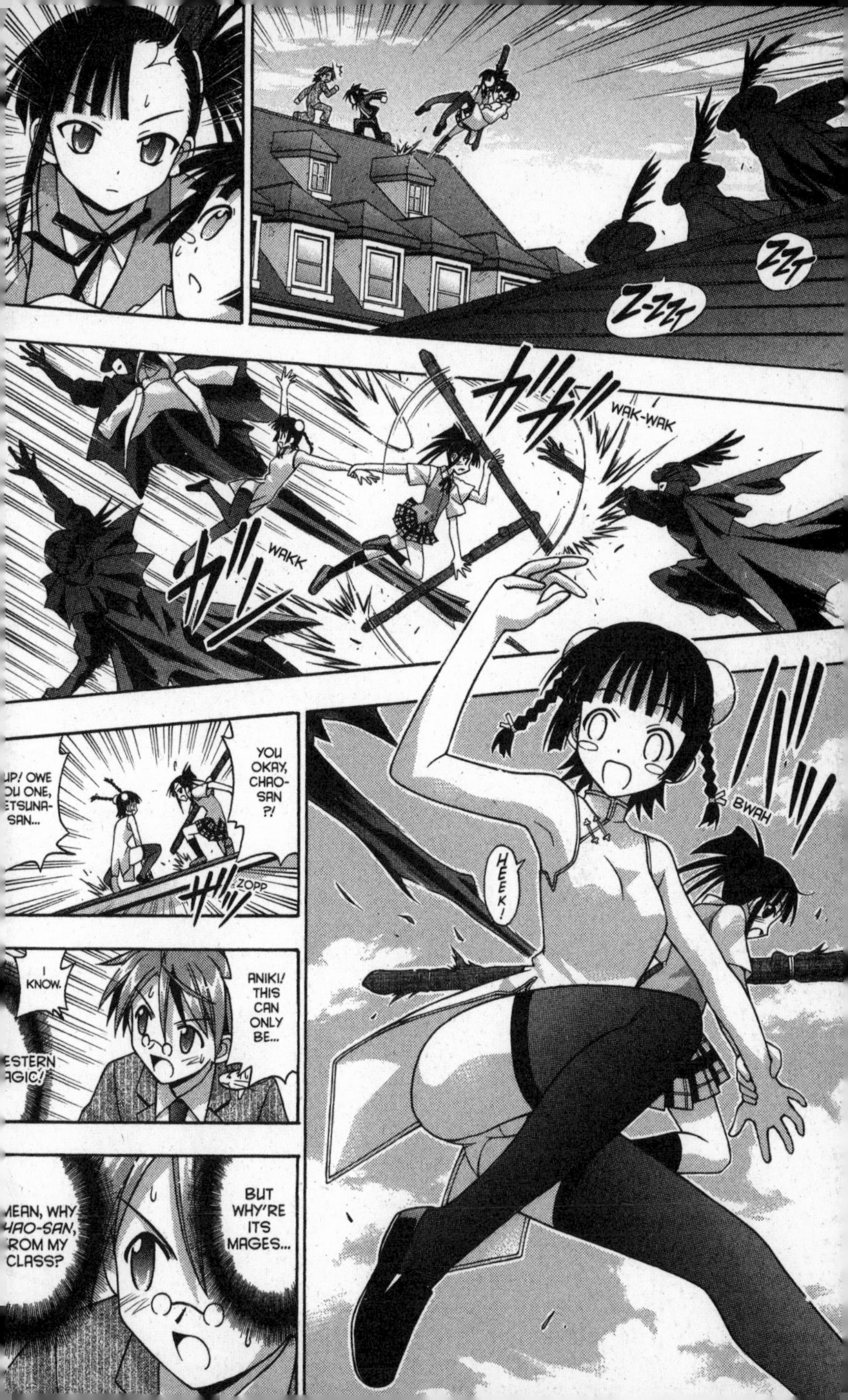
ZZZT
Z-Z-ZZT
WAK-WAK
WAKK
BWAH
HEEEK!
YOU OKAY, CHAO-SAN?!
UP! OWE OU ONE, ETSUNA-SAN...
ZOPP
ANIKI! THIS CAN ONLY BE...
I KNOW.
ESTERN AGIC!
BUT WHY'RE ITS MAGES...
MEAN, WHY HAO-SAN, ROM MY CLASS?

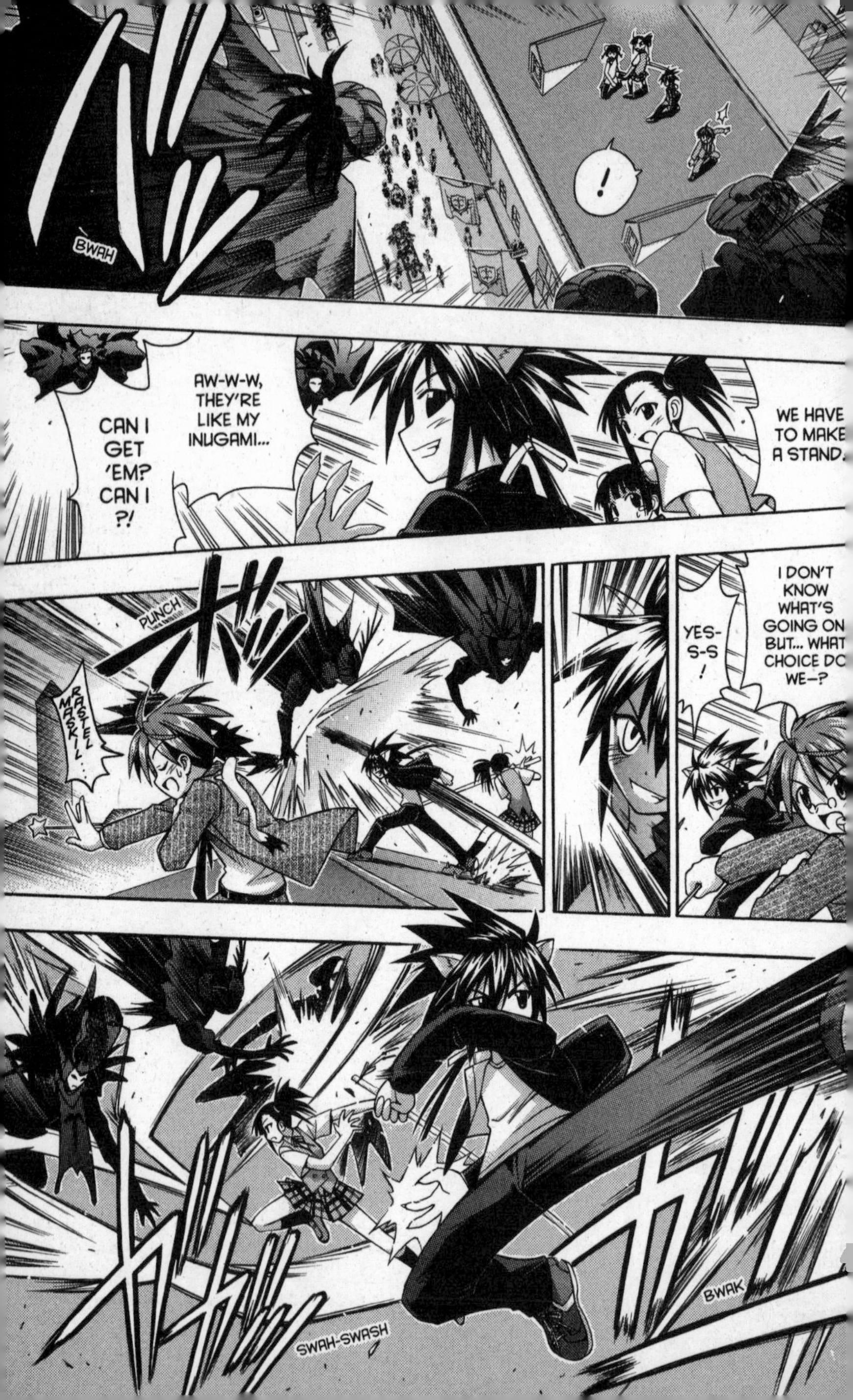
!
BWAH
WE HAVE TO MAKE A STAND.
AW-W-W, THEY'RE LIKE MY INUGAMI...
CAN I GET 'EM? CAN I ?!
I DON'T KNOW WHAT'S GOING ON BUT... WHAT CHOICE DO WE–?
YES-S-S!
PUNCH
RASTEL MASKIL...
BWAK
SWAH-SWASH

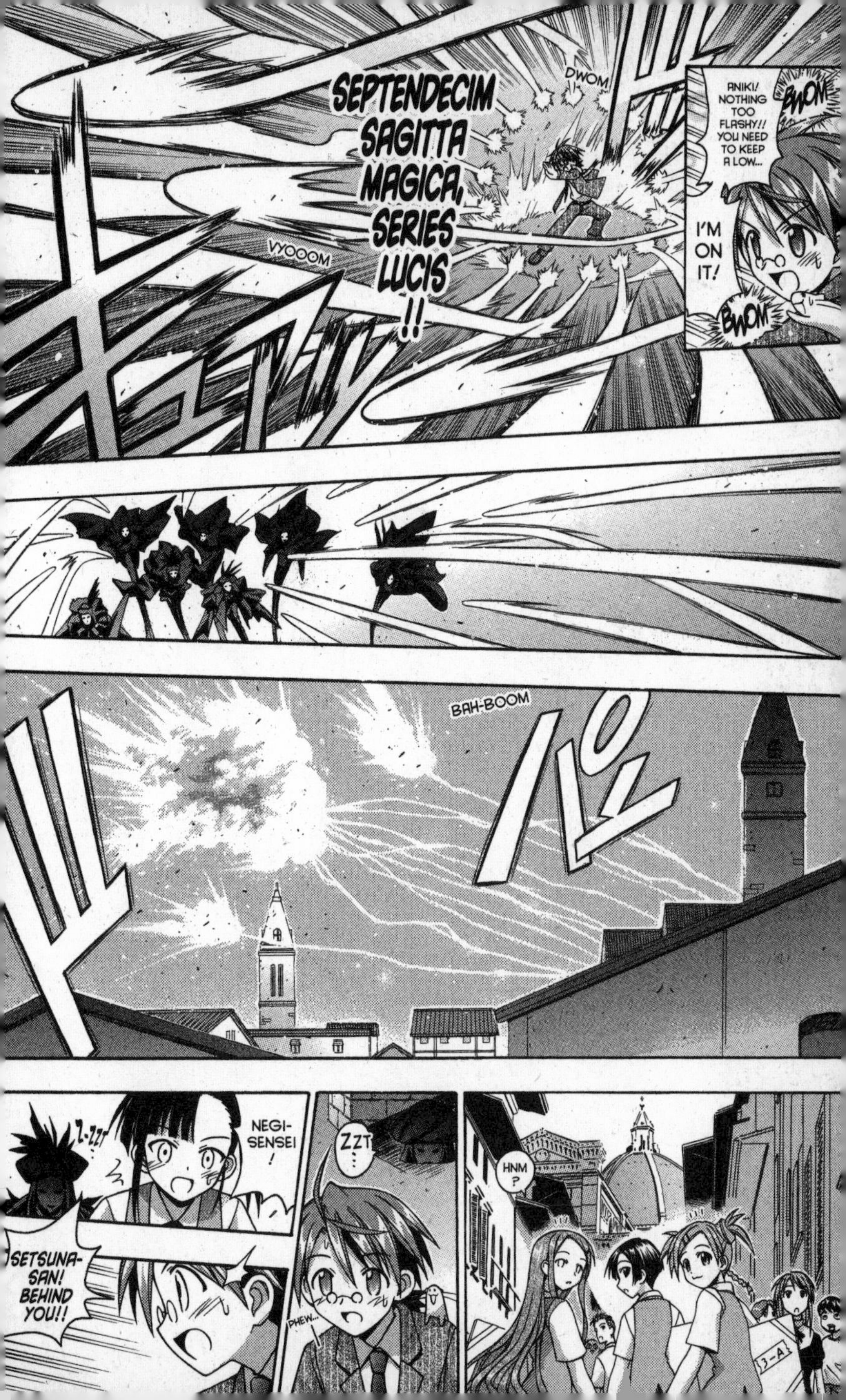
ANIKI! NOTHING TOO FLASHY!! YOU NEED TO KEEP A LOW...
BWOM
I'M ON IT!
BWOM
DWOM
SEPTENDECIM SAGITTA MAGICA, SERIES LUCIS!!
VYOOOM
BAH-BOOM
HNM ?
ZZT...
PHEW...
NEGI-SENSEI!
Z-ZZT
SETSUNA-SAN! BEHIND YOU!!

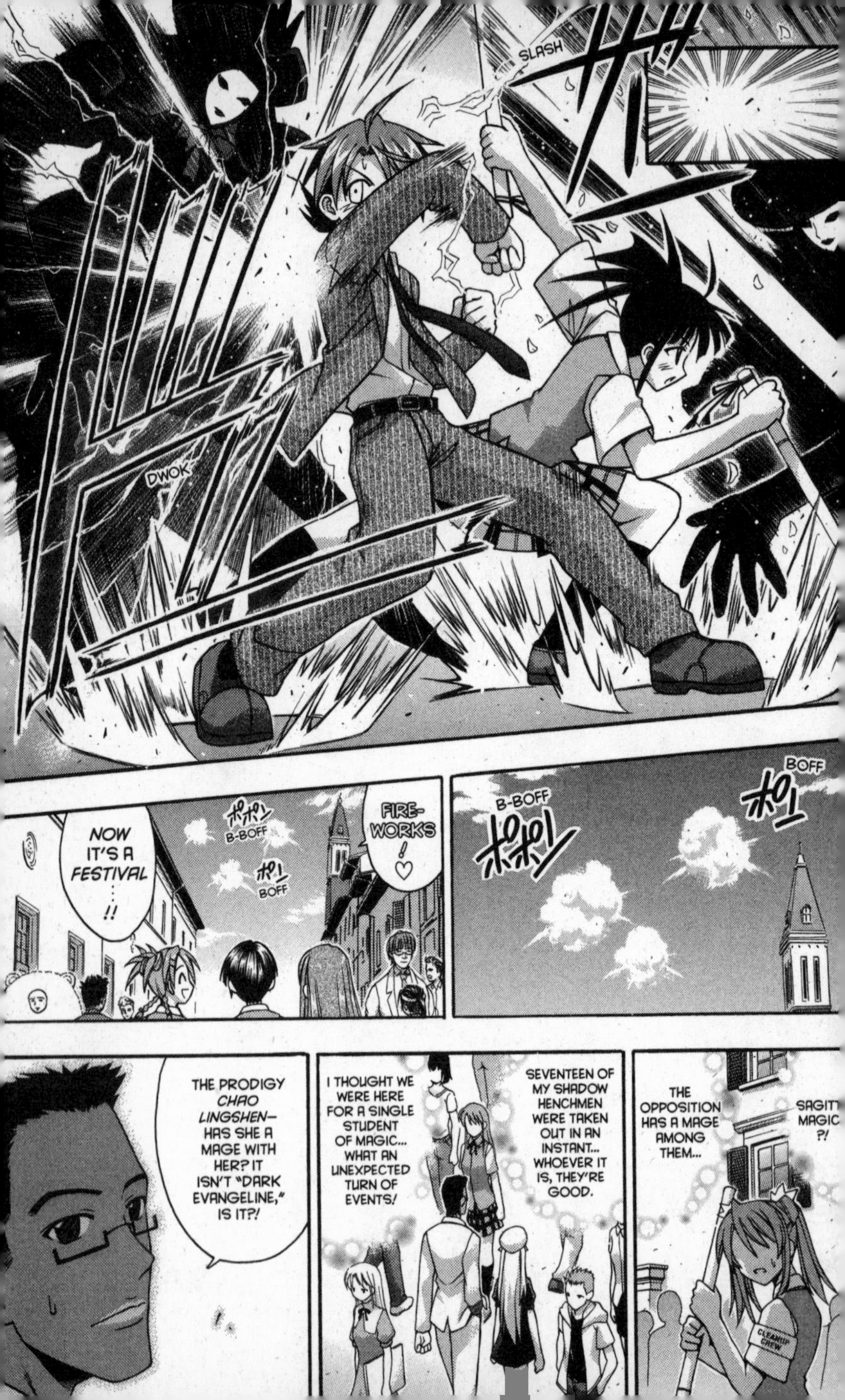

SLASH
DWOK
BOFF
B-BOFF
FIRE-WORKS! ♡
B-BOFF
BOFF
NOW IT'S A FESTIVAL...!!
SAGIT MAGIC ?!
CLEANUP CREW
THE OPPOSITION HAS A MAGE AMONG THEM...
SEVENTEEN OF MY SHADOW HENCHMEN WERE TAKEN OUT IN AN INSTANT... WHOEVER IT IS, THEY'RE GOOD.
I THOUGHT WE WERE HERE FOR A SINGLE STUDENT OF MAGIC... WHAT AN UNEXPECTED TURN OF EVENTS!
THE PRODIGY CHAO LINGSHEN—HAS SHE A MAGE WITH HER? IT ISN'T "DARK EVANGELINE," IS IT?!

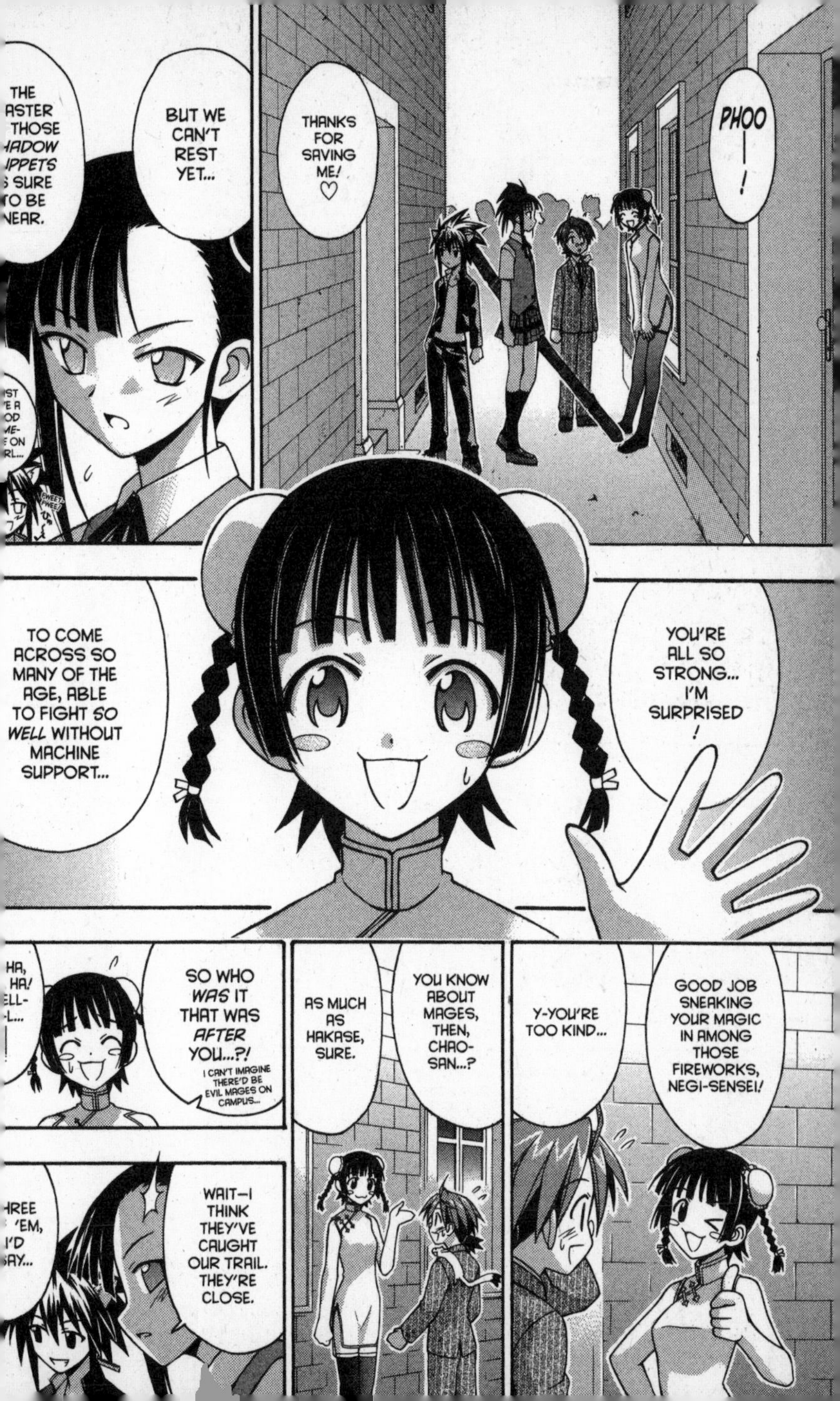
PHOO—!
THANKS FOR SAVING ME! ♡
BUT WE CAN'T REST YET...
THE ASTER THOSE HADOW IPPETS S SURE TO BE NEAR.
YOU'RE ALL SO STRONG... I'M SURPRISED!
TO COME ACROSS SO MANY OF THE AGE, ABLE TO FIGHT *SO WELL* WITHOUT MACHINE SUPPORT...
GOOD JOB SNEAKING YOUR MAGIC IN AMONG THOSE FIREWORKS, NEGI-SENSEI!
Y-YOU'RE TOO KIND...
YOU KNOW ABOUT MAGES, THEN, CHAO-SAN...?
AS MUCH AS HAKASE, SURE.
SO WHO *WAS* IT THAT WAS *AFTER* YOU...?!
I CAN'T IMAGINE THERE'D BE EVIL MAGES ON CAMPUS...
HA, HA!
WAIT—I THINK THEY'VE CAUGHT OUR TRAIL. THEY'RE CLOSE.
HREE 'EM, I'D SAY...

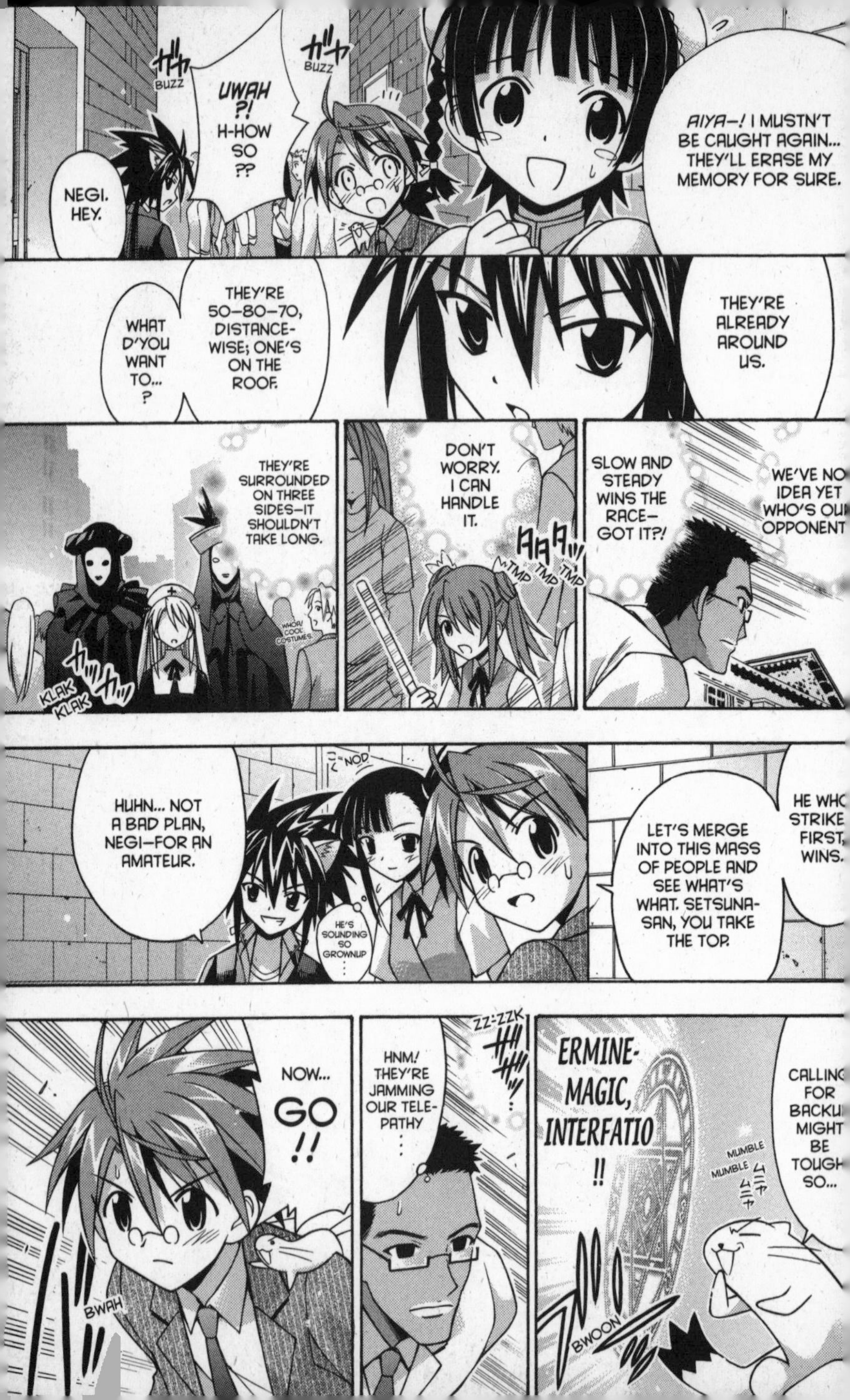
AIYA—! I MUSTN'T BE CAUGHT AGAIN... THEY'LL ERASE MY MEMORY FOR SURE.
BUZZ
UWAH ?! H-HOW SO ??
BUZZ
NEGI. HEY.
THEY'RE ALREADY AROUND US.
THEY'RE 50—80—70, DISTANCE-WISE; ONE'S ON THE ROOF.
WHAT D'YOU WANT TO... ?
WE'VE NO IDEA YET WHO'S OU OPPONENT
SLOW AND STEADY WINS THE RACE—GOT IT?!
DON'T WORRY. I CAN HANDLE IT.
TMP TMP TMP
THEY'RE SURROUNDED ON THREE SIDES—IT SHOULDN'T TAKE LONG.
WHOA! COOL COSTUMES.
KLAK KLAK
HE WHO STRIKE FIRST, WINS.
LET'S MERGE INTO THIS MASS OF PEOPLE AND SEE WHAT'S WHAT. SETSUNA-SAN, YOU TAKE THE TOP.
NOD
HUHN... NOT A BAD PLAN, NEGI—FOR AN AMATEUR.
HE'S SOUNDING SO GROWNUP ...
CALLING FOR BACKU MIGHT BE TOUGH SO...
MUMBLE MUMBLE
ERMINE-MAGIC, INTERFATIO !!
BWOON
ZZ-ZZK
HNM! THEY'RE JAMMING OUR TELE-PATHY ...
NOW... GO !!
BWAH

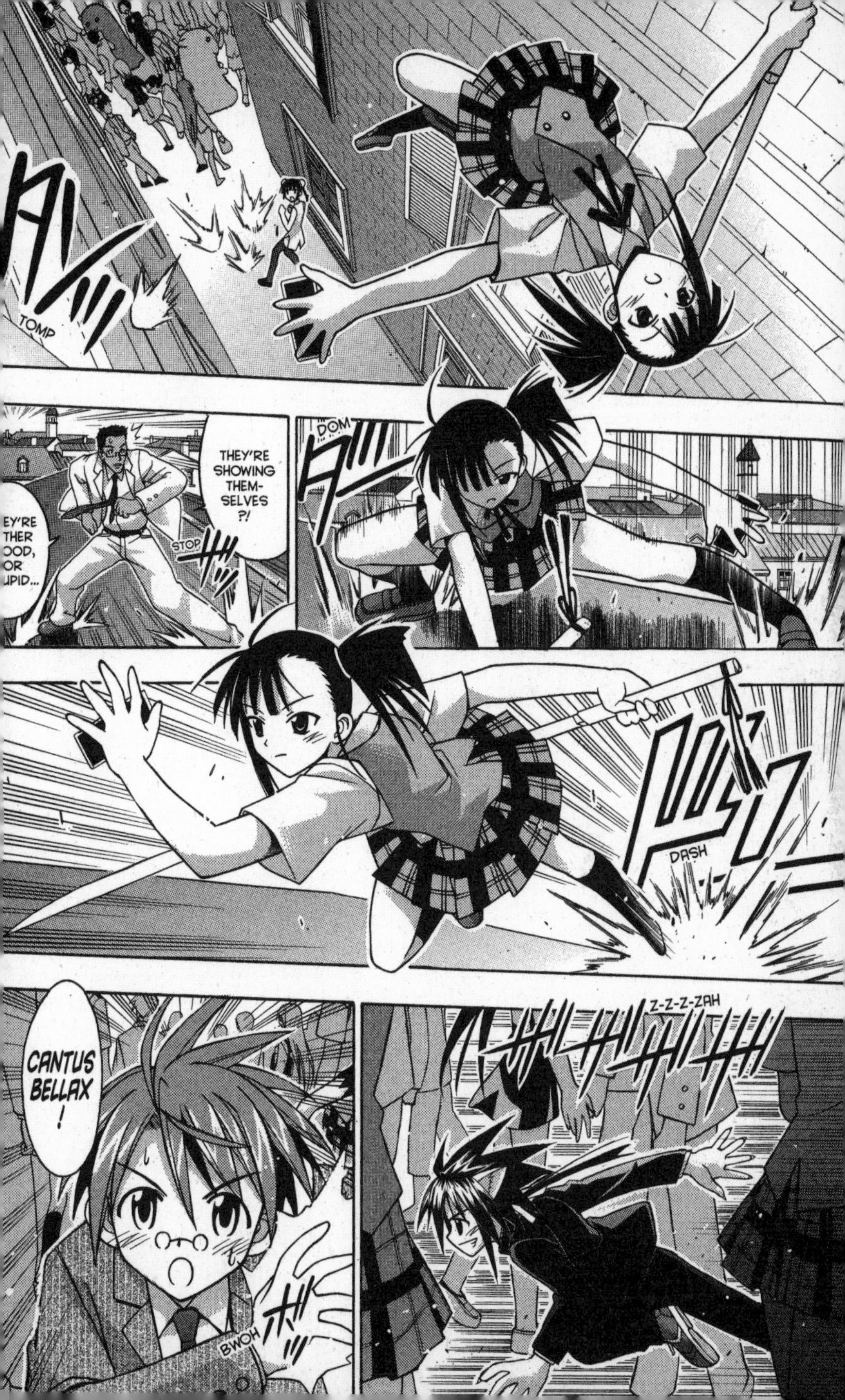
TOMP
DOM
THEY'RE SHOWING THEM-SELVES ?!
STOP
EY'RE THER OOD, OR UPID...
DASH
Z-Z-Z-ZAH
CANTUS BELLAX !
BWOH

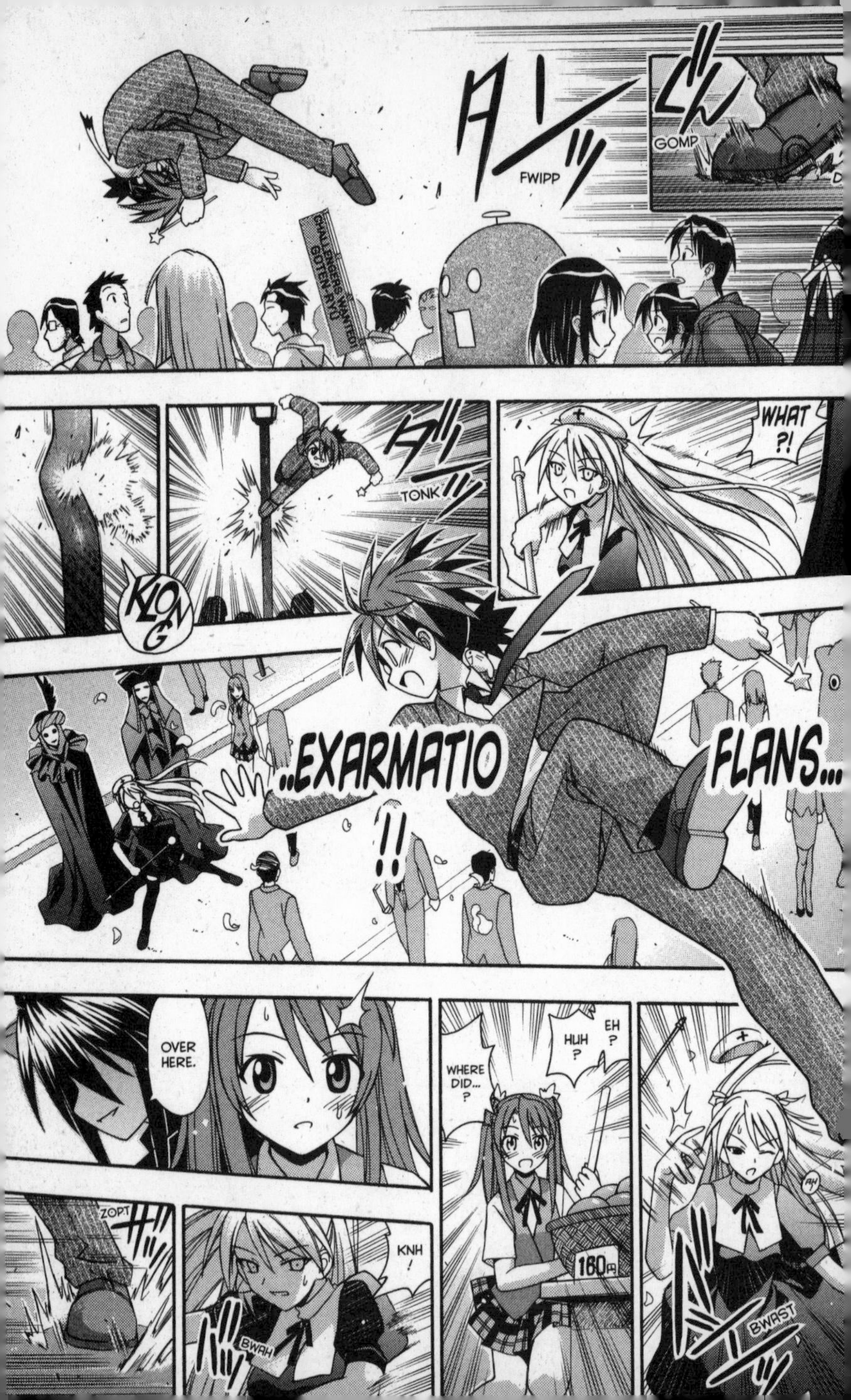

GOMP
FWIPP
CHALLENGERS WANTED! GOTEN-RYU
WHAT ?!
TONK
KLONG
..EXARMATIO
FLANS...
!!
BWAST
AH
HUH ?
EH ?
WHERE DID... ?
160円
OVER HERE.
KNH !
BWAH
ZOPT

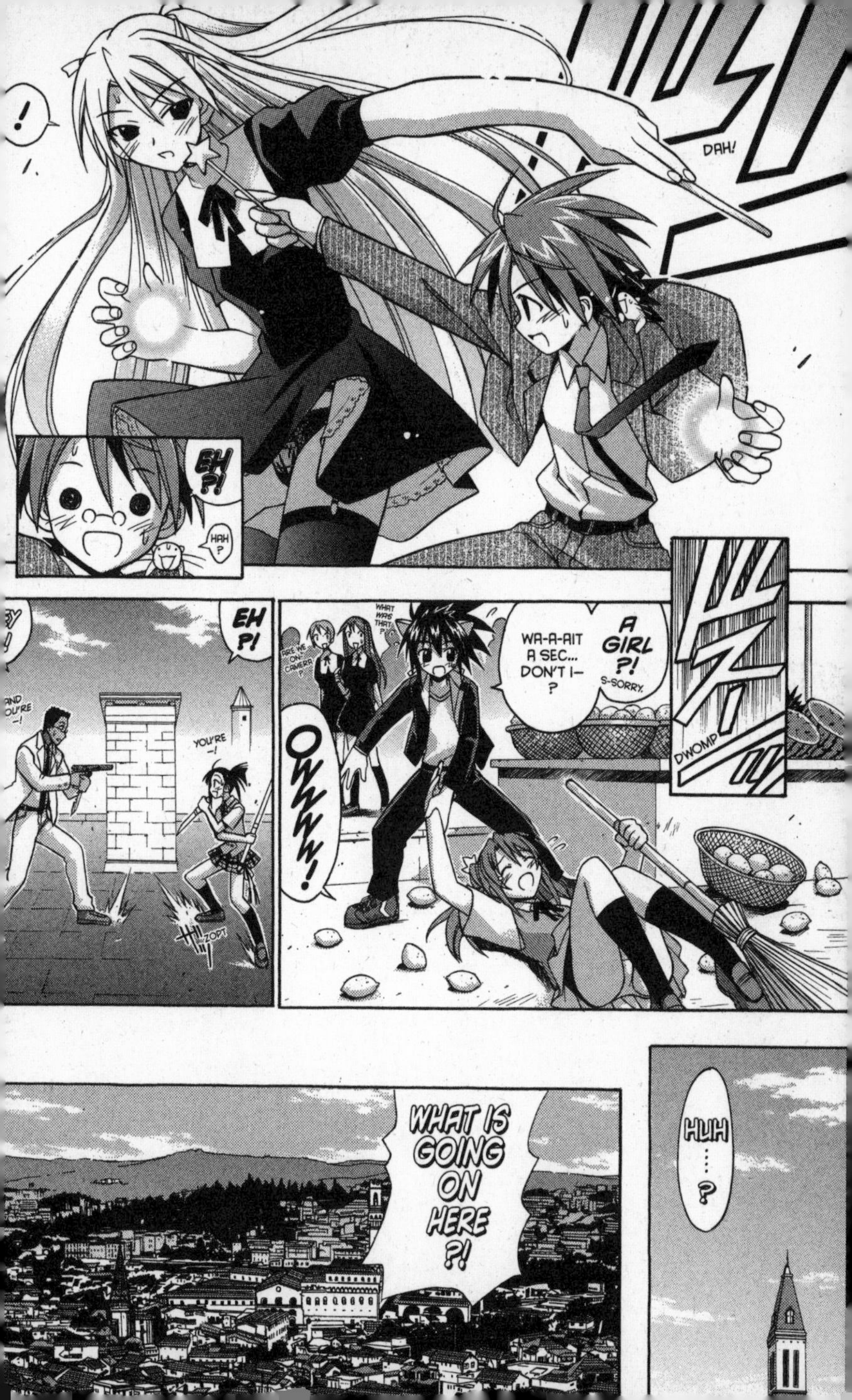
DAH!
!
EH ?!
HAH ?
A GIRL ?!
WA-A-AIT A SEC... DON'T I- ?
S-SORRY.
DWOMP
WHAT WAS THAT ?
ARE WE ON-CAMERA ?
OWWWW!
EH ?!
YOU'RE —!
ZOPT
HUH ....?
WHAT IS GOING ON HERE ?!

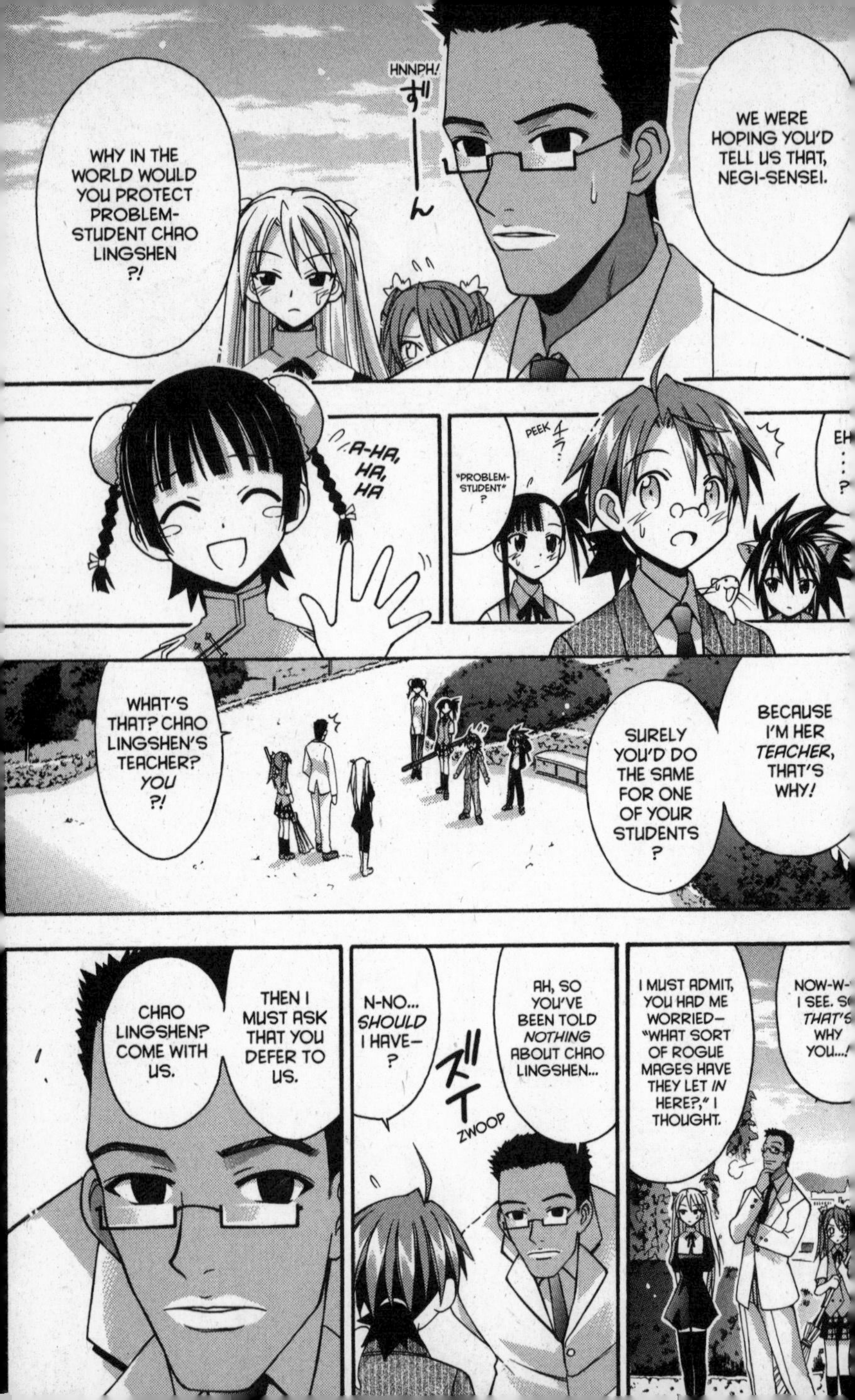
WE WERE HOPING YOU'D TELL US THAT, NEGI-SENSEI.
HNNPH! ずーーん
WHY IN THE WORLD WOULD YOU PROTECT PROBLEM-STUDENT CHAO LINGSHEN?!
EH...?
PEEK
"PROBLEM-STUDENT"?
A-HA, HA, HA
BECAUSE I'M HER TEACHER, THAT'S WHY!
SURELY YOU'D DO THE SAME FOR ONE OF YOUR STUDENTS?
WHAT'S THAT? CHAO LINGSHEN'S TEACHER? YOU?!
NOW-W- I SEE. S THAT'S WHY YOU...!
I MUST ADMIT, YOU HAD ME WORRIED— "WHAT SORT OF ROGUE MAGES HAVE THEY LET IN HERE?," I THOUGHT.
AH, SO YOU'VE BEEN TOLD NOTHING ABOUT CHAO LINGSHEN...
ズイ ZWOOP
N-NO... SHOULD I HAVE—?
THEN I MUST ASK THAT YOU DEFER TO US.
CHAO LINGSHEN? COME WITH US.

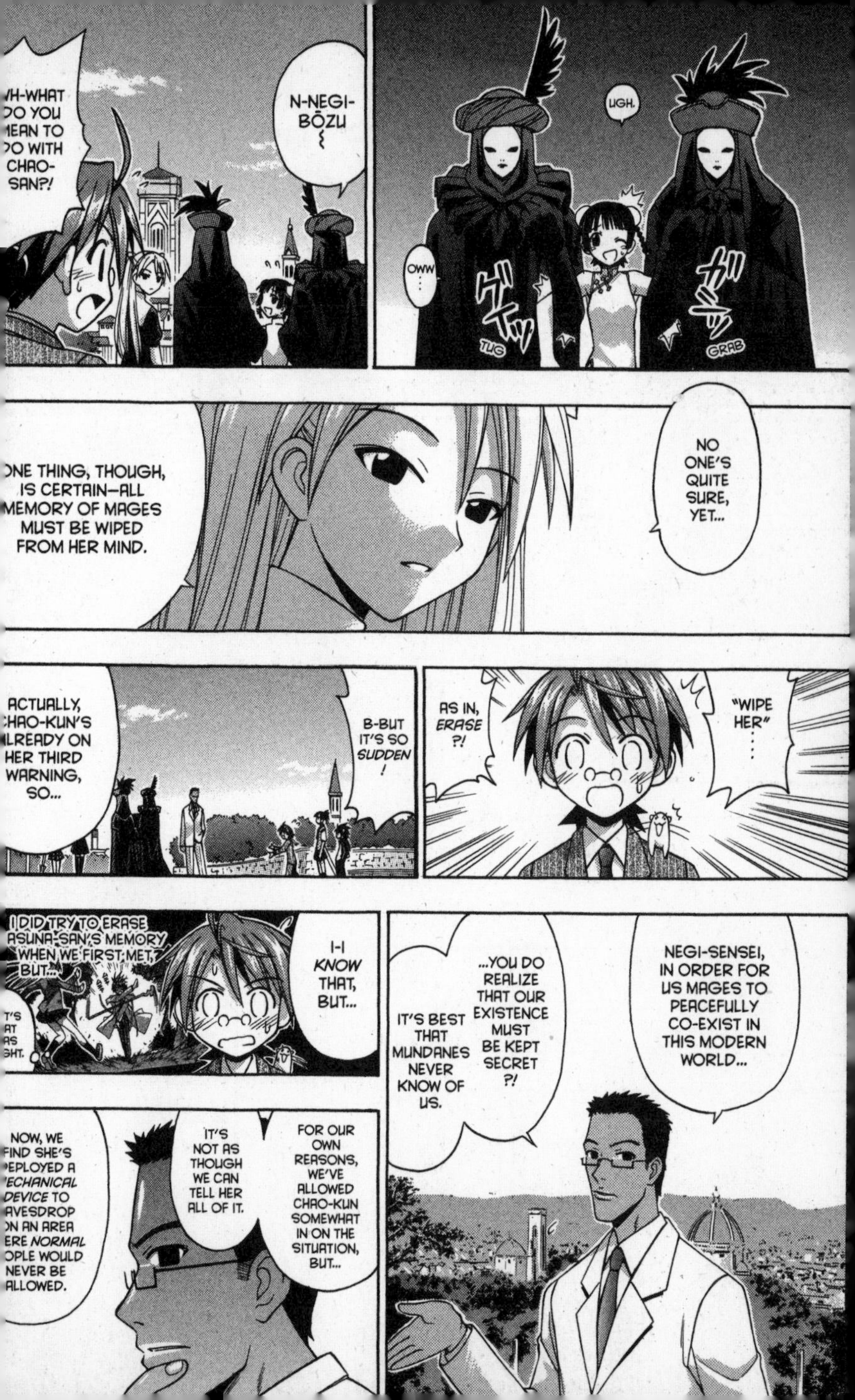
UGH.
OWW...
TUG
GRAB
N-NEGI-BŌZU~
WH-WHAT DO YOU MEAN TO DO WITH CHAO-SAN?!
NO ONE'S QUITE SURE, YET...
ONE THING, THOUGH, IS CERTAIN—ALL MEMORY OF MAGES MUST BE WIPED FROM HER MIND.
"WIPE HER"...
AS IN, *ERASE*?!
B-BUT IT'S SO *SUDDEN*!
ACTUALLY, CHAO-KUN'S ALREADY ON HER THIRD WARNING, SO...
NEGI-SENSEI, IN ORDER FOR US MAGES TO PEACEFULLY CO-EXIST IN THIS MODERN WORLD...
...YOU DO REALIZE THAT OUR EXISTENCE MUST BE KEPT SECRET?!
IT'S BEST THAT MUNDANES NEVER KNOW OF US.
I-I *KNOW* THAT, BUT...
I DID TRY TO ERASE ASUNA-SAN'S MEMORY WHEN WE FIRST MET, BUT...
FOR OUR OWN REASONS, WE'VE ALLOWED CHAO-KUN SOMEWHAT IN ON THE SITUATION, BUT...
IT'S NOT AS THOUGH WE CAN TELL HER ALL OF IT.
NOW, WE FIND SHE'S DEPLOYED A *MECHANICAL DEVICE* TO EAVESDROP ON AN AREA WHERE *NORMAL* PEOPLE WOULD NEVER BE ALLOWED.

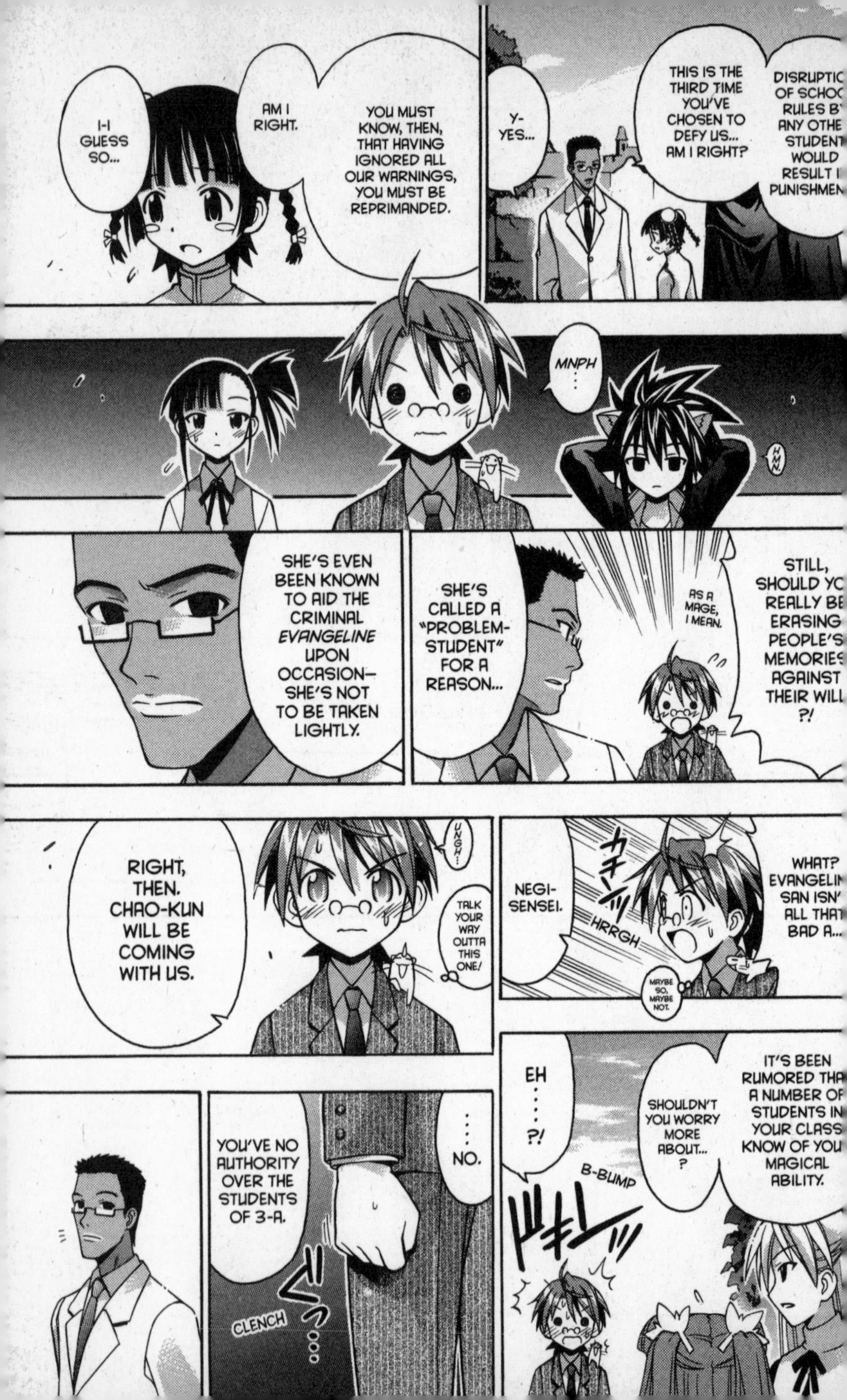
DISRUPTIC OF SCHOC RULES BY ANY OTHE STUDENT WOULD RESULT I PUNISHMEN
THIS IS THE THIRD TIME YOU'VE CHOSEN TO DEFY US... AM I RIGHT?
Y-YES...
YOU MUST KNOW, THEN, THAT HAVING IGNORED ALL OUR WARNINGS, YOU MUST BE REPRIMANDED.
AM I RIGHT.
I-I GUESS SO...
HMN.
MNPH...
STILL, SHOULD YO REALLY BE ERASING PEOPLE'S MEMORIES AGAINST THEIR WILL ?!
AS A MAGE, I MEAN.
SHE'S CALLED A "PROBLEM-STUDENT" FOR A REASON...
SHE'S EVEN BEEN KNOWN TO AID THE CRIMINAL EVANGELINE UPON OCCASION— SHE'S NOT TO BE TAKEN LIGHTLY.
WHAT? EVANGELIN SAN ISN' ALL THAT BAD A...
HRRGH
MAYBE SO, MAYBE NOT.
NEGI-SENSEI.
UNGH...
TALK YOUR WAY OUTTA THIS ONE!
RIGHT, THEN. CHAO-KUN WILL BE COMING WITH US.
IT'S BEEN RUMORED THA A NUMBER OF STUDENTS IN YOUR CLASS KNOW OF YOU MAGICAL ABILITY.
SHOULDN'T YOU WORRY MORE ABOUT... ?
EH......?!
B-BUMP
...NO.
YOU'VE NO AUTHORITY OVER THE STUDENTS OF 3-A.
CLENCH

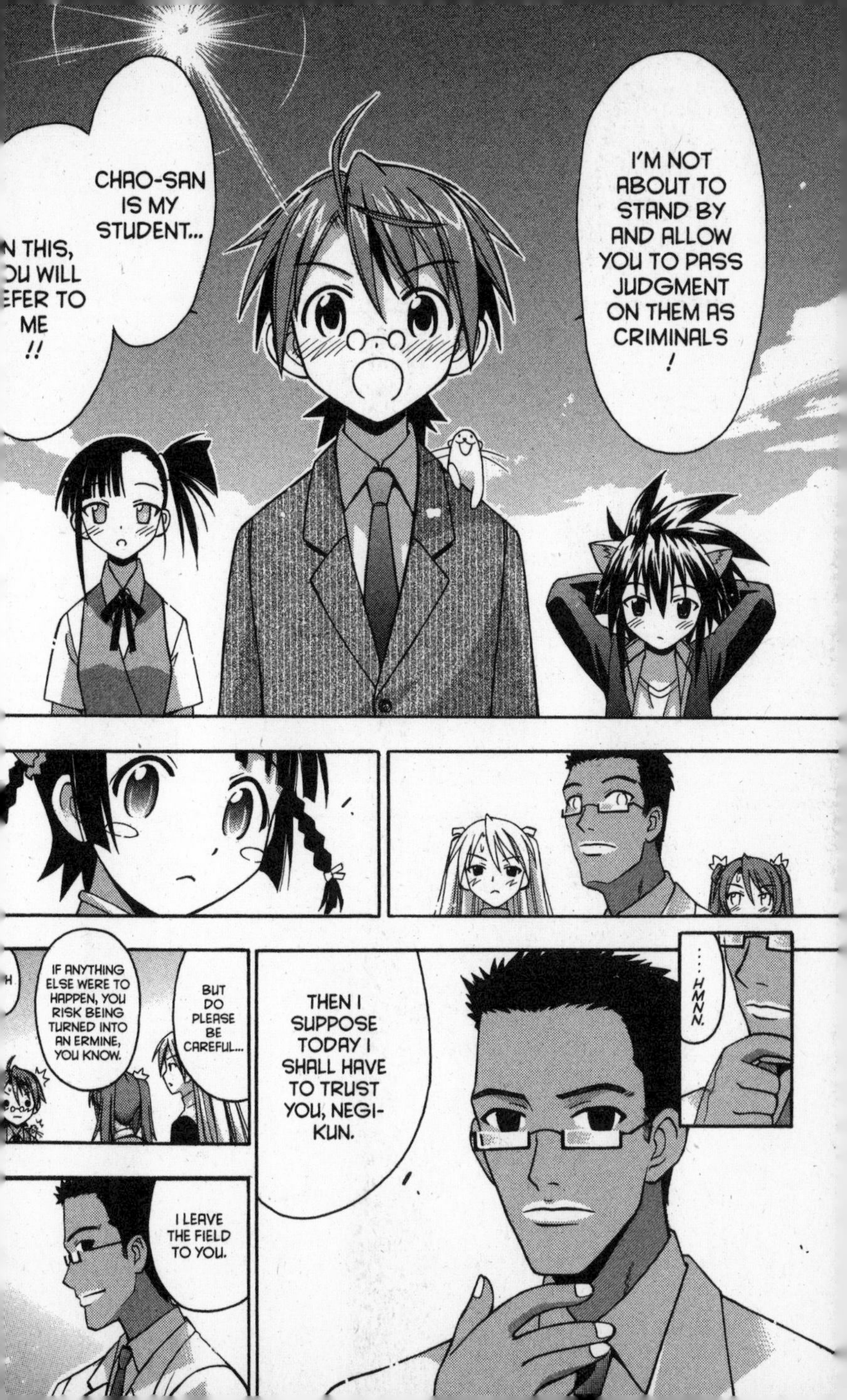
I'M NOT ABOUT TO STAND BY AND ALLOW YOU TO PASS JUDGMENT ON THEM AS CRIMINALS !
CHAO-SAN IS MY STUDENT...
N THIS, OU WILL EFER TO ME !!
....HMNN.
THEN I SUPPOSE TODAY I SHALL HAVE TO TRUST YOU, NEGI-KUN.
BUT DO PLEASE BE CAREFUL...
IF ANYTHING ELSE WERE TO HAPPEN, YOU RISK BEING TURNED INTO AN ERMINE, YOU KNOW.
I LEAVE THE FIELD TO YOU.

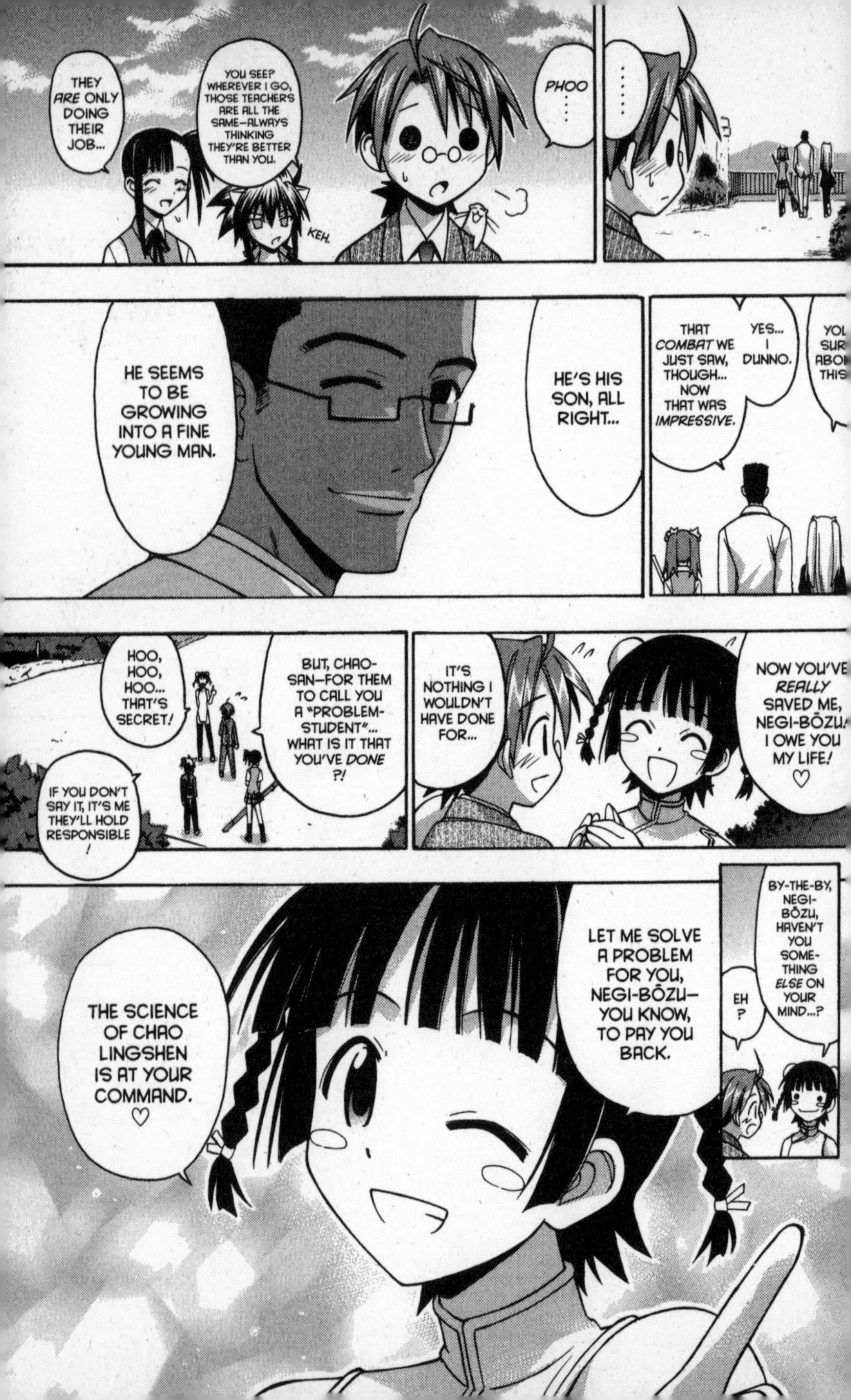
......
PHOO......
YOU SEE? WHEREVER I GO, THOSE TEACHERS ARE ALL THE SAME—ALWAYS THINKING THEY'RE BETTER THAN YOU.
THEY *ARE* ONLY DOING THEIR JOB...
KEH.
YOU SUR ABO THIS
YES... I DUNNO.
THAT *COMBAT* WE JUST SAW, THOUGH... NOW THAT WAS *IMPRESSIVE.*
HE'S HIS SON, ALL RIGHT...
HE SEEMS TO BE GROWING INTO A FINE YOUNG MAN.
NOW YOU'VE *REALLY* SAVED ME, NEGI-BŌZU! I OWE YOU MY LIFE! ♡
IT'S NOTHING I WOULDN'T HAVE DONE FOR...
BUT, CHAO-SAN—FOR THEM TO CALL YOU A "PROBLEM-STUDENT"... WHAT IS IT THAT YOU'VE *DONE* ?!
HOO, HOO, HOO... THAT'S SECRET!
IF YOU DON'T SAY IT, IT'S ME THEY'LL HOLD RESPONSIBLE!
BY-THE-BY, NEGI-BŌZU, HAVEN'T YOU SOMETHING *ELSE* ON YOUR MIND...?
EH?
LET ME SOLVE A PROBLEM FOR YOU, NEGI-BŌZU—YOU KNOW, TO PAY YOU BACK.
THE SCIENCE OF CHAO LINGSHEN IS AT YOUR COMMAND. ♡

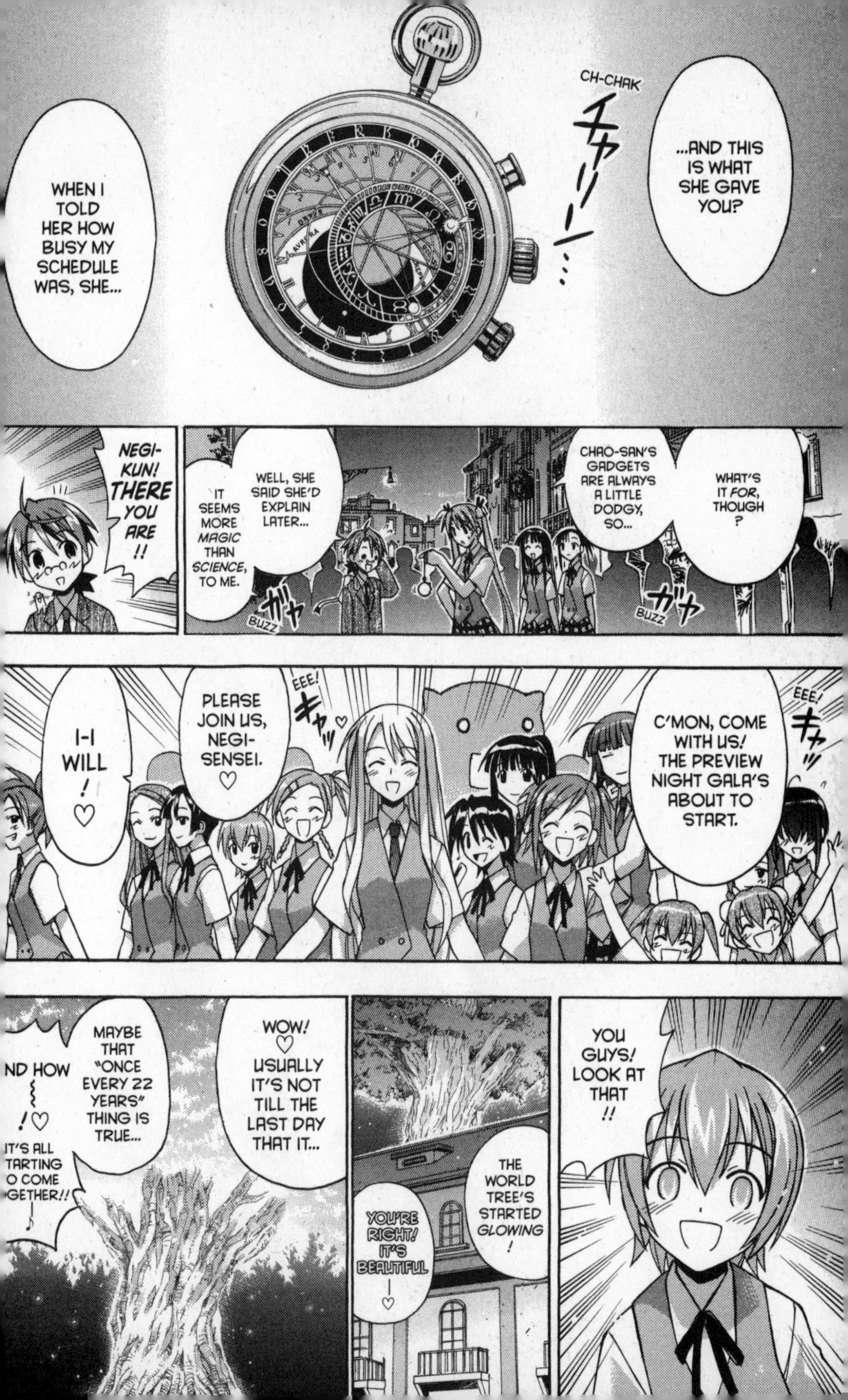
...AND THIS IS WHAT SHE GAVE YOU?
CH-CHAK
WHEN I TOLD HER HOW BUSY MY SCHEDULE WAS, SHE...
WHAT'S IT *FOR*, THOUGH?
CHAO-SAN'S GADGETS ARE ALWAYS A LITTLE DODGY, SO...
BUZZ
WELL, SHE SAID SHE'D EXPLAIN LATER...
IT SEEMS MORE *MAGIC* THAN *SCIENCE*, TO ME.
BUZZ
NEGI-KUN! THERE YOU ARE!!
EEE!
C'MON, COME WITH US! THE PREVIEW NIGHT GALA'S ABOUT TO START.
EEE!
PLEASE JOIN US, NEGI-SENSEI. ♡
I-I WILL! ♡
YOU GUYS! LOOK AT THAT!!
THE WORLD TREE'S STARTED *GLOWING*!
YOU'RE RIGHT! IT'S BEAUTIFUL—♡
WOW! ♡ USUALLY IT'S NOT TILL THE LAST DAY THAT IT...
MAYBE THAT "ONCE EVERY 22 YEARS" THING IS TRUE...
ND HOW~! ♡
IT'S ALL TARTING O COME GETHER!! ♪

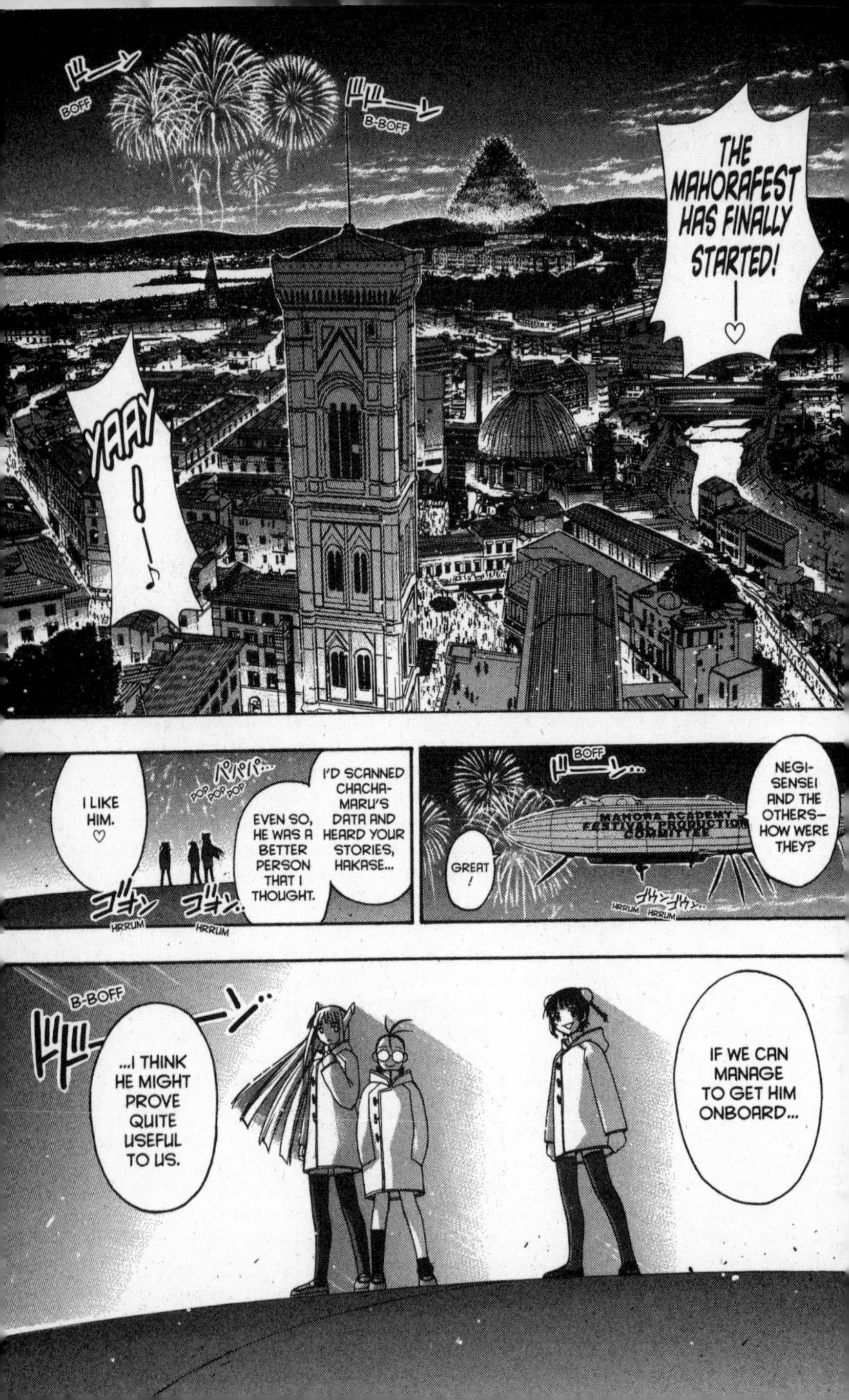
B-BOFF
THE MAHORAFEST HAS FINALLY STARTED! ♡
BOFF
YAAY ♪
BOFF
NEGI-SENSEI AND THE OTHERS— HOW WERE THEY?
MAHORA ACADEMY FESTIVAL PRODUCTION COMMITTEE
GREAT!
HRRUM HRRUM
I'D SCANNED CHACHAMARU'S DATA AND HEARD YOUR STORIES, HAKASE...
EVEN SO, HE WAS A BETTER PERSON THAT I THOUGHT.
POP POP POP
I LIKE HIM. ♡
HRRUM HRRUM
IF WE CAN MANAGE TO GET HIM ONBOARD...
...I THINK HE MIGHT PROVE QUITE USEFUL TO US.
B-BOFF

***NEGIMA!* EIGHTIETH PERIOD: LEXICON NEGIMARIUM**

■「『念波妨害』」
インテルファーティオー

INTERFATIO

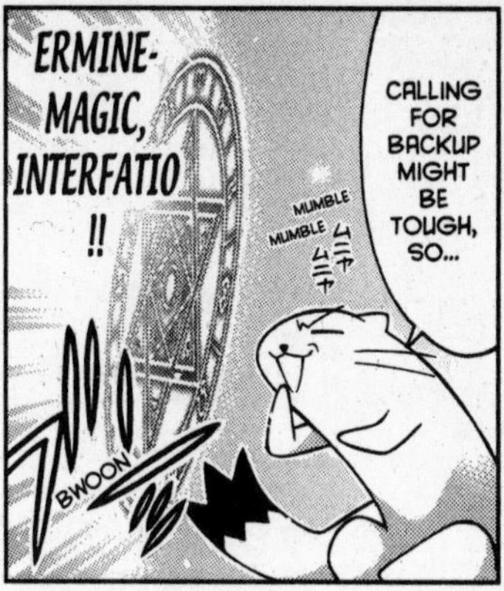
CALLING FOR BACKUP MIGHT BE TOUGH, SO...
ERMINE-MAGIC, INTERFATIO !!
MUMBLE MUMBLE
BWOON

Many users of magic or Magi have ESP (*extrasensoria perceptio*) and are able to read the minds of others (1st Period, 16th Period), distinguish among particular magic powers (8th Period, 16th Period, 20th Period, 23rd Period, 42nd Period, 46–47th Periods, 49th Period, 68th Period, 79th Period), perceive future events (15th Period), detect infiltration into a specified area (18th Period, 67th Period), be aware when one's self is being observed (27th Period, 79th Period), sense the feelings of one to whom one is close (29th Period, 35th Period, 53rd Period, 55th Period), note the presence of a spiritual being (73–74th Periods, 78th Period), see through an illusion (78th Period), detect the presence and location of another Magi (80th Period), among other forms of truly extraordinary, extrasensory perception.

As phenomena without overt, outward manifestation which may be rationalized without empirical evidence even by those who are not of the magical world, those abilities which fall beneath the rubric "ESP" tend to be less popular than those of a more easily perceptible, external character (i.e., conflagration) insofar that, among the magically inclined, abilities of a perceptive or intuitive nature tend to be seen as rather more practical and, therefore, less exciting. Even in the quotidian world of corporate business, for example, it is not uncommon to retain (however discreetly) fortunetellers as company consultants. In this sense, the career path chosen by Negi's schoolmate, Anya, is not at all unusual.

ESP, as the acronym puts it quite plainly enough, refers to perception outside the realm of the "normal" senses (sight, hearing, touch, smell, taste). When the perception is sight, that which is sensed are electromagnetic waves—vibrations of electric and magnetic fields which form the visible spectrum; when auditory, vibrations in the air; when temperature (touch), vibrations on the molecular level. Each of the "ordinary" senses, then, is perceived across its various mediums, while ESP—being of an "extraordinary" nature—has as its home the spiritual plane, and therefore cannot be perceived by the common individual.

As regards the matter of telepathy between Magi, communication is effected across a similar medium—that of the spiritual plane. To explicate further, just as the commonborn communicate via voice (vibrations in the air), or through written words (characters relayed across the visible spectrum), so too do the magically gifted communicate, albeit in a manner wholly unlike "speech" or "words" appearing in the receiver's mind, but as something completely different.

In Latin, *interfatio* means "speaking between," or "interruption." The purpose of this spell, then, is to disrupt telepathic communication by filling the medium across which it travels with something like static, or "white noise." Another way to think of it would be to imagine a person right next to you, shouting in your ear, while you and someone else are trying to have a conversation.

- STAFF -

Ken Akamatsu
Takashi Takemoto
Kenichi Nakamura
Masaki Ohyama
Keiichi Yamashita
Chigusa Amagasaki
Takaaki Miyahara

Thanks To

Ran Ayanaga

NEGIMA!

CHARACTER POPULARITY POLL

HERE ARE THE RESULTS OF THE FOURTH (ANNUAL?) *NEGIMA!* CHARACTER POPULARITY POLL, A.K.A. THE "NEGI-PRIX 4." BELIEVE IT OR NOT, SETSUNA'S TOPPED THE CHARTS TWO TIMES IN A ROW (!), ALTHOUGH THIS TIME, THE VOTES *ARE* MORE EVENLY DISTRIBUTED. THINK WE'LL SEE AN UPSET NEXT TIME 'ROUND...?

RESULTS OF THE THIRD *NEGIMA!* POPULARITY POLL

RANK	CHARACTER	TOTAL VOTES
1ST	SAKURAZAKI, SETSUNA	2,272
2ND	MIYAZAKI, NODOKA	2,051
3RD	KONOE, KONOKA	1,658
4TH	KAGURAZAKA, ASUNA	1,111
5TH	AYASE, YUE	807
6TH	NAGASE, KAEDE	803
7TH	SASAKI, MAKIE	750
8TH	MURAKAMI, NATSUMI	544
9TH	MCDOWELL, EVANGELINE A.K.	526
10TH	IZUMI, AKO	463
11TH	ASAKURA, KAZUMI	355
12TH	YUKIHIRO, AYAKA	283
13TH	KAKIZAKI, MISA	251
14TH	AKASHI, YŪNA	209
15TH	KUGIMIYA, MADOKA	198
16TH	SHI'INA, SAKURAKO	165
17TH	HASEGAWA, CHISAME	147
18TH	KARAKURI, CHACHAMARU	142
19TH	NABA, CHIZURU	122
20TH	KASUGA, MISORA	120
21ST	CHAO LINGSHEN	95
22ND	TATSUMIYA, MANA	87
23RD	RAINYDAY, ZAZIE	84
24TH	OKŌCHI, AKIRA	83
25TH	KŪ FEI	62
26TH	NARUTAKI, FUMIKA	56
27TH	AISAKA, SAYO	54
28TH	YOTSUBA, SATSUKI	51
29TH	SAOTOME, HARUNA	43
30TH	HAKASE, SATOMI	36
31ST	NARUTAKI, FŪKA	22

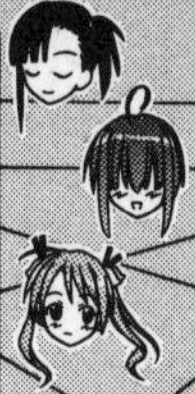

RESULTS OF THE FOURTH *NEGIMA!* POPULARITY POLL

RANK	CHARACTER	TOTAL VOTES
1ST	SAKURAZAKI, SETSUNA	1,633
2ND	MIYAZAKI, NODOKA	1,307
3RD	KAGURAZAKA, ASUNA	1,015
4TH	KONOE, KONOKA	966
5TH	MURAKAMI, NATSUMI	914
6TH	MCDOWELL, EVANGELINE A.K.	803
7TH	AYASE, YUE	628
8TH	SASAKI, MAKIE	604
9TH	NAGASE, KAEDE	593
10TH	KARAKURI, CHACHAMARU	583
11TH	IZUMI, AKO	567
12TH	YUKIHIRO, AYAKA	402
13TH	AKASHI, YŪNA	348
14TH	NABA, CHIZURU	321
15TH	CHAO LINGSHEN	320
16TH	AISAKA, SAYO	255
17TH	KAKIZAKI, MISA	226
18TH	OKŌCHI, AKIRA	223
19TH	SAOTOME, HARUNA	212
20TH	TATSUMIYA, MANA	198
21ST	KUGIMIYA, MADOKA	185
22ND	YOTSUBA, SATSUKI	176
23RD	ASAKURA, KAZUMI	124
24TH	HASEGAWA, CHISAME	113
25TH	KŪ FEI	105
26TH	RAINYDAY, ZAZIE	64
27TH	NARUTAKI, FŪKA	55
28TH	NARUTAKI, FUMIKA	53
29TH	HAKASE, SATOMI	42
30TH	SHI'INA, SAKURAKO	38
31ST	KASUGA, MISORA	27

NEGIMA!

FAN ART CORNER

I'M GOING TO INTRODUCE THE FAN ART SENT IN BY YOU READERS THIS TIME, AS WELL. (^^)

TEXT: ASSISTANT Max

WELL WISHES MOST HUMBLY ACCEPTED (HEH).

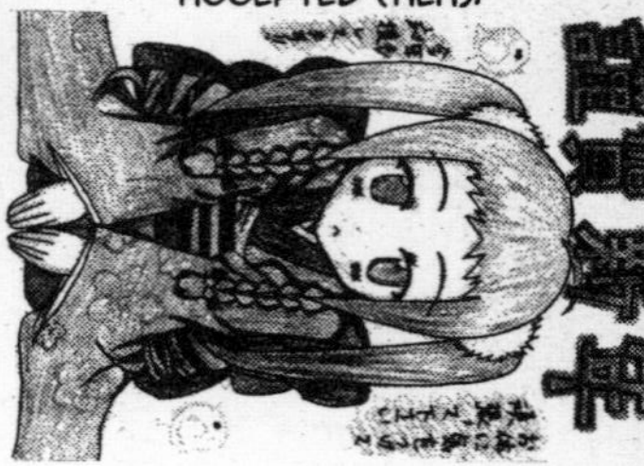
謹賀新年

YIKES! GUESS WE'D BEST NOT FORGET YOU NAGI FANS, HUH? (HEH.)

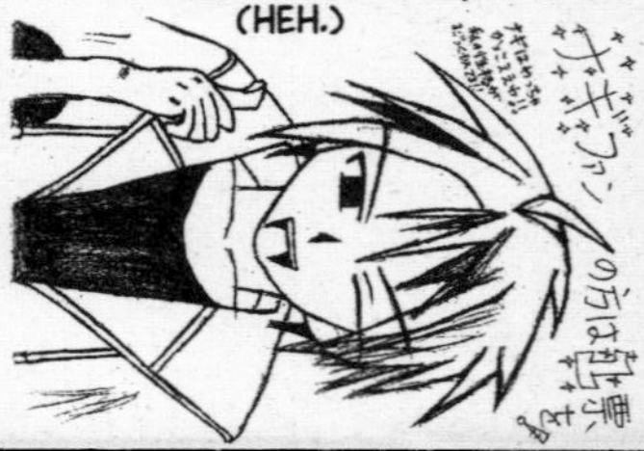

HOW CUTE IS THIS KOTARŌ, HUH?!

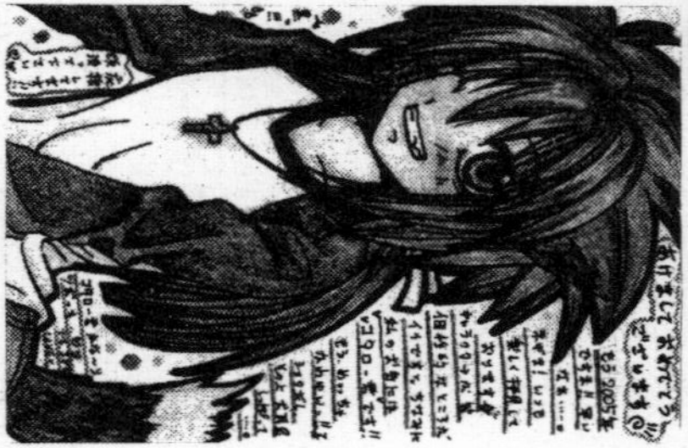

LOVE THE WAY THE "BAKA BLACK" NICKNAME IS WORKED IN, HERE.

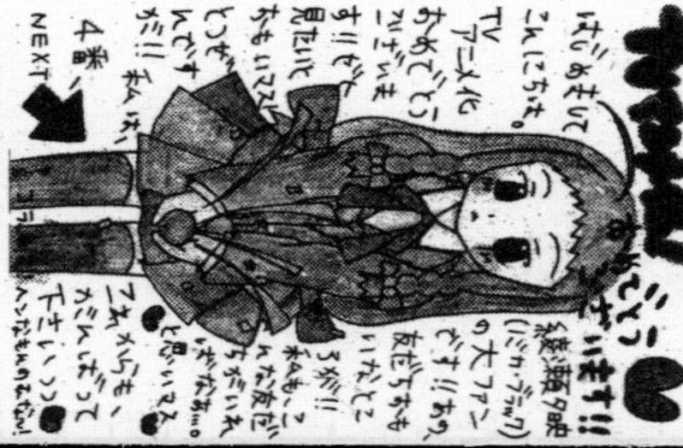

A PICTURE MADE FROM CUT-OUTS! VERY RARE, INDEED.

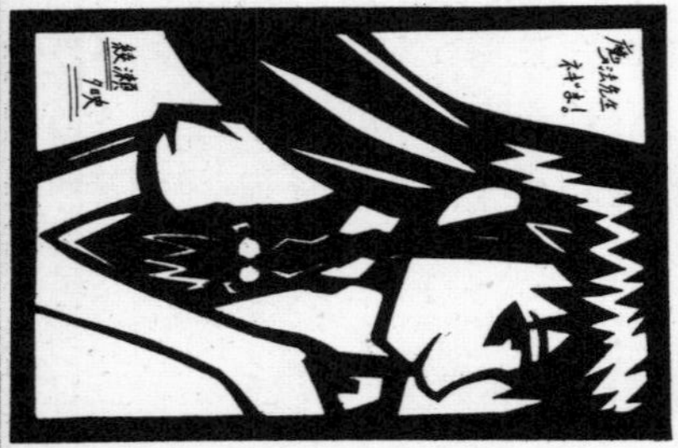

AYAKA LOOKS ESPECIALLY SPARKLY IN THIS ONE.

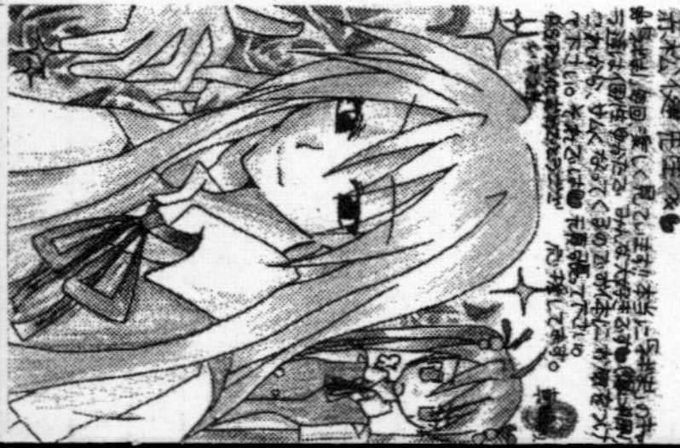

NEGIMA!

PRELIMINARY DESIGN COLLECTION

~CHARACTER CONCEPT SKETCHES~

[SAYO AISAKA]

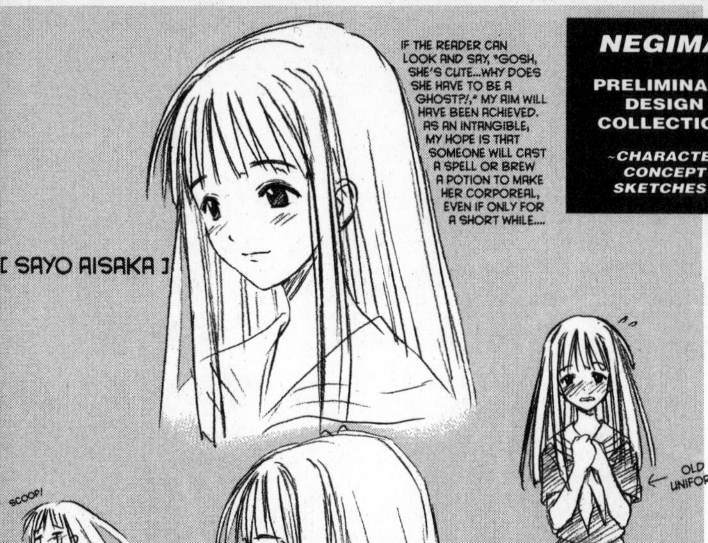

IF THE READER CAN LOOK AND SAY, "GOSH, SHE'S CUTE...WHY DOES SHE HAVE TO BE A GHOST?!," MY AIM WILL HAVE BEEN ACHIEVED. AS AN INTANGIBLE, MY HOPE IS THAT SOMEONE WILL CAST A SPELL OR BREW A POTION TO MAKE HER CORPOREAL, EVEN IF ONLY FOR A SHORT WHILE....
OLD UNIFORM
SCOOP!
UWAAH!
THE CLASSROOM'S TIMID GHOST.

DATING ALL THE WAY BACK TO THE EARLY DAYS OF THE SCHOOL'S FOUNDING, SAYO IS A GHOST WHO FELL VICTIM TO A SERIES OF SCHOOL MURDERS. A GOOD GIRL—SHE IS! REALLY!—SHE'S EVEN ABLE TO BECOME PART OF THE SCHOOL'S NEWSPAPER CLUB THANKS TO HER ABILITY TO GO THROUGH WALLS.

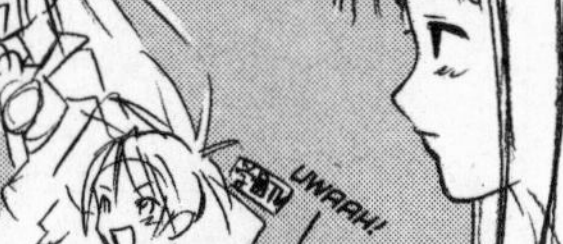

SKIRK!
SAD SHE COULDN'T MAKE THE SCHOOL FIELD TRIP.

ONCE HER MURDER IS BROUGHT TO LIGHT BY SCHOOL JOURNALIST KAZUMI, SAYO'S INITIAL "CLASS GHOST" RANGE-LIMITATION OF 500 METERS IS EXPANDED TO WHEREVER SHE MIGHT LIKE TO GO—INCLUDING THE ABILITY TO "MOVE ON," ALTHOUGH THE NEW FRIENDSHIPS SHE FINDS CONVINCE HER TO STICK AROUND A WHILE LONGER.

I'VE NEVER BEEN ABLE TO BUILD MUCH OF SAYO'S BACKSTORY INTO THE MAIN PLOT. (^^;) NOT MEANT TO BE MUCH MORE THAN A GHOST AT THE START, BEFORE I KNEW IT, SHE'D BECOME THIS SLIGHTLY DAZED, BUMBLING, LOVABLY GOOFY GIRL... BUT THAT'S OKAY, THOUGH, 'CAUSE SHE'S CUTE, RIGHT? RIGHT?! (HEH.)

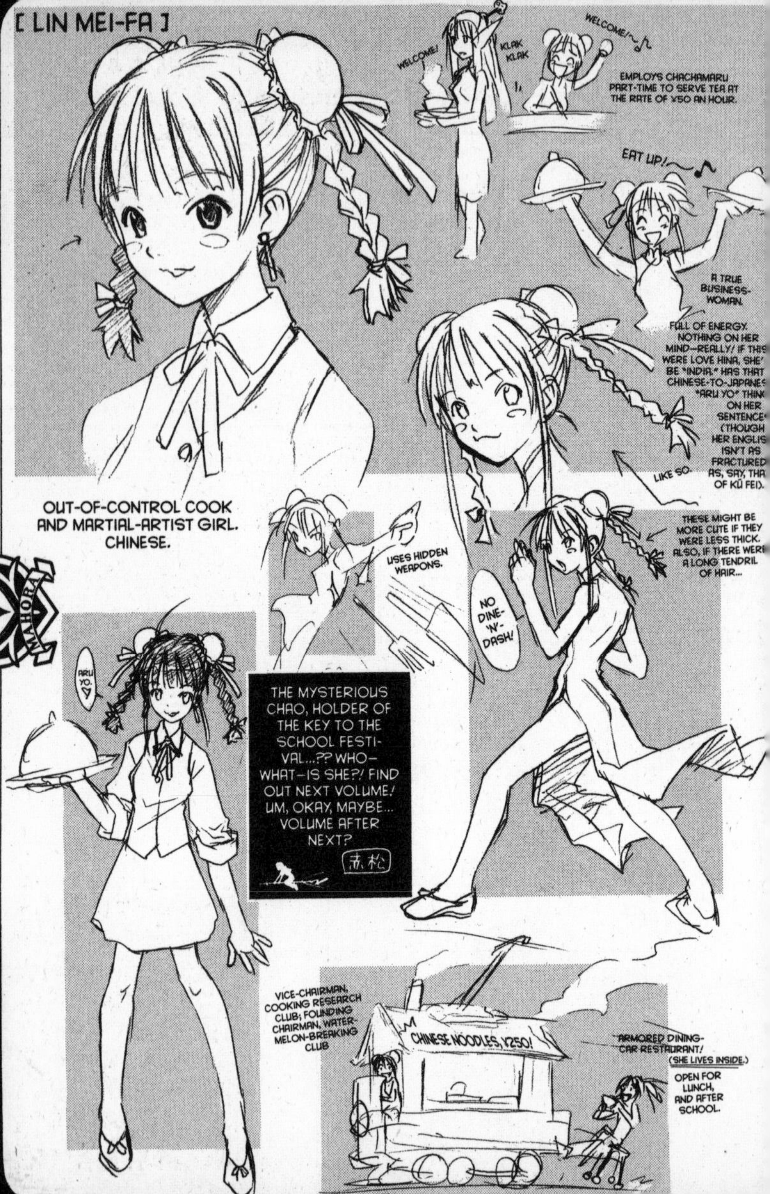
[LIN MEI-FA]
WELCOME!~♪
EMPLOYS CHACHAMARU PART-TIME TO SERVE TEA AT THE RATE OF ¥50 AN HOUR.
KLAK KLAK
WELCOME!
EAT UP!~♪
A TRUE BUSINESS-WOMAN.
FULL OF ENERGY. NOTHING ON HER MIND—REALLY! IF THIS WERE LOVE HINA, SHE' BE "INDIA." HAS THAT CHINESE-TO-JAPANES "ARU YO" THIN ON HER SENTENCE (THOUGH HER ENGLIS ISN'T AS FRACTURED AS, SAY, THA OF KŪ FEI).
LIKE SO.
OUT-OF-CONTROL COOK AND MARTIAL-ARTIST GIRL. CHINESE.
THESE MIGHT BE MORE CUTE IF THEY WERE LESS THICK. ALSO, IF THERE WER A LONG TENDRIL OF HAIR...
NO DINE-'N'-DASH!
USES HIDDEN WEAPONS.
THE MYSTERIOUS CHAO, HOLDER OF THE KEY TO THE SCHOOL FESTI-VAL...?? WHO—WHAT—IS SHE?! FIND OUT NEXT VOLUME! UM, OKAY, MAYBE... VOLUME AFTER NEXT?
赤松
ARU YO. ♥
ARMORED DINING-CAR RESTAURANT! (SHE LIVES INSIDE.)
OPEN FOR LUNCH, AND AFTER SCHOOL.
CHINESE NOODLES, ¥250!
VICE-CHAIRMAN, COOKING RESEARCH CLUB; FOUNDING CHAIRMAN, WATER-MELON-BREAKING CLUB

3-D BACKGROUNDS EXPLANATION CORNER
BACKGROUNDS CREATED FOR VOLUME 9 IN 3-D EXPLAINED HERE!

MAHORA ACADEMY JUNIOR-HIGH GIRLS' SCHOOL BUILDING

SCENE NAME: SCHOOL POLYGON COUNT: 288,583

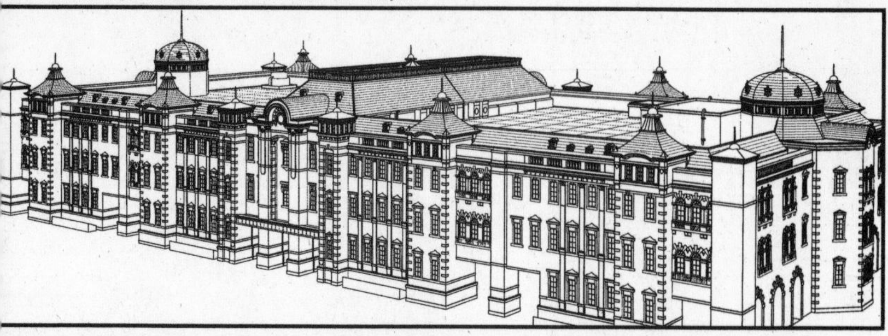

TILL NOW, THE SCHOOL'S ALWAYS BEEN A PHOTOCOPY OF THE INITIAL, HAND-DRAWN SKETCH, BUT WE FINALLY WENT AND MADE A PROPER 3-D VERSION OF THE MAHORA ACADEMY JUNIOR-HIGH GIRLS' SCHOOL BUILDING. IT'S REALLY BIG! AND COMPLICATED! IT TOOK MUCH LONGER TO RENDER THAN THAT OF THE WORLD-TREE SQUARE, WHICH WAS INTRODUCED IN THE PREVIOUS VOLUME (^_^;). MARVEL, IF YOU WILL, AT THE SHEER DETAIL OF THIS KEY LOCATION WITHIN THE SPRAWLING ACADEMY CITY.

HERE'S THE MOST RECOGNIZABLE DETAIL OF THE JUNIOR HIGH, THE CLOCK TOWER AT THE FRONT OF THE BUILDING. WE'VE EVEN DONE SOME FINE DETAIL-WORK IN THE MASONRY BUT, SINCE IT'S SO SMALL, MOST PEOPLE WON'T EVEN NOTICE. (^_^;)

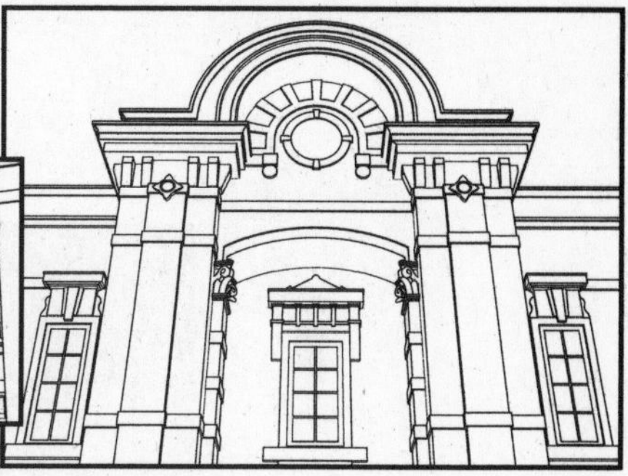

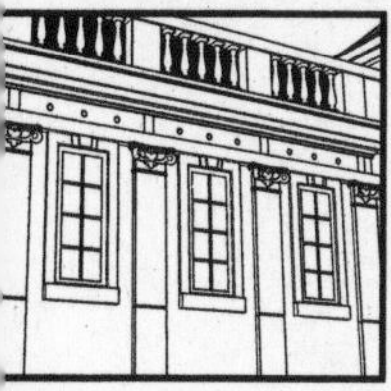

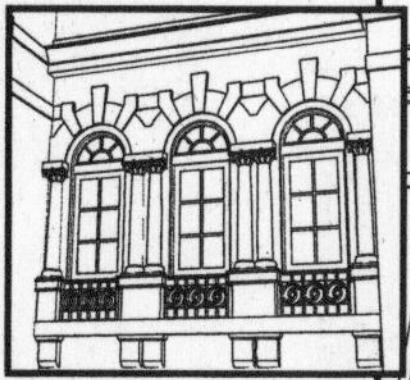

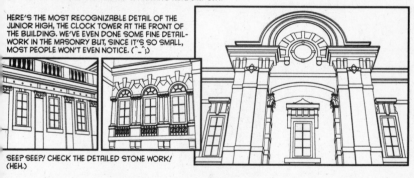

SEE? SEE?! CHECK THE DETAILED STONE WORK! (HEH.)

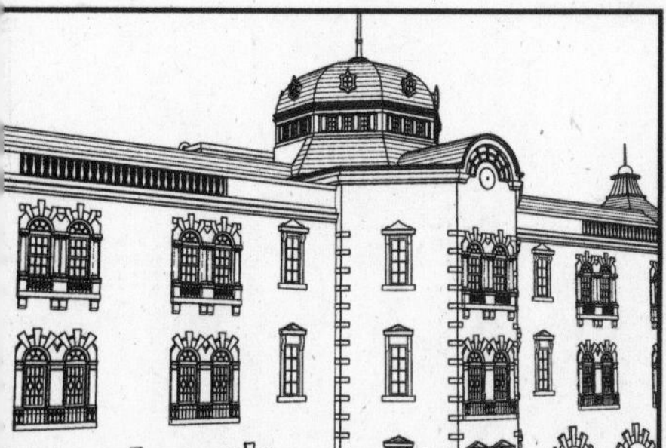

OUTSIDE OF CLASSROOM 3-A. THE PERSPECTIVE OF THE FACADE YOU SEE BELOW IS THE FIRST TIME 3-A'S EVER BEEN SHOWN FROM THE OUTSIDE.

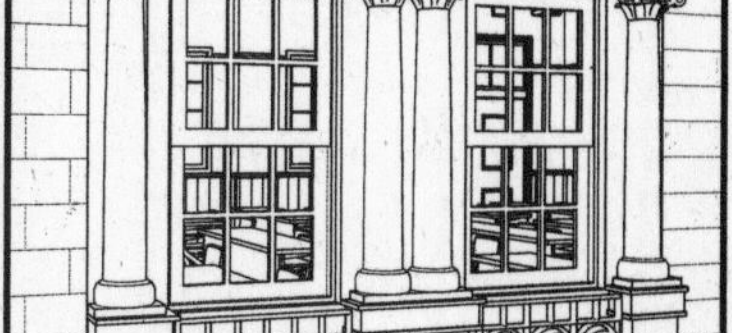

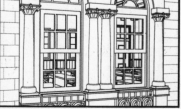

• CHAO'S DINING-CAR RESTAURANT

SCENE NAME: CHAO'S_TRAM_ POLYGON COUNT: 34,885

TILL3-D COMPUTER GRAPHIC OF CHAO'S CONVERTED DINING-CAR RESTAURANT, CHAO BAO ZI. THE SCHOOL FESTIVAL REALLY SEEMS TO BE KEEPING THE PLACE HOPPING! I'D LIKE TO SEE IT SHOW UP IN THE MAIN STORYLINE, AS WELL.

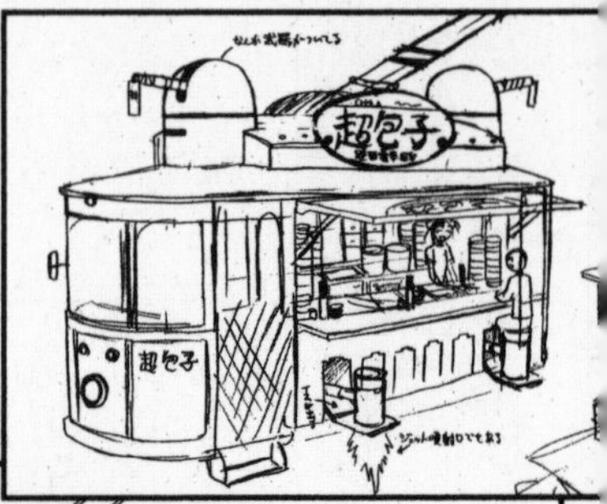
超包子

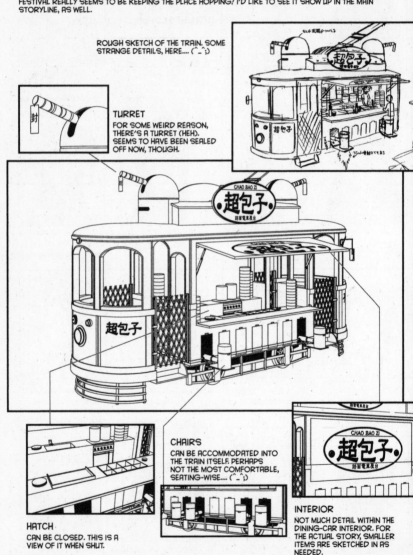

ROUGH SKETCH OF THE TRAIN. SOME STRANGE DETAILS, HERE.... (^_^;)

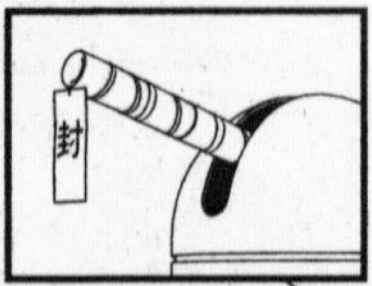
封

TURRET

FOR SOME WEIRD REASON, THERE'S A TURRET (HEH). SEEMS TO HAVE BEEN SEALED OFF NOW, THOUGH.

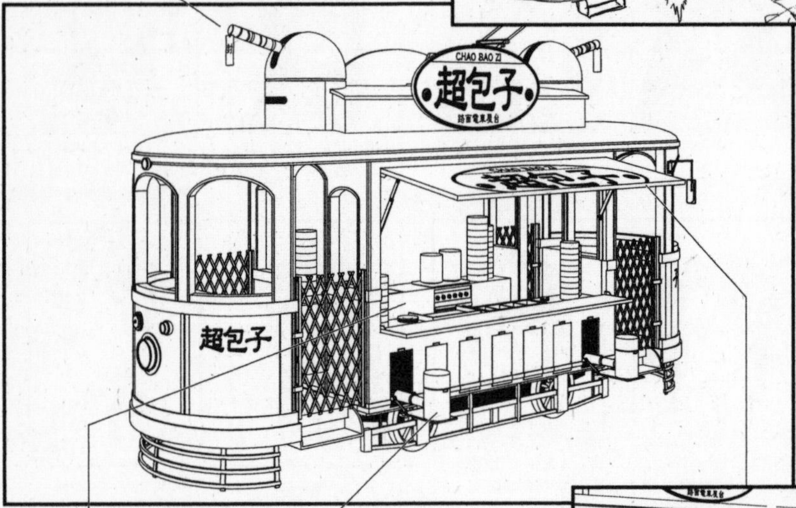
封
CHAO BAO ZI
超包子
路面電車屋台
超包子

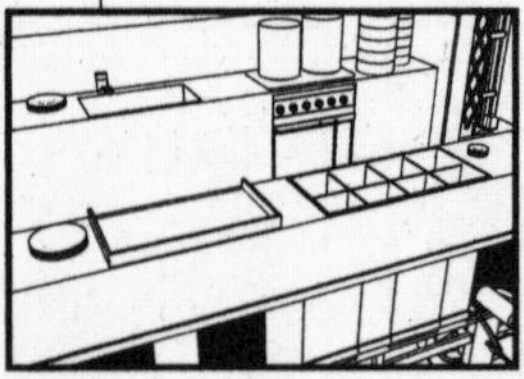

HATCH

CAN BE CLOSED. THIS IS A VIEW OF IT WHEN SHUT.

CHAIRS

CAN BE ACCOMMODATED INTO THE TRAIN ITSELF. PERHAPS NOT THE MOST COMFORTABLE, SEATING-WISE.... (^_^;)

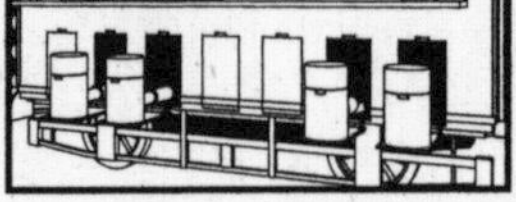

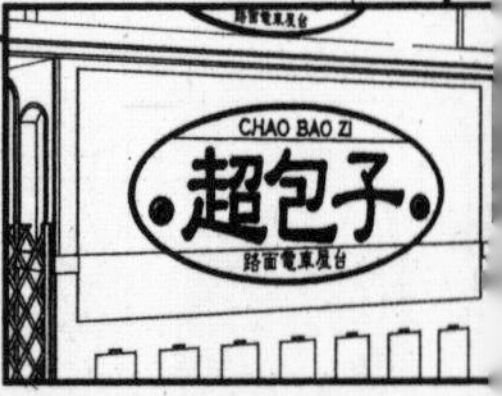
CHAO BAO ZI
超包子
路面電車屋台

INTERIOR

NOT MUCH DETAIL WITHIN THE DINING-CAR INTERIOR. FOR THE ACTUAL STORY, SMALLER ITEMS ARE SKETCHED IN AS NEEDED.

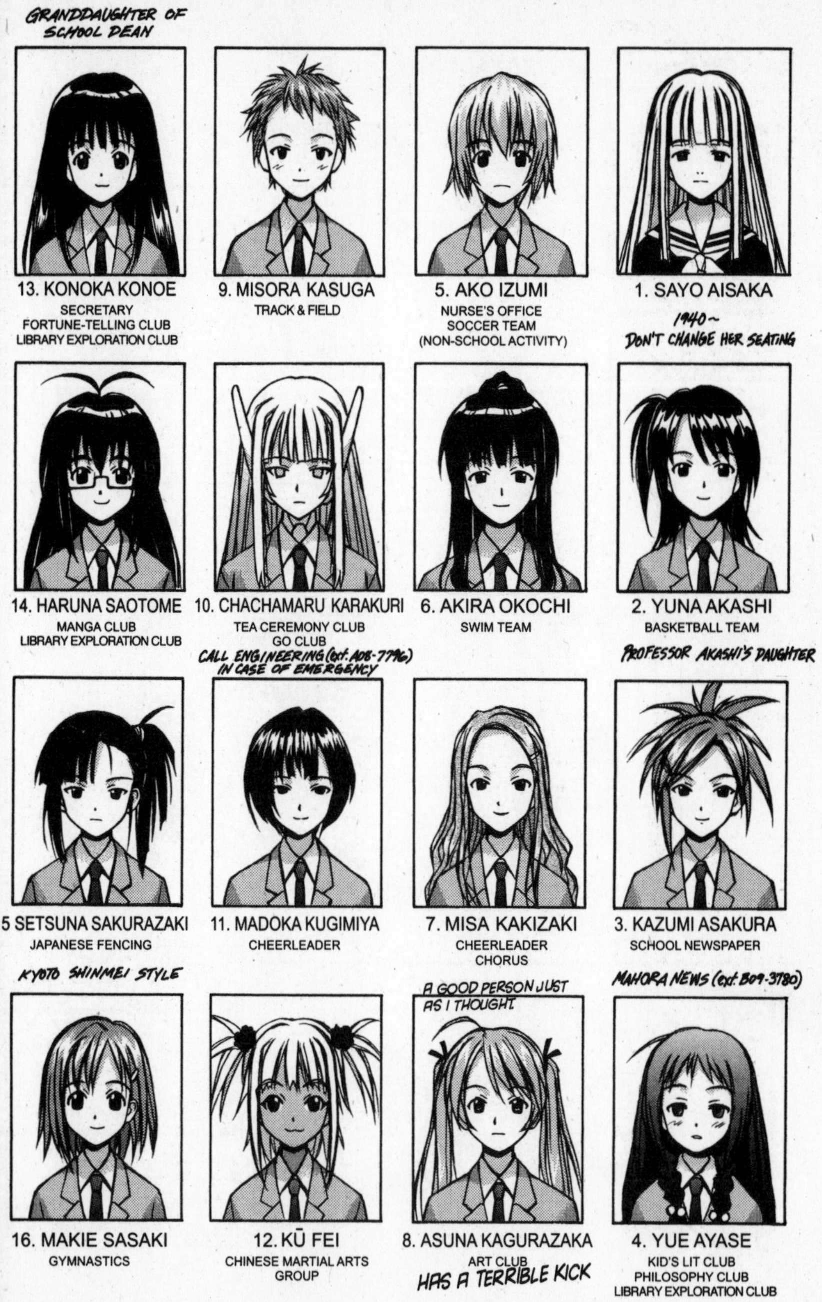
1. SAYO AISAKA
1940~
DON'T CHANGE HER SEATING
5. AKO IZUMI
NURSE'S OFFICE
SOCCER TEAM
(NON-SCHOOL ACTIVITY)
9. MISORA KASUGA
TRACK & FIELD
GRANDDAUGHTER OF SCHOOL DEAN
13. KONOKA KONOE
SECRETARY
FORTUNE-TELLING CLUB
LIBRARY EXPLORATION CLUB
2. YUNA AKASHI
BASKETBALL TEAM
PROFESSOR AKASHI'S DAUGHTER
6. AKIRA OKOCHI
SWIM TEAM
10. CHACHAMARU KARAKURI
TEA CEREMONY CLUB
GO CLUB
CALL ENGINEERING (ext. A08-7796) IN CASE OF EMERGENCY
14. HARUNA SAOTOME
MANGA CLUB
LIBRARY EXPLORATION CLUB
3. KAZUMI ASAKURA
SCHOOL NEWSPAPER
MAHORA NEWS (ext. B09-3780)
7. MISA KAKIZAKI
CHEERLEADER
CHORUS
11. MADOKA KUGIMIYA
CHEERLEADER
5 SETSUNA SAKURAZAKI
JAPANESE FENCING
KYOTO SHINMEI STYLE
4. YUE AYASE
KID'S LIT CLUB
PHILOSOPHY CLUB
LIBRARY EXPLORATION CLUB
A GOOD PERSON JUST AS I THOUGHT.
8. ASUNA KAGURAZAKA
ART CLUB
HAS A TERRIBLE KICK
12. KŪ FEI
CHINESE MARTIAL ARTS GROUP
16. MAKIE SASAKI
GYMNASTICS

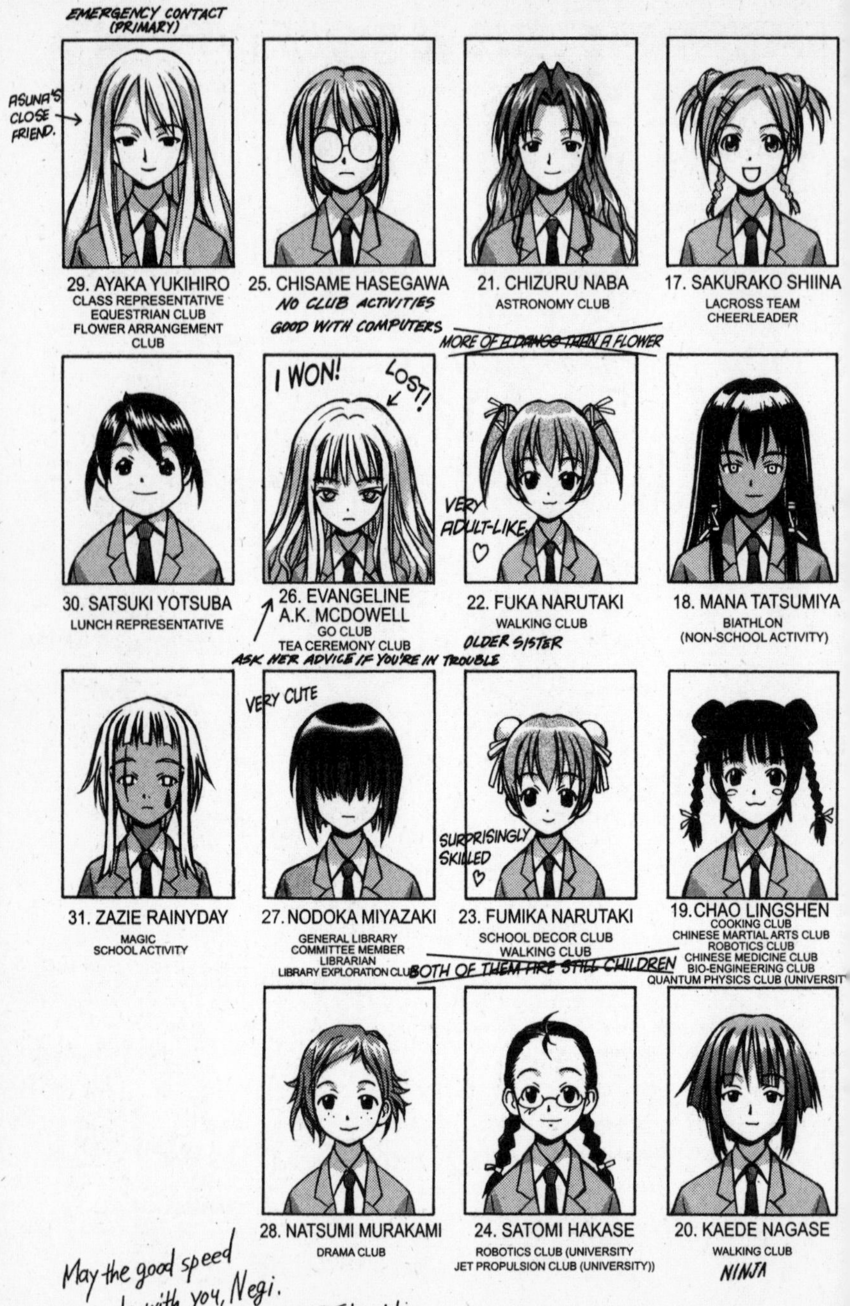
17. SAKURAKO SHIINA
LACROSS TEAM
CHEERLEADER
MORE OF A DANGO THAN A FLOWER
21. CHIZURU NABA
ASTRONOMY CLUB
25. CHISAME HASEGAWA
NO CLUB ACTIVITIES
GOOD WITH COMPUTERS
EMERGENCY CONTACT (PRIMARY)
ASUNA'S CLOSE FRIEND.
29. AYAKA YUKIHIRO
CLASS REPRESENTATIVE
EQUESTRIAN CLUB
FLOWER ARRANGEMENT CLUB
18. MANA TATSUMIYA
BIATHLON
(NON-SCHOOL ACTIVITY)
VERY ADULT-LIKE ♡
22. FUKA NARUTAKI
WALKING CLUB
OLDER SISTER
I WON!
LOST!
26. EVANGELINE A.K. MCDOWELL
GO CLUB
TEA CEREMONY CLUB
ASK HER ADVICE IF YOU'RE IN TROUBLE
30. SATSUKI YOTSUBA
LUNCH REPRESENTATIVE
19.CHAO LINGSHEN
COOKING CLUB
CHINESE MARTIAL ARTS CLUB
ROBOTICS CLUB
CHINESE MEDICINE CLUB
BIO-ENGINEERING CLUB
QUANTUM PHYSICS CLUB (UNIVERSIT
SURPRISINGLY SKILLED ♡
23. FUMIKA NARUTAKI
SCHOOL DECOR CLUB
WALKING CLUB
BOTH OF THEM ARE STILL CHILDREN
VERY CUTE
27. NODOKA MIYAZAKI
GENERAL LIBRARY
COMMITTEE MEMBER
LIBRARIAN
LIBRARY EXPLORATION CLUB
31. ZAZIE RAINYDAY
MAGIC
SCHOOL ACTIVITY
20. KAEDE NAGASE
WALKING CLUB
NINJA
24. SATOMI HAKASE
ROBOTICS CLUB (UNIVERSITY
JET PROPULSION CLUB (UNIVERSITY))
28. NATSUMI MURAKAMI
DRAMA CLUB
May the good speed be with you, Negi.
Takahata.T.Takamichi.

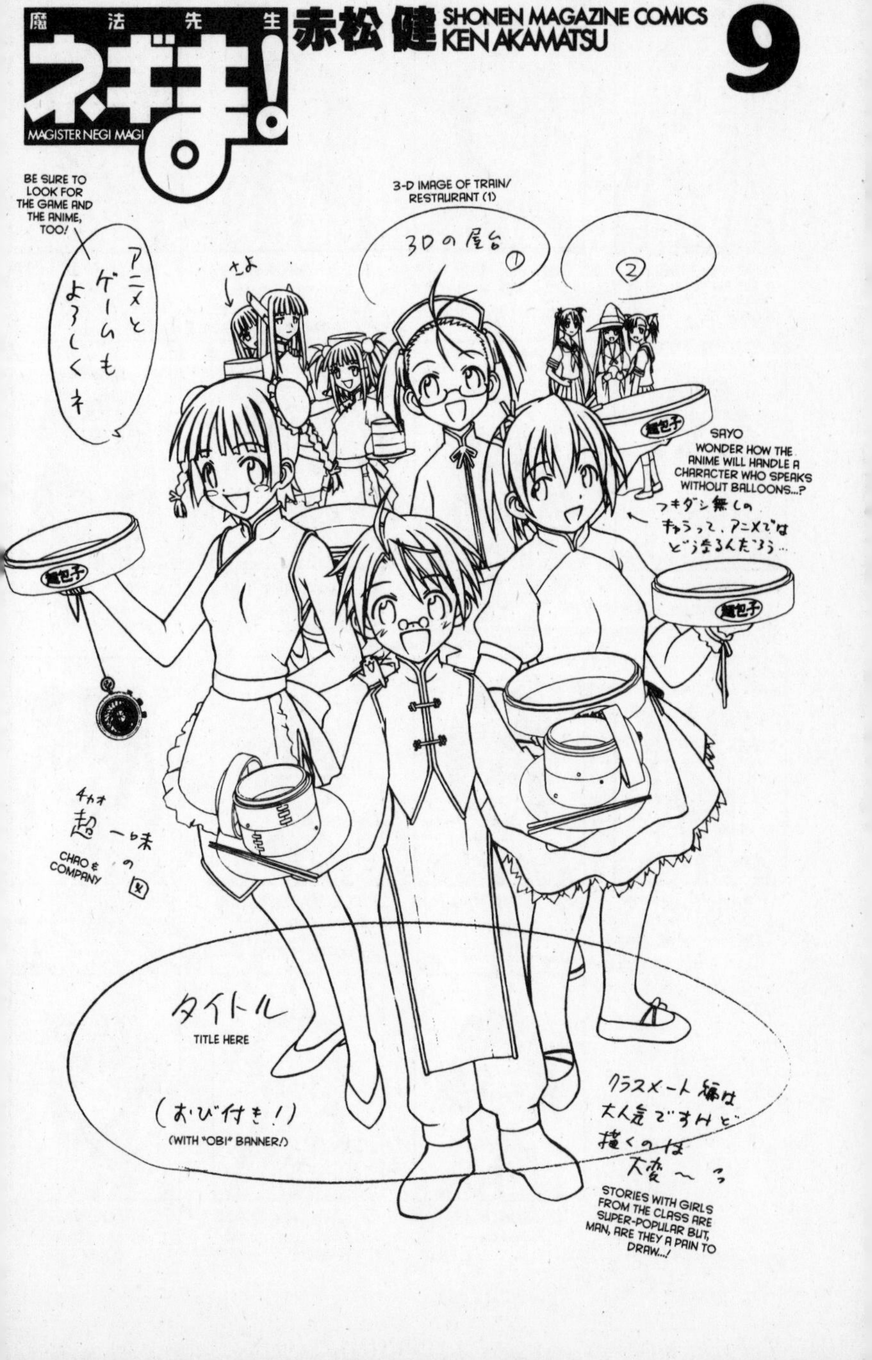
魔法先生
ネギま!
MAGISTER NEGI MAGI
赤松健
SHONEN MAGAZINE COMICS
KEN AKAMATSU
9
アニメとゲームもよろしくネ
BE SURE TO LOOK FOR THE GAME AND THE ANIME, TOO!
3Dの屋台①
3-D IMAGE OF TRAIN/ RESTAURANT (1)
②
さよ
SAYO
麺包子
フキダシ無しのキャラって、アニメではどうなるんだろう…
WONDER HOW THE ANIME WILL HANDLE A CHARACTER WHO SPEAKS WITHOUT BALLOONS...?
4カオ
超一味の図
CHAO & COMPANY
タイトル
TITLE HERE
(おび付き!)
(WITH "OBI" BANNER!)
クラスメート編は大人気ですけど描くのは大変〜っ
STORIES WITH GIRLS FROM THE CLASS ARE SUPER-POPULAR BUT, MAN, ARE THEY A PAIN TO DRAW...!

キャラ解説
CHARACTER PROFILE

① 相坂さよ
SAYO AISAKA

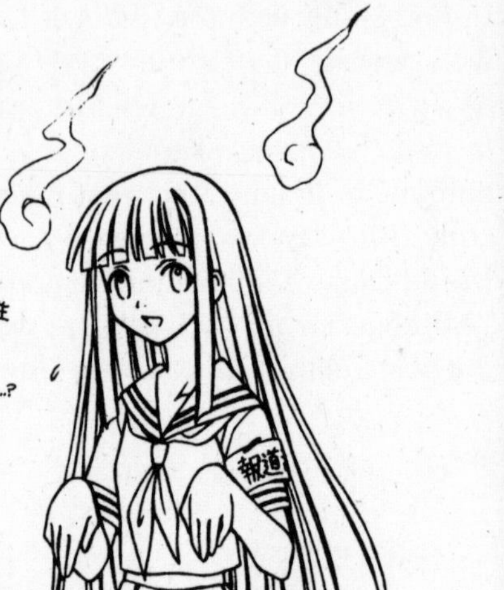

大人気のユーレイです。
THE EVER-POPULAR GHOST!

(しのむ＋むつみ)÷2 みたいな属性
IN LOVE HINA TERMS, I GUESS MAYBE SHE'D BE SHINOMU
でしょうか。 アワアワ ボケボケ キャラ？
+ MUTSUMI ÷ 2 (IN OTHER WORDS, NERVOUS TENSION + AIRHEAD)...?

コノカとかに似たデザインなので、
SINCE SHE'S SO POTENTIALLY SIMILAR TO KONOKA,
鼻とか瞳のテカりとかで必死に
I WORKED REALLY HARD TO CHANGE THE "FEEL" OF HER NOSE,
違いを出そうとしたのですが(笑)
AS WELL AS HOW THE LIGHT SHOWS IN HER EYES...DID IT WORK? (HEH.)
やっぱ同じですよね。スミマセン？
PROBABLY THEY STILL DO LOOK PRETTY SIMILAR...SORRY 'BOUT THAT.

声優はベテランの白鳥由里さん。
FOR THE ANIME, HER VOICE-ACTOR IS YURI SHIRATORI, A REAL VETERAN.
アニメでは出番が多いようで、
IT SEEMS SAYO WILL HAVE AN EVEN BIGGER PART IN THE ANIME THAN IN THE MANGA,
今から楽しみです。
SO I'M LOOKING FORWARD TO THAT.
(主役の回もあるらしい…)
(SUPPOSEDLY SHE'LL EVEN HAVE HER OWN EPISODE.)

次の10巻からは、いよいよ
AS OF VOLUME 10—NEXT VOLUME!—
学園祭のスタートです！
IT'S FINALLY THE START OF THE SCHOOL FESTIVAL.
ぜひ見てね！
BE SURE NOT TO MISS IT!

赤松
(AKAMATSU)

About the Creator

Negima! is only Ken Akamatsu's third manga, although he started working in the field in 1994 with *AI Ga Tomaranai* (released in the United States with the title *A.I. Love You*). Like all of Akamatsu's work to date, it was published in Kodansha's *Shonen Magazine*. *AI Ga Tomaranai* ran for five years before concluding in 1999. In 1998, however, Akamatsu began the work that would make him one of the most popular manga artists in Japan: *Love Hina*. *Love Hina* ran for four years, and before its conclusion in 2002, it would cause Akamatsu to be granted the prestigious Manga of the Year award from Kodansha, as well as going on to become one of the best-selling manga in the United States.

Translation Notes

Japanese is a tricky language for most Westerners, and translation is often more art than science. For your edification and reading pleasure, here are notes on some of the places where we could have gone in a different direction in our translation of the work, or where a Japanese cultural reference is used.

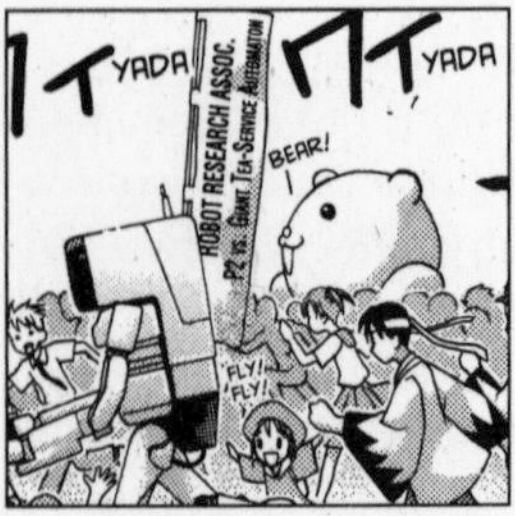
YADA
YADA
ROBOT RESEARCH ASSOC.
P2 vs. GIANT TEA-SERVICE AUTOMATON
BEAR!
FLY! FLY!

P2 Robot, page 10

A prototype humanoid "walking robot" in development by auto manufacturer Honda since the mid '80s (starting with the E0 or "Experimental Model 0" in 1986 and continuing up to the E6 in 1991), the robot you see running alongside the students on this page is the P2. In 1993, Honda entered the prototype phase, and created the P1 (the frame of the P2 model seen in this panel was created in 1996). A year later (in the summer of '97), Honda created the first-to-look-mostly-humanoid P3; in 2000, the final evolution of the Honda robots culminated in the creation of the ASIMO (for more info, see asimo.honda.com).

Saratoga Cooler, page 15

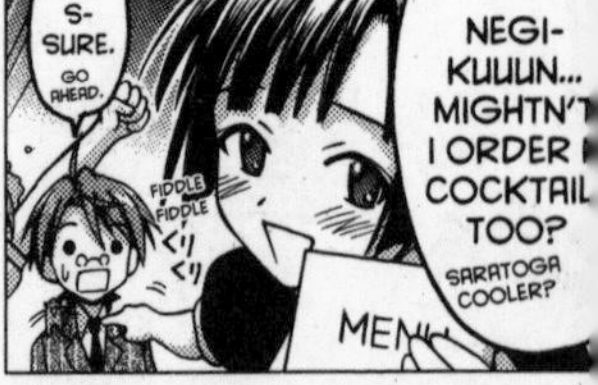
NEGI-KUUUN... MIGHTN'T I ORDER COCKTAIL TOO?
SARATOGA COOLER?
MEN
S-SURE. GO AHEAD.
FIDDLE FIDDLE

The drink Madoka asks Negi if she may order during his "education" on the world of "Adult Cafés." A non-alcoholic beverage made with lime juice and grenadine, added to a glass of crushed ice, topped off with ginger ale and garnished with lime, a Saratoga Cooler is essentially the better-known Moscow Mule...except, of course, without the vodka.

"All-Girl Swimsuit Expo Café," page 27

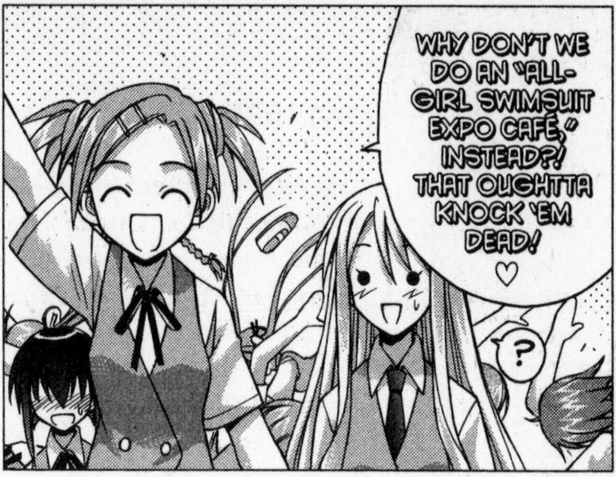
WHY DON'T WE DO AN "ALL-GIRL SWIMSUIT EXPO CAFÉ," INSTEAD?! THAT OUGHTTA KNOCK 'EM DEAD! ♡
?

Known perhaps more properly (and definitely more naughtily) in Japan by the proper title *DOKI! Onna-Darake no Idol Mizuki Taikai* ("BAH-BUMP! The Nothing-But-Idol-Girls Swimsuit Suit-Off"), the show itself is not only real but just one of a series of similarly titled programs featuring swimsuit-clad female idol-singers gamely attempting various pool-based obstacle courses while singing their latest hits in-between. (The Japanese sound-effect *porori*, incidentally, refers to a "wardrobe malfunction" of the type which, amazingly enough, happens only to "B"-list idols—never to those on the "A"-list.) Needless to say, ratings on this and other such late-nite TV "specials" in Japan are said to be very high with teenage and young adult male audiences.

"No-Panties Café," page 28

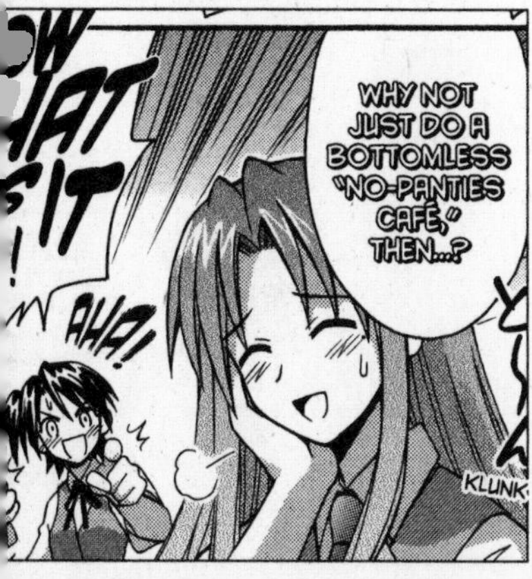
WHY NOT JUST DO A BOTTOMLESS "NO-PANTIES CAFÉ," THEN...?
AHA!
KLUNK

In the '80s, in the floating world known as Japan's colorful sex trade, there once was a place known as a "No-Panties Café (*No-Pan Kissa*)." Much like any other coffee shop but with two major differences, the point of a "no-panties café" was, of course, that the waitresses wore no undergarments...and that the floor was mirrored. With typical pricing for a cup of plain, house coffee—no refills!—said to have run around ¥2,000–3,000 (US$18.00–27.00 at today's exchange rates), one supposes the customer got what he paid for....

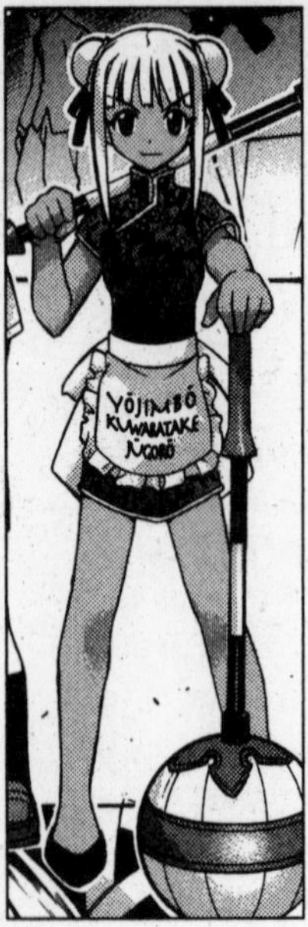
YŌJIMBŌ
KUWABATAKE
JŪGORŌ

Yōjimbō Kuwabatate Jūgorō, page 33

...is what's written on Kū Fei's apron. An obvious reference to the famed Kurosawa film of the same name, a *yōjimbō*, of course, is a bodyguard. In the film, when the Toshirō Mifune character is asked his name, he replies falsely, "Kuwabatake Sanjūrō...although I'm close to 'Shijūrō,' now"—the joke being, "Sanjūrō" refers both to a common Japanese first name as well as to an age, 30, while "Shijūrō" means 40. Kū Fei, whose apron reads "Jūgorō" (as in jūgo, 15), is Akamatsu's nod to Mifune's pun.

Satomi Hakase, page 62

In Japanese, *hakase* means "professor," so even though Satomi's last name is written with different *kanji*, interpreting her nickname as "Professor Professor" would not be, technically speaking, incorrect.

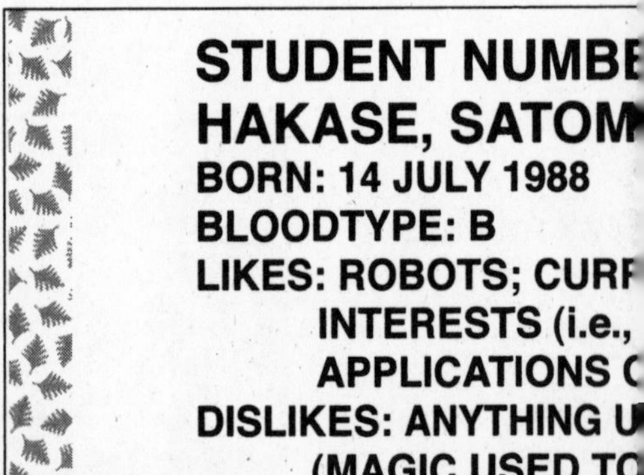
STUDENT NUMBE
HAKASE, SATOM
BORN: 14 JULY 1988
BLOODTYPE: B
LIKES: ROBOTS; CURF
INTERESTS (i.e.,
APPLICATIONS C
DISLIKES: ANYTHING U
(MAGIC USED TO

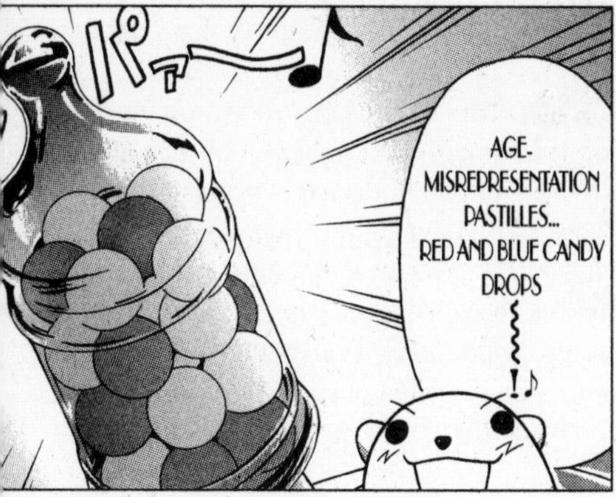
AGE-MISREPRESENTATION PASTILLES... RED AND BLUE CANDY DROPS

Red and Blue Candies, page 93

An homage to *Manga no Kami-sama* or "God of Comics" Osamu Tezuka's '70s manga *Fushigi na Merumo* ("Marvelous Melmo"), in which a girl is given a jar of red and blue candies by her mother (who is in Heaven), so that her daughter might overcome various obstacles. In Tezuka's original story, the red candies make Melmo ten years younger, while the blue make her ten years older. In *Negima!*, the effect of the colored candies is reversed, and there is no ten-year restriction.

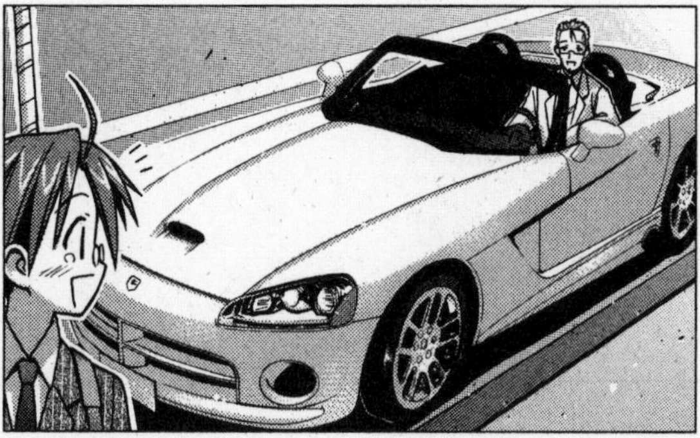

Takamichi's Tight Ride, page 119

A Dodge Viper SRT-10 Convertible, featuring a 500 HP 8.3 Liter V10 engine with a top speed of 306km/h... just in case you were wondering.

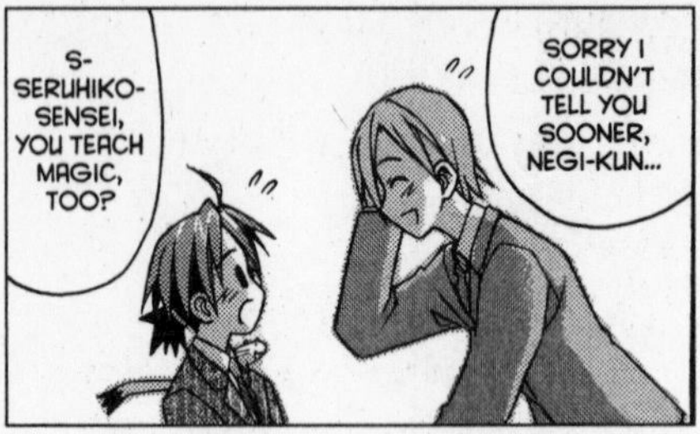
SORRY I COULDN'T TELL YOU SOONER, NEGI-KUN...
S- SERUHIKO-SENSEI, YOU TEACH MAGIC, TOO?

Seruhiko-sensei, page 144

A character who's appeared (perhaps more mysteriously) several times in the past, now that it's been revealed that Seruhiko-sensei is a magic teacher like Negi, it can be noted that "Professor Seruhiko" is also Akamatsu's homage to the "Serpico" character in fellow author Kentarō Miura's manga, *Berserk* (note the resemblance?).

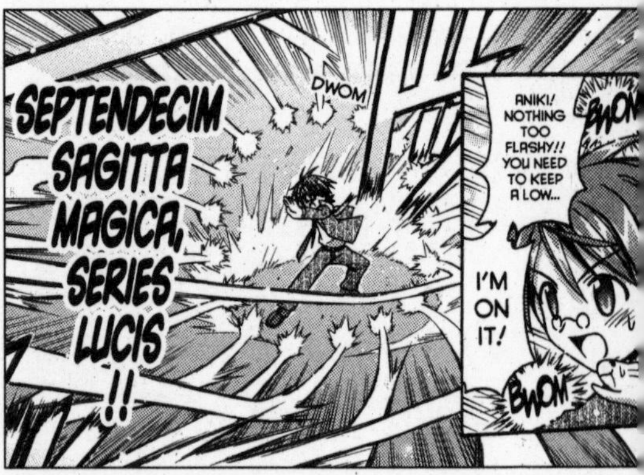
BWOM
ANIKI! NOTHING TOO FLASHY!! YOU NEED TO KEEP A LOW...
I'M ON IT!
BWOM
DWOM
SEPTENDECIM SAGITTA MAGICA, SERIES LUCIS !!

Sagitta Magica, page 160

By now we know of course that "Sagitta Magica" means "magic arrow(s)," but here's something you may not have noticed—every time Negi casts the spell, *the number of arrows is always a prime number* (1, 17, 19, 199, et cetera). According to Akamatsu, although he'd decided to go with the prime-numbers concept for the manga, once the series came out for the PlayStation, for game reasons the idea had to be abandoned.

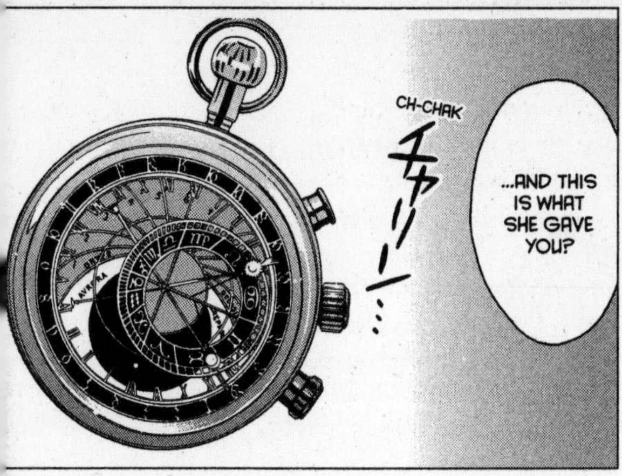
...AND THIS IS WHAT SHE GAVE YOU?
CH-CHAK
チャリーー…

Chao's Watch, page 172

The timepiece given to Negi by Chao plays a major (more like *the* major) role in the next volume, but here's a bit of information ahead of time. Chao's watch is named "Cassiopeia," and though we won't give away what it does quite yet, we *will* tell you that the design for its face is taken from the Orloj, the world-famous Astronomical Clock located on the former City Hall of Prague (for more, Orloj.com).

Preview of Volume Ten

Because we're running about one year behind the release of the Japanese Negima! manga, we have the opportunity to present to you a preview from volume ten. This volume is available in English now.

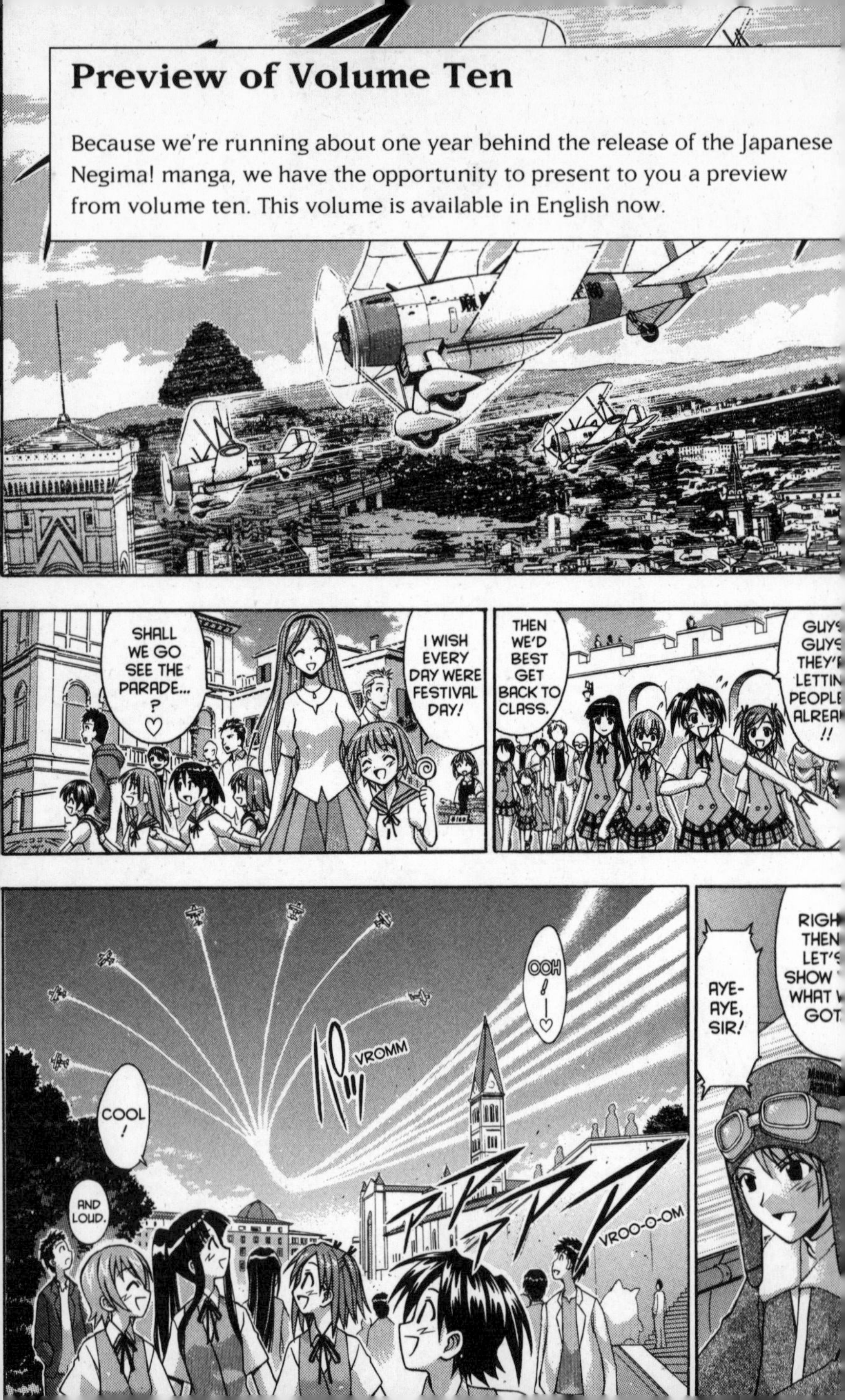
GUYS GUYS THEY'R LETTIN PEOPLE ALREA !!
THEN WE'D BEST GET BACK TO CLASS.
I WISH EVERY DAY WERE FESTIVAL DAY!
SHALL WE GO SEE THE PARADE...? ♡
RIGH THEN LET'S SHOW WHAT GOT
AYE-AYE, SIR!
OOH!—♡
VROMM
COOL!
AND LOUD.
VROO-O-OM

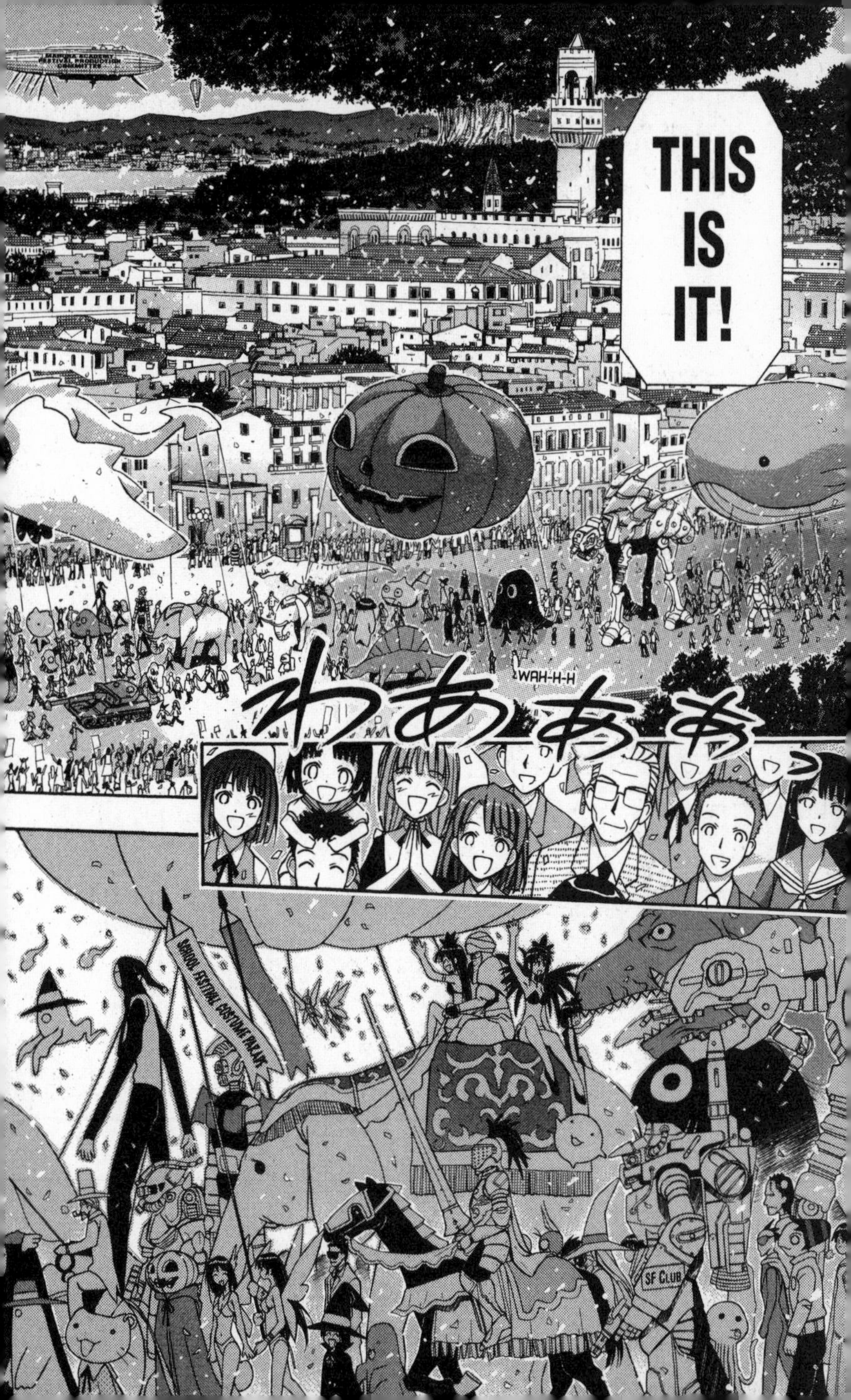
MAHORA ACADEMY FESTIVAL PRODUCTION COMMITTEE
THIS IS IT!
WAH-H-H
わあああっ
SCHOOL FESTIVAL COSTUME PARADE
SF CLUB

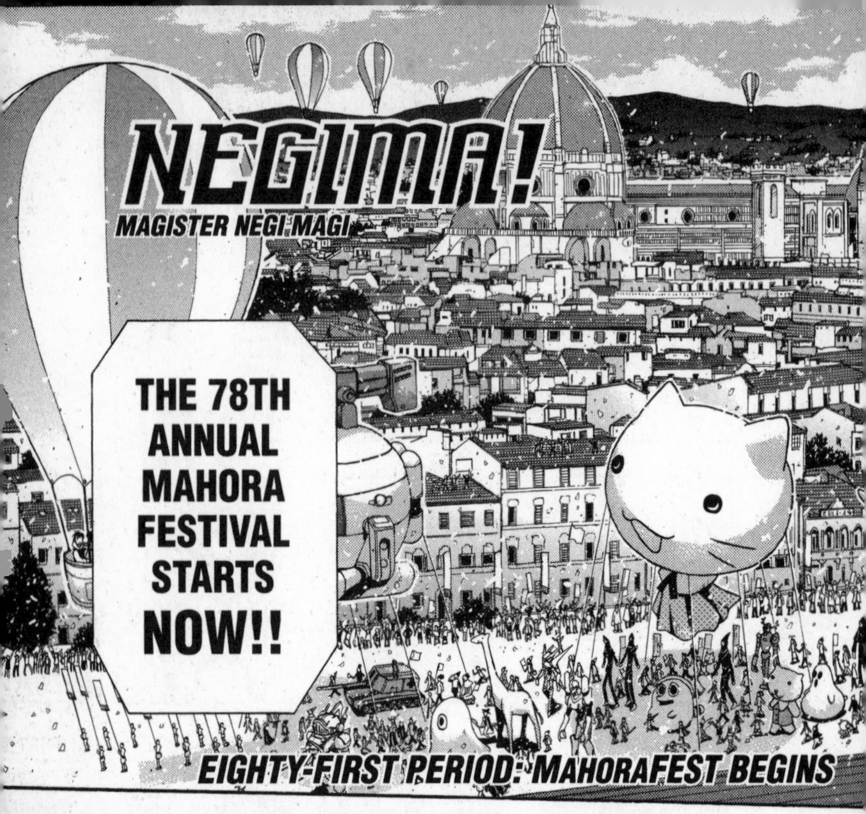
NEGIMA!
MAGISTER NEGI MAGI
THE 78TH ANNUAL MAHORA FESTIVAL STARTS NOW!!
EIGHTY-FIRST PERIOD: MAHORAFEST BEGINS

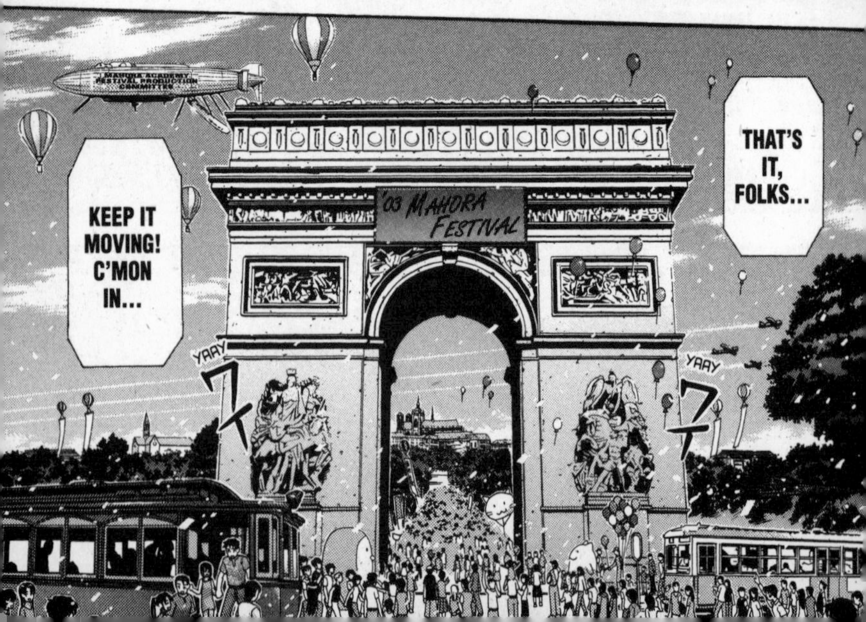
THAT'S IT, FOLKS...
'03 MAHORA FESTIVAL
YAAY
KEEP IT MOVING! C'MON IN...
YAAY

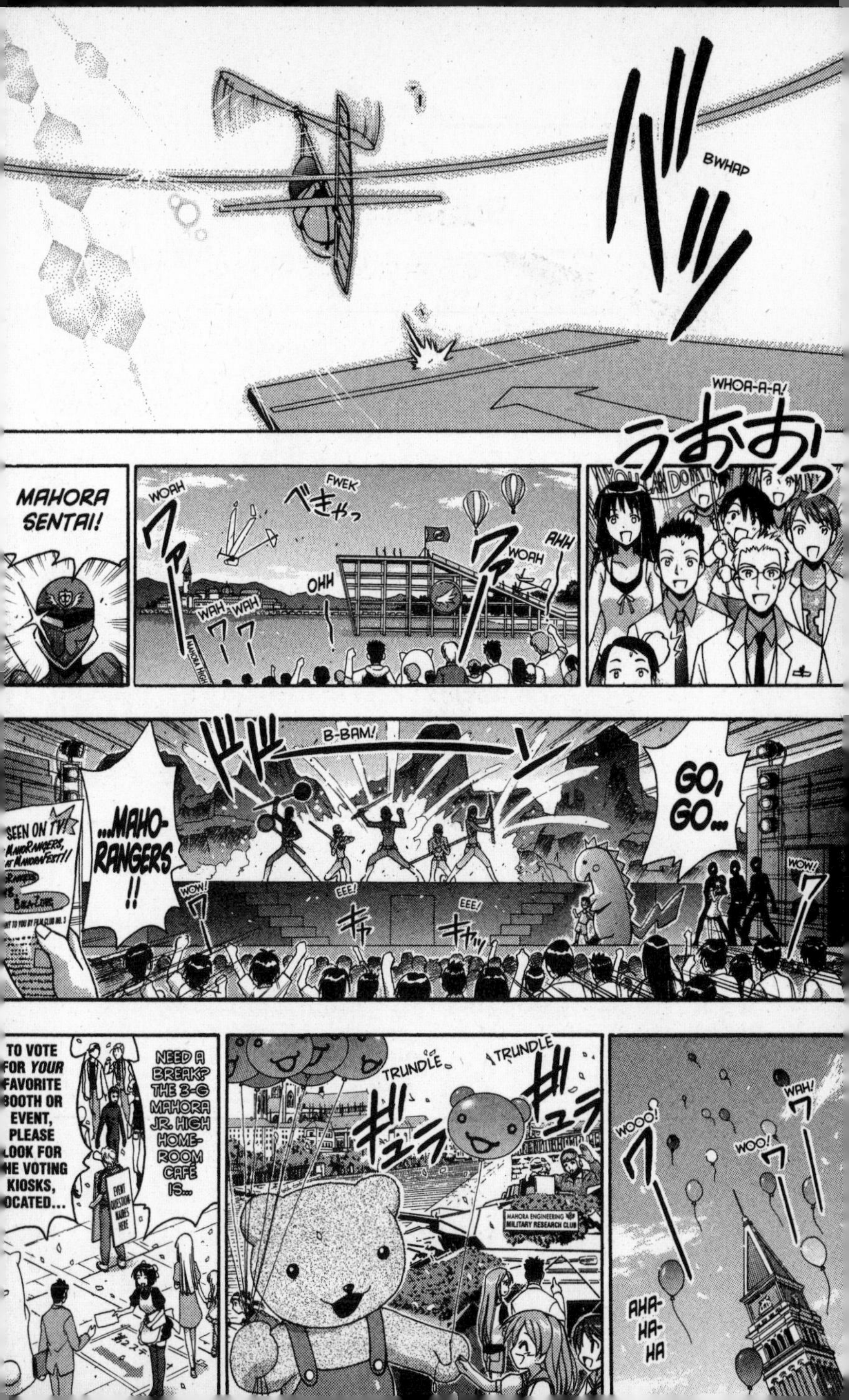

BWHAP
WHOA-A-A!
うおおっ
FWEK
べきゃっ
AHH
WOAH
ファー
OHH
WOAH
ファー
WAH WAH
ワワ
MAHORA HIGH
MAHORA SENTAI!
GO, GO...
B-BAM!
...MAHO-RANGERS!!
SEEN ON TV!
MahoRangers, at MahoraFest!!
WOW!
EEE!
キャ
EEE!
キャッ
WOW!
WAH!
ワー
WOO!
ワー
WOOO!
ワー
AHA-HA-HA
TRUNDLE
TRUNDLE
MAHORA ENGINEERING MILITARY RESEARCH CLUB
NEED A BREAK? THE 3-G MAHORA JR. HIGH HOME-ROOM CAFÉ IS...
TO VOTE FOR YOUR FAVORITE BOOTH OR EVENT, PLEASE LOOK FOR THE VOTING KIOSKS, LOCATED...
EVENT QUESTION-NAIRES HERE

BY CLAMP

Watanuki Kimihiro is haunted by visions. When he finds himself irresistibly drawn into a shop owned by Yûko, a mysterious witch, he is offered the chance to rid himself of the spirits that plague him. He accepts, but soon realizes that he's just been tricked into working for the shop to pay off the cost of Yûko's services! But this isn't any ordinary kind of shop . . . In this shop, Yûko grants wishes to those in need. But they must have the strength of will not only to truly understand their need, but to give up something incredibly precious in return.

Ages: 13+

Special extras in each volume! Read them all!

VISIT WWW.DELREYMANGA.COM TO:
- View release date calendars for upcoming volumes
- Sign up for Del Rey's free manga e-newsletter
- Find out the latest about new Del Rey Manga series

Gacha Gacha

By Hiroyuki Tamakoshi

Kouhei is your typical Japanese high school student—he's usually late, he loves beef bowls, he pals around with his buddies, and he's got his first-ever crush on his childhood friend Kurara. Before he can express his feelings, however, Kurara heads off to Hawaii with her mother for summer vacation. When she returns, she seems like a totally different person . . . and that's because she is! While she was away, Kurara somehow developed an alternate personality: Arisa! And where Kurara has no time for boys, Arisa isn't interested in much else. Now Kouhei must help protect his friend's secret, and make sure that Arisa doesn't do anything Kurara would regret!

HIROYUKI TAMAKOSHI

Ages: 16+

Special extras in each volume! Read them all!

Guru Guru Pon-Chan

BY SATOMI IKEZAWA

WINNER OF THE KODANSHA MANGA OF THE YEAR AWARD!

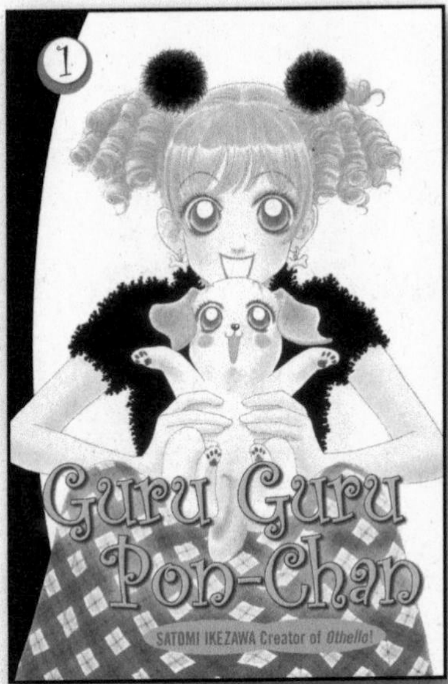

1
Guru Guru Pon-Chan
SATOMI IKEZAWA Creator of Othello!

Ages: 13+

Ponta is a normal Labrador retriever puppy, the Koizumi family's pet. Full of energy, she is always up to some kind of trouble. However, when Grandpa Koizumi, a passionate amateur inventor, creates the "Guru Guru Bone," which empowers animals with human speech, Ponta turns into a human girl!

Ponta dashes out into the street and is saved by Mirai Iwaki, the most popular boy at school! Her heart pounds and her face flushes. Why does she feel this way? Can there be love between a human and a dog?

The effects of the "Guru Guru Bone" are not permanent, and Ponta turns back and forth between dog and girl.

Special extras in each volume! Read them all!

DEL REY

VISIT WWW.DELREYMANGA.COM TO:
- View release date calendars for upcoming volumes
- Sign up for Del Rey's free manga e-newsletter
- Find out the latest about new Del Rey Manga series

TOMARE!

[STOP!]

You're going the wrong way!

Manga is a completely different type of reading experience.

To start at the *beginning*, go to the *end*!

That's right! Authentic manga is read the traditional Japanese way—from right to left. Exactly the *opposite* of how American books are read. It's easy to follow: Just go to the other end of the book, and read each page—and each panel—from right side to left side, starting at the top right. Now you're exp_____ o be.